EXPANDED SECOND EDITION

METHODS for DEVELOPING NEW FOOD PRODUCTS

An Instructional Guide

FADI ARAMOUNI, Ph.D.

Professor of Food Science
Kansas State University

KATHRYN DESCHENES, M.S.

Food Science, Deschenes Consulting, LLC

DEStech Publications, Inc.

HOW TO ORDER THIS BOOK

BY PHONE: 877-500-4337 or 717-290-1660, 9AM–5PM Eastern Time

BY FAX: 717-509-6100

BY MAIL: Order Department
DEStech Publications, Inc.
439 North Duke Street
Lancaster, PA 17602, U.S.A.

BY CREDIT CARD: American Express, VISA, MasterCard, Discover

BY WWW SITE: http://www.destechpub.com

This work is dedicated to the several people
whose immense sacrifices and inexhaustible love
made all the difference in my life:
My mother, Violet, my father, Michael, my wife, Mary,
and my two sons, Daniel and Alexander.

To my husband, Joshua, my parents,
Johnnie and Karen, and my brother, John.
Life is best spent in good company.

Methods for Developing New Food Products

DEStech Publications, Inc.
439 North Duke Street
Lancaster, Pennsylvania 17602 U.S.A.

Printed in the United States of America
10 9 8 7 6 5 4 3 2 1

Main entry under title:
Methods for Developing New Food Products: An Instructional Guide, Expanded Second Edition

A DEStech Publications book
Bibliography: p.
Includes index p. 411

Library of Congress Control Number: 2017947549
ISBN No. 978-1-60595-432-5

Table of Contents

Preface

FOOD product development is a continuously evolving area, which has to reflect market trends, consumer preferences, and, perhaps most importantly, current food laws and regulations. Following publication of the first edition of this book, two key pieces of Federal legislation were issued dealing with food safety and food labeling, namely, the Food Safety Modernization Act (FSMA) and the Nutrition Facts labeling requirements, of which both led to new FDA regulations that are part of the second edition. We took this opportunity to include new information as well as review all of the book's content and make corrections and additions based on recommendations of colleagues and students who used the first edition.

The second edition adds a completely new chapter devoted to the development of pet foods, which have become a major branch of the food industry. For example, in April 2017, the Bureau of Labor Statistics reported that in 2015 U.S. households increased their spending on pet foods to $230 per year from $190 the year before, suggesting this segment is a fertile area for new products. The chapter was written by Dr. Greg Aldrich of Kansas State University, a national expert on pet food processing, in coordination with his graduate student, Ms. Lydia Molnar.

Besides including information needed for the Nutrition Facts panel on packaging, we supplemented many chapters of the first edition with original material. In the area of general product development, new sections appear on how to use market research and how to reverse-engineer competitors' products, as well as descriptions of FPD software and techniques for running an ideation session. The chapter on food chemistry now contains more extensive information on proteins and a case study explaining the effects of caramelization. Food processing chapters have been augmented with details on how operations are scaled up. In this edition, readers are given an account of how to develop a food safety plan that accords with FSMA requirements. Regarding documentation of food ingredients and quality, developers are now provided with samples of a Certificate of Analysis and a Letter of Guarantee.

It is our hope that the new edition will better serve the needs of instructors, students and professionals tasked with teaching, learning, and applying proven and proper techniques for developing food products that are both new and successful.

FADI ARAMOUNI
KATHRYN DESCHENES
Manhattan, Kansas
May, 2017

Acknowledgements

THE authors would like to express their sincere appreciation to the following people for their imput on the textbook material: Dr. Thomas Herald (food chemistry), the late Dr. Carole Setser (sensory testing), Dr. Donald Grickson (financial feasibility), and Dr. Elizabeth Boyle (HACCP). Their advice and expertise were very useful in the completion of this project.

CHAPTER 1

Overview of Food Product Development

Learning Objectives

- Learn the steps involved in food product development.
- Know the definitions of acid, low-acid, and acidified foods along with examples of each.
- Know the feasibility barriers to product commercialization.

FOOD product development involves more than creating the perfect recipe. Companies must plan extensively, work hard, and carry out research for an extended period of time, in order to evolve new food products. Companies engage in product development with the hopes of gaining new customers, expanding into new markets geographically, increasing profits, elevating brand excitement, and, as the foregoing imply, increasing market share. Prior to starting a new development venture, key stakeholders should create specific objectives and timetables that are integrated into the future direction of the business.

Companies large and small introduce thousands of new food products each year. The time spent developing new food products ranges from six months to five years, depending on the degree of new technology and innovation. For example, a line extension from existing items that can be made on equipment already in place at a manufacturing facility usually takes less time than a new product requiring a custom processing line. The failure rate of new products, which is defined as a product no longer on store shelves after five years, can be as high as 90 percent in some grocery categories.

Larger companies rely on multifunctional product development teams that include food scientists, food engineers, regulatory specialists, and marketing and purchasing experts, whereas smaller companies may not even have a research and development department. Smaller

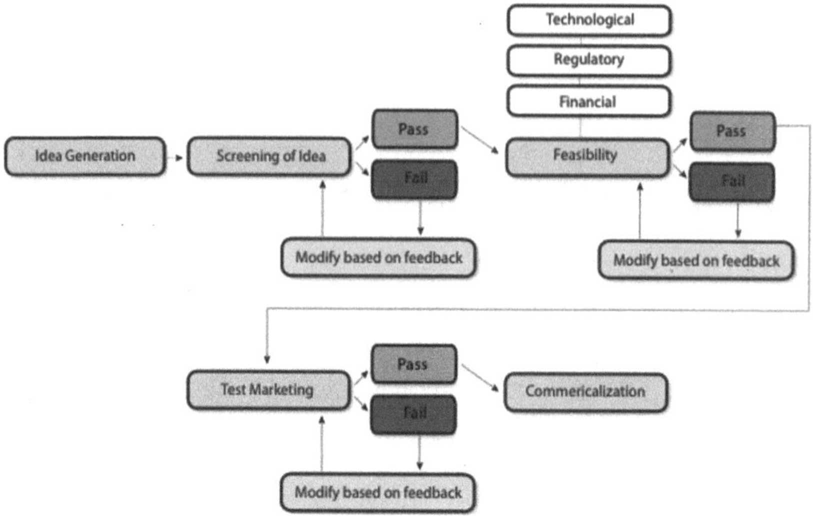

FIGURE 1.1. The Process of Product Development.

companies must rely on outside resources, such as universities, independent laboratories, third-party development firms, or in-house development teams at co-manufacturing facilities, in order to create successful products.

WHY DEVELOP NEW FOOD PRODUCTS?

In recent times, economic progress has been linked to innovation and application of new technologies in many fields, including food. This would not have been possible without spending money on product research and development to drive these new technologies. The development of food products certainly follows this model. Companies develop new food products for financial reasons, with the main driving force being to increase profitability over the long range, despite the initial costs associated with research and development. New product development is mostly market driven, meaning that products are developed in response to consumer trends. Other factors may affect a company's desire to introduce new food products into the market. Chief among these are the following:

a. *Technological advances*, such as improvements in ingredients or packaging. Examples would be the discovery of a new artificial sweetener or of a self-heating food package.

b. *Regulatory/legal rationales*, such as changes in laws, labeling requirements, or agricultural policies. Examples would be banning a certain food additive or allowing a new health claim or nutrient content claim.

IDEA GENERATION

Companies use varying techniques to generate ideas for new products. Marketing teams may be charged with the central development of ideas, with supplementation from researchers. Ideas may also come from consumers. Some companies may not need this step, especially if they thrive on regenerating competitors' products. An example is creating a store-brand product that is very similar to name-brand products already on the market. Ideation sessions using participants from all departments can also be a part of corporate idea generation. After idea generation, the major steps in developing a new food product may be divided into four phases: screening, feasibility, test marketing, and commercialization. Idea generation should be completed by gathering information about trending ingredients and consumer desires, attending trade shows, keeping up to date on new product releases from other companies, scanning research articles and trade publications, and monitoring grocery shelves.

Developing marketable concepts can also be accomplished through the hiring of market research companies or the purchasing of periodical market surveys that large firms publish regarding particular product categories or consumer trends. If this does not fit your budget, your company could do its own research to build a customer database to help you understand which market segments your existing customers fall into and what you could do to increase your market share. Additionally, there is a wealth of free information on websites from government agencies, commodity groups, and trade associations, where companies can tap into data on consumer and product trends. One reliable source of information is the USDA Economic Research Service (ERS) reports on Food Consumption and Demand that cover topics such as Commodity Consumption by Population Characteristics, Food Consumption and Nutrient Intakes, Food Availability (Per Capita) Data System, Food Environment Atlas, and Eating and Health Module (ATUS). Economic Research Service research on food consumption examines: the effects of food consumption choices on agriculture; the behavioral and economic determinants of food and nutrient consumption; interrelationships between spending on food and non-food items; consumer valuation of quality, safety, and nutritional characteristics; and the role of information in determining food choices.

Reverse Engineering Competitors' Products

Reverse engineering is widely used in the food industry, especially to launch generic versions of proven, successful products introduced by national brands. The purpose is to develop a product as close as possible to the one being imitated, but at a lower cost. In general, this means that the two products, original and imitation, must be extremely similar in terms of sensory properties. The ideal process flow to achieve this result is as follows:

- Characterize applicable physical and chemical properties of the original product: shape, size, thickness, weight, density, color, texture, pH, water activity, viscosity, and proximate analysis (moisture, protein, fat, ash, fiber, carbohydrates). This can be done using a variety of analytical instruments and methodologies.
- Characterize the sensory properties of the original product using a trained sensory panel. This procedure does not address likes and dislikes, but rather seeks to produce a descriptive analysis of selected product attributes such as sweetness level, saltiness, intensity of certain flavors, mouthfeel, after-taste, and order of appearance of flavors.
- Identify processing methods and parameters for the product, based on knowledge of unit operations and working closely with engineers. For operations such as extrusion, thermal processing, baking, or dehydration, make sure to provide the engineers with moisture levels of both raw and processed products. Achieving a certain moisture level is a critical metric for many processes and ensures that desired physical and chemical properties can be achieved.
- Starting from the list of ingredients listed on the original product's label and based on the proximate analysis, work with a nutrition labeling software to formulate several products that fit the data provided. One of the biggest challenges at this step is to duplicate the balance of spices in the original product, since names of spices do not have to be listed on the ingredient legend, except for a few that also provide color (e.g., paprika, turmeric, saffron). We have achieved good success with this challenge in our laboratory by simple microscopy:

observing samples of the original product under the microscope at a 10× magnification and comparing the sample's spice particles to the wide stock of individual spices we maintain. By counting the number of specific particles in a field, we obtain a rough estimate of the amount of a certain spice, and then we proceed with numerous sensory tests until we match the spice profile.

- Use your sensory panel to test the formulations you have developed and determine which one has an attributes profile closest to your target product.
- Keep manipulating that formulation and consulting your trained panel until results from the imitation closely match the original product.
- Run a test batch of your product and use it with the control to perform a sensory "triangle test" or a "duo-trio" test to find out if consumers can pick the "different" sample. These tests are explained in Chapter 5. In case these tests prove that consumers can detect the different sample, some finetuning of the formulation may be necessary.
- Finally, perform a statistically significant consumer preference test between your new product and the original product. Make sure your test ballot also has a comment section to get any input on the products. Hopefully your product will be as much, if not more, preferred (it has happened!) than the one you are trying to match. Otherwise, data and comments from the consumer study will guide you to make further changes to your product before you re-test it.

SCREENING

After an idea has been agreed upon, the steps of product development begin. Screening is the most critical step in a product development project. Thorough testing of product concepts can assist a firm in deciding whether to invest time and money in a venture, or to abandon the effort completely. Project ideas, now more carefully refined, must be judged to be congruent with organizational goals. Project managers should repeatedly screen an idea throughout development of the project in order to gauge whether the concept remains acceptable in the target market, ingredients are still readily available, and regulations impacting the product have not changed. Smaller companies may call on outside firms to assist in market screening.

Collaboration of departments during the screening step helps to evaluate individual areas involved in product development, including financial and legal considerations, process and equipment availability,

Questions for Screening Concepts

Companies can begin by asking a series of questions such as:

- Who will use the product?
- How will it be used?
- What preparation is necessary for the consumer?
- How will the consumer benefit from it?
- Does it have any other uses?
- Who is the competition? How is the product different?
- Where will the product be available?
- How will people find out about the product?
- What will the price be?

purchasing power and ingredient accessibility, shifts in the marketplace, and consumer perceptions. Examining markets and conducting consumer research are vital to product screening.

Consumer testing is essential when screening products. Without consumer testing, companies have no way of knowing consumer needs, desires, and willingness to purchase. Initial screening may also reveal useful information for subsequent marketing strategies.

FEASIBILITY

Feasibility considerations for a business include regulations, technology, and finances. By setting up an interdepartmental team, the tools will be available to answer questions of attainability, which may be introduced at any stage during the development process.

Regulations

At the start of a project, firms must be cognizant of the state and/or federal agencies that regulate a product. In general, products sold locally (i.e., do not cross state lines) are regulated by state agencies. A product crossing state lines comes under the United States Food and Drug Administration (FDA) or the United States Department of Agriculture (USDA) jurisdiction, depending on the type of food. Some states allow small food processing businesses to be conducted out of a person's home, but the processing area must be separated from the living quarters by solid walls, and there should be no direct entrance from the living quarters to the food processing area. Other local governments prohibit in-home commercial food processing, so awareness of zoning laws is of utmost importance.

The term “food”—as defined in 21 CFR 321 (f)—signifies the following: (1) articles used for food or drink for man or other animals, (2) chewing gum, and (3) articles used for components of any such article. Legally binding ”standards of identity” stipulate the requirements for individual food products as defined in the Code of Federal Regulations (CFR). Individual products must meet certain guidelines in order to be called by a specific name. Applesauce, for example, has strict guidelines on ingredient inclusion for it to be labeled as such (21 CFR 145.110). Applesauce can legally name a product only with a soluble solids content (measured by a refractometer) of at least 9 percent if unsweetened, and 16.5 percent if sweeteners are added. Apples must be the primary ingredient of the product, but optional ingredients such as water, salt, apple juice, organic acids, nutritive carbohydrate sweeteners, spices, natural flavorings, and a color additive/color preserving agent may be added in limited quantities. The FDA and USDA release publications that give the guiding principles of labeling products under their jurisdiction. These are titled “*Food Labeling Guide*” and “*The Food Policy and Labeling Guide*,” for the FDA and USDA, respectively. In 2015, USDA FDIS stated that they will no longer update their guide and instead will issue compliance policy guides as needed but this document still provides valuable insight into general labeling laws.

Meat and poultry products containing more than three percent fresh meat or at least two percent cooked poultry and intended for sale in interstate commerce are regulated by the USDA Food Safety Inspection Service (FSIS). The FDA regulates all other food products except for seafood, which is regulated by the Department of Commerce and the FDA.

Because of the hazard of botulism, special regulations apply to heat-processed, low-acid canned foods and acidified foods in hermetically sealed containers (CFR 108, 113, and 114.). Acid foods are those that naturally have a pH below 4.6 and/or a water activity (a_w) below 0.85. These regulations are based on the microbiological activity of *Clostridium botulinum* and *Staphylococcus aureus*. Low-acid canned foods are defined as processed foods with a pH greater than 4.6 and an a_w greater than 0.85, except for alcoholic beverages. Water activity is a measure of the water available for microbial growth in a food. Acidified foods are low-acid foods to which acid(s) or acid food(s) are added to reduce the pH to 4.6 or below with an $a_w > 0.85$. All processors of these foods must take an FDA-approved course of study, often referred to as the Better Process Control School. In addition, companies must provide site-specific processing information for FDA approval. Products such as jams and jellies usually have pH values low enough that they do not fall under these regulations. Most canned vegetables and pickled products are subject to low-acid food regulations.

Other regulated areas that require attention fall under two general categories: health safeguards and economic safeguards. Health safeguards protect against adulteration, natural toxicants, unapproved food additives, residues, and unsanitary processing or holding practices. Economic safeguards focus on issues of labeling, especially misleading or false statements, and net contents. More information on these subjects will be covered in Chapter 10—Regulatory Considerations.

It is imperative for the product developer to keep abreast of new approved ingredients and emerging regulations to ensure compliance of the new product with federal and state regulations. The FDA has recently enacted final rules regarding compliance with the Food Safety Modernization Act (FSMA) for development of food safety plans by processors, as well as mandated new formats for the Nutrition Facts panels on food products. Both issues are discussed in more detail in other chapters.

Technology

Before launching a food product, companies must vet all equipment, facilities, and processes needed to manufacture the product. Technological feasibility can be accelerated when companies utilize co-manufacturing facilities in which expertise in specific technologies is established. Co-manufacturing and the utilization of third-party laboratories and consultants are efficient ways to expand a company's capabilities without large investments. If a potential product is found to be not technologically feasible, the project should be terminated.

Formulation

Experimentation with varying ingredients, processing parameters, and packaging options will be carried out to find the best combination to create the desired product. Sound statistical analysis and adequate recordkeeping are critical at this step to ascertain which combinations contribute to the best product. After initial trials, an experimental design will cut down on the number of prototypes to be developed, which saves time and money. All formulas and experiments should be fully recorded in a laboratory notebook or equivalent. Each entry should include detailed information, so colleagues can understand the experiments and results. This is beneficial when projects are temporarily delayed, last for long periods of time, or are passed to other developers in the organization.

Ingredients

Ingredient specifications and quality can directly change the properties of a food product's sensory characteristics and ability to machine. Considerations when choosing ingredients include whether the commodity will be available for purchase year-round or only seasonally. Product developers will generally consider more than one supplier of the same product to test quality, cost effectiveness, and ensure consistent supply. Larger companies may need to find more than one supplier of the same product to fulfill needs. Certain applications require more rigid ingredient specifications than others. If more than one supplier is used, tight deadlines and exacting product specifications must be followed by all suppliers.

Processing

If a new product will be made in an existing facility, you must ask what relevant equipment do you already have? Companies usually try to produce newly developed products on equipment already in place, since adding machinery is a major capital expense. Thus, new product development projects are often based on expanding product lines through the use of existing facilities and equipment. For this reason, product developers should be aware of what equipment is available at the location where the product will ultimately be produced. If the product will be produced in more than one manufacturing location, consideration needs to be given to differences between facilities and how they can be reconciled to produce commercially similar products.

Processing capabilities can be expanded through the use of a co-manufacturing model. Even large multi-national companies may enter into a contract manufacturing agreement to gain access to manufacturing techniques without making significant investments. Quality and food safety personnel review new facilities by auditing their capacities to meet internal company standards and governmental food safety requirements, while at the same time assessing all processes. Auditing of facilities gauges the levels of overall food safety, quality, and environmental practices.

Facilities

Facility capabilities and design are a focal point of multi-functional research and development teams. Teams should consider the capacity of the current equipment to meet the expected product demand, the geographical proximity to raw material, finished good warehouses and retail destinations, the climate in given locations, and predicted capital investment. The qualification of the manufacturing locations should take into account the entirety of process flow: from raw material storage to processing/packaging capabilities to holding/warehousing of the finished product.

The facility's surroundings should be assessed for interior and exterior design. Exterior design (and location) considerations include the risk of environmental contamination and pest issues. Trees and shrubs should be maintained to cut down on pests. The location of the facility should be assessed in terms of temperature, relative humidity, potential for natural disaster, and surrounding businesses and terrain. Will your facility face potential contamination from a nearby sewage treatment facility or insect infestation from a body of water? Exterior placement of security features, such as lighting and openings to the building, are important as well. Loading docks and receiving areas should be separated by enclosures to allow for assessment prior to acceptance of materials. All doors and windows should be sealed and secured.

Safety and quality personnel will also evaluate interior design features. Crosscontamination and allergen control must be limited by operational flow, air conditioning, and employee access to sanitation stations and break rooms. All interior features should be constructed for durability and cleanability, using materials designed to withstand the chemical and physical wear of manufacturing. The conditions inside the plant, such as temperature and relative humidity, should be taken into account. Facilities in areas with high humidity and heat need to modify ambient conditions to produce efficiently throughout the entire year. Additionally, water supply and sewage systems require inspection.

Packaging

Packaging is a critical part of a product's appeal to consumers, especially with first-time purchasers. The aesthetics of a package affect how consumers view what it contains, including the discernment of whether it is a high-quality premium product or a generic grade. Marketing specialists, product developers, and packaging engineers need to examine the types of packaging materials used in competitors' products and decide how to set theirs apart. Additionally, packaging is an important factor in determining a finished product's quality and shelf-life.

Distribution

Distribution must be considered to determine the profitability and feasibility of a product. Products requiring special distribution include frozen and refrigerated foods. Organizations must calculate the costs of higher-level distribution. Other distribution considerations include the radius in which the product will be available and climate effects on the product. The distribution radius will also influence packaging needs.

Shelf-life

Shelf-life is the determination of how long a product will maintain quality as perceived by customers. The shelf-life of a product is important when considering distribution channels. Shelf-life can be calculated through the use of accelerated or realtime testing. Product degradation occurs as a result of factors such as exposure to varying temperatures, light, and product chemistry and property changes over time. The most important determination to be made about a new food product with regard to shelf-life is the expected Mode of Failure, which points to the one quality-related property affecting acceptability that will fail first. Depending on the product properties, the Mode of Failure could be staling, rancidity, mold growth, color fading, flavor changes, or loss of a certain nutrient. Quantitative methods need to be developed to measure these properties. More information about shelf life and its testing will be given in a later chapter.

Safety

In an age of multiple and well-publicized foodborne disease outbreaks, new product developers must carefully investigate the safety risks of their products. History of contamination of similar products and published safety risks of product categories provide clues to risk factors. For example, peanut butter producers must use controls to test for *Salmonella* contamination, a concern heightened by a large outbreak in early 2009, which sickened 400 people and led to at least 5 deaths. Some products are more susceptible to spoilage and the growth of pathogenic microorganisms. Physical contaminants, such as metal shavings from processing equipment, can pose safety threats to consumers as well. Allergens in the facility and the processes used to restrict exposure of products to these allergens are a major consideration that should never be overlooked.

Finances

Before a food product is created for sale, an understanding of all development, production, and marketing costs is required. A detailed cost analysis should be carried out prior to manufacture. The two types of costs are annual fixed and variable. Annual fixed costs are those that will not change in any one year, regardless of the level of production. These costs include the values of equipment, buildings, property taxes, and other items that do not fluctuate due to changes in production. Variable costs are expenditures that vary with the volume of production, such as labor, raw ingredients, packaging materials, fuel, electricity, utilities, and other items required to manufacture a specific product. Variable costs need to be carefully examined prior to test marketing and commercialization, in order to set a unit price in line with profit calculations.

TEST MARKETING

Should screening and feasibility tests indicate that a product has potential for launch, the next logical step is actual development and test marketing. Purchasing equipment at this stage is not advisable. The chief costs should be for test packaging materials, test marketing, third-party development (if applicable), and ingredients. Large companies rely on pilot plants to manufacture smaller batches of new food products for test marketing. For start-up companies, pilot plants at regional universities or community centers can be used at minimal charge. Third-party development firms or comanufacturers with small-batch capabilities can also be utilized at this stage. Alternatively, the test product could be manufactured at an approved food processing facility in your area with the proper equipment. Consumer tests at this stage are sometimes conducted as in-home use tests. Consumers should provide assessments of the product prior to the food manufacturer engaging in capital investments and launching a larger marketing scheme.

Market testing is most effective when planned well in advance with the help of an expert. Ask for assistance from marketing and consumer testing specialists who can devise a plan and interpret the results of your test, if the in-house cross-functional team does not include a professional trained in this area.

Test marketing should address formulation, processing, and packaging. At the time of test marketing, a final formula is no longer a "recipe," and ingredients should be expressed on a weight/percent basis. Multiple sources for all ingredients should be located. These should be of high quality with very little variability between shipments.

Processing techniques and ideal product qualities should be defined at this juncture. The process must be adequate to routinely deliver a high-quality, safe product. Check for state or federal regulations on processing parameters, such as final internal temperature requirements, for specific products. Packaging must be designed to appeal to the consumer, while providing protection from contamination. Codes on packaging can be helpful in keeping track of shelf-life and distribution.

Documentation is critical to assess the success or failure of your market test. Records should be kept for all processing steps and controls, including quality and temperature of raw ingredients, final cooking temperature, weight of every ingredient used in the batch, chemical and physical tests performed, net content of containers, and the number of defective units. Assessment of each step can identify product and processing flaws that can be devastating to product launches.

For test marketing, it is best to limit the distribution area. The target market should be defined by this point. Questionnaires should be provided for consumers, so they can evaluate the quality of the product. Keep in touch with store managers selling your product, and take frequent trips to determine who is buying and where and how the product is displayed at the retail level. Keep a detailed record of the market test and ask for help in analyzing the data to determine whether you should take the next step—commercialization.

COMMERCIALIZATION

Should your market test prove successful, the product will be ready to commercialize. The product can still be produced at an existing food processing plant; otherwise, the main concern at this stage is to find a location to manufacture larger quantities of the product. To set up a processing facility, a firm must address issues that include finding a location, building, equipment, utilities, and personnel. Consumer concerns remaining from test marketing need to be addressed, and a second round of testing may be conducted if deemed necessary.

Product promotion will be an integral part of commercialization. Companies with the leverage to fund national marketing schemes use many avenues to get their products noticed. Common methods of advertising new products include savings coupons, national television, internet, and product placement strategies.

Finally, product maintenance must be covered in commercialization. Maintenance should concentrate on quality and profit improvements, including sustaining the initial quality and, where feasible, enhancing it. Quality factors are maintained by noting potential defects in the product as it is handled in processing, distribution, and display. Cutting costs rather than raising the price can achieve profit improvement without deterring potential consumers. Investigating ways to improve process efficiency, save on labor costs, and find alternate suppliers of ingredients is essential to boost profits. While the product is new, solicit consumer reactions, to help identify alternative flavors and packaging.

INNOVATION MANAGEMENT SYSTEMS

Streamlining the innovation process and creating set steps for each milestone increase efficiency in product innovations. Often, organizations will subscribe to a specific innovation management system, such as the Stage-Gate® International "Idea-to-Launch model" or internally developed procedures. Innovation management systems guide organizations to make systematic decisions throughout the process, requiring one set of tasks to be finished before moving to the next.

Innovation systems should include the basic development steps outlined in this chapter, coupled with deliverables at each step. Once all mandatory tasks at a certain level are completed, the project team can move to the next step. Generally, innovation management systems begin with the idea-generation phase and end when the product is launched. Each step should be accompanied by a checklist that must be completed before going to the next step. Some systems allow for conditional passing to the next step, with an explicit acknowledgment of risks and sign-off by management.

The idea-generation phase should begin widely and end narrowly, with the output of a well-defined concept. This phase should include defining the basic parameters in terms of which product concept is to be developed. From the outset, the company should understand how the product concept will fit into a portfolio, have potential buyers in mind, and comprehend the general feel and appeal of the product, including details such as concept flavors and desired claims. At the end of this initial phase, the product should be easily explainable to the research and development team. Once the concept is well defined, the product goes to the screening phase.

Screening of products includes major steps to ensure the product hits the mark with consumers and can provide a path to profitable production. Product screening is calibrated by the basic standards set by the company. What percentage of consumer acceptance in a screening test should be accepted? This is dependent on the degree of risk a company is willing to accept and the business case for the product. As a part of a system, if a consumer concept test shows that potential consumers have little interest in the product or the concept is not well accepted, the project should either be redefined in the idea-generation phase or dropped from the innovation pipeline. Likewise, if the business case for the product cannot be realized or does not look like a promising road to profit, the concept should be discarded. Screening will differ based on product complexity. That is, a line extension may take less time in the screening process, if the original product has been wildly successful.

The adherence to innovation management systems continues in a similar fashion—assigning specific tasks and benchmarks in order to continue to the next step, until the final step, the launch. Initially, certain concepts may not be ready to introduce to market. However, these concepts should be filed and revisited. As markets change and mature, an older idea may become the perfect product concept. Innovation management systems allow organizations to make educated, logical decisions about development, while limiting verdicts based mainly on emotion. (Emotion should not be discounted, but rather heeded with caution.)

The Stage-Gate® Process (http://www.stage-gate.com/)

Stage-Gate® International is a private entity that created a system for developing all kinds of new products from idea to launch. The system sets a number of serial activities (stages) monitored by management decisions (gates). Teams must successfully complete a prescribed set of activities at each stage, which are reviewed by management for approval prior to proceeding to the next stage.

The Stage-Gate® Process has five stages (Stages 1 to 5) besides Idea Discovery (Stage 0): Idea Discovery, Scoping, Building a Business Case, Development, Testing and Validation, and Launch. The structure of each stage is similar in that each requires Activities, Integrated Analysis, and Deliverables. "Gates" separating each of these stages are structured into Review of Deliverables and Criteria for Decision making, which often are supplemented by scorecards. Criteria for decision making are what the project is judged against in order to make the go/kill and prioritization decisions. These criteria are usually organized into a scorecard and include both financial and qualitative standards. Outputs are results of the "gate" review. Gates must have clearly articulated outputs, including a decision (go/kill/hold/recycle) and a path forward (approved project plan, date, and deliverables for the next gate agreed upon).

PRODUCT LIFECYCLES

Are products from your childhood still for sale and others no longer on store shelves? The product lifecycle registers the various points throughout a product's time on the shelf, until a point in which it is no longer sold. Products go through cycles during their period of sales. When a product is first launched, companies heavily promote it. products. In-store demonstrations are sometimes used to lure customers who might not try the product otherwise. Discounts and coupons can help spike sales of a new product as well. Initial advertising costs are high, and the returns are minimal directly after launch.

The next phase in the cycle is a strong growth period. At this time, repeat buyers may decide to purchase the product on a regular basis. Word of mouth may begin to attract new customers. Expansion to new markets can also assist in generating sales. Costs continue to be high, but profits are improving.

The next phase is a decline in the growth rate. Repeat buyers decline, new markets have been tapped out, the competition begins to grow, and added costs associated with trying to attract attention to the product start to rise. Nonetheless, profits are still good in this phase.

This stage is followed by a stability period that experiences no growth in sales, as a result of consumer fatigue. There is little excitement about the product, and sales stagnate. Costs and profits break even, and profits may begin to decline.

In the product decline phase, competing products erode the product's market share, and promotions prove too costly to be effective. Sales decline further, and the product becomes unprofitable to maintain. At this point, companies must decide if it is necessary to cease manufacturing the product. The lifecycle described above is condensed, and it must be noted that some new products do not enter the decline phase for extended periods of time.

SUMMARY

Product success is dependent on multiple factors. Realistic goals and sound financial analysis can make a product more apt to prosper. Collecting ample product research assists in creating competitive products that match consumers' desires. A good business plan with adequate lists of all necessary tools is essential for building a realistic, profitable product. Developing a winning product also requires good correct timing and luck.

KEY WORDS

Acid foods—processed foods that naturally have a pH below 4.6 and/or a water activity below 0.85.

Acidified foods—low-acid foods to which acid(s) or acid food(s) are added to reduce the pH to 4.6 or below with a water activity greater than 0.85.

Food—as defined by FDA in 21 CFR 321 (f) means (1) articles used for food or drink for man or other animals, (2) chewing gum, and (3) articles used for components of any such article.

Hermetically sealed container—as defined by the FDA in 21 CFR 113.3 (f), "a container that is designed and intended to be secure against the entry of microorganisms and thereby to maintain the commercial sterility of its contents after processing."

Innovation management systems—a prescribed methodology that guides organizations to make systematic decisions throughout the innovation process, requiring prescribed sets of tasks, with each set to be accomplished before moving to the next set.

Low-acid canned foods—processed foods in hermetically sealed containers with a pH greater than 4.6 and a water activity greater than 0.85, except for alcoholic beverages.

Product lifecycle —the various points throughout a product's time on the shelf and until it is no longer sold.

Shelf-life—the determination of how long a product will retain its quality as perceived by customers.

Water activity (a_w)—the measure of the water available for microbial growth in a food.

COMPREHENSION QUESTIONS

1.1. What are the four steps in product development?

1.2. What are the three types of feasibility product development teams must be concerned about?

1.3. Find the standard of identity for ketchup from Title 21 CFR. (Hint: Go to FDA.gov and search for 21 CFR, then search within 21 CFR.) List the ingredients allowed in, and the allowable labeling of, ketchup.

1.4. What must a producer do if its canned product has a pH > 4.6 and a water activity > 0.85 in order to manufacture the product as one that is considered a low-acid or acidified food?

CHAPTER 2

Consumer Preferences, Market Trends, and Creativity

Learning Objectives

- Learn about influences of consumer preferences.
- Explore market trends.
- Become more familiar with activities that stimulate creativity and new idea generation.

THE involvement of food scientists in the creative process of new product development varies in the industry. Research and development teams, no matter their direct involvement in concept generation, should be aware of trends in the market, consumer preferences, and how concepts are developed in an organization.

CONSUMER PREFERENCE FACTORS

A myriad of influencers play into decisions by consumers to purchase or leave a product at the retailer. Consumers are influenced by age, religion, ethnicity, non-religious beliefs, and their experiences (e.g., income and community). Product developers should understand their target markets in order to devise a product that meets consumer standards, which might dietary restrictions. Information of this type must be gathered prior to innovation of a product.

Age

Age affects consumer preferences because of the culture, experiences, or scientific beliefs of individuals in a given age cohort. If you grew up eating margarine and were told it was a good alternative to butter, there is a chance you may, in a supermarket, choose margarine rather than butter. In addition, specific food choices are age related. Prunes are more appealing to aging consumers, whereas fruit snacks shaped like the latest action-movie hero are more likely to be eaten by those in a younger demographic population. With the baby boomer generation aging, there is a push to create products strictly geared toward this group. With age also comes diet restrictions that correspond with illnesses, such as diabetes, heart disease, and high blood pressure.

Religion

Religious denominations dictate the preferences of the foods consumed by their followers. Whether based on Jewish, Catholic, Muslim, Hindu, or a range of other beliefs, dietary customs vary widely. Each religion has its own reasons for requiring its guidelines, which range from the cleanliness of a species to the notion a spice will make a person angry.

Roman Catholics and some Protestant sects fast or abstain from eating meat on certain holidays. Traditionally, Catholics may substitute fish items for meat on Fridays during the Lenten season, the 40 days before the Easter holiday.

Those who practice Islam may consume only foods that meet halal standards. Foods that are not permitted are referred to as "haram," which covers items such as alcohol, pork, animals not slaughtered according to standards, and foods containing pork gelatin.

Adherents of certain forms of Judaism are restricted to eating foods prepared according to kosher laws. Kosher law does not permit the consumption of pork products, crustaceans, animals not slaughtered according to standards, and items containing gelatin from pork. In addition, there are guidelines for baked goods and avoiding meals with both meat and dairy in them.

Ethnicity

Ethnic background also affects food choices. For example, a family with Hispanic roots would have an affinity for different types of food than a family raised in India. The kinds of food a person consumes during childhood help shape his or her food cravings during adulthood.

Non-religious Beliefs

Have you ever asked a vegetarian why she practices vegetarianism? Common answers to this question include the beliefs that animals raised for meat are mistreated, that it is healthier, or that farm animals contribute to pollution. Those who limit their eating habits to local or organic foods may harbor purely secular values that guide their decision to live a certain way, such as to avoid foods or ingredients derived from genetically modified organisms (GMOs). Persons who adhere to restrictive diets may entertain a belief that their food choices contribute to overall wellness, and they may appeal to scientific studies to support their position.

Health

Other than eating food for survival and/or enjoyment, consumers may choose to include or eliminate certain foods from their diets for health reasons. Health trends are frequently influenced by new studies on food-related medical conditions or risk reduction through selective diets. Recent trends have included avoidance of allergenic ingredients, foods high in calories and added sugars, corn syrup, and food additives. Foods selected by more consumers than in previous years include organic, local, antioxidant-rich, high-protein, and high-fiber.

Income

As customers become more affluent, their shopping behaviors change. An extremely low income usually discourages consumers from selecting organic or local foods, whereas higher income has consistently been linked with shoppers who purchase these types of foods (Zepeda and Nie 2012). Customers with lower incomes tend to shop at retail stores different from the ones frequented by individuals with greater discretionary income.

Community

Location also plays a role in food choice. Cities and states can cultivate community organization or cultural tendencies that encourage distinctive eating patterns. If a person lives in a city with many farmers' markets, there is a higher likelihood of purchasing his or her food there. States that produce high quantities of livestock often have a higher proportion of persons who consume meat. Geographical proximity to food types dictates that consumers in Kansas may, on average, eat less fish than their counterparts in Maine. Similarly, citizens of rural areas may have a limited number of food product choices, especially when compared to the range of items available to urbanites.

MARKET TRENDS

Market trends stem from many sources—celebrity diets, the latest scientific research, or suddenly popular ingredients. Companies producing foods often try to be on the front end of trends, so that new products they introduce will reflect the newest trends. Diet-based trends can come and go quickly, but it can be financially lucrative to introduce products that align with the latest customer demands.

Current hot trends include gluten-free, ancient grains, and redesigning packaging to be more environmentally friendly. Consumers with sufficient income may decide to choose one product over another merely from personal belief or a sense they have the power to make a better world by purchasing more earth-friendly products or to support companies that seem to make an effort to give back. In such instance, customers are paying more to buy an item that reinforces an idea they cherish. New product ideas that disregard current consumer fixations are generally less successful than others, unless they can gain attention through low prices or catchy marketing.

As a new product developer, it is important to be cognizant of the ever-changing trends in the food industry. Constantly asking how a new product will fit into the current line of products and assessing market needs is important.

One area commonly overlooked in the study of new food product development is the food service industry. Restaurants, including fast food chains, are always seeking to add new menu items. There has been a big shift from the sole dependence on chefs to develop new items to a reliance on teams of chefs AND food scientists to introduce a successful new menu offering. The nature and properties of successful restaurant foods provide advance clues to what consumers may prefer in meals prepared at home.

CREATIVITY

Not every person is born with creativity. Still, companies can facilitate creativity in their employees by encouraging and nurturing it. A certain amount of creativity can be "taught," e.g., through short courses that introduce techniques for brainstorming. The best ideas are sometimes found by accident or with a team of people putting their heads together. The most important piece of brainstorming for a new product is to not discourage any ideas that seem out of touch. Today's conceptual clunker could be tomorrow's star. Ideation sessions should include a "no put down" rule, to facilitate an open environment. When you have a great idea, hammer out possible details of how the product would be packaged and marketed to the intended demographic.

As a product developer, you may be asked to facilitate or be part of a structured ideation session. A practical way to perform an ideation session is to follow the steps listed below.

1. Sit around a table and start with a briefing of the following:
    a. Main objective of the session: Create a new food product in an indicated category.
    b. Current consumer trends and existing products: Forms, ingredients, packaging, price.
    c. Rules for brainstorming activity: No personal attacks on teammates; critique rather than criticism of ideas.
2. Brainstorming activity
    a. Break into small groups of 3 to 4 people each. Give groups about an hour for this activity and provide each group with Post-it® notes to record ideas. Emphasize *quantity* rather than quality of ideas at this point.
    b. Bring groups back together and cluster similar ideas on poster boards.
    c. Engage in a group discussion of each idea, followed by a secret individual ranking of the ideas.
3. Ideation
    a. Regroup participants based on their own choice of which ideas they want to explore.
    b. Charge the newly formed groups with providing more details of their product concept. A rough description of product properties relating to shape, form, size, flavor, and color should be developed. If possible, a rendition of the product drawn on a piece of paper is very helpful to the product development team in making a prototype for further discussions.

COMPREHENSION QUESTIONS

2.1. Give 2 examples of current hot market trends. Think of a product that you would create to match these trends.

2.2. What is the best way for you to think creatively? Are you an innately creative person?

2.3. Give a few examples of your own consumer preference factors. How do your preferences affect how you spend your grocery dollars?

2.4. If a fast food chain asked you to help them create a new menu item that satisfies current consumer trends, what would you recommend?

REFERENCE

Zepeda, L., and Nie, C. "What are the Odds of Being an Organic or Local Food Shopper? Multivariate Analysis of US Food Shopper Lifestyle Segments." *Agriculture and Human Values, 29*, no. 4 (2012): 467–480.

CHAPTER 3

Functionality of Food Components

Learning Objectives

- Learn the functionality of carbohydrates, lipids, water, and proteins.
- Roles of food components in systems.
- Learn about reactions that can occur in food systems.

UNDERSTANDING the internal components of foods helps product development teams formulate stable, palatable food products. The major food components consist of carbohydrates, lipids, water, and proteins. Together these make up 97% of the mass of foods (Vieira 1999). This chapter will not dwell on the chemical and molecular structure of these compounds. Such information is best found in food chemistry textbooks. Rather, it will focus on the functionality of these components as it relates to food product development. Understanding food properties helps predict reactions during food processing and assists in troubleshooting. An infinite variety of minor food components can be in a formulation, including vitamins, minerals, and food additive components consisting of fiber, gums, and emulsifiers. By understanding the functions of each ingredient and their interactions during processing, product developers can better align ingredients, processing conditions, and product properties.

CARBOHYDRATES

A carbohydrate is an organic compound composed of carbon, hydrogen, and oxygen. Carbohydrates, the most abundant organic molecules on earth, serve as the main source of energy for animals. Each gram of carbohydrate produces 4 kilocalories of energy. Sugar and starches are the main sources of carbohydrate energy.

Types of Carbohydrates

Simple sugars, or monosaccharides, are the most basic units of carbohydrates. Glucose, fructose, and galactose are examples of monosaccharides. Sugar molecules consisting of 2 to 10 monosaccharides units are called compound sugars or oligosaccharides. Sucrose (table sugar) is a disaccharide composed of glucose and fructose. Other oligosaccharides include maltose (in corn syrup), lactose (in milk sugar), raffinose, and stachyose (in soybeans). Polysaccharides are carbohydrates that consist of more than ten monosaccharide units. These may be made of a single monosaccharide, such as glucose in starch, or more complex chains made of multiple monosaccharides, e.g., as found in xanthan gum. Table 3.1 details the functions of mono- and oligosaccharides in food systems.

Sweeteners

Formulations for products include sweeteners to impart desirable flavors, colors, and sweetness. Processed foods in the United States are noted for containing added sugars, which can contribute to a higher than recommended daily sugar intake. Studies by the Centers for Disease Control and Prevention (CDC) National Center for Health Statistics have found that children consume most added sugar calories in processed foods (Ervin *et al.* 2012).

Sweeteners can be nutritive or non-nutritive. Nutritive sweeteners are ones that add calories to food. Common nutritive sweeteners in the food industry include table sugar, corn syrup, fruit juice concentrates, molasses, nectars, and honey. Non-nutritive sweeteners contribute either a very small number of calories or no calories at all. Sweeteners that do not supply calories are often used in low-calorie options.

Reducing sugars are those with a carbonyl compound that will react with an amine group from an amino acid and initiate a Maillard reaction

TABLE 3.1. Function of Mono- and Oligosaccharides in Food Systems.

Function	Example
Hydrophilicity	Ability to bind water and control water activity, humectancy
Binding of flavors ligands	Sugar-water + flavorant → sugar-flavorant + water
Contribute brown color	Maillard browning reaction
Contribute sweetness	Sucrose, corn syrups and dextrose

under certain conditions. The Maillard reaction results in brown color formation and toasted flavors. Higher cooking temperatures increase the rate of this reaction (Side 2002). The Maillard reaction can be desirable or undesirable, depending on the application. This reaction is discussed later in this chapter.

Carbohydrate Sugars

Brown sugar is partially refined sucrose with a distinctive brown coloration—the result of residual molasses. The sugar is characterized based on its color and may come in light and dark varieties depending on the molasses concentration. Brown sugar contains more water than table sugar. A list of carbohydrate sweeteners with their descriptions is presented in Table 3.2.

Corn syrup is a viscous, clear sweetener made of glucose and short polymers, which can improve the humectancy of baked goods. Hydrolyzing corn starch produces corn syrup. Dextrose equivalent (DE) is used to distinguish varieties of corn syrup. The DE is the amount of total reducing sugars expressed as dextrose and calculated as a percentage of the total dry product. Hydrolyzed starch with a DE of less than 20 is considered maltodextrin. Maltodextrins are used as thickeners and stabilizers.

Fructose is a monosaccharide that can be used in place of sucrose. Hydrolyzing sucrose, resulting in the split of the simple sugars fructose and dextrose, produces fructose. Crystalline fructose has a sweetness level of about 1.3 relative to sucrose (represented as 1). Fruits contain fructose, hence, the reference to this sugar as "fruit sugar." The solubility of fructose is higher than sucrose and dextrose at all temperatures. Fructose contributes to the browning of baked goods, because it is a reducing sugar.

Glucose is a monosaccharide found in grains, fruits, and blood. It is commercially produced by hydrolyzing starch completely. Glucose is also available as a syrup and is commonly used in fermentation and confectionary applications.

Polyhydric alcohols contain several hydroxyl groups, enabling them to be used as sweeteners. They are commonly used in chewing gums and hard candies. Examples of polyhydric alcohols are sorbitol, mannitol, xylitol, and maltitol. These sugar substitutes are non-cariogenic, but can have a laxative effect when consumed in large quantities.

Dextrose equivalent (DE) is the amount of total reducing sugars expressed as dextrose and calculated as a percentage of the total dry

TABLE 3.2. Description of Common Carbohydrate Sweeteners.

Name	Description
Agave syrup	The nectar of the agave plant, which is sweet.
Brown rice syrup	A not-as-sweet syrup created from cooking brown rice with enzymes to create a sweet syrup product; half as sweet as sugar.
Brown sugar	Partially refined sucrose.
Corn Syrup	Sweet syrup of glucose and short polymers produced by hydrolysis of corn starch. DE above 20.
Fructose	Monosaccharide used in place of sucrose.
Glucose	A monosaccharide found in grains, fruits, and blood, and produced commercially by hydrolyzing starch completely.
Grape juice concentrate	The juice from grapes made into a concentrated form, which is sometimes used to sweeten products in which added sugar is undesirable.
"Higher" sugars (oligosaccharide)	Sugar molecules containing two or more monosaccharide units.
High fructose corn syrup (HFCS)	Especially sweet corn syrup made by using isomerase to convert some glucose to fructose.
Invert sugar	A blend of mixed sized sugars with a collective DE of less than 20.
Liquid sugar	Sucrose in enough water to keep a product fluid.
Maltodextrins	A blend of mixed sized sugars with a collective DE of less than 20.
Maltose	A disaccharide of two glucose units produced commercially by partial hydrolysis of starch.
Molasses	Sweetener produced as a byproduct of the refining of sucrose.
Pear juice concentrate	The juice from pears made into a concentrated form which is sometimes used to sweeten products in which added sugar is undesirable.
Powdered sugar	Pulverized granulated sugar with cornstarch.
Reducing sugar	Sugars with reducing ends that will react with copper ions and will initiate the Maillard reaction under certain conditions.
Sucrose	A disaccharide produced by condensation of glucose and fructose.
Table sugar	Refined sucrose.
Turbinado sugar	Unrefined sugar which still retains some of the brown color from molasses containing particles, sometimes referred to as "raw sugar."

Case Study: Consumer Perception of High Fructose Corn Syrup (HFCS)

High-fructose corn syrup (HFCS) at one time was just an ingredient taken for granted in food. Consumers could purchase corn syrup in the store, and its reputation was neutral. The consumer perception was that it was just liquid sugar. In 2006, consumers were not very familiar with HFCS. (Borra and Bouchoux, 2009). The impression of corn syrup changed when media outlets began to print articles alluding to a link between obesity and the sweetener (White, 2009). Although a weak association between HFCS and obesity was found in some studies, the public interpreted this as a telltale sign they should not consume products with HFCS. As a result, many companies began frantically replacing HFCS with other sweeteners. Consumers' perceptions, based on fact or fiction, drive the market to act upon their current views.

1. How might changing from HFCS to another sweetener affect a product's quality?

2. What sweetener would be best suited to take the place of HFCS and why?

weight. DE is also related to acid conversion, discussed below in connection with acid modified starch. Glucose syrup is a concentrated solution obtained from starch and has a DE of 20 or more.

OTHER COMPONENTS OF CARBOHYDRATES

Starch

Starches are dense, insoluble carbohydrate molecules that serve a variety of functions in food systems. Starch is generally composed of two polymers: amylose and amylopectin. Amylose is a straight-chained, smaller molecule, whereas amylopectin is highly branched. The characteristics of amylose and amylopectin are detailed in Table 3.3. Starches vary in their amylose and amylopectin compositions, giving each native starch different characteristics. Starches are generally insoluble in cold water, and heat increases their solubility (Vieira 1999).

Starches in prepared foods are derived from corn, wheat, rice, potato, and waxy maize. They are added to food systems to thicken or gel. The variable composition of the starches leads to differing functional prop-

TABLE 3.3. Amylose and Amylopectin Characteristics.

	Amylose	Amylopectin
Shape	Linear	Branched
Linkage	α–1,4 (some α–1,6)	α–1,4 and α–1,6
Molecular Weight	< 0.5 million	50–500 million
Films	Strong	Weak
Gel Formation	Firm	Non-gelling to soft
Color with Iodine	Blue	Reddish Brown

erties. Modification of food starches creates starches fit for a variety of food processing conditions—from the high heat of canning to stability through freeze-thaw cycles (Vieira 1999) .

Starches used for thickening act like balloons, taking up water and space (Imeson 2010). The balloon action of the starch creates higher viscosity in the system (Vieira 1999). Potato starch is an effective thickening starch, whereas wheat starch is the least effective for increasing viscosity (McWilliams 2001).

Starches used for gelling must be broken down within the system in order to form a gel. Gel strength and retrogradation characteristics are dependent on the amylose and amylopectin makeup of the starch (Imeson, 2010). To form a gel, heat is used to dissociate the molecules, and the gel structure forms during cooling. Wheat starch, potato starch, and rice starch form strong, medium, and weak gels, respectively (McWilliams 2001).

Modified Starches

Modified starches are starches that have been altered from their native state through physical or chemical means. Modification allows starches to serve more targeted functions in food systems. Applications for modified starches include emulsification, thickening, or the prevention of crystallization due to freezing of food products. Modified starches are commonly made from tapioca, corn, and potatoes.

Pre-Gelatinized Starch

Pre-gelatinized starch is created by heating a starch suspension above its gelatinization temperature, followed by suspension drying.

This process provides a product that gels and is soluble in cold water. Products that use pregelatinized starch include instant puddings, cake mixes, whipped desserts (in combination with gelatin), and instant potatoes and rice (McWilliams 2001).

Acid-Modified Starch

Acid-modified (also called thinboiled) starches are obtained by treating starch with acid in water suspensions at sub-gelatinization temperatures. A property of acid-modified starch includes decreased viscosity modification and decreased gel strength. Acid-modified starches are used in the manufacture of gum candies and confections in which a hot mixture must first flow and then cool to form a firm gel.

Oxidized Starch

Oxidized starches are produced by subjecting an acid-modified (thinboiled) starch to an alkaline (sodium hypochlorite) treatment below gelatinization temperatures. Oxidized starch is used as a lower-viscosity filler for salad dressings and mayonnaise. Unlike thinboiling starch, oxidized starch does not retrograde nor does it set to an opaque gel (McWilliams 2001).

Cross-linked Starch

Cross-linking is created through covalent bonding of two starch molecules to make a larger molecule. The starch granule gelatinization temperature increases in proportion to the extent of cross-linking, whereas the swelling power decreases (McWilliams 2001). Cross-linked starch is used when high starch stability is demanded. These starches are used in fruit paste fillings and salad dressings because of their ability to resist acid hydrolysis and remain stable at extreme pH values.

Other Starches

Freeze-thaw stability of products distributed or retailed frozen can be maintained through the use of starch phosphates or starch ethers (McWilliams 2001). Starch phosphates and starch ethers are generated through chemical means. Both products can be used to obtain non-opaque pastes to improve the quality of frozen foods.

RESISTANT STARCH

Resistant starch derives its name from the fact that it resists full digestion in the small intestine and is partially fermented by bacteria in the colon. Resistant starches are classified into five classes. They can be found naturally in some legumes, grains, and seeds or can be produced via chemical modification. For the product developer, the use of resistant starch in food formulations will allow for the benefits and functionality of starches, while reducing the caloric content of the finished food from 4 to 0.6 calories per gram of non-resistant versus resistant starch. The CODEX definition of dietary fiber now includes resistant starch.

Applications of Starches

Baking applications use starches widely, and they are also used in other processed foods. Starches can replace up to 30 percent of flour in cakes to improve volume, symmetry, and tenderness. Cakes also use starches to control the viscosity of the batter, a correlating factor in cake structure. Cookies use starch to control spread and thickness. Canned goods utilize starch to help give a clear flavor release in baby foods and improve texture and mouthfeel of pudding products. Dry mixes use starch products to control the absorption of fat and water. Starches control the spread and thickness of pancakes made from dry mixes. Starches are even added to control the viscosity, body, and texture of sour cream and dips. Ready-to-eat cereals may use starches to achieve puffiness or flake strength.

Maltodextrins

Maltodextrins are starches that are further hydrolyzed to have a DE of less than 20. Maltodextrins can be prepared from any starch. As the DE goes up, the degree of polymerization decreases and the hygroscopicity, solubility, sweetness, freezing point, and browning efficiency increase. Lower DEs lead to an increase in viscosity, binding ability, and crystal formation inhibition.

Maltodextrins' multifunctional uses are detailed in Table 3.4. They are used as a binder in granola bars and meat analogs. With artificial sweeteners that are less bulky and sweeter than sugar, maltodextrins can be used to provide bulk. Frozen applications and confections utilize low DE maltodextrins to reduce crystal formation.

TABLE 3.4. Functions of Maltodextrins and Their Applications.

Function	Food Application
Agglomerating agent	Water soluble gums
Binder	Frozen meat analogs, granola bars
Bulking agent/carrier	Artificial sweeteners, dry milk flavoring mixes, dry sauce/soup mixes, spice blends
Coatings	Dry roasted peanuts, panned candies
Crystallization inhibitor	Confections, frozen foods/desserts
Fat replacers	Bakery fillings, fat free confections, salad dressing, yogurt
Processing aid	Cheese powder, extruded products

Fiber

The ingestion of fiber in western diets decreased as a result of the processed food revolution and the expanded consumption of refined grain products. Fiber includes substances, e.g., plant cell walls, that are indigestible by human enzymes in the stomach. The intake of certain fibers has been shown to reduce the risk of heart disease and some cancers.

Soluble and insoluble fibers are found in the same foods, but each functions differently. Soluble fiber is partially digested and provides limited calories. Soluble fiber has also been credited with reducing cholesterol levels (McWilliams 2001). Insoluble fibers speed up the time it takes for food to be digested, and they also add bulk to stool. However, no energy is received from their ingestion (McWilliams 2001). Citrus fruit, oats, and legumes provide soluble fibers, whereas wheat and rice furnish insoluble fibers (McWilliams 2001). Health professionals in the United States and elsewhere have recently been recommending a higher intake of fiber by consumers, mainly through inclusion of more whole grains in the diet.

Dietary fiber that can be declared on the Nutrition Facts label includes certain naturally occurring fibers that are "intrinsic and intact" in plants according, and added isolated or synthetic non-digestible soluble and insoluble carbohydrates that FDA has determined have beneficial physiological effects to human health.

The FDA's approved dietary fibers not intrinsic and intact in plants are:

- Beta-glucan soluble fiber
- Psyllium husk

- Cellulose
- Guar gum
- Pectin
- Locust bean gum
- Hydroxypropylmethylcellulose

Hydrocolloids (Gums)

A hydrocolloid is a long-chain molecule that dissolves or swells in water and brines. Hydrocolloids improve water-holding capacity, structure, mechanical properties, and adherence in food applications. Table 3.5 offers details on common hydrocolloids and their sources, including plants, seaweeds, microorganisms, and animals.

Carrageenan is a hydrocolloid derived from red seaweed. There are three main classes of carrageenan in food applications: Kappa, iota, and lambda, all of which are soluble in hot water. Carrageenan is best used in foods that have pH above 4.3. The most common application of this additive is in dairy products, such as chocolate milk and yogurt, but it is also utilized in the meat industry for hot dogs and hamburgers. Carrageenan can also be combined with other hydrocolloids to produce a desired texture in food systems.

Xanthan gum is derived from microorganisms. It is soluble in hot or cold water and functional across a wide pH range. Temperature has no effect on the viscosity of xanthan gum solutions. The gum functions better with careful hydration. The most effective method of preparing xanthan gum dispersions is to use a mixer with a high shear rate. Xanthan gum can be found in salad dressings, beverages, and baked goods.

Cellulose is a polysaccharide chain of repeating glucose units. The hydroxyl groups can be substituted with methyl, hydroxypropylmethyl, or carboxymethyl groups. These cellulose ether derivatives are "cellulose gums," used in low-calorie foods as a binder and a thickener. Cellulose retards crystal growth, inhibits syneresis, contributes mouthfeel, and is odorless and tasteless.

Alginate is found in the form of alginic acid, a polymer. Alginate solutions gel quickly when used with calcium ions (calcium citrate). Bakery fillings and artificial cherries use alginate as a gelling agent. Alginic acid is insoluble in water.

Food scientists employ hydrocolloids in food systems to form products that have textures and consistencies that are desirable to the consumer. With the wide variety of products and uses in the hydrocolloid group,

TABLE 3.5. Hydrocolloids and Their Sources, Characteristics, and Applications.

Source	Examples	Characteristics	Application
Plants	Guar gum	Non-gelling, increases viscosity, water binding	Desserts, baked goods, ice cream stabilizer, salad dressings
	Gum Arabic	Dissolves in hot or cold water, soluble, emulsifying agent	Candies, soft drinks, beer (foam stabilizer)
	Locust bean gum	Soluble in water above 95°C, gels with xanthan gum	Ice cream stabilizer, bologna, cheese, sauce, processed meat
Seaweed	Carrageenan	Protein binding, traits dependent on types	Pet food, low sugar jam, chocolate milk, bakery fillings
	Alginate	Irreversible gel with calcium in cool water, thickener, emulsifier	Salad dressing, lemon pie, fruit for baking
	Agar	Strong gelling agent, insoluble in color water, very soluble in hot water	Stabilizer in puddings, cheese, sherbets
Microorganisms	Xanthan Gum	Soluble in hot or cold water, stable to heat and pH, good freeze thaw stability	Frozen dough, meringues, ice cream, gluten free baked goods
	Gellan gum	Strong gels, soluble in hot water, gels upon cooling	Icings
Animals	Gelatin-derived protein prepared from collagen	Strong gels	Gelatin dessert products, marshmallows
Synthetic	Cellulose gum	Water soluble, thickener in cool water, thins with heat	Bulking agent in low calorie foods
	Microcrystalline Cellulose	Stable to acids, increases film strength, stabilizer	Oil replacement in emulsions
	Methylcellulose	Soluble at cool temperatures, gels at high temperatures	Batters for fried foods, sauces, gluten free baked goods
	Hydroxypropyl Methylcellulose	Soluble at cool temperatures, gels at high temperatures	Batters for fried foods, gluten free baked goods

Sources: Imeson 2010; McWilliams 2001; Igoe 1989.

choosing the right hydrocolloid may take research, trial, and error. Suppliers can assist in finding the best hydrocolloid for specific applications.

Bulking Agents

Food systems utilize bulking agents to increase product volume. Foods modified for special dietary needs, such as fat-free or sugar-free, need bulking agents. Commonly used bulking agents include maltodextrin, hydrocolloids, and polydextrose.

Maltodextrins are non-sweet, nutritive (4 kilocalories per gram) carbohydrates that have a DE of less than 20. Polydextrose (1 kilocalorie per gram) is a polysaccharide gum that functions as an emulsifier, crystal inhibitor, and viscosity improver. It also plays a role in flavor retention, water activity control, and staling retardation. Polydextrose can be used as a bulking agent, a sweetener, and a humectant.

Chemical Reactions of Carbohydrates

Chemical reactions involving carbohydrates include: caramelization, the Maillard reaction, gelation, starch gelatinization, and retrogradation. Some carbohydrates are formulated into food for their ability to react, whereas others are added to prevent reactions that are undesirable.

Caramelization

Caramelization is the direct heating of carbohydrates, usually sugars and sugar syrups. The reaction is facilitated by small amounts of acids and certain salts. Sucrose melts at 160°C (320°F) and breaks down into glucose (glucosan and levulosan) anhydride. Caramelization of sucrose requires a temperature of 200°C (392°F). As sucrose is heated, it loses some of its water molecules, and the final product of caramelization (as heating continues at > 200°C) is $C_{125}H_{188}O_{80}$, which is called caramelin. Caramelin is a dark, bitter, and insoluble pigment. This product is to be avoided. Prior to the production of caramelin, desirable flavors occur that are the result of a number of sugar fragmentation and dehydration by-products, including diacetyl and acetic acid. Baking soda is often used to remove the bitter flavor from caramelization reactions.

Commercial types of caramel color include acid-fast, brewer's color, baker's color, and others. Acid-fast caramel color uses an ammonium bisulfite catalyst to produce cola color. Brewer's color is the product of heating a sucrose solution with ammonium ions. Through the pyrolysis of sucrose, a burnt sugar color is produced, which is called baker's color.

The Maillard Reaction

The Maillard reaction is a non-enzymatic browning reaction occurring when a protein and a reducing sugar are heated or stored together over time. This reaction is significant in foods due to its ability to affect color, taste, and texture. The Maillard reaction leads to a desirable color during the browning of meat or the undesirable browning of spray dried egg whites or fruit. The Maillard reaction also produces flavors that are preferable in applications such as bakery items and roasted coffee. Later stages of the Maillard reaction may result in the development of toxicity in foods and the reduction of nutritional value.

It is important for food product developers to know that all monosaccharides are reducing. Table sugar (sucrose) is NOT a reducing sugar, but lactose and maltose are. The browning reaction is catalyzed by heat. In some cases, the occurrence of the Maillard reaction is incorrectly referred to as "caramelization."

Starch Gelatinization

Native starch granules are insoluble in cold water due to the association of amylopectin with amylose to form regions of crystalline micelles. However, they can swell slightly and become partially hydrated. As the granules are heated, the weak hydrogen bonding in the crystalline micelle is disrupted. The crystal starts to swell and forms a sticky starch suspension with highly swollen intact granules dispersed in a solution of free starch molecules (granules released during swelling). Continued swelling of the starch granules causes a breakdown in internal crystal structure. The amylose molecule is then solubilized, partially leaching out from the swollen starch granule into solution. The solubilized amylose begins to form an intergranular matrix, which causes an increase in viscosity. Molecular associations among the amylose molecules and with other constituents (lipids, proteins, etc.) occur. The swollen starch granules may break down into fragments and are more susceptible to mechanical shearing. Changes in gelatinization take place starting at 52°C (126°F) depending on the type of starch. A continuous increase in temperature causes the granule to collapse and rupture. The degree of starch hydration depends on temperature, pH, shear, and concentration of water to starch.

Gelation

Gel formation occurs when hydrogen bonds with the straight-chained amylose and water. This occurs, for example, as a starch paste is cooled. The starch chains become less energetic, and the hydrogen bonds become stronger, giving a firmer gel. As a gel ages or if it is frozen and thawed, the starch chains have a tendency to interact with each other and force out water. The release of water from the gel is called syneresis. Amylose content and the molecular size of the amylose fraction influence the tendency of starches to thicken or gel. Gelling is a function of amylose, whereas swelling is a function of amylopectin. Gelation is demonstrated in gelatins, pie fillings, and puddings.

Case Study: The Product Developer and the Heated Carbs Dilemma

Stan had been working for 14 months on the development of a new sweetened chip made from a variety of vegetables and tubers. The formula had been finalized and the process developed to fry the formed chip at a temperature of 177°C (350°F) for 10 minutes to develop the nice flavor and brown color. One month before launch, out of the blue came a report from Europe that carbohydrates heated to a temperature above 120°C (248°F) contain a chemical called acrylamide and that the World Health Organization stated that the level of acrylamide in foods poses a "major concern" as a potential carcinogen! The product development team charged Stan with altering the process parameters to lower the risk of acrylamide formation. Back to the drawing board and after some literature search, Stan decided to blanch the vegetables prior to frying, decrease the cooking time, and then dry the chips in an air oven after frying. This produced good quality chips, except that the desired brown color was not achieved. The simplest solution was the addition of caramel color, after which Stan announced to the team that the product was ready for launch again . . . at least until that night when all news channels reported that public health researchers were warning that people may be exposing themselves to a potentially cancer-causing byproduct of the caramel coloring used in some types of sodas! The byproduct is 4methylimidazole (4-MEI) and can be found in other foods in which certain caramel colors are added as well. The next few weeks, Stan worked on incorporating beets into his formula, resulting in a chip with a red tinge that consumers expected to find in a beet-containing product.

Retrogradation

Retrogradation is the crystallization of a starch chain in the gel. During storage, amylose molecules re-associate, and hydrogen bonding occurs. Amylose is more susceptible to retrogradation than amylopectin. Retrogradation, which is chiefly responsible for the staling of bread, is generally a slow reaction, even though it starts soon after bread is baked. Additives such as diacetyl tartaric acid ester of mono- and diglycerides (DATEM) can be included in baked goods' formulations as anti-staling agents. Also, packaging in moisture-barrier films can slow down the retrogradation process.

LIPIDS

Lipids, found in animal and plant tissues, are defined as water-insoluble organic substances that are widely classified as fats and oils. Lipids that are solid at room temperature are referred to as fats, whereas lipids that are liquid at room temperature are oils. Lipids are extractable by nonpolar solvents (chloroform, hexane and ether). Lipids consist of: (1) fatty acids, (2) glycerides, (3) non-glyceride lipids, and (4) complex lipids.

Lipid Applications in Food

The principal functionality of lipids in the food system is to provide body, mouthfeel, plasticity, moistness, color, and flavor. Both fats and oils are routinely incorporated into foods or used as a medium for processing. The type of fats used in new food products impacts the shelf-life and stability of the product. Fats also influence sensory characteristics.

Baked Goods

The volume and textural characteristics of baked goods are directly related to the kind and amount of lipids present in the system. When lipids are incorporated, they are dispersed throughout the batter or dough. The dispersed lipid tenderizes the baked product by coating ingredients and interfering with the development of gluten and starch structures that reinforce rigidity in baked goods.

The dispersal of lipids varies with the baked product. For example, cake fat is finely dispersed, whereas large dispersions of fat are encouraged in pastry dough to achieve flakiness. In pastries, expansion of water vapor separates the layers of dough to create a flaky texture. Lipids contribute to the enjoyment of foods, but also significantly increase the amount of kilocalories intake. Lipids provide 9 kilocalories per gram, the highest of any food component (Shewfelt 2009). For this reason, companies producing baked goods have replaced lipids with other ingredients that mimic the mouthfeel of lipids.

Confectionary Products

Confectionary products use fats and oils from various sources to increase viscosity, prevent or promote crystallization, and provide desired sensory effects. In crystalline candies, lipids increase the viscosity of the syrup and interfere with the growth of sucrose crystals. Amorphous candies, such as toffee and caramels, use a high proportion of lipids to prevent the crystallization of sucrose. Lipids serve as the base for coatings and for the foundation of certain confections. In confections, lipids improve the sensory characteristics by providing the desired mouthfeel and flavor, while helping to suspend solids, such as sugar.

Processing with Lipids as a Cooking Medium

Oil as a cooking medium is utilized in processing many foods, including potato chips and donuts. The type of lipid chosen as a cooking medium is important, because some oils deteriorate at low temperatures. Shortenings and butter are poor frying lipids because they have low smoke points and rapid rancidity formation. Oils are usually the best choice for frying, but not all oils are suitable for these applications. To process foods using oil, maintenance of oil quality and temperature control are essential. Temperature control affects how much oil a product absorbs. Suppliers can generally direct their clients on the best oils for frying applications.

Characteristics of Lipids

Crystallization

Plasticity of fat is a physical characteristic, such as spreadability (e.g., in margarine) and depends on the amount of solids and the melting point. Fat can be visualized as a mass of interlocking crystals (solid phase) holding a liquid phase. The plasticity of fat depends on the proper proportion between the solid and liquid phase. In a plastic fat, such as hydrogenated shortening, the solid phase consists of crystals of fat surrounded by a liquid phase of oil.

Hydrogenation

Hydrogenation is a process for improving the oxidative and thermal stability of fats and oils and for converting vegetable oils to plastic fats with a desired level of hardness. Hydrogenation involves the catalytic addition of hydrogen to the double bonds of fatty acids. After hydrogenation, liquid shortenings are charged with inert nitrogen gas, cooled rapidly, and agitated. Unfortunately, hydrogenation of oils results in the formation of trans fats, which have been associated with increasing the levels of LDL cholesterol in the blood and thus heightening the risk of coronary heart disease and stroke. In the early 2000s, the FDA required that trans fats be listed on the nutrition facts panels of packaged foods, and in 2013, the FDA made a preliminary determination that partially hydrogenated oils are no longer considered generally recognized as safe (GRAS) substances. Consequently, most companies moved to eliminate trans fats from their products. Product developers who replaced hydrogenated fats in their formulations with more unsaturated oils had to rely on the addition of antioxidants to make up for the loss in shelf-life. Additionally, because of the trend toward "clean" labels, traditionally used antioxidants such as butylated hydroxyanisole (BHA) and butylated hydroxytoluene (BHT) had to give way to "natural" antioxidants such as tocopherols (vitamin E) or rosemary extract.

Deterioration of Fats

The quality of lipids is affected by chemical reactions and handling over the life of the product. Chemical degradation causes rancidity, which leads to disagreeable odors and flavors in the fatty substance. Heat and storage conditions are major factors in the breakdown and quality degradation of lipids.

Rancidity

Lipids in which rancidity has occurred produce off-flavors, which

TABLE 3.6. Types of Rancidity.

Type of Rancidity	Description	Prevention Strategies
Lipolysis (hydrolytic rancidity)	Water present in product splits the glycerol from the fat molecules.	• Reduce water content • Use packaging with moisture barrier
Oxidative rancidity	The uptake of oxygen by an unsaturated fatty acid.	• Chelating agents • Antioxidants • Prevention of temperature and light abuse

are unacceptable to consumers. Types of rancidity include lipolysis (hydrolytic rancidity) and oxidative rancidity, as indicated in Table 3.6. Rancidity reactions require specific environmental factors. Oxidative rancidity needs oxygen to occur, whereas lipolysis requires water.

The hydrolysis of ester bonds in lipids may take place by enzyme action (lipase) or by heat (frying)/moisture, resulting in the liberation of free fatty acids. Free fatty acids are unstable pieces of lipids. Ultimately, the breaking-off of free fatty acids causes rancid odors and flavors. This reaction is common in products with higher moisture and fat in the same system, such as butter.

Molecules of fat containing unsaturated fatty acid are prone to oxidative rancidity. Oxidative rancidity can occur only in the presence of oxygen, but metals such as copper and iron will facilitate the reaction (McWilliams 2001). Light and warm temperatures can also accelerate this type of rancidity. The unpleasant odor of rancid lipids is attributed to the formation and breakdown of hydroperoxides.

Antioxidants are effective in slowing down oxidation and increasing the induction period. Antioxidants such as BHA, BHT and tertiary butylhydroquinone (TBHQ) reduce oxidation by preventing formation of radical chains through the donation of a hydrogen atom. Other antioxidants, such as ethylenediaminetetraacetic acid (EDTA) and citric acid, retard rancidity by binding metals in the food system. Food scientists choosing antioxidants should consider the legal status, type of fat or oil, application method, and ease of dispersion. Environmental factors can also slow down degradation. Vacuum or modified atmosphere packaging, controlling temperature, and excluding light can all delay the onset of rancidity.

Effect of Heating Fats. Along with accelerating oxidative rancidity, heating also causes polymer formation. The free fatty acids from lipolysis continue to degrade and form polymers as the free fatty acids couple together (McWilliams 2001). Polymer formation results in increased viscosity, which may increase foaming in frying fat.

The smoke point is different for each fat and gradually changes throughout its life. Fats and oils can be heated to high temperatures when they are fresh, but degradation by heat causes the smoke point to drop over time. Reductions in smoke point temperatures are caused by hydrolysis of free fatty acids, which in turn causes excess glycerol to accumulate. The smoke point of a fat depends on the percentage of free glycerol in the fat or the ease with which the molecules are hydrolyzed to free glycerol. Monoglycerides hydrolyze more readily than triglycerides.

Quality Determinants of Lipids

The quality of fats is determined by color, sensory properties, and shelf stability. Color testing can be done with the Lovibond method, or a comparison to color standards, or by using a spectrophotometer. Sensory properties including odor and degree of rancidity can be tested through organoleptic sensory testing procedures. Rancidity and quality degradation are also determined through other analytic methods, which are detailed in Table 3.7. Shelf stability of oils is tested through the Schaal oven storage protocol, an accelerated test that determines shelf-life characteristics over time. The oils being tested are stored at a set temperature and tested periodically for off-odors and tastes.

TABLE 3.7. Tests Used for the Determination of Lipid Oxidation.

Test	Measures	Use
Peroxide Value	The formation of peroxides by milliequivalents (meq) of peroxide	Quality testing of packaged products such as chips and peanuts
Free Fatty Acid	Free fatty acids content, hydrolytic rancidity	Liquid fats
Chromatographic Analysis	Free fatty acids	Liquid fats
Thiobarbituric Acid (TBA) Analysis	Formation of monoaldehyde, shown to correlate with peroxide formation; correlates well with sensory testing over time	Any foods susceptible to oxidation, especially meats
Iodine Value	Degree of unsaturation (higher iodine number = more unsaturation)	Characterizing oil

Source: Nielsen 1998.

SPECIALTY FATS AND FAT SUBSTITUTES

Medium Chain Triglycerides (MCT)

Medium chain triglycerides or MCTs are specialty fats composed primarily of saturated 8 and 10 carbon fatty acids (caprylic and capric). These fats exhibit: (1) low viscosity, (2) bland odor and taste, (3) absence of color, and (4) heat stability. Like carbohydrates, MCTs are not metabolized through the gut but rather in the liver. The caloric value of MCTs is 8.3 kilocalories per gram.

MCTs have many food applications. They are used as flavor carriers due to their bland odor and neutral taste, which will not interfere with the main flavor contributor. In confectionary applications, these fats provide gloss and prevent sticking because of their low viscosity. MCTs have been directly substituted for vegetable oils in salad dressings to create a reduced-calorie product.

Fat Replacers and Substitutes

Fat replacers are important to the food business, as more and more customers look to trim their waistline. The obesity problems in the United States have prompted the food industry to find better-tasting fat substitutes, while at the same time retaining fat-related texture and taste qualities. Many fat-replacing products are on the market. As with other additives, it is important to work with suppliers to find the best additives that fit the food system.

Olestra

Olestra (sucrose polyesters) is a mixture of hexa-, hepta-, and octesters of sucrose with long-chain fatty acids from vegetables, which have been used to replace fat. The first product to use Olestra was potato chips. Olestra is stable during heating and provides texture and mouthfeel similar to the products they are replacing. The biggest benefit of the fat replacer is that it is not digested and therefore provides zero calories. Possible side effects of Olestra include stomach cramping and diarrhea.

Maltrin

Maltrin (040 Maltodextrin) is a spray-dried non-sweet carbohydrate

TABLE 3.8. Tested Formulations for Sugar-free and Low-fat Muffins

Ingredients	Control	Sugar Free	Low Fat
Cake flour	100.0	100.0	100.0
Sucrose	51.0	—	51.0
Vegetable shortening	21.1	21.1	7.0
Fluid whole milk	75.0	75.0	—
Skim milk	—	—	75.6
Beaten liquid egg	26.0	26.0	26.0
Sucralose	—	0.1	—
Maltodextrin DE ≤ 3	—	51.0	60.0
Xanthan gum	—	0.1	0.1
Water	6.0	35.0	45.0
Baking powder	4.3	4.3	4.3
Salt	2.1	2.1	2.1

Source: Khouryieh, J., Aramouni, F.M., and Herald, T. 2005. Evaluation of sucralose, maltodextrin, and xanthan gum in low-fat/sugar-free muffins. *J. Food Quality. 28* (439–451).

made from hydrolyzed corn starch. The product has a bland flavor and smooth mouthfeel. It contributes 4 kilocalories per gram of product. Maltrin fat replacer can be used in many different types of foods, including baked goods, frozen desserts, and dressings.

There is no silver bullet to replace fat in a food. The product developer has to rely on various ingredients to make up for the loss in texture, taste, and color that accompany fat reduction or elimination. Extensive testing for physical, chemical, microbiological, and sensory properties must be performed whenever fats (or sugar) are being replaced or reduced in a food product. Table 3.8 gives tested formulations for sugar-free and low-fat muffins.

WATER

Water is the key ingredient in any food product, as it controls the appearance, texture, and flavor of foods. The high content of water in fruits and vegetables provides crunch and crisp texture, whereas the water-holding capacity of meat influences color and texture. In addition, water is a dispersion medium for food and makes possible ionization of acids and bases as demonstrated by the leavening action of baking powder in bakery products. In the presence of water, acids can hydrolyze sucrose to glucose and fructose, which is desirable in fruit pectin jellies and bread dough. Microorganisms spoil highmoisture foods quickly. Tap water has a pH range of 7.5 to 8.5.

Factors Affecting Boiling Point of Water

The boiling point of water is affected by atmospheric, geographic, and other factors. Altitude lowers water's boiling point. For each 960-foot increase above sea level, the boiling point decreases 1°C because of a decrease in air pressure. Increased barometric pressure increases the boiling point. For example, cloudy days with lower barometric pressure may decrease water's boiling point. Steam pressure, as in a pressure canner, may also raise the boiling point above 100°C (212°F). Adding solutes also increases boiling points and freezing points. Sugar, for example, increases the boiling point 0.52°C (0.94°F) per mole in a solution, whereas salt increases the boiling point by 1.04°C (1.87°F) per mole due to ionization.

Types of Water

The basic types of water are soft and hard. Soft water is classified as water with some organic matter but no mineral salts. In contrast, hard water contains both organic matter and mineral salts. Distilled water contains no mineral salts or organic matter.

An effective method for reducing mineral salts in water is heating. Mineral salts are eliminated upon boiling, which can under some circumstances eliminate hardness. Heat converts soluble bicarbonates into insoluble carbonates and removes unwanted Ca^{2+} and Mg^{2+} ions. More permanent hardness in water is caused by the presence of Ca, Mg, and $FeSO_4$, which do not precipitate upon boiling. Instead, these insoluble salts interact with soap and decrease the cleansing effectiveness of hard water. Hard water in cooking can interfere with tenderizing.

WATER MANAGEMENT IN NEW FOOD PRODUCTS

When developing a new product, one of the first issues to consider is the amount of water in the food, since water content affects the product's properties, stability, processing yield, and safety. The initial and final moisture contents often dictate the processing method and packaging options, as well as the ultimate nutrient density. Large deviations in water content will cause errors in nutrition facts panels because of a dilution or concentration effect on the nutrients. Therefore, once you develop a prototype of your new product, make sure you run a moisture test. Based on the prototype's sensory properties, a decision can then be made on whether to do the following:

1. Increase the moisture content by adding water or other moist ingredients to the formula; to counter any negative effect of the added water on product shelf-life, water binders such as salt, sugar, maltodextrins, and gums can be added to lower the water activity;
2. Decrease the moisture content by reducing the amount of water added, adjusting the heating process time and/or temperature, or using one of the many drying options available. In some instances, the decrease in moisture will have a negative effect on the sensory properties. If a moist mouthfeel and shiny appearance are desired, then the addition of humectants such as glycerol, propylene glycol, or sugar alcohols is warranted. This approach can also be used for the development of intermediate moisture foods (IMFs), which have been popular for years in the pet food industry but have not been used extensively outside it.

PROTEINS

Proteins are complex macromolecules that are made up of the 21 amino acids. In food systems, they provide structure and function through creating foams, increasing gel strength, and extending water-holding capacity. Proteins have a high nutritive value and are major components in animal-derived foods.

Functions of Proteins in Food

The food product developer needs to be familiar with the functionality of proteins, because such knowledge is valuable for formulating new products and for troubleshooting problems that may arise during processing. Proteins are easily modified through heat processing and chemical agents, which can be witnessed in everyday cooking. The coagulation of egg whites from heat is an example of a physical agent changing a food. Another instance of protein change is the shrinking of steaks when they are cooked. Because the protein chains shrink, the meat shrinks as well. Recent trends in food proteins include the extensive use of whey proteins in body-building powders and drinks; the development of non-traditional sources of flours from foods like peas, lentils, sorghum, and almonds; the use of ancient grains like amaranth and teff in breadmaking; the use of textured and flavored fish protein from inexpensive fish to produce surimi, a product used extensively in the manufacture of imitation seafood; and the attempt to incorporate insect flours into mainstream foods because of their high protein content.

Water Binding and Viscosity Effects

Proteins can bind large amounts of water in food systems, which in turn affects the viscosity of a food. This property is used in bread-making, meat products, and gelatin desserts. Proteins have minimum functionality at certain pH values. Viscosity of a protein solution will depend on the solubility of particular proteins, which is affected by factors such as pH, salt concentration and temperature. Each protein has an isoelectric point, which is the pH at which the protein has its minimum solubility and a net charge of zero in solution. Fluid sources of protein, such as milk, are likely to coagulate at the isoelectric point. The protein becomes more positively charged as the pH goes below its isoelectric point. Coagulation is the process of precipitating proteins, mostly by heat, enzymes, or pH, which leads to aggregation of the molecules (McWilliams 2001).

Denaturation can also occur due to exposure to heat, acids, or solvents (Vieira 1999). Denaturation is a change in a protein's structure without the breaking of covalent bonds. Denaturation is accompanied by decreased solubility (McWilliams 2001; Vieira 1999). When denaturation occurs, the function of the protein is altered. The denaturation of proteins is desirable in selected food processing applications. For example, cheese and yogurt are the products of denaturation in fluid milk. (Vieira 1999).

Cohesiveness and Elastic Properties in Dough

Proteins are responsible for providing a cohesive, elastic network in dough. Wheat gluten is the most effective protein for this function. Recently, with the popularity of gluten-free foods, various proteins from other grain flours have been tried with different degrees of success. In order to make gluten-free bread from these flours, it is often necessary to add gums to bind the water in the system.

Emulsifying Agents

Emulsions are the dispersion of one liquid in another that are not readily soluble. The emulsion capacity is the ability of a protein solution or suspension to emulsify oil. Some proteins have an emulsifying capacity, enabling them to bind both hydrophilic and hydrophobic molecules. This property is exploited in the processed meats industry to manufacture sausages and hot dogs. Factors such as pH and ionic strength can be manipulated to increase protein extraction from meat and improve their emulsifying properties.

Contribution to Color

Myoglobin is responsible for the red color in meat. Chemical changes due to oxidation-reduction reactions and exposure to various gases affect the color of the red meat pigment and have been extensively studied for their impact on consumer acceptance and products' shelf-life. Also, the Maillard reaction needs proteins in order to occur. Thus, proteins are partially responsible for the formation of pleasant, volatile flavoring compounds, as well as brown pigments in food products.

Enzymatic Activity

Enzymes are proteins that play a role in biological systems and affect food acceptability and shelf-life. Enzymatic activity can be reduced or eliminated by the same factors that affect protein solubility, such as heat, pH, or reducing agents. Thus, to extend their shelf-life, fruits and vegetables are blanched in steam or hot water to inactivate polyphenol oxidase, the enzyme responsible for enzymatic browning, and to inactivate pectinases responsible for softening in produce. Other enzymes act to develop food flavors and to speed up fermentation reactions.

Forming Food Foams

Proteins have a vital role in the development of food foams, such as egg white foams used to make meringues, toppings, and cookies, or milk proteins used to make foam toppings in coffee drinks. The foaming ability of proteins is affected by the nature and the concentration of the protein, pH, temperature, and mixing time. Proteins form foams due to their ability to decrease interfacial tension at the air-liquid interphase.

Examples of proteins in food are given in Table 3.9.

TABLE 3.9. Proteins in Food.

Type of Protein	Source	Properties
Albumins	Egg white, milk	Coagulate when heated, soluble in water
Globulins	Meat and legumes	Coagulate when heated, limited water solubility
Glutenins	Wheat	Helps give structure, elastic protein
Prolamins	Wheat, rye, and other grains	Protein with low lysine values
Fibrous proteins (i.e., collagen)	Meat and poultry	Insoluble
Casein	Milk	Begins to precipitate at pH 4.6

SUMMARY

The components of whole foods and ingredients are important to understand whenever adding them to food products. Food scientists should investigate and consult with suppliers about what properties will factor into creating the targeted food item. Understanding the science behind ingredient functionality in a product system will contribute to higher prototype success rates.

KEY WORDS

Caramelization—the direct heating of carbohydrates, usually sugars and sugar syrups, to facilitate the melting and breakdown of sugar into glucose.

Coagulation—precipitating proteins, mostly by heat, enzymes, or pH, which leads to aggregation of molecules.

Denaturation—a change in a protein's structure without the breaking of covalent bonds.

Dextrose equivalent (DE)—the amount of total reducing sugars expressed as dextrose and calculated as a percentage of the total dry product.

Isoelectric point—the pH at which a protein has its minimum solubility and a net charge of zero in solution.

Maillard reaction—a reaction that results when proteins and reducing sugars are joined together, leading to the onset of brown pigments; catalyzed by heat.

Reducing sugars—sugars with reducing chain ends that will react with copper ions and initiate the Maillard reaction under certain conditions.

COMPREHENSION QUESTIONS

3.1. Answer True or False:

a. Sucrose is commonly responsible for Maillard browning reactions.
b. Hydrogenation makes lipids both less stable and solid.

3.2. Explain two reactions that contribute to changes in the color of red meat products.

3.3. Fill in the following blanks:

a. ________________ is also referred to as glucose.
b. ________________ is often used to help remove the bitter flavor from caramelization reactions.
c. ________________ is the protein found in eggs.
d. ________________ and ______________ are the proteins found in wheat, whereas ____________ is the protein found in corn.

3.4. Give the meaning of the acronym DE and explain the term.

3.5. How would a producer eliminate hardness from water?

3.6. List three ways to modify starch.

3.7. What is the relative sweetness of the following compared to sucrose?

a. Fructose
b. Honey
c. Aspartame
d. Acesulfame Potassium
e. Sucralose
f. Molasses

3.8. List five functional properties of sugar in foods.

3.9. Define isoelectric point.

3.10. If you were developing a baked good that contained lower fat, what ingredients might you use to replace the lipids in the formulation?

REFERENCES

Borra, S., and A. Bouchoux. "Effects of Science and the Media on Consumer Perceptions About Dietary Sugars." *The Journal of Nutrition 139*, no. 6 (2009): 1214S–S1218.

Ervin, B. R., B. K. Kit, M.D. Carroll, and C. L. Ogden. *Consumption of Added Sugar Among U.S. Children and Adolescents (Data Brief No. 2012-1209).* (Atlanta: U.S. Department of Health and Human Services National Center for Health Statistics, 2012).

Igoe, R. S. *Dictionary of Food Ingredients*, 2nd ed. (New York: Chapman & Hall, 1989).

Imeson, A. *Food Stabilisers, Thickeners and Gelling Agents.* (City: John Wiley & Sons, 2010).

McWilliams, M. *Foods: Experimental Perspectives*, 4th ed. Upper Saddle River, NJ: Prentice-Hall, 2001).

Nielsen, S. S., ed. *Food Analysis*, 2nd ed. (Gaithersburg, MD: Aspen Publishers, Inc., 1998).

Shewfelt, R. L. *Introducing Food Science.* (Boca Raton, FL:CRC Press, 2009).

Side, C., ed. *Food Product Development Based on Experience.* (Ames, IA: Iowa State Press, 2002).

Vieira, E. R. *Elementary Food Science*, 4th ed. (Gaithersburg, MD: Aspen Publishers, 1999).

White, J. "Misconceptions About High-Fructose Corn Syrup: Is it Uniquely Responsible for Obesity, Reactive Dicarbonyl Compounds, and Advanced Glycation End-Products. *The Journal of Nutrition 139*, no. 6 (2009):1219–1227.

CHAPTER 4

Physical and Chemical Properties of Food

Learning Objectives

- Role of chemical properties on characteristics of food.
- Role of physical properties on characteristics of food.
- How to determine chemical and physical properties of foods.

FOOD SCIENTISTS must pay close attention to the properties of foods being developed, in order to determine quality, create standards for production, and ensure safety. The properties of raw ingredients may need to be measured as they are brought into a plant, from the protein content of a new year's harvest of wheat to the brix of grapes for wine. The properties of food raw ingredients contribute to the overall quality of the final product and should be measured for processing stability.

ACIDITY

Many foods, including yogurt, need an acidic environment for preparation. Other foods, such as sauerkraut and pickles, need an acid environment to kill harmful bacterial and enhance flavor. The basic concepts for understanding pH and acidity start with the Bronsted-Lowery theory, which states that an acid is a proton donor, (H^+) and a base is a proton acceptor (OH^-). The reaction of an acid and a base will yield salt and water. This is considered a neutralization reaction.

Acid and base reactions can cause dissociation/ionization in dilute solutions. Strong acids, including hydrogen chloride (HCl), will ionize in solution to H^+ and Cl^-, and strong bases will ionize to Na^+ OH^-. Weak acids (e.g., acetic acid) and weak bases (e.g., ammonia) dissociate only slightly. Most foods contain a mixture of weak acids. The ori-

$$\text{Acid }(H^+) + \text{Base }(OH^-) \xleftrightarrow[\text{(neutralization)}]{} H_2O + \text{Salt}$$

FIGURE 4.1. The reaction of an acid and a base.

gins of acids in food products include natural compounds (e.g., tartaric acid in grapes), acids produced by microorganisms (e.g., *Aspergillus niger* produces citric acid), or ones added during manufacture (e.g., acetic acid for pickles). Fumaric acid is added to tortillas to lower the pH, which increases the effectiveness of mold inhibitors and helps with machinability.

Acidity in foods can be measured in two ways: by determining pH or titratable acidity. With pH, active or effective acidity is expressed as a function of hydrogen ions that exist in solution at any one time. Strong acids almost completely dissociate, whereas acetic acid (weak acid) has little dissociation. Titratable or total acidity is measured through a titra-

TABLE 4.1. Role of Acid and Bases in Food Systems.

Role of Acid	Acid Used	Example
Chemical leavening	Tartaric acid, sodium aluminum phosphate	Baked goods
Chelating agents	Citric acid, EDTA	Canned beans, fats and oils, beverages
Microbial inhibitor	Sorbic acid, benzoic acid	Food and drinks
Pectin gel formation	Citric acids	Jams, jellies
Flavor	Hyrdronium ion, short chain fatty acids, malic acid, phosphoric acid, citric acid	Any food item with sour taste, sour candy apples, phosphoric acid (commonly added in cola drinks), citric acid (added to fruit drinks to assist in tangy flavor)
Role of Base	**Base Used**	**Example**
Chemical leavening	Sodium bicarbonate	Baked goods
Enhancement of color and flavor	Sodium hydroxide	Ripe olives (darker color and remove bitterness), pretzels (alter browning and smoothness), tortilla dough
	Sodium bicarbonate	Peanut brittle (enhances Maillard reaction, CO_2 makes porous structure), cocoa processing (gives darker color)
Promotes gelation	Tetra-sodium pyrophosphate + disodium phosphate + calcium	Instant milk-gel puddings
Peeling of root and tuber skins	Sodium hydroxide (3% at 80°C)	Potatoes

tion in which all of the hydrogen molecules in the solution are replaced by a metal (neutralization of the acid with an appropriate amount of base).

pH

pH is an indicator of the amount of acid or base present in a food system. The pH scale ranges from 0 to 14. The pH scale is determined by the negative logarithm of the H^+ or OH^- concentration in solution. The pH of pure water is equal to 7. The pH of blueberry juice is 3. Keep in mind that a decrease in pH value of one integer corresponds to an increase in $[H^+]$ of ten times the original value. The value pH 2, for example, represents a $[H^+]$ of 0.01 moles per liter.

The majority of foods are acidic. In food production, the pH of food products is sometimes altered using an acidifying agent, to meet safety standards and extend shelf-life. The pH of food can be lowered by adding agents such as citric, malic, or fumaric acid. Table 4.2 lists the effects of acids and bases on selected categories of foods.

Determining the pH of a Product. To test the pH of a product, pH meters are most commonly used. In order for pH meters to operate properly, it is important to maintain the instrument in good working condition. Meters should be calibrated before each use by means of two-point calibration (by utilizing two different standard buffers, commonly at pH 4.0 and 7.0). After the instrument is calibrated, it should be immersed in the product to be tested. Always follow the manufacturer's instructions when using and maintaining a pH meter. Most pH meters are equipped with automatic temperature compensation (ATC), which corrects for slight changes in temperature. The sensitivity of pH meters is very important to consider, especially when measuring canned foods close to pH 4.6. By comparison, testing the pH of products with pH strips is inaccurate and imprecise.

TABLE 4.2. Description and pH Ranges of Common Foods.

Description	pH Range	Product Examples
Alkaline	7.0–9.6	Egg white, hominy, soda crackers
Neutral	6.5–7.0	Milk, chicken meat
Low acid	5.3–6.5	Bacon, canned vegetables, fresh meat
Medium acid	4.5–5.3	Canned soup, soft cheese, ravioli
Acid	3.7–4.5	Mayonnaise, yogurt, orange juice, tomatoes, berries
High acid	pH < 3.7	Pickles, most canned foods, lemon juice

When testing the pH of solid foods, surface pH meters or other approved methods can be used. Approved methods for determining the pH of solid foods can be found in the American Association of Cereal Chemists (AACC) or Association of Analytical Communities (AOAC) approved methods. A general method to test the pH of solids is to mix them with a small amount of deionized water and thoroughly mix or place in a Stomacher device. Surface and probe pH meters are available to test the pH of solid foods as well.

pH and Microorganisms

All microorganisms have a minimum, maximum, and optimum pH for growth. Bacteria tend to prefer high pH (above 4.6), whereas molds and yeasts prefer lower pH. It is important to note that *Clostridium botulinum* (*C. botulinum*) grows and produces deadly neurotoxins as low as pH 4.8 (upper pH for acid foods is 4.6). Product ingredients may also have a certain buffering capacity, resulting in pH changes over time. In addition, the growth of molds and yeasts in canned foods using acids as an energy source can cause the pH of the product to rise. This may make the product more susceptible to bacterial growth and will become a concern if the pH goes above 4.6, because of the risk of botulism.

The pH of foods determines how they are processed. For example, low-acid foods such as green beans require pressure canning to attain temperatures of 240° to 250°F, in order to destroy spores of *C. botulinum*. Fruits and vegetables have lower pH values; meats and milk are

TABLE 4.3. Legal Definition of Low-Acid, Acidified, and Acid Foods.

Legal Classification	Definition	pH	a_w
Low acid food	Any foods, other than alcoholic beverages, with a finished equilibrium pH greater than 4.6 and a a_w greater than 0.85. Tomatoes and tomato products having a finished equilibrium pH less than 4.7 are not classified as low-acid foods (21 CFR 113.3).	> 4.6	> 0.85
Acidified food	Low-acid foods to which acid(s) or acid food(s) are added and have a_w greater than 0.85 and a finished equilibrium pH of 4.6 or below (21 CFR 114.3).	< 4.6	> 0.85
Acid food	Foods that have a natural pH of 4.6 or below (21 CFR 114.3).	< 4.6	< 0.85

CFR = Code of Federal Regulations.

Case Study: The "Cheesecake in a Jar" Dilemma

The product development team at Company X was in the process of developing a line of "cheesecake in a jar" products for sale during the holiday season. Initial testing in our laboratory indicated that the product as formulated had a pH of 5.6 and a a_w of 0.87 making it, by definition, a low acid food. To manufacture a safe product, this would require processing in a retort under pressure at a temperature of 250°F. As expected, the quality of the cheesecake, especially texture and color, deteriorated drastically such that the product was not acceptable. The recommendation was made to add chemical preservatives to the formulation and market the product refrigerated. Company X insisted on having a shelf stable product. Therefore, the cheesecake was acidified to a pH of 4.5 and processed in a boiling water bath. The resulting product taste was deemed unacceptable by the company sensory panel and described as "too acidic for a cheesecake". What was the alternative? Bringing the water activity down to < 0.85, so the product is a_w controlled. This was achieved by putting less cream in the formula and adding more sugar to bind the water. A water activity of 0.83 was targeted and the jars were processed in boiling water bath for extended shelf-life. The cheesecake was less moist and sweeter, but it still scored high in a sensory test.

close to neutrality; and egg white may have a pH up to 7.9. A fresh egg has a pH of approximately 7.6. However, over time, H_2CO_3 in the albumen breaks down and forms CO_2, which escapes through the shell and increases the pH. The pH values of common foods are listed in Table 4.3.

The legal definition of a canned acid food is any food with a pH of less than 4.6, as seen in Table 4.3. If a product has a pH of greater than 4.6 and a water activity (a_w) of greater than 0.85, then the product is classified as a low-acid canned food. The pH value of 4.6 is based upon the growth of the pathogen *Clostridium botulinum*, which, as noted above, produces spores than can germinate at a pH of 4.8, but not at 4.6.

Food Fermentation and Acid Production

Fermentation is the conversion of a biodegradable food constituent (carbohydrates, sugar) by controlled biochemical decomposition (microbiological) into a more stable substance (e.g., acid) capable of preventing or inhibiting further microbial activity (glucose → lactic acid). As a result of this conversion, the stability of the product is increased both by removing the degradable element and converting it into a natural preservative. As indicated in the following passages from the CFR, fermented products such as sauerkraut are exempt from low-acid food regulations. "Fermented foods (such as some kinds of sauerkraut, cucumber pickles, and green olives) are low-acid foods subjected to the action of acid-producing microorganisms to reduce the pH of the food to 4.6 or below" . . . "We do not require processors of fermented foods to register their establishment(s) and foods they process (using Form FDA 2541) if these foods do not also meet the definition of an acidified food (or if these processors do not process other foods subject to 21 CFR part 113 or part 114). We also do not require such processors to provide us with information on scheduled processes for their foods (using Form FDA 2541a)." However, "low-acid foods to which acid(s) or acid food(s) are added and that have a pH of 4.6 or below and a water activity above 0.85 are acidified foods subject to the requirements in 21 CFR 108.25 and part 114, irrespective of whether the low-acid food is also subjected to the action of acid-producing microorganisms" (21CFR108.25).

pH and Food Quality

The pH of foods also has an effect on the qualities of foods. Canned vegetables have a relatively high pH, making it necessary to can them at higher temperatures. Cooked green vegetables receive their olive green cooked color because under acidic conditions the Mg^{+2} is removed from the chlorophyll molecule causing a color change. Angel food cake gets its distinctive white color because the cream of tartar retards browning reactions and influences the anthoxanthin pigment. The addition of acid decreases the net negative charge on pectin molecules in fruit jellies, allowing them to be less repelled by each other. Sugar also further stabilizes pectin cross-bonding.

TABLE 4.4. Acids and Their Molecular Weights and Milliequivalent Weights.

Acid	Molecular Weight	Meq. Wt
Citric acid	192	0.064
Acetic acid	60	0.060
Lactic acid	90	0.090
Malic acid	134	0.067
Oxalic acid	90	0.045
Tartaric acid	150	0.075

$$\text{Titratable Acidity (T.A.)} = \text{Volume of base (mL)} \times \text{Normality} \times \text{Meq. wt acid} \times 100$$

FIGURE 4.2. Equation for the calculation of titratable acidity.

Titratable Acidity

Titratable acidity (TA) is an approximate measure of total acidity in a sample determined through the amount of an alkaline solution it takes to neutralize an acid. Titratable acidity is a commonly controlled parameter used for the quality control (QC) of fresh fruit products, fermented foods, and soft drinks. This is because food flavors are influenced by the degree of acidity. Titratable acidity values may be as low as 0.5% in some cheeses to as high as 6.0% in vinegar. Titratable acidity is normally expressed as a percentage of a dominant acid in a food, e.g., lactic in whole milk or buttermilk; citric in soft drinks; acetic in vinegar).

The brix/acid ratio is more commonly used as an index of flavor. *Brix* is a measure of percent soluble solids. The proportion of brix to acid is a better determinant of food flavor and quality than brix or acid measurements alone (Nielsen 1998). The fruit industry relies widely on the brix/acid measurement to determine ripeness and optimum harvest times.

WATER ACTIVITY

Controlling the amount of available water for microbial growth and spoilage has been a technique for centuries. Water activity represents the amount of water available for chemical reactions and microbial growth. Water activity is important to control in foods because it determines the stability and influences the odor, color, flavor, texture, and shelflife of products. Water can act as a solvent in foods and is highly reactive in chemical and biochemical reactions, such as non-enzymatic browning (Nollet 2004). The values of a_w in foods can assist in predicting microbial activity, as well (Chinachoti and Vittadini 2006). Water activity is a much more accurate indicator of food stability than the measuring of moisture content.

Water activity and microbial growth are highly correlated. Microorganisms may be beneficial in some foods, but are detrimental where the organisms are pathogenic. Spoilage organisms cause foods to become unappetizing, but consuming them would probably not lead to a hospital stay. On the other hand, pathogenic bacteria can be present in a food

TABLE 4.5. Water Activity (a_w) of Common Foods*.

a_w Range	Product Examples
> 0.98	Fresh meat and fish, milk, canned vegetables
0.93–0.98	Evaporated milk, bread, lightly cured meats
0.85–0.93	Semi-dry salami, mature cheese, sweetened condensed milk
0.60–0.83	Dried fruit, jams, jellies, dried salted fish
< 0.6	Chocolate, crackers

*Water activity values range from 0 to 1 (pure water).

that looks and tastes completely appetizing. Water activity is important to control the growth of all microorganisms, because water must be present for most microbes to grow. Reducing a_w can limit the quantity of water used by microorganisms. Microorganisms do not grow at an a_w below 0.91 (except *Staphylococcus aureus*, which grows at an a_w of 0.86 under certain conditions) (Nollet 2004). The minimum a_w for mold growth and spoilage yeasts are 0.70 and 0.88 respectively (Nollet, 2004). Table 4.5 shows the a_w of common foods.

When product developers are looking to modify the a_w of a product, they can add ingredients to bind water. Sugar, salt and selected gums are effective binders of water, helping to reduce a_w. Foods with a_w below 0.85 are likely to be stable at room temperature, even with pH values above 4.6.

Determining the a_w of a Product

The most common method for determining a_w is using a dewpoint a_w meter. The dewpoint method is determined by reflecting an infrared beam on a mirror located in the instrument. The dewpoint temperature of the sample is determined, which can be used (along with the sample temperature) to calculate the a_w. Other methods include water-holding capacity and freezing-point depression studies. Still, the most widely used is the dewpoint meter, because it produces results in fewer than five minutes and has acceptable accuracy (Nollet 2004). Handheld dewpoint a_w meters are also available for use on processing lines or other applications in which portable instruments are more convenient. All a_w meters should be calibrated prior to use and kept in good working order. Calibration is usually done with supplier-provided solutions of sodium, potassium, or lithium chloride. The mirror in dewpoint meters can get dirty, causing skewed results.

MOISTURE

Moisture, like aw, is important for determining shelf life. Higher-moisture products are more perishable than those with lower moisture content. Also, water is more easily released from certain food systems than others. Water can exist as free water, adsorbed water, or bound water (Nielsen 1998). Free water is that which is available for microbial growth, whereas adsorbed water is being employed in the system. Bound water is chemically secured by another compound through hydration. Adsorbed water is more difficult to release than free water, and bound water cannot be released. Table 4.6 shows the approximate moisture in common products.

Moisture content can be determined through direct or indirect methods. Direct methods include removing the moisture through oven drying, vacuum oven, the Karl Fischer titration method, or desiccation. Indirect methods include the dielectric method, infrared analysis, and the microwave absorption method.

Direct Methods for Moisture Determination

Oven Drying

Weighed samples are heated under controlled conditions, then their weight is determined following drying. Calculation of the moisture is determined by the amount of weight lost in relation to the amount of

TABLE 4.6. Percentage Moisture of Common Foods.

Approximate % Moisture	Product Examples
79–96	Vegetables
81–91	Fresh fruits
63–75	Meat, poultry, fish
1.5–3	Nuts
16	Butter, salted
35	White bread
10–12	Flour
3.8	Ready to eat cereals
4.3	Crackers
10	Macaroni pasta

*Based on information from the USDA Nutrient Database for Standard Reference. Release 24 (March 2012) http://ndb.nal.usda.gov/.

the sample weight at the beginning of the experiment. Oven drying, though, is highly dependent on the type of oven used and the conditions within the oven. Oven drying results are dependent on the environmental factors of the study, such as temperature control, airflow, and the pans that are used (Nielsen 1998). Disposable pans with fiberglass covers are commonly used. Pans need to be handled very carefully with tongs and never touched with bare hands. Forced draft ovens can be used to decrease drying times. Oven drying is one of the most common methods used for determining moisture content, although there are significant disadvantages to this method. The latter include: sample variability, difficulty in removing all water, loss of volatile compounds, and decomposition of the sample (Nollet 2004).

Vacuum Oven

Vacuum ovens provide the most accurate drying method to determine moisture content (Nollet 2004). Vacuum drying, with its reduced pressure, can accelerate the time needed to complete moisture analysis. Advantages over the oven drying method include higher reproducibility, lower heating temperatures, and uniform heating (Nollet 2004).

Karl Fischer Titration Method

The Karl Fischer titration method has become a standard for moisture determination of low-moisture foods because of its selectivity, precision, and speed (Nollet 2004). The Karl Fischer titration method is the routine test for the determination of moisture in dried fruits and vegetables, candies, chocolate, roasted coffee, oils and fats, or other foods with high sugar or protein (Nielsen 1998). To determine the moisture concentration, a reagent of iodine, pyridine, sulfur dioxide, and methanol is used (Nollet 2004). The endpoint of the titration with water occurs when a brown color appears. Official methods for determining moisture content of foods are given in the Association of Analytical Chemical (AOAC) official methods. Automated equipment is available for this test (Nielsen 1998).

Desiccation

Desiccation is a method that is accurate with volatile compounds is chemical desiccation (drying out). This method is best employed when using a strong moisture-absorbing chemical substance in a desiccator (Nollet 2004). The effectiveness of the moisture absorption depends on the chemical. Recommended desiccating agents include calcium sulfate, phosphorus pentoxide, barium oxide, and magnesium perchlorate. Calcium sulfate is widely used as a desiccant, but it is not as effective as the other compounds.

Indirect Methods for Moisture Determination

Dielectric Method

The moisture content of foods can be measured using electrical currents (Nielsen 1998). In this method, a sample's capacity to alter current flow is measured by placing it between two metal plates with opposite charges (Nollet 2004). The dielectric method is commonly used for grain products.

Infrared Analysis

Infrared spectroscopy provides insight into food composition by measuring the absorption of radiation by food products (Nielsen 1998). When determining the moisture content of foods, the researcher identifies a set of bands in the food product being tested. The bands from the analyzed food product are compared to standardized bands for varying concentrations of water and matched to determine the amount (Nollet 2004).

Microwave Absorption Method

Microwave absorption methods are popular in food companies to rapidly measure moisture and make adjustments to the food prior to moving to the next processing step. New technologies can determine the moisture of a food product in about 10 minutes with the accuracy of a 5-hour vacuum oven test (Nielsen 1998). Factors affecting microwave absorption readings include leakage of microwave energy, the temperature of the sample, particle size, and soluble salts present in the sample (Nollet 2004). The microwave method gives rapid readings, but is not as accurate as alternative methods.

TEMPERATURE

Food processors must pay close attention to temperature guidelines, in order to destroy potentially hazardous and spoilage microorganisms in foods that are perishable.

Meats and other products that are cooked should reach the minimum temperatures recommended for them, as displayed in Table 4.7. Ground meats have a higher recommended heating temperature because of their greater surface area and higher projected microbial loads. Eggs as a food ingredient must also be heated to prescribed temperatures.

Foods that require refrigeration should be held at a temperature less than 41°F (5°C). Regulating food storage areas and checking temperatures periodically are important. Frozen foods should be held at a temperature that keeps them thoroughly frozen. Both refrigeration and freezer units fluctuate in temperature and must maintain a temperature so that food is always in the safe zone. The temperature danger zone (Figure 4.3), between 41°F (5°C) and 135°F (57°C) has been established because this is the range where pathogenic bacteria can survive. Pathogens grow very quickly between temperature 70°F (21°C) and 120°F (49°C). Food service operations must establish hot holding and cold holding procedures and check temperatures for both.

Although the temperature that products are heated to is vital, temperature and time go hand in hand. If processors wish to heat a product to a lower temperature, they may do so, if the product is heated for a longer amount of time. Time and temperature recommendations must be made through a process authority or governmental guidance.

Determining the Temperature of a Product

Temperatures of products should be determined throughout processing, especially if heating is a vital step in the prevention of foodborne illness in the product. Temperatures are recorded by means of in-line

TABLE 4.7. Proper Cooking Temperatures for Meat Products.

Proper Cooking Temperature	Type of Food
165°F (74°C)	Poultry
160°F (71°C)	Ground meat of all types
145°F (63°C)	Seafood, steaks, and other cuts of pork, beef, veal, or lamb

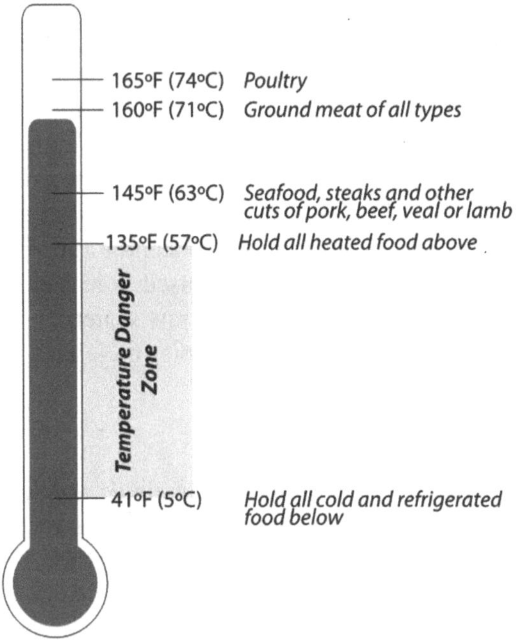

FIGURE 4.3. Demonstration of the temperature danger zone.

detectors or thermometers. Thermometers should be calibrated at the beginning of each shift, in order to ensure their accuracy. One common way to calibrate stem thermometers is the ice point method. This entails placing the thermometer in an ice-water bath and adjusting the temperature to 32°F or 0°C. Care must be taken when calibrating a thermometer by the boiling point method. A reading of 212°F is appropriate at sea level, but the boiling point of water changes with altitude (decreasing by about 1°F for each 500-foot elevation) and barometric pressure. Many food processing plants and food service establishments also have their thermometers calibrated by the manufacturer once per year. The temperature at which products are processed affects quality parameters such as the color, flavor, and texture when developing a product. Product developers need also to be aware of regulations governing the heat treatment of certain foods. These will be covered in the chapters on unit operations and on food laws and regulations.

BRIX

The Brix value is a measure of soluble solids content. A refractometer is used to measure light passing through the solids content. It is expressed as the degrees (°) Brix, the equivalent to the weight of sugar. The ratio of the speed of light in a vacuum to the speed of light in a particular substance is referred to as its refractive index. The refractive index is then calculated to ° Brix, which relates it to the percentage of sucrose (Nollet 2004). Most refractometers are set to give readings as a percentage of sucrose. The accuracy of refractometers is dependent on the temperature, product composition, concentration of solids, and purity of the sample (Nollet 2004). Brix is used in research and development and processing to test the solids of raw materials, such as grapes and potatoes, and as a quality factor in jams and jellies.

COLOR

Color is a vital component in quality standards and consumer acceptance. Foods with unexpected colors are generally not well received. To consumers, color is representative of the flavors of food—for example, yellow may represent lemon and green may signify lime or apple flavors. Enhanced color intensity has also been shown to increase the perceived flavor of food products (Francis 1999). In addition to flavors, the quality and perceived freshness of foods (especially meats, fruits, and vegetables) are initially judged by the color of a product (Lawless and Heymann 2010). Some products, such as soft drinks and ice creams have an unattractive or low-intensity natural color. To these types of products, colorants must be added to make them appear more appetizing (Francis 1999).

Color is the perception by the human brain of pigments created by light reflected from, or transmitted through, an object (Francis 1999; Lawless and Heymann 2010). The perception of a certain color is affected by the background in which it is seen, the individual viewer, and the spatial arrangement. Spatial color perception variation can be illustrated by the perceived change in color from that on a paint chip to that on a wall painted with the same color. The color on the wall is a little different from the one expected. Hues are the properties of colors, by which they can be perceived as ranging from red through yellow, green, and blue, as determined by the dominant wavelength of light. Lightness is the dimension of color of an object, by which the object appears to reflect or transmit more or less light. Saturation is a measure of the vividness of the hues and their degree of difference from a gray of the same lightness.

Methods of Color Measurement

Methods of color measurement can be visual or instrumental. Visual color differences can be determined using consumer testing or descriptive analysis by a trained panel. Other visual color grading systems include the Munsell system, as well as standards made from glass or plastic. Instrumental measurements are done using spectrophotometers, tristimulus colorimeters, or other specialized colorimeters.

The Munsell system is a three-dimensional system comprised of colored chips. It was first devised in the 1900s to be a mathematical system of color comparisons. The three dimensions are hue (H), value (V), and chroma (c) (Lawless and Heymann 2010). The Munsell system contains 1,225 color chips for visual matching purposes (Francis 1999). Other visual standards can also be used, such as painted paper chips, plastic color standards, or glass standards (mostly used for sugar products) (Lawless and Heymann 2010).

A common instrument for measuring color is the Hunter Lab Colorimeter. The Hunter color system, as illustrated in Figure 4.3, measures colors using *L*, *a*, and *b* values. The *L* corresponds to lightness and darkness, whereas the *a* and *b* values correlate with red-green and yellow-blue spectrums, respectively. Red is positive on the a spectrum, whereas green is represented by negative a values. Yellow is positive for *b* values; negative *b* values corresponds to blue. Hunter Lab instruments rapidly give these values based on the Hunter diagram for comparative purposes.

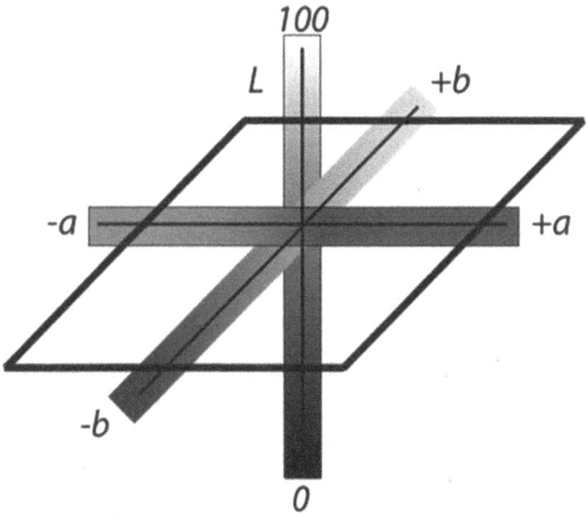

FIGURE 4.4. *The Hunter color system.*

Plant Pigments

Vegetables and fruits contain colors generated by chemical reactions in their cells. With certain limitations, "natural," plant-based pigments may be added to food products.

Chlorophyll

Chlorophyll is the green pigment well-known for its role in photosynthesis. It is fat soluble and occurs in large quantities in nature. As a pigment, it is extremely sensitive to light, changes in pH and is sensitive to acid degradation in the presence of heat. Chlorophyll is not permitted as a food color in the United States.

Carotenoids

Carotenoids are yellow, red and orange pigments naturally present in plants and animals such as carrots, red tomatoes, paprika, and salmon. These fat soluble pigments are classified into carotenes-carotenoid hydrocarbons and xanthophyll.

Carotenes are a group of carotenoids containing only hydrogen and carbon in a polymer of isoprene. These include β-carotene and lycopene. Lycopene is found in tomatoes, pink grapefruit, and watermelon and is the most predominant carotenoid. Carotenoids are precursors of vitamin A.

Xanthophyll (or oxycarotenoids) are oxygen-containing carotenoids in a polymer of isoprene. In oranges, about 50% of the carotenoids are xanthophylls. Annatto is the plant pigment extract that, when heat treated, undergoes some isomerization from trans to cis, creating an oil-soluble red color.

Flavonoid

Flavonoids are intensely colored water-soluble orange, red, and blue pigments responsible for the color of grapes, strawberries, raspberries, blueberries, cranberries, apples, roses, and Indian corn. Flavonoids are more stable under acidic conditions. Types of Flavonoids include anthocyanin, anthoxanthin, and anthocyanidin.

Discoloration of flavonoids is a common occurence resulting in the following color reactions:

- Canned pears and white potatoes may turn pink as a result of a high processing temperature and delayed cooling.
- Bananas, apples, cherries, or avocados may exhibit a browning blackening due to bruising, cut, or exposed surface. The browning is due to polyphenol oxidases, a group of enzymes capable of oxidizing flavonoid compounds.

Disadvantages in the use of naturally colored foods

Naturally occurring color as ingredients in other food products can result in challenges such as imparting unwanted flavors and discoloration over the shelf life of the product. For example, beet and cranberry juices will color foods red, but they also impart an undesirable flavor or an astringent taste. These coloring agents are known for low pigment concentration, low stability, and poor color uniformity.

Synthetic Colors

Synthetic colors are the primary sources of commercial colorants. Dyes permitted in foods are called "FD&C" because they are allowed for use in foods, drugs, and cosmetics by the Federal Food, Drug, & Cosmetic Act of 1938.

FD&C dyes are water-soluble compounds, manufactured in the form of powders, granules, liquids, blends, pastes, and dispersion that can be used at less than 300 parts per million (ppm). F&C lakes are aluminum hydrate extensions of dyes formed by chemically extending the corresponding dye onto an aluminal hydrate substratum. The dye content generally varies from 10% to 40%. The color of lakes is manifested through dispersion rather than solubilization, as in dyes. Typical applications include icings, coatings, donut mixes, hard candy, and gum products.

PARTICLE SIZE

Particle size affects the texture, density, and mouthfeel of certain foods (Smith 2011a). The particle size of flour affects the characteristics of baked goods made from it. Particle size can be determined though sieves, photo analysis, or laser diffraction. Sieves allow handheld determination of particle size. Screens are stacked from large at the top to small at the bottom in order to determine the particle size differences throughout a food, such as flour. The material on each sieve is weighed to determine the percentage of particles that represents a certain size. Photo analysis provides faster analysis, in that a picture is taken and then analyzed using computer software.

Rheology

Rheology is the study of the flow and changing shape of products during processing or in use (Nielsen 1998). For example, rheological properties may describe the flow of milk from a carton or the breaking of hard candy. Stress and strain are important factors in determining rheological properties of given products. Rheological properties of foods include viscosity, viscoelasticity, shear rate, and strain. The measurement of these attributes can help determine how easy a sauce will flow from a bottle or compare the capacities of a tortilla product to be rolled or stretched. Rheological properties are also important for plant applications, such as flow through pneumatic valves.

TEXTURE

Texture represents those qualities that are experienced by the tongue, palate, and teeth during eating (Vieira, 1999). Textural attributes include structure, mouthfeel, and ease of breakage—all factors that contribute greatly to the liking of food products. How good would potato chips be without their crisp texture? Children sometimes display a disapproval of some textures, including the crust of bread and the skin of apples.

One goal of food processing is to make foods easier to eat by altering the textures of ingredients (Bourne 1982). For example, wheat is milled into flour and used in formulated foods to make baked goods. Other food processes that modify texture include freezing, dehydration, canning, and tenderizing of meats. When developing food products, a person can add many ingredients to modify texture: Lipids in cake to increase smoothness, pectin in jelly to form a gel, or calcium chloride to make firmer pickles.

Texture can be grouped into two categories—the rheological properties and the sensory properties. Rheological properties are generally measured with instruments, whereas sensory attributes are measured by means of sensory panels. A number of texture analysis instruments, such as those listed in Table 4.8, can bridge the gap between the two.

Viscosity

Viscosity is an especially important factor in the creation of fluid foods. Viscosity, by definition, is the tendency to resist flow through internal friction (Bourne 1982). Though this definition seems to include liquid foods, such as soda, and to exclude solid foods, viscosity can be measured in solid foods that exhibit liquid characteristics under stress. Measuring the flow of foods is important when food engineers must determine the feasibility of transporting ingredients through pneumatic pipes. Measuring rheological properties goes far beyond viscosity and includes gel strength, consistency, extensibility, hardness, cohesiveness, and other attributes. The Rapid Visco Analyzer (RVA) is an effective instrument widely used for determining the cooked viscous properties (pasting profile) of starches, grain products, flours, and other foods.

Colloids and Emulsions

Colloids are mixtures that are not homogeneous, yet not heterogeneous. Colloids consist of particles (solids, liquids, or gases) suspended

TABLE 4.8. Common Rheological Tests Used in Product Development*.

Test	Purpose
Farinograph	Consistency of dough
Brabender	Dough extensibility
Tarr-Baker Jelly Tester	Firmness of pectin jellies
Warner-Braxler Shear	Tenderness of meat
Armour Tenderometer	Tenderness of meat
Bloom Gelometer	Gel strength for pectin jellies
Rotary Viscometer	Measures torque and viscosity
Brabender Struct-o-Graph	Snapping of product
Penetrometers	Firmness of cheeses, tenderness of fruits/vegetables, force required to penetrate a material
Instron	Compression, tensile, harness, and impact testing; gives Instron Texture Profile (ITP)
Bailey Shortometer	Snapping properties of baked goods
Bostwick Consistiometer	Measures consistency and flow rate
Line spread test	Consistency of liquids
Texture Profile Analysis (TPA)	Fracturability, cohesiveness, adhesiveness, springiness, hardness, gumminess, and chewiness (Imitative test that has action similar to human eating)

**Source:* Bourne 1982; Smith 2011b.

in a medium, which can itself be a solid, liquid, or gas. Food colloids include liquid in liquid (salad dressing), liquid in solid (jelly), gas in liquid (foam), and gas in solid (meringue). In contrast with colloids, emulsions are dispersions of one liquid in another, which are not readily soluble. The components of emulsions are called the continuous and the dispersed phases. The continuous phase represents the fluid that is more prevalent in the mixture. As illustrated in Figure 4.4, the dispersed phase is suspended in the continuous phase.

The most important variables determining emulsion properties are the type of emulsion, droplet distribution (for example, smaller drops generally provide more stable emulsions), composition and thickness of the surface layer around the droplets, and composition of the continuous phase. The viscosity of the continuous phase has a pronounced effect on creaming. Types of emulsions and examples of emulsion processed foods are listed in Table 4.9.

Emulsion capacity, the ability of a protein solution or suspension to emulsify oil, is determined by electrical conductivity. For example, testing is used to determine how much corn oil could be emulsified into 100 mL of protein solution. Emulsion capacity is expressed as the maximum volume of oil (mL) that can be emulsified by a protein without phase inversion or collapse of emulsion. To test for emulsion capacity, oil is added at a given rate until viscosity decrease or inversion occurs.

Emulsion stability is the ability of an emulsion to resist coalescence, i.e., a tendency of particles to merge and thus break down an emulsion's structure. Emulsion stability is limited by the temperature, gravitational field strength, and concentration of oil in the emulsion. Emulsion stabil-

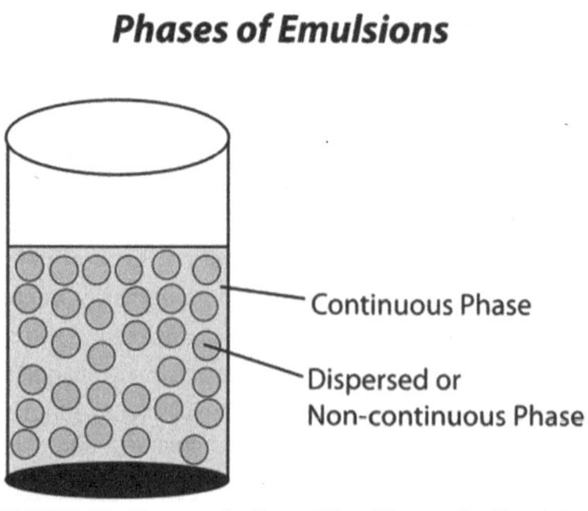

FIGURE 4.5. Demonstration of the Phases in Emulsions.

TABLE 4.9. Types of Emulsions.

Type of Emulsion	Example
Oil in water	Milk, soups, sauces
Water in oil	Butter, margarine

ity is commonly measured in terms of the amount of oil and or cream separating from an emulsion during a certain period of time at a stated temperature and gravitational field. The time required for a specified degree of breakdown to occur is also used as a measure of stability. Another simple test is to take 100 grams of fat and slowly add water while mixing with an electric beater until the emulsion breaks. Record the volume of water taken up by 100 grams of fat.

Sensory

Sensory tests measure the perceived properties of food, such as texture, based on responses from trained specialists. Panelists are taught to rate textural attributes of food, such as hardness, fracturability, chewiness, gumminess, adhesiveness, and viscosity. Other sensory tests to measure texture include squeeze tests, in which panelists squeeze a food product, or viscosity and consistency measurements, in which panelists stir a sample with their finger or a spoon (Meullenet, Lyon, Carpenter, & Lyon, 1998). Sensory analysis for other food properties is covered more thoroughly in a later chapter.

The correlation between texture profiling by a sensory panel and a texture profile analysis by an instrument has been found to be significant in some areas and insignificant in others. Hardness and springiness factors from sensory data correlate well with instrumental data, while cohesiveness and chewiness do not correlate (Meullenet *et al.* 1998, 77–93). Even when sensory and instrumental results do not correlate, both sets of readings supply valuable product input.

THERMAL PROPERTIES OF FOOD

During heating, food undergoes phase transitions that affect its texture, structure, and function. Three key phase transitions are (1) water/ice, (2) protein denaturation, and (3) starch gelatinization (Peleg and Bagley 1983). Many transitions take place in the presence of heat. Glass transition is a change in amorphous solids from a hard state to a rubberlike phase. The glass transition temperature (T_g) should be considered, especially when developing low-moisture or frozen foods. Glass transition temperature measurements can be complicated if a product being developed is encapsulated or coated with an edible film. Additionally, some foods may have more than one T_g.

Differential Scanning Calorimetry (DSC)

Differential scanning calorimetry (DSC) is a method for studying the thermal properties of food and ingredients that quantifies and records data regarding the amount of heat involved in physical state changes. Differential scanning calorimetry works by comparing the changes in enthalpy in a sample with a reference material and can measure starch gelatinization temperatures and protein denaturation points. Differential scanning calorimetry is used in the food industry to study important variables, such as the amount of freezable/non-freezable water in a system, glass transition in wheat, the influence of water on a variety of starches, changes in phase transitions from the addition of ingredients, and the gelatinization of starches (Nielsen 1998).

DENSITY

The density (or specific gravity) of foods can be an important calculation for the quality of some foods, including baked goods and fresh vegetables. Density measures the mass of a unit per its volume. For example, the density of peas or corn is determined for grading purposes. The vegetables are first weighed in air, then weighed in a solvent (water), and the specific gravity is calculated (Nielsen 1998). The United States Department of Agriculture (USDA) Agricultural Marketing Service (AMS) determines grading standards, and individual companies may have their own internal standards of quality.

MICROBIAL PROPERTIES

The microbial properties of foods are dependent on the products being tested. Cultured products such as yogurt naturally support and thrive on non-pathogenic bacteria to create their unique flavors. Microbial standards for bacteria are regulated by governmental standards for certain products. Microbial testing is vital in production operations measuring risk of contamination.

Processors and regulators can both establish unofficial standards for particular products, which are referred to as "guidelines." Microbiological guidelines set an approximate or a maximum level for the microbial load that should be attainable when good manufacturing practices and proper plant procedures are met (Banwart, 1989). The Food and Drug Administration (FDA) recognizes that foods contain microbes and has published guidelines stating when the number and nature of microbes rise to the level of a "defect," where processors and producers must take action to address threatening microbial loads. These are called "defect action levels." Defect action levels are addressed by the FDA in 21 CFR 110, subpart G, § 110.110—"Natural or unavoidable defects in food for human use that present no health hazard." The FDA standards for molds and microorganisms can be used as guideline levels for plant personnel. The defect action levels are listed in the Defect Levels Handbook, which is available on the FDA website. If foods are found to be above the defect action levels, the food can be deemed adulterated. Examples of defect action levels for common foods are given in Table 4.10.

Food producers may set more stringent specifications at the request of buyers or retailers. Specifications may even be lower than the FDA prescribed action levels, in order to satisfy a buyer's needs. Food processing standards are based on the type of food that is being produced. Ready-to-eat products must be handled carefully to ensure that they contain a lower microbial load than the load in a product meant to be cooked.

SUMMARY

The properties of food contribute to the processing techniques used, safety of the product, and its sensory properties. Product developers should be cognizant of the properties of their raw materials and the final food product. Taking measurements often to determine the presence and level of each property is recommended, especially if its effect is unknown. The properties of food products are critical variables, when it comes to safety and flavor.

KEY WORDS

Brix—a measure of percent soluble solids.

Density—the mass of a unit per its volume.

TABLE 4.10. Defect Action Levels for Common Foods.

Product	Defect Action Level
Apple Butter	• Average of mold count is 12% or more • Average of four or more rodent hairs per 100 g of apple butter • Average of five or more whole or equivalent insects (not counting mites, aphids, thrips, or scale insects) per 100 g of apple butter
Apricots, canned	• Average of 2% or more by count has been damaged or infected by insects
Beets, canned	• Average of 5% or more pieces by weight with dry rot
Berries, canned or frozen	• Average mold count is 60% or more • Average of 4 or more larvae per 500 g or average of 10 or more whole insects or equivalent per 500 g (excluding thrips, aphids, and mites)
Broccoli, frozen	• Average of 60 or more aphids, thrips, and/or mites per 100 g
Cinnamon, ground	• Average of 400 or more insect fragments per 50 g • Average of 11 or more rodent hairs per 50 g
Corn, sweet, canned	• Insect larvae (corn ear worms, corn borers) two or more 3 mm or longer larvae, cast skins, larval or cast skin fragments of corn ear worms or corn borer, and the aggregate length of such larvae, cast skins, larval or cast skin fragments exceeds 12 mm in 24 lb
Olives, pitted	• Average of 1.3% or more by count of olives with whole pits and/or pit fragments 2 mm or longer measured in the longest dimension
Black olives, imported	• 10% or more olives by count showing damage by olive fruit fly
Peanut Butter	• Average of 30 or more insect fragments per 100 g • Average of 1 or more rodent hairs per 100 g • Gritty taste and water insoluble inorganic residue is more than 25 mg per 100 g
Tomatoes, canned	• Average of 10 or more fly eggs per 500 g or 5 or more fly eggs and 1 or more maggots per 500 g or 2 or more maggots per 500 g
Wheat flour	• Average of 75 or more insect fragments per 50 g • Average of 1 or more rodent hairs per 50 g

Source: FDA Defect Levels Handbook (revised 1998).

Differential Scanning Calorimetry (DSC)—a method for studying the thermal properties of food and ingredients that quantifies and records data regarding the amount of heat involved in physical state changes.

Emulsions—dispersions of one liquid in another that are not readily soluble.

Emulsion capacity—the ability of a protein solution or suspension to emulsify oil.

Emulsion stability—the ability of an emulsion to remain stable and unchanged in the face of coalescence.

Fermentation—the conversion of a biodegradable food constituent (sugar) by controlled biochemical decomposition (microbiological) into a more stable substance (e.g., acid) capable of preventing or inhibiting further microbial activity.

Hues—the properties of colors by which they can be perceived as ranging from red through yellow, green, and blue, as determined by the dominant wavelength of light.

Hunter color system—measures colors using *L*, *a*, and *b* values. *L* corresponds to lightness and darkness, while the *a* and *b* values correlate with red-green and yellow-blue spectrums, respectively.

Lightness—the dimension of color of an object by which the object appears to reflect or transmit more or less light.

Munsell system—a three dimensional system color system that is comprised of colored chips.

pH—an indicator of the amount of acid or base present in a food system based on a scale of 0 to 14 and determined by the negative logarithm of the H^+ or OH^- concentration in solution.

Saturation—the vividness of the hues, and their degree of difference from a gray of the same lightness.

Titratable acidity—approximate measure of total acidity in a sample determined through by the amount of an alkaline solution it takes to neutralize the acid, which is expressed as free hydrogen ions and as hydrogen ions till bound to undissociated acids.

Viscosity—the tendency to resist flow through internal friction.

Water activity (a_w)—the amount of water available for chemical reactions and microbial growth.

COMPREHENSION QUESTIONS

4.1. *Answer True or False:*

a. Egg whites are one of the only foods that are not naturally acidic.

b. If vinegar has a pH of 2 and orange juice a pH of 3, the vinegar is 100 times more acidic than the orange juice.

c. There are no microorganisms that can grow below a a_w of 0.91.

d. Food should never be held between 21°F and 145°F, also called the temperature danger zone.

4.2. Match the following acids to the foods in which they are commonly used in.

a. Citric	___Tortilla
b. Malic	___ Orange juice
c. Fumaric	___ Pepsi Cola
d. Phosphoric	___ Sour apple candies

4.3. *Fill in the blanks:*

a. Most pH meters are equipped with __________________ that correct for slight changes in temperatures.

b. ____________________ should be calibrated at the beginning of each shift in order to ensure their accuracy.

c. Cinnamon is allowed to have an average of ____ insect fragments per ____ gram sample according to the FDA's Defect Action Levels.

d. In the Hunter color system, *L* refers to ______ and ________, a corresponds to the __________-_________ spectrum, and b corresponds to the __________-__________ spectrum.

4.4. What type of equipment would be used to measure the ° Brix of a product?

4.5. Legally define an acid food and give the two microorganisms for which this definition is based upon.

4.6. Describe the difference between hydrolytic and oxidative rancidity.

4.7. Discuss the relation of pH to microbial growth in foods.

4.8. How many times more acidic is cranberry juice (pH of 3.2) compared to banana pineapple juice (pH of 4.2)?

4.9. Choose one natural pigment and discuss the effects of pH on that pigment.

4.10. What is emulsion capacity and how does one test for it?

4.11. List two types of emulsions and give an example of each.

REFERENCES

Bourne, M.C. 1982. *Food texture and viscosity.* New York: Academic Press.

Chinachoti, P., and Vittadini, E. 2006. Water stress of bacteria and molds from a NMR water mobility standpoint. In M.d.P. Buera, J. Welti-Chanes, P.J. Lillford and H.R. Corti (eds.), *Water properties of food, pharmeceutical, and biological materials* (pp. 167–190). Boca Raton, FL: Taylor & Francis Group, LLC.

Francis, F.J. 1999. *Colorants.* St. Paul, MN: American Association of Cereal Chemists, Inc.

Lawless, H.T., and Heymann, H. 2010. *Sensory evaluation of food: Principles and practices.* New York: Springer.

Meullenet, J., Lyon, B.G., Carpenter, J.A., and Lyon, C.E. 1998. Relationship between sensory and instrumental texture profile attributes. *Journal of Sensory Studies. 13*(1), 77–93.

Nielsen, S.S. ed.. 1998. *Food analysis.* Gaithersburg, Maryland: Aspen Publishers, Inc.

Nollet, L.M.L. ed.. 2004. *Handbook of food analysis.* New York, NY: Marcel Dekker, Inc.

Peleg, M., and Bagley, E.B. eds.. 1983. *Physical properties of foods.* Westport, Connecticut: AVI Publishing Company, Inc.

Smith, B. 2011a. *Particle size.* Manhattan, KS: Kansas State University.

Smith, B. 2011b. *Texture analysis.* Manhattan, KS: Kansas State University.

CHAPTER 5

Sensory Analysis and Consumer Evaluation in Food Product Development

Learning Objectives

- What the basic sensory attributes are.
- How companies use sensory analysis in product development.
- What sensory tests are commonly used.

SENSORY ANALYSIS is an essential tool in product development for measuring product differences, perceived characteristics of products, and the acceptability of what we produce. Sensory analysis is a scientific discipline designed to evoke, measure, analyze, and interpret reactions to material characteristics and traits of food, as they are perceived by sight, smell, taste, touch, and hearing (Stone *et al.* 2012). Product development relies on the work of sensory scientists, who seek to determine consumer preferences and how changes made to a food product affect perception and liking.

Sensory traits associated with food products include everything from appearance to texture. Appearance attributes include color, size, shape, and the opaqueness or clarity of the product. Aroma is important with some types of products. Are there off-odors? Texture, an important piece of the eating experience, is analyzed by sensory testing. Is the product crunchier than the consumer expected? Does it stick to the consumer's teeth? Panelists measure flavor as well. Does the flavor match the concept? Is it what the consumer expected?

SENSORY EVALUATION IN FOOD PRODUCT DEVELOPMENT

Sensory evaluation is a critical phase of product development. The

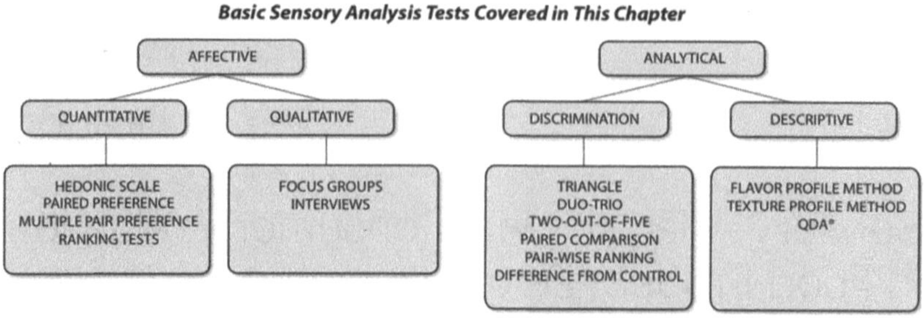

FIGURE 5.1. A basic overview of the sensory tests explained in this chapter for a food scientist doing product development. There are many more sensory tests that are applicable to product development.

sensory appeal of food must meet consumer expectations for the product to be a success. The results of sensory analysis tests determine whether a product moves forward in development or is scrapped. Figure 5.1 provides an overview of sensory tests performed by food product developers.

Sensory analysis techniques provide tools for product developers to determine the acceptability of a product, preferences of consumers, and implications of ingredient or processing changes. Acceptability and preference tests are subjective tests that can be carried out in a variety of ways including in-home, focus groups, and central location tests (Fuller 2011). Objective sensory tests completed by trained panelists include discrimination testing and descriptive analysis.

Companies rely on data from properly executed sensory tests to determine if a new or reformulated product is fit to launch or if the company should invest elsewhere. Focus groups can also aid in idea generation, concept definition, and product design. Two types of sensory tests are used in the selection of ingredients. Difference testing is used to determine if ingredients make a significant change in the flavor formulation. Triangle tests can predict whether a larger population will be able to detect formulation or processing changes. If the objective is to replace an ingredient without changing the flavor, a similarity test is appropriate. Similarity tests are conducted the same as difference tests, but the statistical analysis determines the beta risk rather than the alpha risk. Difference and similarity tests are valuable in cost-reduction projects, where formulas are changed slightly to reflect lower ingredient costs for the company. Consumers also provide guidance for continued product development. For example, ranking studies can be used to rank several prototype flavors or formulations developed, along with two or three products (flavors) already on the market. To ensure test results are accurate, randomizing the order of presentation or presenting samples sequentially are methods for controlling error.

TYPES OF SENSORY TESTS

The type of sensory test used is highly dependent on the goals of the study. Prior to starting trials, researchers should define their goals and consider what sensory tests are applicable. Figure 5.2 shows common objectives of sensory testing, and which test should be utilized for each objective.

Analytical Tests

Analytical tests measure the attributes of a product through quantitative and qualitative measures using highly trained personnel. Testing procedures and the participants are highly dependent on the test objective. Analytical tests involve distinguishing between products, and in some cases, their attributes.

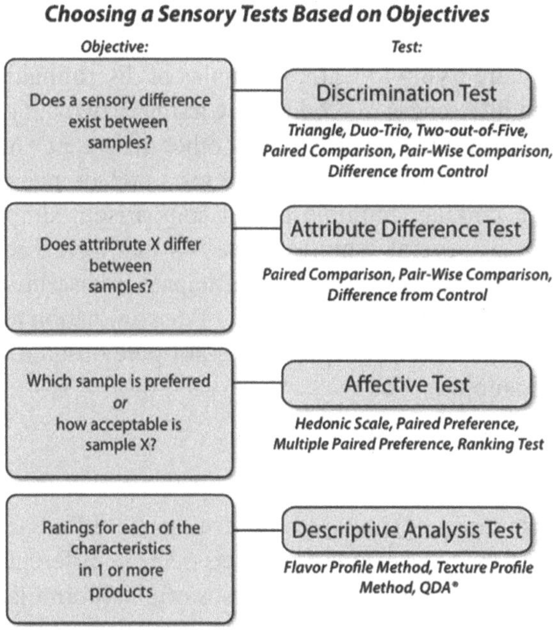

FIGURE 5.2. The objective or goals of a study are the basis for determining which sensory test should be used.

Trained panels are a part of some companies, whereas others train contracted panels for specific projects. In order to keep a panel well trained, regular meetings are necessary. Biases must be monitored and factored in as much as possible. For example, untrained employees of a company that produces a product could be disposed to favor it. Trained panel members should be sequestered in a controlled sensory facility and should be taught the correct procedures for testing and learning through repeated tasting of the products they will be reviewing. With minimal orientation, you can conduct acceptability and preference tests, simple difference tests, and difference from control tests. Minimal training is required for scaling of selected, easily recognizable characteristics. For detailed product descriptions, extensive training and monitoring of panelists are a must and require considerable investment in time and money. The cardinal rule in sensory is that trained panelists should be used to provide product descriptions, and consumers should be used for acceptability (affective) tests.

Discrimination Tests

In order to have meaningful difference tests, one essential condition is that samples are identical except for the single attribute under consideration. If this is not done, ratings will be based on information other than what you are trying to learn. Examples of discrimination tests for distinguishing differences in products are triangle, two out of five, duo-trio and difference from control, among other difference and similarity tests. Attribute difference and similarity tests include paired comparison, pair-wise ranking, multiple paired comparison, simple ranking, and the rating of several samples. Panelists that have been screened for sensory acuity are best suited to participate in discrimination tests (Lawless and Heymann 2010). The goal of discrimination tests is to establish if there are discernible product or attribute differences between two or more samples.

Triangle Test

The triangle test is a simple test to distinguish differences in products. Companies may wish to test products made in different processing facilities (or a cost-reduced product versus original formulation) to see if any differences are realized. In this test, three samples are presented simultaneously or successively. Two of the samples are the same, rep-

FIGURE 5.3. *Triangle tests are presented with three randomized samples. Two of the samples are identical to one another, and the participant should pick the one that is different.*

resenting a single lot, and the third represents another lot and might be different. The subject is required to pick the sample he believes is different. The orders in which samples are presented must be balanced or randomized to prevent bias. In order to obtain reliable results, at least 12 responses should be obtained.

Duo-Trio Tests

In duo-trio tests, the sample set is like that for the triangle test; however, one of the identical samples is identified as the "control," and the panelist must choose the unidentified sample that is different from the control. The control can remain constant in the test, or can be alternated between the two samples. The duo-trio test should have no fewer than 16 participants. The ideal number of participants is greater than 32.

FIGURE 5.4. *Duo-trio tests are presented with one reference and two randomized samples. The panelist should identify which sample is different than the control.*

Two-Out-of-Five Test

Like the other discriminative tests, the two-out-of-five test is used to identify differences in samples. Panelists are given five samples and asked to identify the two that are different from the other three. Because five samples are used, the panelists have less opportunity to guess the correct samples by chance. The chance of picking the two correct samples is 1/10—a chance much lower than the paired comparison (1/2) or the triangle test (1/3).

Paired Comparisons for Attributes

The paired comparison method employs a standard external to the test itself. As illustrated in Figure 5.5, two samples are presented, and the panelist chooses one of the samples on the basis of the specified characteristic or attribute. An example of a question that might be asked in a paired comparison test is: *Which of the samples is sweeter*? Panelists usually taste several pairs of samples and indicate which exemplifies the attribute.

Pair-Wise Ranking Test for Attributes

The pair-wise ranking test for attributes involves ranking several

EXAMPLE BALLOT

You have two samples to evaluate for each set. Taste each of the coded samples from left to right in the sequence presented. You do not have to use the entire sample. Do not retaste. Circle the number of the sample that is saltier. Rinse with water between pairs and expectorate all samples. Then proceed to the next set and repeat the tasting sequence.

286 935

FIGURE 5.5. *Paired comparison tests are used to determine if attributes are different in two products. An example ballot is given showing how a paired comparison test might be given.*

samples that are grouped into pairs to test the differences of a single attribute, such as sweetness. Samples are presented in randomized pairs, using every possible combination for each panelist. The panelist indicates which item within the paired samples exhibits more of the attribute for each of the pairs, until all possible combinations have been scored.

If four different juice drink formulas are being evaluated for sweetness called A, B, C, and D, and there are twelve participants for the pairwise ranking test, then there would be six different pair combinations: AB, BA, BC, CB, CD, and DC. These would be served in a different order to each participant. Each sample in the study should be given a separate three-digit code to eliminate any bias.

Difference from Control Tests

A difference from control test combines aspects of difference and scaling testing. Subjects are asked to rate the size of difference between each sample and a control on a scale. Some test samples can be the same as the control. The scale ranges from no difference (0) to extreme difference (X). The mean difference from control for each sample and for the blind controls is calculated. The results are analyzed using the statistical method analysis of variance, which reveals the samples that are statistically different. The difference from the control test can also be used to determine the degree of difference between samples.

Descriptive Tests

Descriptive tests involve both the discrimination and description of the characteristics of products. Such tests typically require fewer panelists and more training. Panels can be as small as 6 people and as large as 20, but a typical number of participants is from 10 to 12 (Stone *et al.* 2012). Generally, more modestly sized sensory programs will not become involved with such tests except perhaps to scale selected key attributes (generic descriptive scaling). Descriptive test results can be ranked against levels of chemical and physical attributes derived from instrumental data. Common descriptive tests include Quantitative Descriptive Analysis® (QDA®), flavor profiling, and texture profiling.

Every company uses its employees to evaluate products at some point. Biases can occur because of vested interests in the products, but employee training, careful test design, and application of statistics can lessen the concerns. Personal likes and dislikes lead to biases more than any other cause, so training is necessary to prevent their influence in analytical tests. The ability of trained individuals to detect differences with great accuracy helps companies make unerring conclusions in projects, thus serving as an invaluable tool in research and development (Stone *et al.* 2012).

Training of panelists is vital to descriptive analysis along with determining scales. The use of language is important in quality attribute analysis. Defining the meaning of words used in testing so that the entire panel understands is critical to ensuring valid information. Physical reference standards and training must also be explicitly defined, although easily understood attributes, such as sweet or bitter taste, or firmness, can be assessed with minimal panelist training. Just as instruments need calibration, trained panel members should undergo regular sensory exercises and screenings to ensure quality readings.

A simple numerical scale is only one of the types of scales that can be used, but it is easily understood and uncomplicated for participants. An example of a scale for rating the intensity of a single attribute is given in the following explanation:

> In order to rate the level of sweetness of a product, panelists could be given references of sweet solutions of 2%, 5%, and 15% sucrose (sucrose [weight]/distilled water [volume]) that correspond to values on a scale of 2, 6, and 9, respectively.

When using a panel, the panelists should verify the rankings for all reference materials by adjusting their position on the hedonic scale if there is a disagreement. All panelists might agree that the 5% solution is really not that sweet and will use this as a reference for the scale value of 5. Before moving the reference point, all participating panelists should agree and rate the unknown samples using the same reference values. Longer scales can be shortened and the reference values adjusted accordingly. Generally, panelists who have less training do not have a lot of difficulty with somewhat shorter 7- or 9-point scales.

Flavor Profile Method

Trained panelists can be used to determine the profiles of products and the intensity of their attributes. Prior to beginning the assessment of a product, panelists are trained on reference foods and identifying their traits on a relevant scale. Then, six screened panelists carefully study the product and discuss its attributes in an open session (Stone *et al.* 2012). When the panelists come to an agreement about the descriptive traits of the product, the results are shared in a report.

Texture Profile Method

After the flavor profile method was developed, the General Food Company developed the texture profile method. This method defined specific reference materials and scales that could be used for all tests. Terms that describe textural characteristics were defined and categorized in order to produce universally uniform descriptions (Stone *et al.* 2012). Texture profiling is completed in a similar way to the flavor profile method by using reference materials for the textural attribute of food (e.g., hardness, viscosity, and adhesiveness). Limitations to texture profiling include the separation of textural traits from the overall food and the rigidness of the reference scaling.

Quantitative Descriptive Analysis®

Quantitative Descriptive Analysis (QDA)® is a descriptive analysis technique that uses a panel of 10 to 12 highly trained participants to characterize and compare products. Participants are trained on a certain product and agree upon references prior to testing. Each panelist individually rates products on a line scale, and then all individual scores are compiled on a chart (Stone *et al.* 2012). Graphical representation, such as the one seen in Figure 5.6, can be created for the QDA to represent how samples scored compared to one another. QDA analysis represents all sensory data including textural and flavor profiles.

Affective Tests

Affective tests assess the personal response by potential consumers to a product, a product idea, or specific product attributes. Consumers are used for these tests. Affective tests of acceptability and preference measure subjective attitudes about a product. All participants should be screened for product usage prior to participation in a study (i.e., cereal studies should use participants that eat cereal). As suggested in Stone

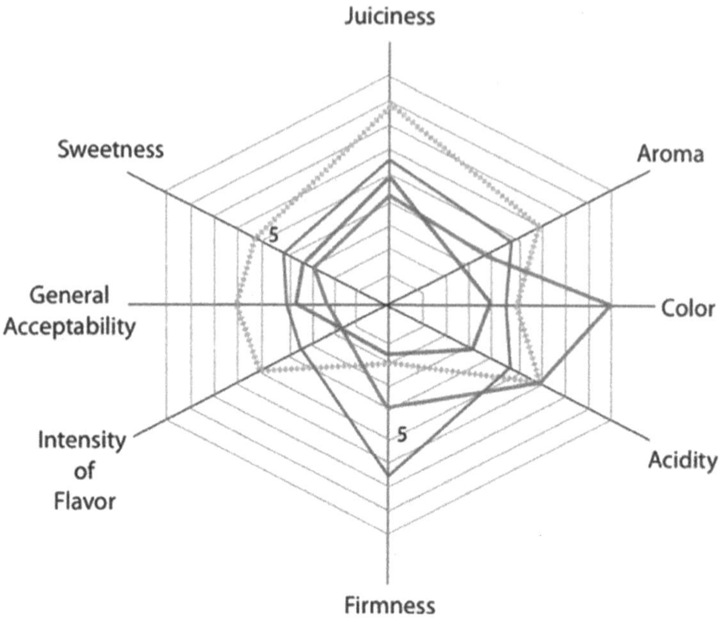

FIGURE 5.6. Based on the statistical results for QDA®, a graphical representation, often called a sensory map or "spider web," can be devised to illustrate the relationship between samples. The gray concentric shapes on the plot represent an attribute scale without anchors, with the very center being zero (Stone et al. 2012). Each colored line in this illustration represents a different sample.

et al. (2012), sensory scientists should consider the following criteria prior to beginning an affective test:

- objectives of the research
- tests to be executed (to fulfill objective)
- criteria for consumer participation
- essential outcomes of the test

Quantitative Affective Tests

Popular examples of quantitative acceptability tests are hedonic scale tests and paired-preference tests. Preferences and acceptability in consumer tests have an obvious connection—if significantly more consumers rate product A higher in preference than product B, then product A would be the more acceptable product. Before companies invest time and equipment in the development of a food, unbranded sensory research can be completed to assess true liking and the potential for repeat purchases (Stone *et al.* 2012).

Central location testing is done using persons not involved in technical or marketing aspects of the product with 25 to 50 respondents. Organizations may also enlist in-home use tests in order to measure the acceptance and use of a product in an unbiased setting. Because the environment cannot be controlled in these tests, the sample size needs to be larger (75 to 200). The overall goal of quantitative affective sensory tests is to determine what the best product for the target audience should be.

Paired Preference Test

Participants are tasked to choose one sample over another. Samples are offered simultaneously and scientists record which is preferred. Multiple samples should be randomized and given unique three-digit codes. The paired preference test is easy for participants to understand, but information about why a consumer may not like the sample is not apparent. Similar testing can also be completed with proper randomization on more than two samples. This testing is called the *multiple pair preference test.*

Hedonic Tests

Hedonic tests are a scale method for measuring the level of liking for foods. Samples are presented in succession, and the subject is asked to indicate how much she likes or dislikes each one on a scale. The traditional scale, developed by the U.S. Army Food and Container Institute in the 1940s, associates a numerical scale with nine degrees of liking and not liking, as illustrated in Figure 5.7 (Lawless and Heymann 2010). Eliminating the neutral category, using more like than dislike categories, switching to more or fewer categories, and replacing verbal categories with caricatures (such as smiley faces), are examples of the many variations that are used. Smiley faces are commonly used for tests involving children. Some variations can cause drastic changes in response. The standard 9-point scale is the safest and easiest to analyze and interpret for novice panelists. No fewer than 25 panelists (repetitions) should be used for hedonic testing, even early in the product development cycle. The hedonic test is also appropriate for in-home use.

Ranking Tests

For three or more samples, a relative order of preference can be deter-

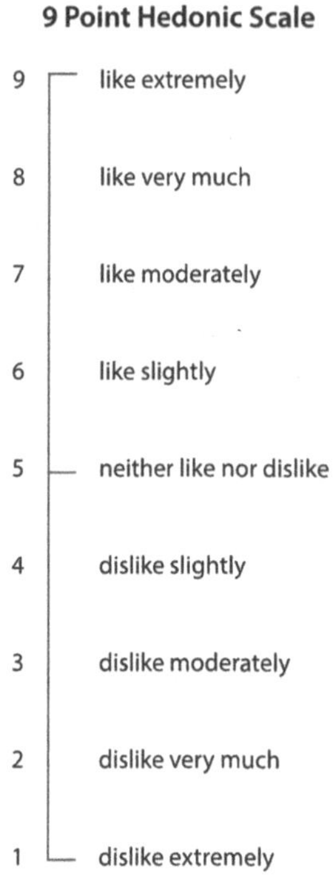

FIGURE 5.7. The 9-point hedonic scale is commonly used in sensory testing to determine liking. An example of commonly used markers is given in this illustration.

mined. Neither the ranking test nor the paired preference test indicates whether any of the products are liked or disliked. These tests indicate only the order in which product samples are preferred. The samples are presented in balanced or random order. The rank sums are calculated and evaluated using Friedman's test (Meilgaard *et al.* 1990).

Qualitative Affective Tests

Qualitative affective consumer tests aim to collect information from consumers regarding their acceptance of products or product concepts. Qualitative affective tests are used to gather data directly from consumers. A sensory department may conduct focus groups or consumer interviews as a solo exercise or as a follow-up to quantitative affective tests.

Focus Groups

Focus Groups consist of a group of 6 to 12 pre-screened consumers that match the demographics of the target audience and are asked about their opinions, beliefs, and habits. Research and development departments may utilize focus groups to gather information about the acceptance of product concepts. Developers can then establish sensory attributes that fit with consumer perception of an idea. Another rationale of focus groups is to gather information about a product prototype that the participants use in their home prior to the focus group meeting. Several focus groups with similar or varying target audiences can be conducted for the same concept.

Conducting a focus group entails establishing what points are important to the research and determining the objectives. Organizers should devise a moderator's guide that includes the purpose of the study, introductions, guidelines for participation, questions, activities, and closing statements. Generally, questions regarding broad product behaviors begin the session, followed by more direct ones. Focus groups normally last from two to three hours; therefore, activities that generate discussion are encouraged.

Moderators are trained discussion leaders who elicit conversation and keep the group discussing the topic at hand. Talented moderators can assist in getting quiet participants to give their opinion and also to prevent talkative participants from taking over the group. Prior to conducting a focus group, the moderator and test coordinator should validate the goals of the study and establish key components that should be covered.

Focus groups should be conducted in a controlled environment with sufficient lighting, limited distractions, and a viewing area separated by a two-way mirror to enable observation by those conducting the study. Audio recording or videotaping can help organizers recall key points after the panel is completed.

Interviews

Companies can conduct interviews with targeted consumers about how they use a product or what they think about a product concept. These interviews are sometimes conducted after other sensory testing to gather more detailed information about a product's acceptability. Interviews could also be conducted following in-home use tests. The interviewer should be trained to conduct consumer research, and those being interviewed need to be screened prior to participation.

Focus groups can suggest a direction that the business might take

Case Study: What Would You Do?

A company is developing an apple flavored hard candy. They have developed two concepts that they believe to fit the concept, so they plan a consumer panel utilizing a central location test with over 100 participants. When the sensory scientist arrives at the test, the facility has the aroma of bleach. The scientist quickly attempts to find other accommodations for the test, but risks not obtaining the number of participants needed due to a change in accommodation. What would you do?

and give insight on the consumer perception of an idea. However, they should not be used as a basis for financial decisions. The data from focus groups is not definitive and can be biased due to the low number of participants.

SENSORY TESTS FOR PRODUCT MATCHING

Some companies try to mimic competitor's products. When trying to match a competitor's product, it may be useful to enlist sensory tests. Focus groups can help determine what the key attributes of the product are, along with qualities of the product consumers like. Descriptive tests can answer what the attributes of the benchmark product are and describe how prototypes differ from the competitor's product. After changes to the prototype have been made or several mock-ups are ready, descriptive tests can also help determine which one is closest to the target sample. Difference testing can also be used to determine if the prototype matches the benchmark model.

SENSORY TESTS FOR PRODUCT REFORMULATIONS

Companies often reformulate products to meet nutritional or cost initiatives or due to a change in the ingredient supply chain. Consumers, on the other hand, come to expect products to have certain sensory characteristics, and do not always appreciate change. Therefore, it is essential for organizations to evaluate product changes and their effect on consumer liking. Difference tests can be used to indicate if consumers will notice a difference in the product. Descriptive analysis can determine if quality has been affected, and what changes have occurred. Acceptability tests can evaluate how much change can occur in the product before consumer acceptance declines.

UTILIZING SENSORY TESTS TO DETERMINE SHELF STABILITY

Sensory tests are used to determine the length of shelf-life for new or reformulated products. Companies need to successfully determine shelf-life in order to gather information about when they should advise distributors and retailers that a product is no longer of acceptable quality. Although microbiological hazards are of interest in shelf-life testing, other changes can occur that make products unpalatable for consumers. Typical modes of failure include texture change, loss of color, nutritional deterioration, or change in functional properties (Fuller 2011). Textural changes can be noticed in products, such as crackers that may stale. Although stale crackers are unacceptable to the consumer, it is unlikely that they would pose any microbiological hazard. Sensory testing can be utilized in this case to measure the degree of staling and consumer acceptability to the end of shelf-life. Loss of functional properties examples are the loss of ability to leaven in the case of yeast, or to set in the case of pectin or gelatin desserts.

SUMMARY: HOW TO GET THE MOST OUT OF SENSORY ANALYSIS

Sensory data can easily become erroneous. In order to repeatedly acquire sufficient data, a sensory scientist and statistician should work together to eliminate common mistakes. Errors can usually be controlled through the use of solid experimental design. Balancing and randomizing the order of product presentation to panelists can help eliminate bias. Experiments need to be replicated when necessary, and sample sizes should be as recommended in order to obtain statistically significant results (i.e., one that a business can use to make decisions).

KEY WORDS

Affective test—assesses the personal response by potential consumers to a product, a product idea, or specific product attributes.

Analytical test—measures the attributes of a product through quantitative and qualitative measures using highly trained personnel.

Consumer testing—uses untrained, unbiased consumers to assess liking or preference for products.

Descriptive analysis—involves both the discrimination and description of the characteristics of products. Typically requires fewer panelists and more training.

Duo-trio test—one of the identical samples is identified as the "control," and the panelist must choose the unidentified sample that is different from the control.

Focus group—a group 6-12 pre-screened consumers that fit into a certain target audience and are asked about their opinions, beliefs, and habits.

Hedonic scale—a scale used in market research and sensory analysis to measure the level of liking of products.

Triangle test—three samples are given wherein two are the same, representing a single lot, and the third represents another lot and might be different.

COMPREHENSION QUESTIONS

5.1. Explain the triangle test.

5.2. Explain the difference between affective and analytical tests.

5.3. Name one of the two methods for controlling error in sensory analysis.

5.4. As a product development technician for a national food company, you have reformulated one of your best-selling products to have a lower cost formulation. The goal of this project was to create a lower cost formulation without sacrificing consumer acceptance. Explain how you would ensure that you are meeting this goal. Give specific examples of tests you would recommend to the rest of your team.

5.5. When should a company use consumers for sensory tests and when should it use a trained panel?

REFERENCES

Fuller, G. *New Food Product Development From Concept to Marketplace*, 3rd ed.. (Boca Raton, FL: Taylor & Francis, 2011).

Lawless, H. T., & H Heymann. *Sensory Evaluation of Food: Principles and Practices*, 2nd ed.. (New York: Springer, 2010).

Meilgaard, M., G.V. Civille, & B.T. Carr. *Sensory Evaluation Techniques* 2nd ed.. (Boca Raton, FL: CRC Press, 1991).

Stone, H., R.N. Bleibaum, & H.A. Thomas. *Sensory Evaluation Practices* 4th ed.. (San Diego: Academic Press, 2012).

CHAPTER 6

Food Additives

Learning Objectives

- Learn about the different categories of additives.
- Know how to find regulations regarding additives.
- Learn the types of food additives and their uses in foods.
- Learn the implications of the Delaney Clause.

FOOD ADDITIVES are included in products for many reasons—to improve the nutritional quality, improve sensory characteristics, increase acceptability, enhance freshness and shelf-life, and assist in processing. A food additive is defined as any substance, natural or artificial, that is added to a food product during any phase of production which includes processing, packaging, and storage. The Food and Drug Administration (FDA) groups food additives into four categories: (1) direct additives, (2) indirect additives, (3) prior-sanctioned, and (4) generally recognized as safe (GRAS) additives. Currently, more than 2,800 different substances are intentionally added to the food supply, whereas as many as 10,000 other substances constitute the category of incidental food additives.

REGULATION OF FOOD ADDITIVES

Regulating and policing food additives is the responsibility of the Food and Drug Administration (FDA). Requirements governing the quantities and quality of additive products must be met in order for the substances to be used. Food additives are tested for safety on at least two animal species (e.g., mice and rats) in order to receive approval. Scientists determine the no observable effect level (NOEL), which corresponds to the highest dose of an additive producing no unexpected adverse health problems in the laboratory animals. Results are extrapolated to humans, usually with a safety factor of 100—10 times, to reflect differences between species, and 10 times for differences within species.

Direct additives are those that are purposefully added to foods in order to serve a function. For example, lemon flavoring added to prepackaged lemon bars is an ingredient intended to enhance the taste. Provisions for direct food additives (found in 21 CFR Part 172.5) also dictate not adding substances in an amount greater than "reasonably required" to achieve the nutritional goal, physical attribute, or sensory quality desired. The FDA may approve the safety of substances for nutritive use, while not endorsing claims regarding effectiveness. The list of direct food additives found in 21 CFR Part 172 details individual ingredients that are permitted in foods and specific guidance for each ingredient. Dried yeasts, listed in 21 CFR Part 172.86, can be added directly to foods, provided the folic acid content does not exceed 0.04 milligram per grams of yeast. Prior to including any ingredient in a formula, a product developer should review any regulations regarding its use.

The Delaney Clause, a 1958 amendment to the Federal Food, Drug, and Cosmetic Act (FFDCA), states that additives exhibiting the ability to cause cancer cannot be used as an ingredient in food. This prevents the intentional addition of a compound that has been shown to cause cancer in animals or humans. The Delaney Clause pertains to all food additives, including pesticides. If a carcinogenic pesticide is found in a processed food tested by the FDA, it is deemed adulterated. It is important to note that the Delaney Clause is enforceable only on food additives.

Many substances added to food are considered safe according to experts. Approximately 600 GRAS substances are used in the food industry. GRAS substances include spices, natural seasonings, baking powder, citric acid, malic acid, mono- and diglycerides, and numerous others. Determination of an additive as GRAS does not qualify it for use in all applications; the limitations on use are listed in the Code of Federal Regulations (21 CFR Ch.1 Part 182, 184, 186).

Views on food additives and their suitability in the food supply can morph over time. The process for hydrogenating oils was developed in the 1930s, leading to widespread commercial use of partially hydrogenated oils in products like margarine by the 1940s. Partially hydrogenated oils were granted GRAS status by the FDA, but this determination was overturned in November 2013. FDA granted manufacturers a comment period in order to help determine whether the substances should be eliminated from foods, as well as the request to help determine an appropriate length of time to allow reformulations. The FDA issued its official revocation on June 16, 2015, allowing manufacturers three years to remove partially hydrogenated oils from their products. The GRAS status of partially hydrogenated oils was heavily influenced by scientific studies linking trans fat consumption to negative health outcomes.

In the situation of non-GRAS substances, approval by the FDA is granted upon submission of scientific data showing that the substance is harmless in the intended food application at a specific level. The FDA sets limits on the type of foods in which the additive may be used and the maximum concentration of the additive. Therefore, a food additive may be permitted at a level of 100 parts per million (ppm) in one food, 50 ppm in another, and not allowed in the third. For example, BHT (butylated hydroxytoluene), listed in 21 CFR § 172.115, can be used in emulsion stabilizers for shortening at a level of 200 ppm, whereas the amount allowed in dry breakfast cereals is 50 ppm.

Manufacturers must present information in a petition to the FDA for a new substance to be approved for addition to foods. A petitioner must establish that the new ingredient is safe and is necessary in the production of a specific food product. Food and Drug Administration petitions take time to be accepted, but companies that provide all vital information can drastically speed up the approval time.

MAJOR USES OF FOOD ADDITIVES

Food additives must have a purpose to be added to a product. Food additives may not be used to cover up product deficiencies or deceive the consumer. Major functions for food additives include preservation, enrichment, improvement in color and flavor, alteration of texture, and processing and/or preparation aids.

Preservation

One main function of food additives is to preserve safety and quality. Without the addition of preservatives, products would spoil at a more accelerated rate than expected by the American consumer, and some would present risk of foodborne illness. The typical consumer is used to fresh, high-quality products. In order to achieve freshness for a longer period of time, additives are included in products to ensure consumer satisfaction. Without preservatives, it would be more common to see bread veiled in mold or milk containing sour or off flavors.

Because the nutrient content of food provides a supportive medium for microorganisms, preservatives are added to control microbial growth. Included in the vast array of preservatives used for the sole purpose of limiting microbial interactions are organic acids and their salts, sulfites, nitrites, parabens, and a host of other compounds. These compounds help to increase shelf-life and reduce the risk of foodborne illnesses.

Certain antimicrobial agents have other functions. For example, salt and sugar can assist in reducing microbial growth by decreasing the amount of water available. Acidulants that reduce the pH of a product can help reduce microbial growth because acidic environments with a pH less than 4.6 tend to preclude microbial expansion. Lysozymes, present in eggs and milk, are naturally occurring antimicrobial agents.

Choosing preservatives is an important part of developing foods. It is critical to inhibit the growth of pathogenic microorganisms throughout the shelf-life of the food, which in turn eliminates the risk of recalls due to contamination. Food scientists need to know the factors (pH, water activity, heating) limiting microorganisms that could possibly thrive in a product. Ready-to-eat products should be treated with great care.

Enrichment

Enrichment is a further function that food additives perform. Enrichment refers to the addition of certain nutrients in amounts that do not exceed those found in the food before processing. Foods with an enriched claim must contain at least 10 percent more of the Recommended Daily Intake (RDI) for vitamins and minerals or of the Daily Recommended Value (DRV) for protein, dietary fiber, and potassium (expressed as a percent of the Daily Value) per reference amount customarily consumed than an appropriate reference food similar in nature.

Vitamin degradation can occur in processes such as milling, canning, and heating, as well as freezing and storage. Various cereal grain products are enriched to restore the original amount of nutrients prior to processing. A typical example of an enriched product is bread. Without the addition of thiamine (B1), riboflavin (B2), and niacin (B3), bread would be deficient in these B-complex vitamins, as well as the mineral iron. Enriching helps ensure that proper proportions of nutrients are contained in the final product. Flour (21 CFR 137.165) and bread (21 CFR 136.115) have more specific regulations in order to use the claim that they are enriched.

Fortified foods are similar to enriched, except that the vitamins and minerals added were not present in the food prior to processing. Like enriched foods, fortified products should have 10 percent more vitamins or minerals (based on RDA) and dietary fiber, protein, and potassium (based on DRV) than a product without fortification. A common example of a fortified product is vitamin D milk. Fortified foods are generally represented as having vitamins and minerals given as a percentage of the RDA. Nutrition labels are required on products that make nutritive claims or have added nutrients.

Improvement in Color

Eating food involves a wide variety of sensory experiences with texture, flavor, odor, and color. As noted in Chapter 4, consumers rely on colors to identify flavors and determine acceptance of products. Just imagine you are in the grocery store looking for produce or meat. How do you determine which product to buy? Most shoppers look at the commodity, smell it, and choose the item that best fits their perception of what's good. Color also pertains to consumer perception of safety.

Because color is an important factor in food choice, added colors are utilized by the food industry to make foods more appealing. Motivations for adding colorants, natural or synthetic, are to:

- Create attractive appearance by restoring natural colors that are lost during processing or storage
- Give color to foods with little color otherwise—such as ice creams, confections, and soda drinks
- Produce consistent color when raw materials may vary in color intensity
- Improve flavor

Flavoring agents include both natural and synthetic compounds used to incorporate flavor. Synthetic flavor additives can be found in a wide variety of products. Methyl salicylate and benzaldehyde are two commonly used synthetic flavors that impart wintergreen and cherry flavoring, respectively. Artificial flavors (or artificial flavoring) are any substances used to impart flavor that are not derived from spices, fruit or fruit juices, vegetable or vegetable juices, edible yeast, herbs, bark, bud, root, leaf or similar plant material, meat, fish, poultry, eggs, dairy products, or fermentation products. A statement must be placed on labels when artificial flavorings are used. Naturally flavored products can be listed on the label as naturally derived flavor ingredients, whereas artificially derived flavors must be declared on the principal display panel (the part of the package that consumers usually see first) as "artificially flavored," in letters not less than one half the size of the food name.

Plant extracts, essential oils, herbs, spices, and other substances head the list of natural flavors used by industry. Natural flavorings are essential oils, oleoresins, essence or extractives, protein hydrolysate, distillate, or any product of roasting, heating, or enzymolysis, which contain flavoring constituents derived from natural substances (listed in the definition of artificial flavor), and which have a significant function in food as flavoring rather than nutrition.

Spices are a form of natural flavoring and may be listed by their common names. Labels refer to natural ingredients added for flavor as "spice." Spices that are also used for coloring purposes (e.g., saffron, paprika, and turmeric) may be listed as "spices and coloring." Dehydrated aromatic vegetables (e.g., garlic, celery, and onion powders) are recognized by consumers as food and, therefore, should be listed by their common names.

Flavor enhancement technologies have become more prevalent in the food industry. With the task of reducing sodium in processed foods, bitterness blocker technologies have been a topic of experimentation, since potassium chloride, a product with notable bitterness, is widely substituted for salt. Adenosine monophosphate (AMP) is one of the compounds that has been found to block the bitter taste of foods and to contribute to better taste (e.g., in naturally bitter grapefruit juice). Monosodium glutamate (MSG), a flavor enhancer used in processing, is commonly used in broths, snacks, and Chinese food to heighten the umami flavor. MSG is the salt form of glutamic acid, an amino acid. Disodium guanylate (21 CFR 172.530) and disodium inosinate (21 CFR 172.535) are also added to foods as flavor enhancers.

Alteration of Texture

Recipe modification often involves reducing or eliminating the amount of fat in a formulation. Gels, gums, and water-based shortening substitutes are used to eliminate fat and calories without sacrificing texture, mouthfeel, and other sensory characteristics. Similar additives that can alter texture also contribute to the desirable characteristics of a food. The food manufacturer utilizes countless approved ingredients and chemicals to help modify texture in complex food systems.

Even simple compounds, such as sucrose (table sugar), can be applied in varying concentrations to achieve a variety of results. Sugar affects texture differently, depending upon its concentration. In a dilute solution, it adds body and mouthfeel to soft drinks, while in higher concentrations it crystallizes and adds brittleness, as in hard candies.

Processing Aids

FDA regulations (21 CFR Part 173) define secondary direct food additives as substances that are required during the manufacture or processing of a food and are ordinarily removed from the final food. Residual carryover to the final food is likely, but no functional changes in the food are seen. Secondary direct food additives are consistent with FDA's definition of a processing aid and are not declared as an ingredient in food products due to their minuscule quantity. Processing aids, in theory, should not present any risk to human health.

Although secondary direct additives and processing aids do not directly affect product attributes, they do increase efficiency of producers. The United States Department of Agriculture (USDA) and the FDA classify additives as processing aids if they meet three criteria:

1. The substance is added and removed, and is not a significant ingredient in the finished food.
2. The substance is added to a food and then changed into a food component present in an insignificant quantity that does not alter the structure of the food.
3. Substances are added during processing and are present only in an insignificant quantity, and do not alter the finished product's structure or function.

Common functions of processing aids include acting as antimicrobials, clarifying agents, skin removers on roots and tubers, and antifoaming elements. Processing aids commonly used in the food industry include fruit and vegetable washes, such as chlorine rinses, decolorization agents (dimethylamine epichlorohydrin copolymer, for refined sugar) and ingredients for strengthening baked goods (sodium stearoyl lactylate, used in frozen baked goods). Although processing aids are not listed as ingredients, they are regulated in the same manner as all other food additives. The USDA has stated that food producers may not categorize an additive as a processing aid without consent.

CATEGORIES OF COMMON FOOD ADDITIVES

Food additives have been used to flavor, preserve, and perform various functions for thousands of years. However, additives can be the source of misinformation and confusion in consumers. Classification of additives is based on the function of the additive. Individual additives may serve more than one purpose, which entails the same additive may fall under differing classifications. The following is a simple classification of food additives according to function.

Acidulants

Acidulants are pH-adjusting/controlling chemicals that assist in enhancing flavors, controlling microorganism growth, and gelling and coagulation. Properties of food acidulants, such as solubility in water, taste characteristics, and physical form, help the processor choose an acidulant to add to a product. Common food acidulants utilized in the

TABLE 6.1. Common Acidulates Used in Foods.

Acidulant	Common Uses
Acetic Acid	Pickling applications, condiments, baked goods, chewing gum, and dressings
Adipic Acid	Jellies, jams, for leavening, dairy products, frozen desserts
Ascorbic Acid	Fruit drinks, soft drinks, bread dough
Citric Acid, anhydrous	Candy, gelatin, alcoholic beverages, fruit drinks
Citric Acid, monohydrate	Wide variety of foods and beverages
Fumaric Acid	Wine, confections, soft drinks, pie fillings, cakes mixes
Lactic Acid	Salad dressings, biscuits, ready to eat meats, infant formulas
Malic Acid	Fruit juices, sauces, processed meat products, confections, ciders, soybean products
Phosphoric Acid	Sodas and other carbonated beverages, cheese and beer making
Succinic Acid	Bakery items, dry mixes, confections, dairy products, sauces
Tartaric Acid	Baking powder, chewing gum, cocoa powder

food industry are acetic, adipic, ascorbic, citric, fumaric, lactic, malic, phosphoric, and tartaric acids. While many of these acidulants are derived from fruits and vegetables, fermentation and chemical synthesis are also methods for generating acidulants. Common acidulants are listed in Table 6.1. Acids are added to foods in order to inhibit microbial growth, initiate coagulation of milk to make cheese, provide flavor (as in wines), and act as a chelating agent. As a product developer, you need to account for the form that the acid will have when added in the product's formulation, which is commonly an aqueous solution. The time the acid will be introduced into the process is also important. For example, if an acid is added prematurely in jelly making, the result will be a clumpy gel.

Anti-Caking Compounds

Compounds added to dry mixes to prevent clumping and keep powders free flowing are called anti-caking agents. These additives adsorb excess water in order to create a more appealing and useful product for consumers. Anti-caking agents not only keep high-fat foods (especially boxed mixes) from caking together, but also serve as a processing aid. Anti-caking compounds are very fine powders used to separate crystals of substances that would otherwise adhere.

Anti-caking agents can be found in dry mixes (cakes, cheese sauce, etc.), shredded cheese, powdered sugar, instant soups, and table salt. Natural ingredients, such as potato starch, cellulose, and sugarbeet fiber, have also been used for anti-caking purposes. Examples of commonly used anti-caking agents are listed in Table 6.2.

Antifoaming Agents

Processing strategies employing mechanical defoaming equipment or chemical antifoam agents can control foam, an accumulation of bubbles created when certain gases are released into a liquid. Chemical antifoams have proven to be the most effective and economical means of controlling this processing menace. Defoaming agents (21 CFR 173.340) can be used in the processing of foods as long as regulations are followed. Effective antifoaming agents have low surface tension, disperse easily, have low solubility, and have no odor. Antifoaming agents may be used in deep fat frying oil, cocoa, fermentation systems, jam and jelly making, and other processes.

TABLE 6.2. Anti-Caking Compounds and their Regulations.

Anti-Caking Compound	Regulations in 21 CFR	Limitations on Use
Calcium silicate	172.410, 182.2227	Up to 2% in foods, but up to 5% in baking powder
Iron ammonium citrate	172.430	Cannot exceed 25 ppm in salt
Silicon dioxide	172.480	Not to exceed amount needed to prevent caking, and cannot be used over 2% of final food
Yellow prussiate of soda	172.490	Can be used in salt in the amount needed for anti-caking effect, and not over 13 ppm
Aluminum calcium silicate	182.2122	Not to exceed 2% of salt
Magnesium silicate	182.2437	Not to exceed 2% of table salt
Sodium aluminosilicate	182.2727	Not to exceed 2% of finished food
Sodium calcium alumino-silicate, hydrated	182.2729	Not to exceed 2% of finished food
Tricalcium silicate	182.2906	Not to exceed 2% of table salt
Potassium acid tartrate	184.1077	Allowed for use in baked goods, confections and frostings, gelatins and puddings, hard candy, jams and jellies, soft candy
Calcium chloride	184.1193	0.2% for cheese, gravies, and sauces, 0.32% for coffee and tea, 0.05% for food categories not specified in regulation*
Calcium sulfate	184.1230	0.5% for frozen dairy desserts and mixes, 0.4% for gelatins and puddings, 0.07% or less for all other food categories*
Magnesium carbonate	184.1425	Not to exceed amount needed to prevent caking
Magnesium oxide	184.1431	Not to exceed amount needed to prevent caking
Propylene glycol	184.1666	97% for seasonings and flavorings, 5% for nuts and nut products, 24% for confections and frostings, 2% for other food categories*
Sorbitol	184.1835	75% in chewing gum, 98% in soft candy, 12% in all other foods
Carnuba wax	184.1978	Can be used in baked goods and baking mixes, confections and frosting, chewing gum, gravies and sauces, and soft candy

*Only foods that may need anti-caking agent are listed. Other limits are found in the Code of Federal Regulations.

Most antifoam agents consist of silicone and are typically classified as secondary direct additives (processing aids), substances whose functionality is required during manufacture and then removed from the final food or permitted in minute percentages. Products in which antifoams are specifically approved for use are canned pineapple juice, yeast, sugar beets, sliced potatoes, fermentation processes and fruit butters, jellies, and preserves. Consulting with antifoam ingredient suppliers for the best antifoam in processing is recommended.

Antioxidants

Antioxidants, as the name implies, serve to prevent or minimize oxidation. Oxidation is the loss of electrons and gain of O_2, which can cause off-odors and quality degradation. Techniques to reduce oxidation include (1) adding free-radical stoppers, (2) introducing free-radical inhibitors, (3) packaging to remove oxygen, or (4) inhibiting catalysts of oxidation like moisture and light.

Common antioxidants naturally present in food include lecithin, vitamin E, tocopherols, and certain sulfur-containing amino acids. Lecithin is found in soybeans and is obtained for commercial use by solvent extraction. Although antioxidants can be natural, synthetic chemicals are much more effective. Synthetic antioxidants that are commonly used include butylated hydroxyanisole (BHA), butylated hydroxytoluene (BHT), tertiary butylated hydroquinone (TBHQ), and propyl gallate (PG). Butylated hydroxyanisole, BHT, and TBHQ all work to reduce oxidation by acting as free-radical stoppers. Another antioxidant, ethylenediaminetetraacetic acid (EDTA), acts to inhibit free radicals. Considerations when choosing an antioxidant include:

- Potency
- Solubility
- Discoloration
- pH
- Type of process
- Flavor and odor
- Legal and regulatory status

Antioxidants are usually added directly into fats and oils. Suppliers of fats and oils are skilled at using these additives, so that food companies can have them added prior to receiving fat- and oil-based ingredients. For nuts and cereals, antioxidants are dissolved in solvent before

TABLE 6.3. Antioxidants and their Regulations.

Antioxidant	Regulations in 21 CFR	Limitations on Use
Anoxomer	172.105	Not more than 5,000 ppm based on fat or oil content
BHA	172.110	50 ppm: Dehydrated potatoes, potato flakes, sweet potato flakes, dry breakfast cereal* 2 ppm: Beverages and desserts prepared from dry mixes (or 90 ppm in dry mix) 32 ppm: Dry diced glazed fruit 200 ppm: Stabilizers for shortening* 1,000 ppm: Active dry yeast
BHT	172.115	50 ppm: Dehydrated potatoes, potato flakes, sweet potato flakes, dry breakfast cereal* 200 ppm: Stabilizers for shortening* 10 ppm: Potato granules
Ethoxyquin	172.140	5 ppm: Uncooked fat of meat from animals (excluding poultry) 3 ppm: Uncooked liver and fat of poultry 0.5 ppm: Uncooked muscle meat of animals, poultry eggs 100 ppm: Chili powder, paprika, and ground chili
4-Hydroxymethyl-2,6-di-tert-butylphenol	172.150	Can be used alone or in combination with other anti-oxidants at a level that should not exceed 0.2% of the oil or fat content of the food
TBHQ	172.185	Can be used alone or with BHA and BHT, but should not exceed 0.2% of the oil and fat content of the food
THBP(2,4,5-trihydroxy-butyrophenone)	172.190	Can be used alone or in combination with other antioxidants at a level that should not exceed 0.2% of the fat or oil in food
Isopropyl citrate	184.1386	Can be used in margarine, non-alcoholic beverages, and fats and oils
PG	184.1660	Should not exceed 0.2% of the oil or fat content of the food
Propylene glycol	184.1666	97% for seasonings and flavorings 5% for alcoholic beverages, nuts, and nut products 2.5% of frozen dairy products 24% for confections and frostings 2% for other food categories
Sodium carbonate	184.1742	Should not be used at levels that exceed necessity
Stannous chloride	184.1845	Maximum level of 0.0015% or less
Stearyl citrate	184.1851	Can be used in margarine, non-alcoholic beverages, and fats and oils
Tocopherols	182.3890	None

being sprayed onto the foods. Packaging materials can also deliver antioxidants. For example, antioxidants can be impregnated into paperboard, polyethylene, and wax paper materials. Food processors should keep in mind that processing steps can destroy antioxidants; therefore, timing of adding antioxidants is important.

Antioxidant effectiveness is product dependent. Tocopherols are very effective on animal fats and oils, especially in frying processes. They have become the antioxidant of choice for product developers looking for a "clean" label and claiming that the product is "all natural." Vegetable oils are effectively protected from oxidation by TBHQ. Baking applications can benefit from a BHT, BHA, and tocopherol antioxidant cocktail. Nut products are well protected by a variety of antioxidants, but TBHQ is commonly used for nut oil and butters. Dry breakfast cereals commonly use BHA and BHT incorporated into packaging material to help protect flavor.

Bases

Like acidulants, bases provide a means of adjusting or controlling pH. Certain manufacturing processes require adjusting pH during a unit operation. For instance, the vegetable industry often submerges vegetables in a 1 percent lye solution at elevated temperatures to loosen the skins. Because the cost of lye and of treating lye-containing wastewaters can be appreciable, processors will use less expensive techniques (e.g., hot water scalding, steaming, or direct exposure to gases or flame).

Bases also play a key role in color development, alteration of texture, and removal of bitter compounds in certain products. Sodium hydroxide, a base commonly used in the food industry, is frequently added to ripe olives to assist in darker color development and removal of bitter compounds. When dipped in a 1.25 percent sodium hydroxide solution prior to baking, pretzels display a more desirable brown color and a smoother texture than without this treatment. The sodium hydroxide converts to sodium bicarbonate in the baking process through its reaction with carbon dioxide ($NaOH + CO_2 \rightarrow NaHCO_3$).

Dough Conditioners and Strengtheners

Additives for baking processes include dough strengtheners, leavening agents, yeast nutrients, antioxidants, sweeteners, thickeners, emulsifiers, enzymes, preservatives, and vitamins. In dough systems, the formation of a gluten network and retention of carbon dioxide are important. Dough conditioners help control the baking process and create the best crumb structure, volume, and shelf-life.

Gluten networks can be improved through the use of oxidizing and reducing agents. Oxidants elevate bread strength, while reducing agents improve dough extensibility and improve softness. Oxidizing agents encompass calcium peroxide, potassium iodate, azodicarbonamide (ADA), ascorbic acid, calcium iodate, potassium bromate, and calcium bromate. Under-oxidized products lead to soft, weak, sticky, and hard to work with dough, as well as bread with low volume, weak crust, and uneven grain and texture. Over-oxidized products lead to tight dough that tears easily. The bread from an over-oxidized dough will exhibit small volumes, large holes in the bread, and uneven grain. Reducing agents, which can cut down mixing time, are generally used alongside oxidants. Commonly used reducing agents include coated ascorbic acid, sodium metabisulfite, sorbic acid, and L-cysteine hydrochloride. Ascorbic acid acts as an oxidizing agent in the presence of oxygen, and a reducing agent in its absence. Coating the ascorbic acid can delay its effects and ensure it acts as a reducing agent.

Bleaching Agents

Bleaching agents have an important use in the bakery industry, primarily in flour milling and breadmaking. Benzoyl peroxide is applied to wheat flour to remove plant pigments and produce a white product. Hydrogen peroxide is used in the dairy industry to create more desirable color characteristics, especially in milk. Hydrogen peroxide is removed before the milk is packaged and transported through the use of the enzyme, catalase.

Chelating Agents (Sequestrants)

Chelating agents are applied in foods to form a complex with unwanted trace metals and to render them inactive. The most problematic metal ions are iron, copper, nickel, and zinc, because discoloration, turbidity, and oxidation can occur in their presence. Because chelating agents are used to control the reactions of trace metals in food systems, they are often referred to as "metal scavengers." Common chelating agents and their solubility are listed in Table 6.4.

TABLE 6.4. Chelating Agents, Their Solubility, and Regulations.

Product	Solubility (g/100 ml H_2O)	Regulation in 21 CFR Part
EDTA—$CaNa_2 \cdot 2H_2O$	40	172.12
EDTA—$Na_2H_2 \cdot 2H_2O$	10	172.135
Citric Acid	160	184.1033 (GRAS)
Potassium citrate • $2H_2O$	167	184.1625 (GRAS)
Sodium citrate • $2H_2O$	71	184.1751 (GRAS)

Source: (Food Additive 1991).

Without chelating agents, discoloration would appear in foods such as potatoes, where iron reacts with phenolic compounds in the presence of oxygen. Citric acid and polyphosphates are commonly used in the food industry to prevent discoloration, but the most effective sequestrant is ethylenediamine tetra acetic acid (EDTA), which can be added to food as disodium EDTA or calcium EDTA. Applications of chelating agents include phosphates in soft drinks to chelate heavy metal ions that interfere with carbonation and using EDTA in mayonnaise to protect flavor. Other specific applications of chelating agents are detailed in Table 6.5.

Clarifying Agents

The beverage industry relies on clarifying agents to prevent cloudiness in the final product. Agents such as bentonite are used for processing juices, wines, vinegar, and other beverages, which then appear as attractive, clear liquids that appeals to consumers.

Emulsifiers

To stabilize oil and water systems, product developers will use emulsifiers to prevent phase separations, because they have both a hydrophilic and a hydrophobic side. Emulsifiers are active in almost every stage of the baking process. Emulsifiers can compensate for abuse from under- and over-mixing (if it is not too extreme) as well as excessive fermentation length. Emulsifiers are particularly desirable in automated processes. Emulsifiers used in the baking industry include mono- and diglycerides, sodium stearoyl-2-lactylate, calcium stearoyl-2-lactylate, lecithin, and polysorbate 60. These emulsifiers, their typical uses, and FDA limits are outlined in Table 6.6.

TABLE 6.5. Chelating Agents and Common Uses.

Category	Food	Chelating Agent	Function
Beverages	Carbonated beverage (in can)	Calcium EDTA	Flavor retention
	Alcoholic beverages—Distilled	Calcium EDTA	Flavor retention, color retention, product clarity
Dairy	Skim milk	Disodium EDTA	Prevent fats from separating
Fats & Oils	Vegetable oil	Potassium citrate, Sodium citrate	Preservative
	Lard	Potassium citrate, Sodium citrate	Preservative
	Mayonnaise	Calcium EDTA, Disodium EDTA	Preservative
	Salad dressing	Calcium EDTA	Preservative
Fish	Frozen fish	Potassium citrate, Sodium citrate	Color retention, slows rancidity
	Clams (canned)	Calcium EDTA	Color retention
	Crabmeat (canned)	Calcium EDTA	Color retention, prevents struvites
	Shrimp	Calcium EDTA	Color retention, prevents struvites
Meat & Poultry	Beef, cooked	Disodium EDTA	Anti-bacterial
	Chicken, cooked	Disodium EDTA	Flavor improver
	Pork, fresh	Potassium citrate, Sodium citrate	Color retention, flavor retention
Fruit	Apple slices	Disodium EDTA, Potassium citrate, Sodium citrate	Prevents browning
	Bananas	Disodium EDTA	Inhibits discoloration
	Frozen fruit	Potassium citrate, Sodium citrate	Color retention, flavor retention
	Fruit spreads, artificially colored	Disodium EDTA	Color retention
Vegetables	Black eyed peas, canned	Disodium EDTA	Color retention
	Chickpeas, canned	Disodium EDTA	Color retention
	Kidney beans, canned	Disodium EDTA	Color retention
	Potatoes, canned	Calcium EDTA	Color retention
	Potatoes, frozen	Disodium EDTA	Color retention
	Mushrooms, canned	Calcium EDTA	Color retention
	Cabbage, pickled	Calcium EDTA	Color retention, flavor retention, improves final texture
	Cucumbers, pickled	Calcium EDTA	Preservative
Eggs	Egg product	Calcium EDTA	Preservative

TABLE 6.6. Emulsifiers Used in Baked Goods.

Emulsifier	Typical Use Levels	Limit (by FDA)
Mono- and diglycerides	0.15–0.75%	No limit*
Sodium stearoyl-2-lactylate (SSL)	0.25–0.5%	0.5% based on flour basis
Calcium stearoyl-2-lactylate (CSL)	0.25–0.5%	0.5% based on flour basis
Lecithins		No limit
Polysorbate 60	0.15–0.4%	0.5% in bread, 0.46% in cakes

*Some types of mono- and diglycerides may have more strict regulations. Refer to 21 CFR for more information..

Depending on the application, emulsifiers can be acquired in liquid, semi-solid, and powder form. The most common source of lecithin is soy, which has to be declared on the label as soy lecithin, a potential concern for those with soy allergies.

Product formulators can avoid the addition of artificial emulsifiers by relying on egg yolk in some baked goods and condiments. Egg yolk is rich in phospholipids and forms the emulsifying backbone in mayonnaise.

Enzymes

Enzymes have specific functions based on the food system where they are applied, and the need for specific substrates. As biological catalysts, enzymes lower the energy required in biochemical reactions and accelerate the rate of the reaction. Enzymes are utilized extensively in the food industry for a variety of applications. Groups of enzymes used for food processing are as follows:

1. *Oxireductases*—Act as catalysts in oxidation or reductions.
2. *Transferases*—Catalyze the shift of one chemical group to another
3. *Hydrolases*—Aid by speeding the reaction of hydrolytic splitting of substrates.
4. *Lyases*—Remove or add groups to their substrates without hydrolysis.
5. *Isomerases*—Catalyze intramolecular rearrangement.
6. *Ligases*—Aid in the joining of two substrate molecules. Also called synthetases.

TABLE 6.7. *Enzymes Used in Food Processing.*

Category	Enzyme	Enzyme Group	Product Usage	Function
Cereals	Amylases	Hydrolase	Bread, other baked goods	Increase fermentation to improve loaf volume. Also benefits crust color and crumb structure
	Proteases	Hydrolase	Biscuits	Reducing mixing time needed for baked goods through modification of gluten
Alcoholic Beverages	Amylases	Hydrolase	Brewing	Decreases viscosity of mash in brewing, aids in conversion of starch to sugars
	Tannase	Hydrolase	Brewing	Removal of polyphenolics
	Glucanases	Hydrolase	Brewing	Assist in filtration, act as extra sugar for fermentation
	Proteases	Hydrolase	Brewing	Add nitrogen for growth of yeast, help in filtration process
	Pectinases	Hydrolase	Wine	Used to clarify; increase the yields of extraction and decreased press times
Non-alcoholic Beverages	Cellulases	Hydrolase	Coffee, Tea	Used to break down cellulose
	Pectinases	Hydrolase	Coffee	Eliminates gelatinous coating
			Cocoa	Separation of pulp from beans
Dairy	Catalase	Oxidoreductase	Milk	To remove H_2O_2 in milk
	Proteases	Hydrolase	Cheese	Casein coagulation
			Evaporated Milk	Stabilizes
	Lipase	Hydrolase	Cheese	Used to develop flavor
Meat & Fish	Proteases	Hydrolase	Fresh meat and fish	Tenderizes, removes oil from tissue of fish
Eggs	Glucose oxidase	Oxidoreductase	Dried egg products	Removes glucose
	Lipases	Hydrolase	Various egg applications	Improves emulsification properties and stabilizes egg white foaming properties
Fruits & Vegetables	Amylases	Hydrolase	Juice	Remove starches to improve extraction
			Vegetables	Tenderizes
	Naringinase	Hydrolase	Citrus juice	Reduces bitter taste
Fats & Oils	Cellulase	Hydrolase	Vegetable Oils	Hydrolyses cell walls

The environment of an enzyme affects its catalytic activity. Factors that can change an enzyme's effects are (1) temperature, (2) pH, (3) concentration of the enzyme and substrate, (4) the presence of inhibitors or activators, and (5) the amount of time it's in the system (also referred to as residence time). Food scientists need to understand the factors influencing enzymes, in order to take advantage of the greatest enzymatic activity. For example, acceleration or retardation of desired reactions can occur with increasing temperatures. If the temperature goes above the temperature of denaturation for a specific enzyme, the enzyme will no longer be active. The optimal pH also varies for enzymatic reactions. Some enzymes need a very specific pH, whereas others can catalyze in a wide range. During production, it is essential to add the enzyme in a range that is appropriate for the desired function.

Enzymes are typically present in small concentrations and, therefore, act as the limiting factor of the reaction. In food systems, the enzyme concentration is usually indicative of the rate of reactions. Although enzyme concentration can prevent catalytic functions from occurring, compounds in the product may affect enzymatic activity as well. Inhibitors are chemical compounds in the system that deter enzymatic reactions from occurring. Metals like copper, iron, or calcium, can also act as inhibitors. On the other hand, enzyme activators in the system will make the environment more stable or increase its function as a catalyst. The catalytic reaction must also have enough time at the controlled environment to be completed.

A common use of enzymes is in the bakery industry, where amylase functions to accelerate the fermentation process. Yeast must have fermentable carbohydrates to produce carbon dioxide and leaven bread. Flour naturally contains α-amylase and β-amylase, but more α-amylase may be needed. This enzyme can be added by incorporating malt flour, fungal amylases (*Aspergillus*, usually added in a tablet or powder form), or bacterial amylases (*Bacillus* species). Other common uses of enzymes in applications are listed in Table 6.7.

In choosing an enzyme for a specific product, the following factors must be considered: cost, legal status, availability, and convenience. As with many additives, some enzymes have received GRAS status, whereas others have limited use.

Flavoring Agents

Flavoring agents can be broken down into food flavors and flavor enhancers. Food flavors comprise more than 1,200 different flavoring materials and constitute the single largest category of food additives. Natural flavoring substances include herbs, spices, essential oils, and plant extracts. However, today there is more emphasis on the use of synthetic flavors because they are more economical compared to natural flavors. Flavor enhancers (or potentiators) are also considered flavoring agents. Unlike food flavors, which contribute flavor, flavor enhancers do not have flavor in themselves, but rather intensify the flavor of other compounds present in foods. Monosodium glutamate (MSG), the most commonly used potentiator in the food industry, is a flavor enhancer. The use of MSG remains controversial due to the sensitivity of some individuals to this additive. Food scientists developing new products should be familiar with labeling regulations concerning flavors. Artificially flavored packaged foods must declare on the Principal Display Panel (PDP) that they contain artificial flavors.

Food Colors

Food colors are added to products for several reasons, as follows:

- To restore the original appearance of the food.
- To ensure uniformity of color due to natural variations in color intensity.
- To intensify colors to the level associated with a specific food type.
- To help protect flavor and light-sensitive vitamins during shelf storage.
- To give an attractive appearance to foods otherwise unattractive or unappetizing.
- To help preserve the identity or character by which a food is recognized.
- To serve as visual indication of quality.

Food products can acquire their final color from natural or artificial sources. Naturally occurring plant pigments (e.g., carotene, chlorophyll, and lycopene) help impart hues of orange, green, and red, respectively. Animal pigments, including myoglobin and heme, serve to incorporate color into products (e.g., meat). Certain red colors, such as kermes and lac, are derived from insects (Food Additive 1991). Algae and fungi also produce color and can be incorporated into specific foods. Without the addition of vegetable dye, cheddar cheese would lack its familiar orange color. Although these colorants come from natural sources, they

TABLE 6.8. Colorants Exempt from Certification in Food Products.

Colorant	Hues	Derived From	Regulation (21 CFR)
Annatto	Reds, Yellows	Tropical shrub	73.30
Beet juice concentrate	Red to yellow	Beets	73.260
Beets (dehydrated)	Red to yellow	Beets	73.40
Cabbage (red)	Red	Red cabbage	73.260
Caramel	Brown	Heating of sugar	73.85
Carmine	Red	Lake of cochineal	73.100
Carrot oil	Yellow	Carrots	73.300
Cochineal extract	Red	Bodies of female cochineal insects	73.100
Fruit juice concentrates	Various	Fruit	73.250
Grape color extract	Red to blue	Grapes	73.169
Grape skin extract	Red to blue	By-product of wine processing	73.170
Paprika	Red	Peppers	73.340
Saffron	Yellow	*Crocus sativus*	73.500
Turmeric	Yellow to green yellow	Dried, ground herb	73.600
Vegetable juice	Various	Various vegetables	73.260

are not categorized as natural colorants, because a natural color can be derived only from food itself.

Artificial colorants are manufactured via chemical synthesis and represent the primary source of commercial colorants. Artificial colorants must be approved by the FDA, and are named with the prefix "FD&C" (food, drug, and cosmetic). A list is provided in Table 6.9. Currently there are nine approved synthetic color additives. Artificial colors can be in lake form or as a pure colorant. Lakes are dyes that have been precipitated with an insoluble base to create a colorant that is insoluble in most solvents. Lakes can be prepared out of all approved FD&C colors except Red #3. Physical and chemical properties of certified food colors include hue range, compatibility with food components, and stability to light, oxidation, and pH change. FD&C Blue #1 (brilliant blue), FD&C Green #3 (fast green), FD&C Red #40 (erythrosine), and FD&C Yellow #6 (sunset yellow) are examples of synthetic colors used in the food industry (Francis 1999).

Sources of naturally occurring colors are endless, but economics usually influence whether to use a natural or synthetic food color. Although naturally occurring colors are often used in food products, artificial coloring is a viable alternative. Artificial colors can be more economi-

TABLE 6.9. Colorants Certified by the FDA.

Colorant Name	Hue	Regulation
Citrus Red No. 2 (only used on citrus fruit)	Red	74.302
FD&C Blue No. 1 (Brilliant Blue)	Greenish Blue	74.101
FD&C Blue No. 2 (Indigotine)	Deep Blue	74.102
FD&C Green No. 3 (Fast Green)	Bluish Green	74.203
FD&C Red No. 3 (Erythrosine)	Bluish Red	74.303
FD&C Red No. 40 (Allura Red)	Yellowish Red	74.340
FD&C Yellow No. 5 (Tartrazine)	Lemon Yellow	74.705
FD&C Yellow No. 6 (Sunset Yellow)	Reddish Yellow	74.706
FD&C Lakes (All except Red No. 3)		

Sources: Francis 1999 and Food Additive 1991.

cal than natural colors, and synthetic colors generally excel in coloring power, color uniformity, and color stability (Francis 1999).

Food Irradiation

Food irradiation, a method of exposing foods to radiation, is an alternative to chemical substances for food preservation. Although food irradiation can be seen as a processing method, it falls under food additives in an FDA regulation found in the 1958 Food Additive Amendment to the Food, Drug, and Cosmetic Act. Applications of irradiation include sprout inhibition, insect disinfestation, sterilization, pasteurization, shelf-life extension, and elimination of parasites. Although irradiation has been authorized for many processes, costs associated with the procedure can be high, and acceptance from the general public has been low for most commodities.

Gases

Industrial gases have a variety of uses and functions in the food industry, with nitrogen and carbon dioxide being the two most widely used. The presence or absence of certain gases can directly influence the shelf stability, color, texture, and flavor of a product. By controlling the amount or level of gases in a food's environment, the processor is able to increase the product's longevity. The combination of gas flushing and food preservation methods (freezing, irradiation, dehydration) will lead to a high-quality product. Gas flushing is commonly used in the packaging of potato chips and meat.

Freezing or Chilling

Carbon dioxide and nitrogen are cryogenic elements used in the freezing and chilling of foods. Cryogenic refers to the capacity to generate very low temperatures. To freeze or chill foods, liquid nitrogen or carbon dioxide (in a liquid or solid state) are allowed to come in contact with the food to be chilled, and upon contact the cryogens undergo a change of state. Changing of state releases the heat from the product being chilled, and the carbon dioxide or nitrogen is released as a gas. Special handling procedures are needed for both these additives.

Controlled Gas Atmospheres

The controlling of a gaseous environment can help maintain product integrity during storage and shipping. There are two options for controlling gases; modified atmosphere or modified atmosphere packaging (MAP). Modified atmosphere is the continuous control of storage conditions under particular atmospheric conditions. MAP refers to replacing the normal air in a package with specific gases, which are allowed to change over time as a result of product changes, bacterial activity, and the penetration of gases through the packaging material.

Modified atmosphere storage is used to prolong the life of fruits, vegetables, meat, and nuts. After harvest, fruits and vegetables begin aerobic respiration, in which they absorb oxygen and begin to degrade. Aerobic respiration can be slowed through the depletion of oxygen present during storage. The best conditions for storing fruits and vegetables depend on the type of product. Meat, poultry, and fish all utilize a modified atmosphere in order to extend their shelf-life. Poultry is best kept under an atmosphere of 30 to 60 percent carbon dioxide and 1–5 percent oxygen, while fish is better at 40 to 110 and 0 to 2 percent respectively. Red meats are best with a higher concentration of oxygen (30–50% carbon dioxide, 50–80% oxygen). Higher oxygen helps preserve the red color of meats. Myoglobin reacts with oxygen to create oxymyoglobin, the bright red pigment that indicates freshness and quality to the consumer. Nuts and snack products with nuts are usually packed in nitrogen atmospheres, which prevent rancidity caused by deterioration of oil.

Other Uses

Carbon dioxide is a common additive in the beverage industry to make soda and other carbonated beverages. Carbonated beverages are usually carbonated under pressure to facilitate a higher rate of carbon dioxide incorporation. The process is responsible for both the fizz in these products as well as some of the sharp flavor. Nitrous oxide is commonly used as a propellant in cans of whipped cream.

Ozone, a strong oxidizing agent, is another gas used in the food industry. Recycled poultry chill water is commonly treated with ozone to destroy objectionable odors, flavors, and to sterilize. Ozone is normally produced onsite by means of ozone generators.

Humectants

The primary purpose of humectants is to bind water that may be present in a food system to retain proper moisture, fresh flavor, and texture. Humectants (e.g., glycerol, propylene glycol, and sorbitol) are often added to products such as candies, shredded coconut, and marshmallows. Sucrose (table sugar) and salt, also fall into this classification as additives due to their ability to bind water.

Leavening Agents

Leavening agents, such as baking soda, baking powder and yeast, play an important role in the bakery industry. They produce carbon dioxide and assist in providing the light texture in baked goods (e.g., cakes and breads). Chemical leavening agents work by a reaction of an acid and a soda, while biological forms (like yeast) work by fermenting carbohydrates in the system. In both cases, carbon dioxide is released into the baking system. A list of common leaveners is provided in Table 6.10.

TABLE 6.10. Chemical Leavening Agents and Common Applications.

Chemical Leavening Agent	Applications
Monocalcium phosphate monohydrate	Pancake, cookie, and angel food cake mixes; double acting baking powder
Sodium acid pyrophosphate	Doughnuts, refrigerated dough, baking powder, mixes
Sodium aluminum phosphate	Baking mixes
Sodium bicarbonate	Baking mixes, cake mixes, pancakes, cookies
Dicalcium phosphate dihydrate	Cake mixes
Sodium aluminum sulphate	Used in combination with fast acting leavener

Sources: Smith 1991.

In order for a chemical leavener to perform, there must be a carbonate that is present as a sodium or potassium salt. There are delaying and fast-acting chemical leavening agents. The delaying agents release about 20 percent of the carbon dioxide during mixing and the rest during baking. An example is sodium aluminum phosphate. Monocalcium phosphate is a fast acting agent, and it will release 80 percent of the carbon dioxide during mixing.

The most common chemical leavening agents are baking soda and baking powder. Baking soda is made up of only sodium bicarbonate; therefore, in order to produce carbon dioxide, an acidic ingredient must be added for it to react. Baking powder, however, is sodium bicarbonate and an acid together. The acid included in baking powder is generally cream of tartar. Baking powder can be single or double acting. The double-acting baking powder helps leaven dough while it sets and then continues to act in the oven as temperatures increase.

Sweeteners

Sugar can denote fructose, sucrose, dextrose, levulose, invert sugar, molasses, brown sugar, and honey. Table sugar or sucrose is the most widely known sweetener. With increasing obesity, cutting out carbohydrates and sugar has been a major focus of the food industry. Sugar is also associated with dental caries. There are a wide variety of sweeteners used to replace table sugar. A number of these and their functions are provided in Table 6.11. Sugar replacers can provide carbohydrates or be non-nutritive. Sugar is a great provider of bulk, as mentioned later in this chapter. Therefore, the use of intense sweeteners to replace sugar may require the addition of bulking agents like maltodextrin.

Sugar substitutes that do not contribute calories are called non-nutritive. Approved nonnutritive sweeteners include aspartame, acesulfame potassium, saccharin, sucralose, and neotame. Aspartame is commonly used in snack foods such as gelatin desserts, diet soft drinks, and other snacks. Acesulfame potassium is approved for use in dry food products and is relatively heat stable. Saccharin can be utilized in low-calorie products such as jams, beverages, and desserts, but may impart a bitter aftertaste and also must carry a notice warning of heightened incidence of bladder cancer in rats that consumed it. Many of these sweeteners are used in combination with one another to create a taste as close to sucrose as possible.

Polyols are sweeteners commonly referred to as sugar alcohols and have low to no carcinogenicity. Polyols are also bulking agents. Xylitol, mannitol, and sorbitol are natural polyols, making their consumer appeal higher than other artificial sugar alcohols. These ingredients are commonly used in sugarless chewing gums. Excessive consumption of sugar alcohols can have a laxative effect. Some require a warning to this effect on the PDP of a package if more than 15g of polyol is contained in one serving. Details on the properties of sweeteners are provided in Table 6.12. Again, it should be noted that many sweeteners have multiple functions as food additives.

Fat Replacers

Presently, there are three primary types of fat substitutes being extensively researched. Reducing the fat of foods can result in a high degree of sensory trait changes; therefore, fat replacers must be carefully deployed to deliver products with the desired textural attributes and flavor. Fat replacers include carbohydrate-based, protein-based, and synthetic compounds (Olestra and caprenin). Although many of these substitutes are partially metabolized by the body, translating

TABLE 6.11. Carbohydrate Sweeteners and their Applications.

Sweetener	Description and Applications
Brown sugar	Partially refined sucrose
Corn syrup	Sweet syrup of glucose and short polymers produced by hydrolysis of corn starch; dextrose equivalent (DE) above 20
Fructose	Monosaccharide used in place of sucrose, sweetness level at 140–170 (compared to sucrose at 100)
Glucose	A monosaccharide found in grains, fruits, and blood, and produced commercially by hydrolyzing starch completely; less sweet than sugar (degree of sweetness: 75)
Oligosaccharides	Sugar molecules containing two or more glucose units; invert sugar: sweeteners produced by catalyzing an aqueous sucrose solution to produce equal quantities of glucose and fructose
Liquid sugar	Sucrose in enough water to keep product fluid
Maltodextrin	A blend of mixed sized sugars with a collective DE of less than 20
Maltose	A disaccharide of two glucose units produced commercially by partial hydrolysis of starch
Molasses	Sweetener produced as a byproduct of the refining of sucrose from sugarcane
Powdered sugar	Pulverized granulated sugar with cornstarch
Sucrose	A disaccharide produced by condensation of glucose and fructose
Table sugar	Refined sucrose

TABLE 6.12. Characteristics of Common Sweeteners.

Sweetener	Sweetness*	Other Characteristics
Saccharin	300–400	Petroleum based with metallic aftertaste
Aspartame	200	4 calories/g; not heat stable, sweet aftertaste
Acesulfame potassium	200	Heat stable, slight bitter aftertaste
Cyclamate	130	Heat stable, distinct aftertaste
Maltitol	65	Non-cariogenic, used in sugar-free chocolate and other confections, hygroscopic, inhibits crystallization
Mannitol	50	Slow absorption rate, does not promote tooth decay, may have laxative effect in large quantities
Sucralose	600–800	pH and heat stable, non-caloric
Sorbitol	50	Slow absorption rate, does not promote tooth decay, may have laxative effect in large quantities, humectant properties, high viscosity
Stevioside	300	Anise aftertaste, slow sweetness onset
Xylitol	100	Cooling effect, used commonly in chewing gum; laxative effect in large quantities

into 1 to 4 calories per gram, they cannot be classified as non-nutritive food additives.

Carbohydrate-based fat replacers can be fully, partially, or non-digestible. These additives must often be used in combination with more than one additive to achieve a desired texture. Reduced fat products that may use multiple additives are dairy-based frozen desserts, salad dressings, baked products, snacks, and frostings. Carbohydrate fat replacers can be one or more of the following products: xanthan gum, gellan gum, pectin, microcrystalline cellulose, pectin, tapioca dextrin, maltodextrin, or polydextrose.

Protein-based fat replacers produce the most similar mouthfeel to fat. Egg whites and wheat can be microparticulated and used as fat replacers. These are easily used in ice creams and salad dressings, but can be undesirable due to allergenic tendencies in consumers. (Eggs and wheat are two of the eight most common food allergens.)

Olestra (manufactured by Proctor & Gamble) is a sucrose-based product that is too large to be split by lipase, causing it to pass through the digestive system. This product has been known to cause negative side effects such as anal leakage and blocking the uptake of fat-soluble vitamins. Olestra was used in many reduced-calorie fried snack products in an effort to reduce the fat contents.

Bulking Agents

Bulking agents are used when fat, sugar, or other components have been eliminated or reduced in a product. These additives are generally made of starch or fiber to minimize volumetric and textural effects. Bulking agents can consist of many different starches and grains, but should be unreactive and bland in the food system, as their purpose is not to add or affect flavor. When sugar (a bulking agent) is replaced with non-nutritive sweeteners (especially ones with higher sweetness levels), bulking agents such as maltodextrin can be added to make up for lost volume.

Nutrient Supplements

Vitamin and mineral supplements are added to foods to improve nutritional quality or to replace nutrients lost during processing. Many common food items are enriched, including flour and white bread. Margarine, milk, and salt are additional examples of foods to which

TABLE 6.13. Fat Soluble Vitamins and Their Usage.

Vitamin	Chemical Names	Product Usage	Considerations
Vitamin A	Retinol Retinyl acetate Retinyl palmitate	Oils and fats, liquid milk, milk powder, infant formula, breakfast cereals	Soluble in fat and oil
Vitamin D_2	Ergocalciferol	Liquid milk, milk powder, oil and fats	
Vitamin D_3	Cholecalciferol	Liquid milk, milk powder, oil and fats, breakfast cereals	Can be found in oil blends (soluble in oil) and dry powders (water dispersible)
Vitamin E	Tocopherol dl-alpha-Tocopherol	Antioxidant in oils, fats, and sausages	Fat and oil soluble
	dl-alpha-Tocopheryl-acetate	Fortification of infant formula, confectionary, oils and fats, fruit drinks, flour, liquid milk, milk powder, breakfast cereal	Water dispersible
Vitamin K_1	Phytonadione	Fortification of infant formula, liquid milk, oil and fats, dietary products	Can be found in oil blends (soluble in oil) and dry powders (water dispersible)

TABLE 6.14. Water Soluble Vitamins and Their Usage.

Vitamin	Chemical Names	Product Usage
Vitamin B_1	Thiamin Thiamin hydrochloride Thiamin mononitrate	Flour, breakfast cereal, infant formula, soup, milk drinks, pasta, meal replacement products
Vitamin B_2	Riboflavin Riboflavin-5'-phosphate sodium salt	Flour, breakfast cereals, sugar, cocoa confections, soups, infant formula, fruit drinks, oils and fats, and meal replacements
Vitamin B_6	Pyroxidine Pyroxidine-hydrochloride	
Niacin	Nicotinic Acid Niacinamide	Flour, breakfast cereal, infant formula, fruit drinks, pasta, meal replacement products
Pantothenic Acid	Pantothenic acid Calcium-D-pantothenate	Infant formula, breakfast cereals, fruit drink, milk drinks, meal replacement products
Vitamin B_{12}	Cyanocobalamin	Infant formula, meal replacement products, and substitute foods
Biotin	Biotin	
Folic Acid	Pteroylglutamic acid	Infant formula, breakfast cereals, fruit drinks, milk drinks, meal replacement products
Vitamin C	Ascorbic acid	Infant formula, breakfast cereals, fruit drinks, milk drinks, meal replacement products, fruit juices, soft drinks, beer, wine, canned fruit and vegetables, potato products, dairy products
	Sodium ascorbate	Curing agent in cured meats, fortification for dairy products
	Calcium ascorbate	Breakfast cereals, low sodium dietetic products
	Ascorbyl palmitate	Antioxidant in oils, fats, fat-based products, uncured frozen sausage, processes potatoes, extruded cereals

vitamin A, vitamin D, or iodine have been added. Adding nutrients has decreased the number of people suffering from vitamin and mineral deficiencies, such as beriberi (thiamin deficiency), pellagra (niacin deficiency), scurvy (vitamin C deficiency), and goiter (iodine deficiency).

Vitamins

In order to add vitamins to a food, it is important to understand the traits of vitamins. Fat-soluble vitamins are A, D, E, and K, which can be added to water-based foods when used with gelatin or sugar. These vitamins, in water-soluble form, usually contain antioxidants. All fat soluble vitamins should be stored in a cool environment, or even a re-

Case Study: Vitamin Rich Dairy Drink

A group of students worked on a dairy drink for a national competition for months. The guidelines were simple—create any dairy beverage that would expand current offerings. The students created a yogurt drink for children that they worked on for months. When it came to the final presentations and report, the group lost major points for over-fortifying the drink with vitamin D. What is the limit on vitamin D? What other food additives can legally be added to a dairy drink? What if it was labeled as a supplement?

frigerator. Vitamin A is highly sensitive to oxygen, light, and heat, and should be tested every 6 months to ensure potency of the additive. The oil based forms of Vitamin A have higher stability than dry products. Vitamin E, when added to food as a source of nutrients, should be used as Vitamin E acetate, its esterified form. Vitamin E in its alcohol form is used as an antioxidant. Vitamin K is not a very common nutritive additive, except in infant formula and some meal replacement products.

All oil-based vitamin additives can crystallize in cool temperatures, and should be brought to room temperature before use. A summary of fat-soluble vitamins is provided in Table 6.13.

Water-soluble vitamins are vitamin C and the B vitamins, which include thiamin (B_1), riboflavin (B_2), niacin/niacinamide, pyroxydine (B_6), cyanobalamin (B_{12}), folic acid, pantothenic acid, and biotin. Water-soluble vitamins come in dry forms and are quite stable. Expected shelf-life is at least one year. When adding vitamins to food products, it is important to ensure that the vitamins will be viable the entire shelf-life. Therefore, overages of vitamins are placed into the product. Food scientists seeking to account for losses of vitamins must consider the method of packaging, the nature of the product, nutrient losses during processing, and how the product will be stored throughout its shelf-life. Fortified and enriched products should be tested during the development stages to ensure vitamin contents are accurately stated. This testing can be done at an accelerated testing condition of 35°C (95°F) and relative humidity of 45%, taking vitamin assays at day 0, week 1, week 2, and every month for about 3 months. An overview of vitamin stability is given in Table 6.15.

Minerals

Minerals may also be added to food products. A food scientist should be aware of the pH, moisture content, particle size, solubility, taste, odor, color, and interactions with vitamins in a food product before adding minerals. The bioavailability and safety of minerals must also be considered. Cost analysis should be done when adding minerals because the cost of adding minerals may outweigh the benefit. During processing and storage, there is very little mineral loss. Overages for minerals are generally not significant.

Stability issues can occur with the addition of minerals in a product. Off odors, colors, and tastes can result from mineral addition, especially with iron. Dry food products generally have fewer stability issues. In high-moisture foods, mineral addition can threaten vitamin and lipid stability. Food minerals, their effects, and bioavailabilities are summarized in Table 6.16.

Added food preservatives contain compounds that aid in the extension of shelf-life by inhibiting microbial growth or by minimizing the destructive effects of oxygen, metals, and other elements that may lead to rancidity. Major food preservatives are presented in Table 6.17, along with an overview of their antimicrobial effects and regulations placed on them.

A common and historical example of a preservative is salt. Salt's effectiveness to suppress microorganisms lies in the fact that only microbes with a high tolerance for salt (halophiles such as *Staphylococcus aureus*) can survive in salted foods.

TABLE 6.15. Vitamins and their Stability in Varying Environments.

Vitamin	Optimum pH	Light Exposure	Mineral Exposure	Oxidation	Heat Stability
Vitamin A	> 6	Yes	Yes	Yes	Semi
Thiamin (B_1)	3–4.5	No	Sulfite	No	No
Riboflavin (B_2)	—	Yes	No	No	Yes
Niacinamide	—	No	No	No	Yes
Pyroxidine (B_6)	—	No	Yes	No	Semi
Vitamin B_{12}	4–5	Yes	No	Yes	Semi
Biotin	—	No	No	No	Yes
Pantothenate	5–7	No	No	No	Semi
Vitamin C	5–7	No	Yes	Yes	No
Vitamin D	—	No	No	Yes	Semi
Vitamin E	—	No	No	No	Yes
Vitamin K	4–7	Yes	No	No	Yes

Source: Food Additive 1991.

TABLE 6.16. Minerals, their Additives, and Conditions for Usage in Food.

Mineral	Additive	Conditions for Usage: Water Solubility	Taste	Bioavailability in Pure Form
Iron	Ferrous sulfate anhydrous	High	Metallic	High
	Ferrous fumerate	Moderate	Slight	High
	Ferric orthophosphate dihydrous	Not	Tasteless	Low
	Reduced iron	Not	Metallic	Moderate
Calcium	Calcium carbonate	Not	Chalky	Moderate–Low
	Calcium glycerophosphate	Moderate	Tasteless	—
	Calcium lactate pentahydrate	High in hot water	Tasteless	Moderate
	Calcium phosphate tribasic	Not	Tasteless	Moderate–Low
	Calcium Phosphate dibasic	Not	Tasteless	Moderate–Low
Magnesium	Magnesium oxide	Moderate	Chalky	Moderate
	Magnesium carbonate hydroxide	Moderate–can give off bubbles	Slightly chalky	High
Zinc	Zinc sulfate monohydrate	High	Astringent	Moderate
Copper	Cupric gluconate monohydrate	High	Astringent	Moderate

The most important preservative in the meat industry is nitrite. Nitrite inhibits the growth of the deadly bacterium Clostridium botulinum and is used extensively in cured meat products. Current trends for natural curing of meats have led to the use of celery powder as a natural source of nitrates. Sodium benzoate or potassium benzoate are typically added to soft drinks. Mold inhibitors like calcium and sodium propionates and sorbates are used in bakery items, such as breads and cakes, whereas natamycin and sorbic acid are utilized in cheeses to prevent molds. Fumigants, such as ethylene oxide and ethyl formate, control microorganisms in spices, nuts, and dried fruits. Sulfur dioxide, which controls browning of fruits and vegetables caused by enzymes, is yet another example of a preservative.

Stabilizers and Thickeners

Stabilizers and thickeners are food additives that provide uniform

TABLE 6.17. Preservatives and their Uses in Food.

Preservative	Antimicrobial Action	Uses in Food
Sorbic Acid	Broad fungicide Bacteriocide—*aerobes, NOT lactic acid bacteria*	GRAS
Benzoic Acid	Fungicide Yeast inhibition Bacteriocide—*food poisoning bacteria, spore forming bacteria, NOT spoilage bacteria*	Should not exceed 0.1% in food
Parabens	Fungicide Yeast inhibition Bacteriocide—*mostly gram +*	Should not exceed 0.1% in food
	Fungicide Yeast inhibition Bacteriocide—*mostly gram +*	Should not exceed 0.1% in food
Propionic Acid	Fungicide, but does not control yeast	No limits
Nitrous Acid (nitrites)	Bacteriocide—*especially inhibits Clostridium botulinum, and also Lactobacillus, Bacillus, Clostridium perfringens, and Salmonella*	Smoke, cured sablefish, salmon, shad—200 ppm sodium nitrite, 500 ppm
Sulfur Dioxide	Bacteriocide	Cannot be used in meats, food recognized as a source of vitamin B1, or fruits and vegetables to be served raw or fresh
Sodium Sulfite	Bacteriocide	
Sodium Bisulfite	Bacteriocide	
Potassium Bisulfite	Bacteriocide	
Potassium Metabisulfite	Bacteriocide	Cannot be used in meats, food recognized as a source of vitamin B1, or fruits and vegetables to be served raw or fresh
Sodium Thiosulfite	Bacteriocide	0.00005% for alcoholic beverages (21 CFR 170.3 (n)(2)) 0.1% for table salt (21 CFR 170.3 (n)(26))
Manganese Sulfite	Bacteriocide	Can be used in baked goods, nonalcoholic beverages, dairy products, fish products, meat products, milk products, and poultry products May be used in infant formulas in accordance with section 412(g) of the FFDCA
Nisin	Bacteriocide *Gram + bacteria, lactic acid bacteria, streptococcus, Bacillus, Clostridium*	Maximum of 250 ppm; used in pasteurized processed cheese products, including those with fruit, nuts, or meat

(continued)

TABLE 6.17 (continued). Preservatives and their Uses in Food.

Preservative	Antimicrobial Action	Uses in Food
Hydrogen Peroxide	Bacteriocide *Best on Gram- bacteria (coliforms), also works against Staph. and lactic acid bacteria* *Least effective against Gram +*	Milk intended for cheese making—0.05% Whey, modified using electrodialysis method, 0.04%
Sodium Chloride	Bacteriocide Gram- *rods, such as Pseudomonas. Lactic acid bacteria*	Salted fish
Calcium disodium EDTA	Bacteriocide *Gram- bacteria*	Dressings (including mayonnaise, salad dressings, and sauces)—75 ppm Sandwich spread—100 ppm Potato salad—100 ppm Oleomargarine—75ppm
Disodium EDTA		Dressings (including mayonnaise, salad dressings, and sauces)—75 ppm Sandwich spread—100 pm
BHA	Most Gram + *(S. aureus, Bacillus, Clostridium)* Some gram- *(Pseudomonas fluorescens, Vibrio)*	Only BHA: Dry diced glazed fruit—32 ppm Dry mixes for beverages and desserts —90 ppm Active dry yeast—1,000 ppm Beverages and desserts prepared from dry mixes—2 ppm BHA alone or in combination with BHT: Dehydrated potato shreds—50 ppm Dry breakfast cereals—50 ppm Emulsion stabilizers for shortenings—200 ppm Potato flakes—50 ppm Potato granules—10 ppm Sweet potato flakes—50 ppm
BHT	*Clostridium botulinum, S. aureus*	BHT alone or in combination with BHA: Dehydrated potato shreds—50 ppm Dry breakfast cereals—50 ppm Emulsion stabilizers for shortenings—200 ppm Potato flakes—50 ppm Potato granules—10 ppm Sweet potato flakes—50 ppm

(continued)

TABLE 6.17 (continued). Preservatives and their Uses in Food.

Preservative	Antimicrobial Action	Uses in Food
TBHQ	*B. subtilis, S. aureus,* most fungi	TBHQ alone or in combination with other antioxidants: The total antioxidant content of a food containing the additive will not exceed 0.02% of the oil or fat content of the food, including the essential (volatile) oil content of the food.
Propyl Gallate	*Clostridium botulinum,* most fungi	The total antioxidant content of a food containing the additive will not exceed 0.02% of the oil or fat content of the food, including the essential (volatile) oil content of the food.
Cultured dextrose	Bacteriocide	Can be used in cheeses, sauces, salad dressings, sausages, soups, deli salads, salsas, pasta, tortillas, muffins, cereal bars, sour cream, yogurt, and hash brown potatoes at 2% or less of the total finished volume

consistency and improve the color, texture, and flavor in candies, chocolate milk, artificially sweetened beverages, ice cream, and other frozen desserts. Other examples of thickeners and stabilizers include vegetable gums, such as carrageenan and guar, pectin, agars, starches, and gelatins. Without stabilizers and thickeners, ice crystals form in ice cream and other frozen desserts more quickly, particles of chocolate separate from chocolate milk, and volatile flavor oils evaporate in cakes, puddings, and gelatin mixes.

Surface Active Agents

Surface active agents (also known as surfactants) are a group of food additives that include emulsifiers, antifoaming compounds, and wetting agents that modify the physical force on the surface of foods. Emulsifiers are used to keep water and oil from separating in products such as margarine, salad dressing, ice cream, and other emulsions. Lecithin, a natural emulsifier obtained from soybeans, and mono- and diglycerides, head the list of emulsifiers used in the food industry. Emulsifiers, composed of chains of unsaturated fatty acids, are capable of depressing foam and serve as antifoaming agents in dairy products and egg processing. An example of an emulsifier that also falls into the detergent category is sodium lauryl sulfate. This compound functions as a whipping aid in marshmallows and angel food cake mixes. Wetting, the promotion of liquid spread over a surface, is another important function of surface active agents. This is important in dessert mixes, drink mixes, and instant breakfast drinks. Surface active agents are used to create emulsions or to improve the consumer quality attributes of foods, such as the hydration of an instant drink mix without clumping.

Consumer Expectations and Demands

Consumption trends in food products change from year to year due to the newest concern in health, the next fad diet, and the latest super food. One consistent growing concern is the consumer desire for a healthier life. With an increasing demand for healthful food products, processors have a responsibility, as well as incentive, to adjust current conventional products to fit consumer needs and desires, including reducing fats and lowering calories. Producers can use food additives to assist in modifying a cookie formulation originally containing 35 percent fat to contain only 5 percent or to extend the shelf-life of flour tortillas by using a potassium sorbate spray. Food processors must be in touch with consumer expectations and tastes when modifying flavors and changing nutrients, which will also include current views on specific food additives. When contemplating any food additives, food scientists should consult with ingredient companies on what the best additive might be, and then test the new ingredient against a previously formulated control.

KEY WORDS

Delaney Clause—1958 amendment to the Federal Food, Drug, and Cosmetic Act (FFDCA) stating that additives exhibiting the ability to cause cancer cannot be used as an ingredient in food.

Food irradiation—a method of exposing foods to radiation to kill microorganisms. Irradiated foods have special labeling requirements.

No observable effect level (NOEL)—corresponds to the highest dose of an additive producing no unexpected adverse health problems in the laboratory animals.

Oxidation—the loss of electrons and gain of O_2, which can cause off-odors and quality degradation.

Surface active agents (surfactants)—a group of food additives that include emulsifiers, antifoaming compounds and wetting agents that modify the physical force on the surface of foods.

COMPREHENSION QUESTIONS

6.1. Define food additive.

6.2. What does the acronym GRAS stand for? Give an example of a GRAS food ingredient?

6.3. Name the type of enzyme that is commonly used as a tenderizing agent in meats.

6.4. Fill in the following blanks:

a. Monosodium glutamate is an example of a ______________ ______________.

b. ________________, present in eggs and milk, are naturally present antimicrobial agents.

6.5. List one example additive in each of the following categories.

a. Antioxidant
b. Emulsifier
c. Base
d. Antimicrobial
e. Binder
f. Chelating agent
g. Anticaking
h. Thickener
i. Bulking agent
j. Curing agent

6.6. Name 3 sources of gums and provide an example of each.

6.7. List 3 strategies to reduce oxidation. Give an example of each.

6.8. List 4 functional properties of acids in foods.

6.9. What is the difference between a dye and a lake?

6.10. What is the difference between baking soda and baking powder?

6.11. Name the 3 classes of plant pigments.

REFERENCES

Ash, M., & Ash, I. (1995). *Handbook of food additives*. London, England: Gower.

Food additive user's handbook (1991). In Smith J. S. (Ed.), (1st ed.). Glasgow: Blackie.

Francis, F. J. (1999). *Colorants*. St. Paul, MN: American Association of Cereal Chemists, Inc.

Igoe, R. S. (1989). *Dictionary of food ingredients* (2nd Ed. ed.). New York, NY: Chapman & Hall.

CHAPTER 7

Formulation and Process Development

> **Learning Objectives**
>
> - Be able to follow the sequence for the formulation of new products.
> - Know where to find basic formulas.
> - Understand important concepts for laboratory experiments and calculations.

NEW products start as ideas. The goal is to create a product that is feasible, cost effective, and meets consumer needs. Basic recipes become scaled-up formulas with extensive experimentation, which in turn can lead to merchandise on the shelf of a grocery store. This chapter will cover the progression from product prototype to full-scale production.

FORMULATIONS

Marketing has a new idea for a product! This concept is assigned to a product developer, who in turn starts researching, experimenting, and ordering samples from suppliers. This is the road to the first prototype. When creating a new product, the first tangible products will be made on a bench top or in small scale. The initial ingredient combinations will be in the form of recipes. These could be based on cookbook recipes, ingredient suppliers, or food processing literature with base formulas. The basic recipe, sometimes referred to as the "gold standard formula," will be converted into a formula that can be scaled up to production. When recipes are transformed into formulas, they should be expressed in numeric units in terms of percentage by weight/weight, weight/volume, or by percentage flour basis (also called baker's percentage).

Flour basis is widely used in the baking industry. These formulas are based on the percentage of ingredients as compared to the amount of flour. With flour basis, the flour or flours used always amount to 100%. Bakers use this formulation, so they can easily characterize whether recipes are sweeter or saltier than others.

To calculate the mass from a baker's weight percentage formula for a chosen flour weight:

$$\text{Desired ingredient weight} = (\text{flour weight} \times \text{baker's percentage of ingredient})/100\%$$

To calculate the mass of an ingredient that you will need in baker's percentage:

$$\text{Baker's percentage of ingredient} = 100\% \times (\text{ingredient mass}/\text{flour mass})$$

The Food and Drug Administration (FDA) has established standards of identity for certain food products. Standards of identity specify ingredients and additive limits allowed for use within a certain food. For example, mayonnaise must contain a minimum of 65% oil by weight and use only egg as an emulsifier. Products that do not meet the standard of identity must use alternative names. Table 7.1 shows the 21CFR, classification numbers of product categories.

The United States Department of Agriculture (USDA) states the identities of its products in the Food Standards and Labeling Policy Book from the Food Safety and Inspection Service (FSIS) which can be found on their website, www.fsis.usda.gov. Table 7.2 shows the USDA food standard products.

INGREDIENT SOURCING

Choosing suppliers for ingredients is an important piece of developing a new product. Products can only meet quality standards that are as high as the quality of their ingredients. In established businesses, contracts for ingredients and approved suppliers may already be in place. New businesses must investigate sources of ingredients that meet quality standards and volume requirements. Ingredient quality is not uniform for all products. Some ingredients are more susceptible to quality deterioration during processing, and these must retain the highest quality possible. Other ingredients are more forgiving of minor changes while being processed. Variability between ingredient lots should be kept at a minimum for color, flavor, and moisture content, factors that need to be discussed prior to investing in a contract

TABLE 7.1. 21CFR, Classification Numbers of Product Categories.

Food	Standards	General
131	131.3 to 131.206	Milk and Cream
133	133.3 to 133.196	Cheeses and Related Cheese Products
135	135.3 to 135.160	Frozen Desserts
136	136.3 to 136.180	Bakery Products
137	137.105 to 137.350	Cereal Flours and Related Products
139	139.110 to 139.180	Macaroni and Noodle Products
145	145.3 to 145.190	Canned Fruits
146	146.3 to 146.187	Canned Fruit Juices
150	150.110 to 150.160	Fruit Butters, Jellies, Preserves, and Related Products
152	152.126	Fruit Pies
155	155.3 to 155.201	Canned Vegetables
156	156.3 to 156.145	Vegetable Juices
158	158.3 to 158.170	Frozen Vegetables
160	160.100 to 160.190	Eggs and Egg Products
161	161.30 to 161.190	Fish and Shellfish
163	163.5 to 163.155	Cacao Products
164	164.110 to 164.150	Tree Nut and Peanut Products
165	165.3 to 165.110	Beverages
166	166.40 to 166.110	Margarine
168	168.110 to 168.180	Sweeteners and Table Sirups
169	169.3 to 169.182	Food Dressings and Flavorings

http://www.ecfr.gov/cgi-bin/text-idx?SID=495c59c5d94f753c9d473204ad4f794d&c=ecfr&tpl=/ecfrbrowse/Title21/21cfrv2_02.tpl

for ingredient sourcing. Other issues in ingredient sourcing include shelf life, safety, and availability.

RULES AND REGULATIONS

For safety purposes, when creating new food products, developers must know government rules and regulations regarding certain products. If a company is not compliant with regulations, the government may seize products or a governing agency may suggest a recall. For example, the USDA regulates the cooking temperature for products containing meat. The FDA defines acceptable processes for low-acid canned foods and acidified canned foods. Details regarding preparation processes must be filed with the FDA in order for a company to be compliant. Product development teams should ensure that their production plans follow all guidelines before investing money on equipment.

TABLE 7.2. Part 319—Definitions and Standards of Identity or Composition.

Subpart A—General	
319.1	Labeling and preparation of standardized products.
319.2	Products and nitrates and nitrites.
319.5	Mechanically Separated (Species).
319.6	Limitations with respect to use of Mechanically Separated (Species).
319.10	Requirements for substitute standardized meat food products named by use of an expressed nutrient content claim and a standardized term.
Subpart B—Raw Meat Products	
319.15	Miscellaneous beef products.
319.29	Miscellaneous pork products.
Subpart C—Cooked Meats	
319.80	Barbecued meats.
319.81	Roast beef parboiled and steam roasted.
Subpart D—Cured Meats, Unsmoked and Smoked	
319.100	Corned beef.
319.101	Corned beef brisket.
319.102	Corned beef round and other corned beef cuts.
319.103	Cured beef tongue.
319.104	Cured pork products.
319.105	"Ham patties," "Chopped ham," "Pressed ham," "Spiced ham," and similar products.
319.106	"Country Ham," "Country Style Ham," "Dry Cured Ham," "Country Pork Shoulder," "Country Style Pork Shoulder," and "Dry Cured Pork Shoulder."
319.107	Bacon.
Subpart E—Sausage Generally: Fresh Sausage	
319.140	Sausage.
319.141	Fresh pork sausage.
319.142	Fresh beef sausage.
319.143	Breakfast sausage.
319.144	Whole hog sausage.
319.145	Italian sausage products.
Subpart F—Uncooked, Smoked Sausage	
319.160	Smoked pork sausage.
Subpart G—Cooked Sausage	
319.180	Frankfurter, frank, furter, hotdog, wiener, Vienna sausage, bologna, garlic bologna, knockwurst, and similar products.
319.181	Cheesefurters and similar products.
319.182	Braunschweiger and liver sausage or liverwurst.
Subpart I—Semi-Dry Fermented Sausage [Reserved]	

(continued)

TABLE 7.2 (continued). Part 319—Definitions and Standards of Identity or Composition.

Subpart J—Dry Fermented Sausage [Reserved]	
Subpart K—Luncheon Meat, Loaves and Jellied Products	
319.260	Luncheon meat.
319.261	Meat loaf.
Subpart L—Meat Specialties, Puddings and Nonspecific Loaves	
319.280	Scrapple.
319.281	Bockwurst.
Subpart M—Canned, Frozen, or Dehydrated Meat Food Products	
319.300	Chili con carne.
319.301	Chili con carne with beans.
319.302	Hash.
319.303	Corned beef hash.
319.304	Meat stews.
319.305	Tamales.
319.306	Spaghetti with meatballs and sauce, spaghetti with meat and sauce, and similar products.
319.307	Spaghetti sauce with meat.
319.308	Tripe with milk.
319.309	Beans with frankfurters in sauce, sauerkraut with wieners and juice, and similar products.
319.310	Lima beans with ham in sauce, beans with ham in sauce, beans with bacon in sauce, and similar products.
319.311	Chow mein vegetables with meat, and chop suey vegetables with meat.
319.312	Pork with barbecue sauce and beef with barbecue sauce.
319.313	Beef with gravy and gravy with beef.
Subpart N—Meat Food Entree Products, Pies, and Turnovers	
319.500	Meat pies.
Subpart O—Meat Snacks, Hors d'Oeuvres, Pizza, and Specialty Items	
Subpart P—Fats, Oils, Shortenings	
319.700	Margarine or oleomargarine.
319.701	Mixed fat shortening.
319.702	Lard, leaf lard.
319.703	Rendered animal fat or mixture thereof.
Subpart Q—Meat Soups, Soup Mixes, Broths, Stocks, Extracts	
319.720	Meat extract.
319.721	Fluid extract of meat.

(continued)

TABLE 7.2 (continued). Part 319—Definitions and Standards of Identity or Composition.

Subpart R—Meat Salads and Meat Spreads	
319.760	Deviled ham, deviled tongue, and similar products.
319.761	Potted meat food product and deviled meat food product.
319.762	Ham spread, tongue spread, and similar products.
Subpart S—Meat Baby Foods [Reserved]	
Subpart T—Dietetic Meat Foods [Reserved]	
Subpart U—Miscellaneous	
319.880	Breaded products.
319.881	Liver meat food products.

Process Development

Processing a food is dependent on multiple factors, including what kind of food is being produced. A new process may need to be created for concepts that have not previously been translated into a successful product. When creating a new process, it is important to carefully plan experiments and keep a detailed experiment notebook. External variables that remain constant in all experiments should remain controlled. Some development projects will require the design and fabrication of new equipment. Order of ingredient addition is important in the production of most products, and must be recorded. For example, when calcium is added to low-sugar jelly that uses low-methoxyl pectin, the calcium should be introduced at the end of the process to eliminate premature gelling. Rates and times of production are also important factors. Other processing elements to take into account are: temperature, time, color, moisture, pressure, viscosity, pH, humidity and more. The processes for many foods have long been established; therefore, it may be beneficial to refer to literature about the basic unit operations for the product of interest.

Standard Operating Procedures (SOPs)

An important part of implementing a process for a new food product is the development of Standard Operating Procedures (SOPs) that describe in great detail each and every step of the process. Written SOPs are needed to ensure product quality and reproducibility. An SOP should clearly indicate what the specific task of an operator is and how it should be carried out. This starts with the type and amount of ingredients to be used; order of addition to a formula; process parameters, especially time and temperature; visual or instrumental checks such as: pH, viscosity, color or %brix; filling, holding, cooling, and packaging criteria; and paperwork to be submitted to supervisors. Below is an example of an SOP for a new pomegranate salad dressing.

1. Who is doing the job or task?

   The kettle operator is responsible for the cooking process.

2. What is the purpose of the job or task?

   The cooking process is designed to make the product safe and appealing by ensuring adequate mixing of all ingredients, heat processing to a safe temperature, and maintaining consistent quality factors especially viscosity, color, pH and %brix.

3. What is the task?

   The kettle operator will measure the correct amounts of ingredients, add them in the prescribed order, and process the batch in compliance with SOPs.

4. What are the detailed steps for completing the job?
   a. Measure 2.5 lb of xanthan gum, 2 lb of spice mix, 10 lb of salt, 3 fl oz of natural pomegranate flavor, and open a barrel of the pomegranate concentrate. On your batch sheet, record ALL the code numbers from each ingredient.
   b. Empty the xanthan gum into the kettle. Turn the mixer on low setting.
   c. Slowly add cold water to the kettle while mixing until the water reaches the 20-gallon mark. Keep mixing until the mixture is thick and clear, and no lumps of xanthan are visible.
   d. Add the pomegranate concentrate to the solution while still mixing at low speed.
   e. Add water to the 60 gal mark on the kettle. Turn mixer to medium speed.
   f. Add salt and spices while mixing.
   g. Pull a sample of product in a cup and take to the QA office to analyze for pH and %brix. QA will let you know if you need to add more pomegranate concentrate or adjust the pH. If they do,

follow their directions and bring back another sample. Wait for the results to get the go-ahead to process the batch.

h. Turn the heat to setting 4 and the mixer to high speed. Keep an eye on the thermometer.

i. When the temperature reaches 180° F, turn the heat setting down to 1 and the mixer to the low setting. Inform the packaging supervisor that the batch is ready. At his/her direction, open the valve from the kettle to the filler line. Do not leave your station till the kettle is empty.

5. What is the frequency of this job?

   Repeat the same procedure for every batch. You should be able to do 4 batches per shift.

6. What is the critical time limit for the task?

   The whole process should take no more than 2 hrs.

7. What corrective action must be taken if the job or task is performed incorrectly?

   If the temperature does not get to 180°F within 2 hr, inform QA and the Food Safety Manager. Fill out a deviation form with batch number, date and time. DO NOT SEND THE PRODUCT TO THE FILLER WITHOUT QA APPROVAL.

Scale-Up

Despite all the hard work that goes into laboratory scale prototype development, a food product developer will face many problems in the scale-up stage. This is when the group approach to product development is most useful. Most scale-up processes are actually handled more by engineers rather than food scientists. While the common goal of every department will be launching the new product, conflicts may arise between food scientists and marketing specialists at this stage due mostly to time constraints, with the former trying to take the necessary time to create the best quality product, while the latter want the new product as soon as possible for consumer testing and test marketing. Large grocery chains plan their product line about a year in advance, and set deadlines for accepting new products. Therefore, if a food company misses the deadline for their targeted new product launch, the delay will incur higher costs, later placement in a store, and missed sales revenue.

In general terms, the following factors affect the scale-up of processing operations:

1. Heat Transfer

   Heat loss and gain play a major role in final product properties. Scale-up of operations may affect heat transfer either through chemical interactions between components or through a change in the proportion of surface area to mass due to larger equipment, which can cause faster evaporation and change laminar and turbulent flow regimes. Some unit operations are easier to scale up than others. For example, a forced-air drying process can be relatively easy to scale up by process engineers who estimate the specific heat and thermal conductivity of the food product, and then calculate the amount of moisture to be removed based on initial and final water contents, air volume, temperature, and residence time. The thermal effects of scale-up in mixing operations, heat processes, and extrusion processing are harder to predict.

2. Mixing and Shear Properties

   Mixing is a common food processing unit operation aiming primarily at the reduction or elimination of undesirable nonhomogeneous phases in a precursor to or a final product. This necessitates elimination of temperature and concentration gradients, which results in improved mass and heat transfer. Mixing efficiency is influenced by the type and amount of material to be mixed, temperature of the mix, and design of the stirrer and mixing regime. All of these factors change when scaling up from benchtop or pilot plant batches and need to be addressed by an engineer.

3. Product Properties

   Raw materials and ingredients may vary significantly, whether they come from one or multiple suppliers. Simple ingredients, like sugar or salt, exhibit various rates of solubility depending on particle size. Spices and other raw ingredients will greatly affect the flavor of the final product based on factors like freshness, titratable acidity, or moisture content. Therefore, raw materials and ingredients must be analyzed to determine their basic constituents and to limit variability resulting from sources and the growing season. This is especially true of grains such as wheat flours, which need to be tested for their protein and moisture contents since these may change with the new crop and will require modification of product formulas. Additionally, the product developer should be sufficiently versed in food chemistry to detect and account for ingredient interactions that may or may not take place during scale-up operations as compared to laboratory-scale processing.

Approaches to Minimize Scale-up Issues at Each Stage

Bench-top batches are of very small size, often 1000–10,000 times less than full production scale. However, benchtop batches are absolutely essential for formulating and process development. Once a satisfactory prototype is made, an evaluation of quality attributes should be performed to determine critical parameters for physical, chemical, sensory and microbiological properties. For each of these, appropriate limits and ranges have to be set to ensure consistency of product quality. Commonly, the major factor to measure is the final moisture content, because this will be used by engineers as a target in scale-up operations. Other important factors are texture, color, and density. Thus, it is critical for the food scientist to retain and store samples of the benchtop prototypes developed, along with a detailed list of their attributes for later reference to share with engineering and marketing staff.

Pilot Plant-Scale Batches

After a robust formula is found, the product is tested in pilot plant batches using equipment that is usually an exact, albeit smaller, replica, of full-scale production equipment. Batches manufactured may be 100–1000 times smaller than production scale batches, but they do allow product developers to predict some of the challenges of larger scale production runs and to determine if the equipment is capable of delivering processes resulting in a quality product. This often requires fine tuning of the processing parameters for quality optimization. Quite frequently, scaled-up formulas require changes in mixing times and temperatures, or may require further ingredients such as stabilizers and preservatives, or are helped via processing aids like anti-foaming agents or food-grade lubricants. Since new products manufactured at a pilot plant will support crucial test-marketing studies, including consumer acceptability and shelf-life evaluations, it is necessary to run as many pilot plant experiments as needed to ensure reproducibility. Larger operations employ statisticians to design experiments and analyze/interpret test data. Changes to the formula should be done one at a time, in order to identify the effects of each individual modification. Based on experience with ingredients' functionality and process parameters that can have an effect on product quality, the food scientist is able to develop a cause and effect diagram and use it to rank process parameters in regard to their impact on product quality parameters. This can be done prior to moving to larger scale batches.

Production-Scale Batches

Production-scale batches are of the size that will be routinely produced for marketing of the product. Even with all previous tests at the benchtop and pilot plant levels, the first samples from production batches rarely look and taste like what the product developer expected. Issues related to heat transfer, mixing, and ingredient interactions, will often force a re-evaluation of process parameters and further formulation. In such instances, a return to pilot plant facilities or even the laboratory is essential to test different approaches or ingredients for manufacturing and packaging before a final round of physical, chemical, sensory, and microbiological evaluations are performed, which define the Gold Standard for product quality.

IMPORTANT EXPERIMENTATION CONCEPTS AND CALCULATIONS

In order to obtain a reproducible product that meets regulatory and consumer standards, basic lab knowledge and techniques are necessary. Simple calculations must be made to determine what level of food additives should be used, or if a producer must claim the use of sulfites on a product. Planning experiments using statistical designs, which are explained in Chapter 8, and keeping current data legibly in a lab notebook, are essential for the creation of a successful new food product.

Accuracy and Precision

Both precision and accuracy are important when creating a new food product. Precision is defined as the agreement among a series of experimental measurements. Therefore, it relates to the reproducibility of the experiment. Accuracy is the agreement of the experimental values with the established or true value. Precise measurements are not necessarily accurate. For example, if you took pH readings of four different jars of salsa from a batch you manufactured at the same time, and your readings were 3.52, 3.51, 3.52 and 3.50, the measurements may be considered precise, but your pH meter may be 0.5 points off if not calibrated properly, and the actual pH could be 3.00 or 4.00. Instruments used for taking experimental data must always be calibrated and maintained as recommended by the manufacturer. If instruments are not accurate when a measured project moves from the pilot plant to a production facility, the food technologist may discover unexpected results.

Working with Chemicals

To protect against accidental chemical injury, dissolve concentrated acid and base solutions under a hood. Add the acid slowly to the water and stir. Pouring water rapidly into a concentrated acid solution causes a violent reaction that may lead to an explosion! Wear goggles to protect your eyes.

Dilutions

There are several conventions for indicating the method of dilution. For example, "1 to 5 dilution" can indicate two different cases. First, one part of the original solution could be diluted with four parts of solvent to give a final diluted volume of five parts. This dilution is 1/5, since the concentration of the diluted solution is 1/5 of the concentration of the original solution. However, "1 to 5" also could indicate that one part of the original solution is diluted with five parts of solvent to give a solution with 1/6 of the original concentration. The latter convention is more suitable and is more frequently used because the dilution factor is immediately apparent. In this case, it is best to read "dilute 1:5" as dilute one part solution with solvent to give six parts of total volume.

Concentrations of Acids and Bases

Molarity (M) is an indication of the number of moles of a solute in one liter of solution, while normality (N) represents a solution of an acid or base which contains 1 g of replaceable H^+ per liter or OH^- per liter. The product of the N of an acid and the degree of ionization equal its $[H^+]$. A 1.0 N acid, which is 100% ionized, contains 1g of H^+/L. All of the replaceable hydrogen is present as H^+. Its $[H^+]$ is 1 mole/L and it has a pH of 0.

TABLE 7.3. Milliequivalent Weights of Commonly Used Acids.

Acid	Molecular Weight (MW)	Milliequivalent Weights (meq. wt)
Citric acid	192	0.064
Acetic acid	60	0.060
Lactic acid	90	0.090
Malic acid	134	0.067
Oxalic acid	90	0.045
Tartaric acid	150	0.075

Source: Smith 1991.

Normality is more convenient than molarity when considering solutions that react with one another; it takes into account the number of replaceable hydrogen atoms or hydroxyl groups.

In terms of active acidity, 0.1N HCl is not equal to 0.1N CH_3COOH. (Approximately 100% of HCl ionizes, while about 0.1% of CH_3COOH ionizes.) However, since both solutions are 0.1N, they react to the same extent with a base in titration (total acidity).

Total/titratable acidity is a commonly controlled parameter used in the quality control of fresh fruit products, fermented foods, and soft drinks. This is because food flavors are influenced by the degree of acidity. Titratable acidity values may be as low as 0.5% in some cheeses to as high as 6.0% in vinegar. In industry, it is normally expressed as % dominant acid in food (e.g. lactic in whole milk or buttermilk; citric in soft drinks; acetic in vinegar).

The formula for determining Titratable Acidity is as follows:

$$\text{Titratable Acidity (T.A.)} = \text{volume of base (mL)} \times N \times \text{meq.wt. acid} \times 100 \text{ vol. in mL or wt. in g of sample}$$

Sample Calculations

1. A baker needs to prepare 50 lb. of bread.
    a. How much salt needs to be added at 2%?
    b. How much calcium propionate (a mold inhibitor) is needed at 0.3%?

Solution:

a. 2 lb. salt/100 lb. bread × 50 lb. bread = 1 lb. salt
b. 0.3 lb. propionate/100 lb. bread × 50 lb. bread = 0.15 lb. propionate

2. A plant uses 200 parts per million (ppm) by weight of smoke flavoring in processing barbecue sauce.
   a. How much flavoring is needed for a 250 lb. batch of barbecue sauce?
   b. How much flavoring is needed for a 45 gal. batch if 1 tbsp. of sauce weighs 15 grams?

Solution:

a. Given: 200 ppm = 200 mg/kg
   250 lb. × (0.454 kg/1 lb.) = 113.5 kg of barbecue sauce is prepared
   113.5 kg × (200 mg/1 kg) = 22,700 mg of flavoring or 22.7 g of smoke flavoring

b. Converting 45 gal. to kg of barbecue sauce:
   45 gal. × (16 c/gal) = 720 cups
   720 cups × (16 tbsp./1 cup) = 11,520 tbsp.
   11,520 tbsp. × (15 g/1 tbsp.) = 172,800 g
   172,800 g/1,000 = 172.8 kg of barbecue sauce
   172.8 kg × (200 mg/1 kg) = 34,560 mg of smoke flavoring or 34.56 grams

3. A manufacturer of low-sugar syrup wants to add 0.08% of sodium benzoate and 200 ppm of xanthan gum (by weight) to her product. How much will she need of each for an 800 kg batch? For a 300 lb. batch? For a 200 gal. batch (1 tbsp. of syrup weighs 18 g)?

Solution:

Step 1. Find how much sodium benzoate is used in 800 kg batch:

800 kg × (0.08/100) = 0.64 kg sodium benzoate

Step 2. Calculate for sodium benzoate in a 300 lb. batch

300 lb. × (.454 kg/1lb) = 136.2 kg
136.2 kg × (0.08/100) = 0.109 kg benzoate or 109 g

Step 3. Calculating amount of sodium benzoate for 200 gal. batch.

921,600 g × 0.08/100 = 737 g

Step 4. Figure the amount of xanthan gum needed (given 200 ppm = 200 mg/kg)

Calculate how much xanthan gum in 800 kg batch

$$800\ kg \times (200mg/kg) = 160{,}000\ mg\ or\ 160\ g\ of\ xanthan$$

Step 5. Calculating for xanthan gum in a 300 lb. batch

$$300\ lb.\ (0.454\ kg/1\ lb.) = 136.2\ kg$$

$$136.2\ kg\ (200\ mg/\ kg) = 27{,}240\ mg\ of\ xanthan\ or\ 272\ g$$

Step 6. Calculating xanthan gum for a 200 gal. batch

$$200\ gal.\ (16\ c/1\ gal) = 3{,}200\ c$$

$$3{,}200\ c\ (16\ tbsp./1\ c) = 51{,}200\ tbsp.$$

$$51{,}200\ tbsp.\ (18g/1\ tbsp.) = 921{,}600\ g\ syrup\ or\ 921.6\ kg.$$

$$921{,}600\ g\ (200\ mg/kg) = 184{,}320{,}000\ mg\ of\ xanthan\ or\ 184\ g$$

Sample Calculation 2: Adjusting Moisture in a Gluten-Free Dinner Roll Formulation

After preliminary work to determine the ingredients to use to obtain an optimal gluten-free (GF) dinner roll formulation as well as the bread-making procedure, the final control formulation was established, as seen in Table 7.4.

The main objective of the study was to quantify the improvement induced by three types of egg ingredients (fresh shell eggs, dried whole eggs, and egg whites), as well as by carob germ flour, on the physical and sensory characteristics of GF bread rolls.

TABLE 7.4. Control Gluten-free Dinner Roll Formulation.

Ingredients	% Flour Basis (%)	Overall Percentage (%)
Sorghum flour	70	33.78
Native potato starch	30	14.48
(Total flour)	(100)	(47.26)
Sucrose	4	1.93
Butter	4	1.93
Non-fat dry milk	4	1.93
Xanthan powder	1.5	0.72
Salt	1.75	0.84
Water	90	43.43
Instant dry yeast	2	0.97
TOTAL	207.25	100

Levels of 30% on a flour basis of fresh eggs or its equivalent in egg ingredients and 10% on a flour basis of carob germ flour were chosen to be tested.

As the base formula does not contain eggs, adjustments needed to be made to obtain an identical moisture content and dough consistency in the control as well as in the egg-containing formulas. A formula specifying 30% of fresh shell eggs on a flour basis was used as a reference for the calculations.

The moisture content of fresh shell eggs, dried whole eggs, and commercial egg whites was analytically determined at 76.73% for the fresh shell eggs, 4.96% in dried whole eggs and 87.39% in the egg whites.

To determine the amount of water to add in the formula containing 30% of fresh shell egg, the following calculation was used:

Water percentage calculation in formula containing 30% fresh shell egg

Percentage of water necessary in formula (%) = x

Water percentage in control (%) = y

Moisture brought by shell eggs (%) = z

$$x = y - z$$

Where y = 90% and z = 23% (egg percentage in formula (%) × egg moisture content (%))

Thus x = 67%

Then, to determine the water adjustments required in the other baking formulas (Table 7.6) a reconstitution table, adapted from a previous study (Yiu 2002), was used (Table 7.5).

TABLE 7.5. Reconstitution Calculation for Egg Containing Formulations.

	Fresh Shell Egg	Dried Whole Egg	Egg Whites
Moisture *y* (%)	76.73%	4.96%	87.39%
Solids (%)	23.27%	95.04%	12.61%
Fresh egg moisture (%) × total solids (%) = *m*		72.92%	9.68%
1 – 0.7673 = *n*		0.2327	0.2327
m/*n* = *x*		313.38	41.58
x – *y* = *z* (water in ml per 100 g of egg sample)		307.42	–45.81
z/(*z* + 100) × 100 = *p* (water percentage to be added per 100 g of egg sample)		75.52%	–84.54%
Fresh egg (%) from formula × (100 – *p*) = egg ingredient (%) in baking formula		7.35%	55.36%
(Fresh egg (%) × *p*) + fresh egg moisture (%) = water(%) in baking formula		89.65%	41.64%

KEY WORDS

Accuracy—the agreement of the experimental values with the established or "true" value.

Baker's percentage—formulas are based on the percentage of ingredients as compared to the amount of flour.

Molarity—an indication of the number of moles of a solute in one liter of solution

Normality (N)—represents a solution of an acid or base which contains 1g of replaceable H^+ per liter or OH^- per liter

Precision—the agreement among a series of experimental measurements.

Standard of Identity—specifies ingredients and additive limits allowed for use within a certain food.

COMPREHENSION QUESTIONS

7.1. Fill in the blanks:

1 Tablespoon =_____ teaspoons =_____fl oz = _____ml

1 gallon =_____ cups =_____Tablespoons =_____l

1 cc of water = _____ml =_____g

1 cup of water =_____ fl oz =_____ml =____ g

1 lb =_____ kg = _______ g

158 degrees F =_____C –40°F =_____C

7.2. A manufacturer of low-sugar syrup wants to add 0.08% of sodium benzoate and 200 ppm of xanthan gum (by weight) to her product. How much will she need of each for an 8000 kg batch? For a 3000 lb batch? For a 200 gal batch (1 teaspoon of syrup weighs 6 g).

7.3. Convert the following pizza dough formula into baker's percent (% flour basis).

Ingredient	Pounds	Ounces	Baker's %
Flour	40	—	
Salt	—	11.2	
Sugar	—	12.8	
Compressed yeast	—	9.6	
Olive oil	1	3.2	
Water	23	3.2	

7.4. List 3 factors that affect product and process parameters during scale-up of operations.

7.5. Besides benchtop-made prototypes of a new food product, what information can a food scientist provide to engineering and marketing specialists to ensure successful scale-up of operations?

REFERENCES

Smith, J. S., ed. *Food additive user's handbook*, 1st ed. (Glasgow: Blackie, 1991).

Graf, E., & Saguy, I. S. (Eds.) (1991). *Food product development from concept to marketplace.* New York: Van Nostrand Reinhold.

Houben A., Hochstotter A., Becker T., 2012. Possibilities to increase the quality in gluten-free bread production: an overview. *European Food Research Technology*, Volume 235, pages 195–207.

Lazaridou A., Duta D., Papageorgiou M., Belc N., Biliaderis C.G., 2007. Effects of hydrocolloids on dough rheology and bread quality parameters in gluten-free formulations. *Journal of Food Engineering*, Volume 79, pages 1033–1047.

McQuaid J, Conor L. 2010 Strategic Approaches to Process Optimization and Scale-up. *Pharmaceutical Technology*. Volume 34, Issue 9.

Mine Y., 2002. Recent advances in egg protein functionality in the food system. *World's Poultry Science Journal*, Volume 58, pages 31–39.

Ott R.L., Longnecker M.T., 2004. *A first course in statistical methods*. Brooks/Cole-Thompson, Belmont, CA, USA. pages 381–400.

Paul, E., *Handbook of Industrial Mixing*, Science and Practice.Wiley (2004)].

Sabanis D., Tzia C., 2010. Effect of hydrocolloids on selected properties of gluten-free dough and bread. *Food Science and Technology International, Volume 17*, pages 279–291.

Sciarini L.S., Ribotta P. D., León A.E., and Pérez G.T., 2010a. Influence of Gluten-free Flours and their Mixtures on Batter Properties and Bread Quality. *Food Bioprocessing Technology*, Volume 3, pages 577–585.

Shieh G., Jan S.-L., 2004. The effectiveness of randomized complete block design. *Statistica Neerlandica*, Vol. 58, n 1, pages 111–124.

CHAPTER 8

Experimental Design in Food Product Development

Learning Objectives

- How to use the appropriate statistical design to get meaningful results from your product development experiments.
- To see how to reduce time and cost in testing new formulations, ingredients or treatments by using appropriate statistical methods.

ELEMENTARY CONCEPTS IN STATISTICS

IT is beyond the scope of this book to teach statistics, a subject that is covered by numerous classes on most campuses. The information provided below assumes that the reader is familiar with the subject, and the following will address the issue of how to use this knowledge in product development. Experiments in the product development process, as in most processes, involve the gathering of data, which is used to make inferences about a certain variable or its effects. It is generally hoped that data gathered follows the normal distribution, i.e., the classic "bell-shaped" curve (see Figure 8.1). The total area under the normal distribution is equal to 1, with the center being the mean of the distribution. A standard normal distribution will have a mean of 0 with a standard deviation of 1.

The empirical rule regarding the standard deviation from the normal distribution is that:

- area in $\mu < \sigma = 0.6826$
- area in $\mu < 2\sigma = 0.9544$
- area in $\mu < 3\sigma = 0.9974$

As an example, what this refers to is that the probability that a val-

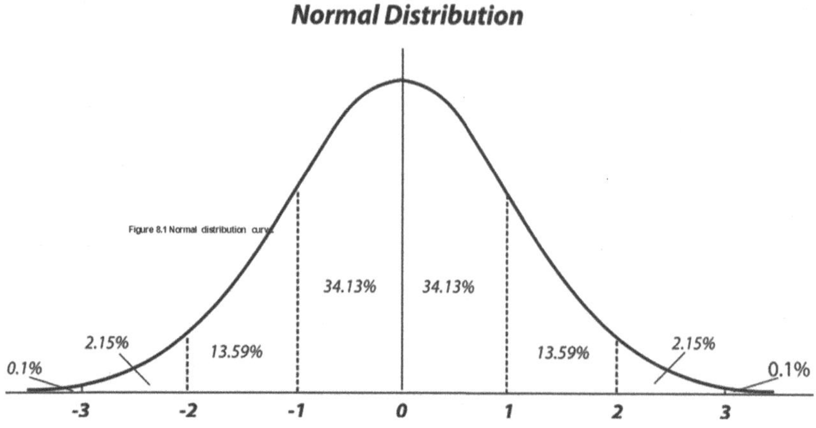

FIGURE 8.1. Normal distribution curve.

ue falling within 1, 2, or standard deviations of the mean is 68.26%, 95.44%, and 99.74% respectively.

INFERENCES FOR NORMAL DISTRIBUTIONS

The above empirical rule is used to define the value a called the confidence level. Therefore, in a set of data where $\alpha = 0.05$, the probability that the interval of values obtained experimentally covers the true value of the parameter is 95%.

Hypothesis Test

When running an experiment in product development, you are often trying to test a certain hypothesis, e.g., if for cost reasons you want to replace sugar with corn syrup in my cake formulation, will it affect cake volume? Therefore, the hypothesis test is the procedure to help you draw a conclusion about a certain parameter:

A hypothesis test consists of 5 steps:

1. Null Hypothesis, H_o

   H_o: $\mu = \mu_o$; in this case, the volumes of the cakes will be the same
2. Alternative Hypothesis, H_a

   Ha: $\mu < \mu_o$ and $\mu > \mu_o$ (one-tailed test); the volume of the cake with corn syrup will be greater or smaller than the cake made with sugar

   $\mu \neq \mu_o$ (two-tailed test); the volumes of the cakes will be different

Practically, you make 3 cakes with sugar and 3 with corn syrup, keeping all other factors the same, and measure the volumes of the cakes. You will then run an analysis of the means of the two treatments, and go to the 3rd step.

3. Test statistic (t or z-value): You test whether these means are the same using an appropriate statistical tool such as a student t-test. The results will tell you if the null hypothesis is correct, i.e., there is no difference in cake volume, or if it is to be rejected, i.e., there is a difference (step 4).
4. *Rejection Region*: You can also tell from the t-test whether the volume of the cake with the syrup is significantly larger or smaller than the control.

   $t > t_a$

   $t < -t_a$

   $|t| > t_a/2$
5. Draw your conclusion.

SPECIAL NOTES ON INFERENCES

- Rejection region depends on specification of desired a (Type I error), most commonly a will be either 0.05 or 0.01.
- Alternatively, we can compute a p-value for the test statistic.
  —The p-value is the probability of observing a test statistic value as extreme as the observed value, assuming that H_o is true.
  —A small p-value, therefore, indicates that such an extreme test statistic is unlikely to occur when H_o is true, leading us to believe that H_o is wrong.
- Failing to reject a null hypothesis does not mean the H_o is necessarily true. Remember it is just a question of probability.

LOGARITHMIC SCALES

Special consideration must be given to pH and microbiological counts, because they are based on logarithmic scales. Differences may be under/over significantly. Changes in microbial counts can multiply very quickly. For example, if you are testing the effect of two acidifying ingredients on the pH of a salsa and your statistical analysis indicates no significant differences between the two means: 4.55 and 4.66. That may be true mathematically, but it makes a very big difference in the safety of the salsa and its regulation. The salsa with a pH of 4.55 will be considered acid or acidified and does not support the growth of botulism, whereas the salsa with a pH of 4.66 will be considered a lowacid food.

In the case of microbial growth, any differences less than 1 log are considered insignificant due to the nature of microbial growth.

STATISTICS BASICS

- *Random sample*—random implies that each sample in the population has an equal chance of being selected
- *Sample mean*—a measure of the "central tendency" of the sample. It is the sum of a set of measurements divided by their number.
- *Sample variance* (s^2) *and standard deviation* (s)—measure the "spread of the sample." The standard deviation is commonly considered the more useful of these, because its units are the same as those for the sample.
- *Estimation*—the process of using a quantity computed on a sample to provide information regarding the corresponding population quantity. We often use the sample mean to estimate the population mean and the sample variance to estimate the population variance.

EXPERIMENTAL DESIGNS

The design of experiments is essential in successful food product development projects. Well-designed studies save money and are easier to analyze. The statistical design of experiments provides confidence that the information you collect is reliable. Experimental design is used mostly in formulating product, process development, sensory testing, and test market analysis. Fortunately, most large companies employ or consult with statisticians to help design experiments and analyze data.

Completely Randomized Design (CR)

Completely Randomized Design (CR) is an experimental design in which the analyst randomly assigns the samples to different procedures. For example, if you are trying to find the best chocolate chip out of four samples that will produce the best taste for a cookie recipe, you could make 3 cookies with each of the 4 chocolates and assign the 12 cookies randomly to 4 judges to score them on chocolate flavor.

Randomized Complete Block Design (RCB)

A Randomized Complete Block Design (RCB) is a restricted randomization of treatments in which the units are sorted into blocks, and the treatments are randomly assigned to units within each block. The block design is considered complete if each treatment is assigned to at least one unit in each block. Otherwise the block design is incomplete. In general, we have t treatments, b blocks, so in a RCB we have $t * b$ experimental units.

In the previous example, you will use a panel of 4 judges to test 4 cookies, each made with a different chocolate, with all other ingredients maintained the same. Each judge is going to test every cookie 3 times, randomly assigned, and score them. Scores are tabulated and data is analyzed for differences among the means.

The advantages of RCB over CR are that this test reduces variability of treatment comparisons by allowing them to be made on more similar units within a block. Variability in experimental units can be introduced deliberately by including a wide variety of blocks, thus broadening the population about which inferences can be made. Randomized Complete Block Design tests are easy to construct and analyze. This type of design is also flexible to the number of treatments and blocks. If the number of treatments is large, you may not be able to find enough similar units to call a block, therefore making other tests a better choice.

Factorial design: Handling many factors simultaneously.

Usually a set of "alphabetic" factor notation will be used to talk about any kind of factorial structure in general.

Factor A has a levels, Factor B has b levels, and so on. When we refer to a factorial structure, we refer to it generically by its level. If we have 3 levels of Factor A and 4 levels of Factor B, we call this a 3×4 factorial structure.

The number of treatment combinations is the product of the levels of the factors: $t = a * b * c$. Factorial designs can be run in any of the following types:

1. Full Factorial Design
2. Fractional Factorial Design

TABLE 8.1. Factorial Design Set Up.

Factor Name	Number of Levels	Subscript on y or μ
A	a	I
B	b	j
C	c	k

3. Response Surface Design: Very commonly used in product development
4. Mixture Designs

Questions to Consider in Factorial Design

- Questions you might want to answer:
  —Is there a Factor A effect?
  —Is there a Factor B effect?
  —Is there any interaction between the different factors?
- Example: You are working on developing a new cherry pie and you want to test the following:
  —3 levels of sugar (high/low)
  —2 suppliers of cherries
  —Butter (B) or margarine (M)
- You can have a 3 × 2 × 2 full factorial design, resulting in 12 different treatments.

SUMMARY

Experimental design in new product development can save companies time and money. By starting with an experimental plan, the product development team can develop a schedule to test each variable in the experiment. Taking detailed notes during all experiments is necessary in case the project is temporarily put on hold or team members are not able to fulfill the entire project.

KEY WORDS

Estimation—the process of using a quantity computed on a sample to provide information regarding the corresponding population quantity. We often use the sample mean to estimate the population mean and the sample variance to estimate the population variance.

Random sample—random implies that each sample in a population has an equal chance of being selected.

Sample mean—a measure of the "central tendency" of a sample. It is the sum of a set of measurements divided by their number.

Standard deviation(s)—commonly considered more useful than the sample variance, because its units are the same as those for the sample.

COMPREHENSION QUESTIONS

8.1. Give two advantages of the Randomized Complete Block Design over the Completely Randomized Design.

8.2. Design a study to correspond to a certain variable you are testing in your own product. Explain why you chose the design you did.

REFERENCES

Hubbard, M. R. (1990). *Statistical quality control for the food industry*. New York: Van Nostrand Reinhold.

CHAPTER 9

Basic Units of Operation

> **Learning Objectives**
>
> - The basic operational units used to produce food products.
> - How to sort for quality at receiving.
> - Which processes to choose for manufacturing your new product.

A unit operation is a physical processing step that cannot be divided into smaller units and that contributes to transforming raw materials into food products. These include events that take place in every step of food processing, including handling and shipping materials, receiving the materials, cleaning and sanitation of equipment, and all processing methods. The reasons for processing food are to prevent spoilage, eliminate waste, preserve quality, enhance convenience, make foods available out of season, and increase the value of the product (Gould 1996).

MATERIAL HANDLING

Material handling is the primary operation in most food plants. Material handling is all movement, packaging, and storing of materials including non-food materials (e.g., packaging material, cleaning chemicals, and sanitation supplies). Material handling operations bind together operations that are productive and nonproductive (Gould 1996). Material handling begins with raw material handling and end with the transportation of foods from the processing plant. When raw materials enter a receiving department, material handlers will check for defects and also ensure a shipment corresponds to what was ordered. Several such steps are presented in Table 9.1.

TABLE 9.1. Attributes to Check at Receiving.

Attribute	Signs of Damage
Quality	Torn packages, off-odor, off-color, heavy ice crystals (on frozen foods)
Condition	Obvious defects, expiration dates, type of product requested
Internal characteristics	Sugar content, soluble solids, pH, temperature

Moving and Storage

After products are accepted at receiving, the raw materials should be moved into storage facilities. If products are delivered on pallets, a forklift can be used to move the material off the delivery vehicle. Other methods of unloading products include unloading by hand and special equipment (e.g., truck lift). If liquid or powder products are being delivered, pumps may be utilized to move the product (Gould 1996).

Just as moving products is dependent on the type of product received, storage is also dependent on product factors. Dry, wet, refrigerated, frozen, food, and non-food storage areas should all be designated within the facility. Storage bins can be utilized for some products. These bins should be designed to operate on a first-in, first out (FIFO) basis, so that the material received last is not used until all of the other products received have been used.

CLEANING

Cleaning is the removal of foreign materials from the raw commodity (e.g., soil and dirt, stones, insect eggs, product debris, and pesticide residue) (Gould 1996). There are two basic methods of cleaning, with and without water. Cleaning methods are commodity specific and some processes are carried out in the field during harvest or prior to shipping.

Dry Cleaning

Dry or waterless cleaning usually involves removing stones and other agricultural debris by means of separating (Gould 1996). One of the most economical methods of dry cleaning is air separation, where light debris is blown off of the product. Other methods include magnetism and direct mechanical, including separation by hand (Fellows 2000).

Dry cleaning is more cost effective than wet cleaning, but it can result in the creation of dust, a potential hazard (Fellows 2000).

Wet Cleaning

Wet cleaning uses water to solubilize the unwanted from the wanted material. Examples of wet cleaning are flotation washing, ultrasonic cleaning, spraying, and soaking (Fellows 2000). Wet cleaning is most effective for removing insect eggs, spray and pesticide residues, rotted areas, and dirt. The water used for wet cleaning must be potable and free of organic and inorganic residues. In some cases, detergents, acids, or alkalis are added to wet cleaning solution. Frequently, chlorine is also added (Fellows 2000).

QUALITY SEPARATION

Quality separation refers to sorting products by specific parameters and quality attributes (e.g., size, color, absence of defects, and maturity). Internal properties (e.g., sugar content, solids content, and acidity) are also parameters by which products are sorted (Gould 1996). Quality separation is done with the goal of eventually grading the products (Gould 1996). Shapes and sizes are sorted by screens or sieves. Machines can sort by color and scan for defects. Weight sorting is done through the use of a detector that redirects products that are too heavy or light. Weight sorting is commonly used in egg processingto sort into small, medium, large, and extra-large sizes. Various techniques for quality separation are listed in Table 9.2.

PEELING

Peels, the protective outer covering on fruits and vegetables, may or

TABLE 9.2. Quality Separation Examples by Type (Hui 2004).

Type of Separation	Example
Solid from solid	Peeling of apples
Solid from liquid	Filtration of apple juice
Liquid from solid	Pressing of grapes for juice
Liquid from liquid	Centrifuging oil from water
Gas from solid or liquid	Canning

may not be edible. Even if peels are edible, they may be unattractive to consumers and require removal. The six common methods for removing the outer peels of commodities are (1) pliers, peeling spoons, or hand-held knife, (2) mechanical knife, (3) brushing with abrasive material, (4) grinding, (5) chemical peeling with alkalis or acids, and (6) steam or high pressure (Gould 1996). Which peeling method to select will depend on the fruit or vegetable being processed and its susceptibility to damage.

DISINTEGRATING

Disintegrating is the process of dividing whole product masses into parts. Disintegration can change the form of the food product, or result in minimal change. Product disintegration that does not change the product significantly includes husking (corn), shelling (peas, nuts), pitting (cherries, peaches), coring (cabbage, apples), and snipping and de-stemming (green beans, strawberries, blueberries) (Gould 1996). Other disintegration processes do alter the form of the product. These include cutting or shredding (lettuce for packaged products), crushing (fruits for pie filling), juicing or extracting (apples for apple juice), homogenization (milk to disperse fat globules), and sheeting (corn for corn chips).

SEPARATION

Separation as a downline unit operation is different from quality separation on food intake, in that it refers to the physical separation of intrinsic parts of the food into various components. These separation techniques, which are frequently carried out together, are filtration, clarification, sieving, sedimentation, etc. (Gould 1996). Deaeration, removal of air dissolved in food, is another separation method that is important in food processing. Deaeration decreases the likelihood of enzymatic browning and foaming, and is performed by passing liquid or particulate product through vacuum chambers (Gould 1996).

PROTECTIVE LINE EQUIPMENT

Protective line equipment is installed on a processing line to eliminate the likelihood of contamination from other materials (Gould 1996). Sieves and screens can be installed in-line to eliminate residual materials left in a product batch after quality separation. Sifters are used for products such as flour and salt both to preserve quality and to prevent ingress of foreign matter. Magnetic and metal detectors are commonly used at the end of a product line to ensure no metal contamination has occurred (e.g., from shavings fallen from the machines used in processing, which are mostly metal).

BLANCHING

Blanching, a brief heat treatment of products, is used to deactivate enzymes, which cause discoloration, texture changes, and flavor loss (Gould 1996). Blanching is usually completed in preparation for other processing treatments. Fruits and vegetables each have their own blanching process, which is based on four factors: (1) the type of fruit or vegetable, (2) size of the pieces, (3) blanching temperature, and (4) method of heating (Fellows 2000). The most common blanching processes are steam and hot water treatments. To test for adequate blanching in vegetables, peroxidase is used. Peroxidase is an enzyme in vegetables that causes discoloration. Blanching helps fruits and vegetables to retain flavor and color, while softening their texture.

PUMPING

Pumping moves liquid or semi-liquid foods from one unit operation to the next. A wide variety of pumps are available; therefore, it is important to know the capabilities of the pumps installed in processing facilities. Important attributes that all pumps should have are the ability to break up foods and ease of cleaning in place (Hui 2004).

MIXING

The objective of mixing is to combine two or more ingredients. The blending of ingredients can be done as a batch or by a continuous method. Mixing is done in kettles with or without steam jackets, vacuum cookers or concentrators, flow mixers, paddle or arm mixers, or tumbling mixers (Gould 1996). The process combines solids with solids (dry cake mix), liquids and liquids, or air and liquids (egg-white foam, or ice cream) (Hui 2004).

COATING

Coating enhances food products by contributing flavor, altering texture, enhancing appearance, providing convenience, or increasing flavor and color options within a food commodity (Fellows 2000). The process of coating usually does little damage nutritionally to the foods (in the way of lost vitamins in processing), but it can add a significant number of calories. Three methods for coating foods are enrobing, dusting, and pan coating. Enrobing involves immersing the product into a tempered coating (such as chocolate or compound coating), whereas dusting is done using dry seasonings or sugars released from a hopper with a mesh screen. Pan coating is common in sugar confections and is done with a revolving pan and a top sprayer. Coating techniques and applications are summarized in Table 9.3.

CHILLING

Chilled food should be held at temperatures between 30°F (–1°C) and 40°F (4.4°C) (Fellows 2000). Enzymes and microorganisms are not killed at reduced temperatures in most cases, but their growth is slowed, which increases shelf-life. Reduction in heat leads to the slowing of microbiological and biochemical deterioration (Fellows 2000). Certain products, such as ones containing uncooked meats, have strict temperature controls that have to be maintained at all times. Chilling systems include air chilling, water chilling, or rapid chilling using liquid carbon dioxide or liquid nitrogen.

Fresh foods, such as fruits and vegetables, rely on chilling to extend a relatively short shelf-life. At the same time, fruits and vegetables must also be stored at precise temperatures to prevent chilling injury. Chilling injuries, including external browning and skin blemishes, occur when the product is held at a temperature below its optimum (Fellows 2000). Products have different optimum temperatures (e.g., bananas have a much higher optimum than broccoli). Banana chill injuries can occur below 53°F (12°C), whereas broccoli's optimum temperature is above 32°F (0°C).

Shelf-lives of processed chilled foods depend on the type of food, degree of microbiological retardation and enzyme deactivation during processing, hygiene control during processing, and the temperatures throughout the product's life from processing to distribution and storage (Fellows 2000). Processed low-acid (pH > 4.6) chilled foods require strict hygienic standards during processing and packaging to resist microbiological contamination (Hui 2004). Microbiological testing and shelf-life studies must be carried out to determine the proper time

TABLE 9.3. Types of Coatings and Uses.

Types of Coating	Description	How it is Used
Batter	A mixture based on flour and water that may have added seasonings	Products are enrobed by batter prior to breading so that the breadcrumbs stick to the product
Breading	Ground previously baked products	Products dipped in batter are then dusted with bread crumbs prior to further processing
Seasoning	Herbs, spices, and cheese added during or after processing	Dusted onto products before or after processing to enhance flavor
Sugar Coatings	Sweet coatings made with sugar that coat the outside of products	Liquid sugar syrups combined with or without flavors are sprayed onto products after processing and drying; used in ready to eat cereal production Pan coating is a batch operation where the product builds up a sugar coating by using a revolving pan Hard coating is the process of slowly building a hard outer shell; mostly used in confectionary applications Soft coating is a mixture of sugar and anti-crystallizing agents that make a soft coating; used on jelly beans
Compound or chocolate coatings	Chocolate or other flavored coatings that are added to products	Enrobing used to cover sweet foods, like confections or ice cream; added as outer coating or dipped on one side
Vitamins	Fortifies product with vitamins and/or minerals	Added during processing or sprayed on the finished product

Source: Gould 1996; Fellows 2000.

products can remain safely on the shelf. Chilling times are also important, especially in the cooling of heat-processed products such as meats. As noted above, many microorganisms tend to grow in temperatures between 40°F (4.4°C) and 70°F (21°C).

EXTRUSION

Extrusion is the process of forcing material through an orifice at high temperatures. The moisture content of the material is usually between 20 and 40 percent (Gould 1996). Popular products made with extrusion include puffed cereals and snacks, and pasta. Extrusion uses high temperatures for a short time to preserve foods and gelatinize starches (Gould 1996). Extruders use dyes at the orifice opening that aid in producing new and unique shapes. Extruders come in many types including single screw, twin screw, and co-extruders for filled products (Hui 2004).

FRYING

Frying is the process of cooking with hot oil. It is done in batches and as a continuous operation. During this process, 75 to 95 percent of water in a product is replaced with oil (Gould 1996). Common fried products available to consumers include potato chips, chicken nuggets, and doughnuts. Frying oils are usually at about 400°F (Gould 1996). Frying is a unit operation that is able to modify texture and flavor, as well as to preserve (Fellows 2000). Shallow fryers and deep-fat dryers are the most commonly used equipment (Fellows 2000). Oil quality and temperature have a major effect on the properties of fried foods that are processed.

FREEZING

Freezing is the process of removing heat from a product, and cooling it rapidly enough to prevent the formation of crystals in or on the product (Gould 1996). Freezing is completed when the water inside the food product goes from the liquid phase to the solid phase. Freezing is a method of preservation due to its reduction of water activity and low temperatures (Fellows 2000).

The quality of frozen foods depends on the time and temperature of freezing rates, especially for fruits and vegetables (Gould 1996). In addition, some frozen foods are better preserved when they undergo a pre-blanching step.

Methods of freezing foods are still-air freezing, forced-air freezing, cooled-liquid freezing, and direct contact freezing. Because ice has a greater volume than water (by 9%), products will expand after being frozen (Fellows 2000).

DRYING AND DEHYDRATION

Drying and dehydration release moisture from product, thereby reducing water activity and leading to better shelf stability. Drying and dehydration normally employ a combination of heat, controlled relative humidity, and airflow conditions (Gould 1996). The temperatures used to dry and dehydrate food are dependent on the properties of the food and need to be controlled to prevent discoloration and off-flavors. Packaging for dried products should have good moisture barriers, since any change in the moisture content will cause rapid spoilage (Fellows 2000). The equipment types for drying include (1) cabinet dryers, (2) conveyor (continuous dryers), (3) fluidized bed dryers, (4) spray dryers, (5) sun drying, and (6) drum dryers (Gould 1996).

Cabinet dryers usually have stacked trays that can be loaded with product (Gould 1996). Air is forced over the product through vents inside the dryer. Cabinet dryers are relatively inexpensive, but do not dry products very quickly. Cabinet dryers are commonly used in smaller-scale production facilities or in pilot plants (Fellows 2000).

Conveyor (continuous) dryers use a mesh conveyor belt to pass food through a chamber that allows for control of relative humidity and heat. These dryers can have different zones of airflow and heat throughout the process, making customized drying schemes possible for a wide variety of products (Fellows 2000).

Fluidized bed dryers utilize forced air along with a bed that moves vigorously to create movement of the product and thereby achieve more uniform drying. These dryers, which can be used in continuous operations, work best with foods that are easily fluidized and not susceptible to breakage (e.g., instant coffee, dried coconut, sugar, yeast, and some ready-to-eat breakfast cereals) (Fellows 2000).

Spray dryers desiccate liquid products, such as milk, through high heating. Products with 40 to 60% moisture are atomized and released into a heated chamber (300°F (150°C) to 575°F (300°C) (Fellows 2000). The product is dried in a matter of seconds. The particle size of the product must be very small in order to be dried effectively.

Sun drying is one of the oldest methods of food preservation. Heat from the sun is used to drive the moisture out of foods and to create a unique product. The disadvantages of sun drying include the time it takes and poor process control. Many developed and developing countries use solar drying techniques at various levels of sophistication. Tomatoes (for sun dried tomatoes) and grapes (for raisins) are products still commonly sun dried.

Drum dryers have a heated, hollow steel drum that rotates and dries by contact (Fellows 2000). Drum dryers have high drying and energy efficiency and can be for products that have larger particle size than those that are spray dried. Examples include instant potatoes and instant soup mixes.

Freeze drying is an expensive process used for high-dollar items such as instant coffee. The product is frozen prior to drying. Following drying, the pressure is dropped to allow the frozen water to undergo sublimation. By skipping the liquid phase, cell structure is better maintained and product quality is higher than with other drying methods.

Whatever method is selected, drying does cause significant changes in the nutritional content, eating quality, and texture of foods (Fellows 2000).

THERMAL PROCESSING

Thermal processing applies heat for set times, both to cook a product and to ensure microbial safety. The time necessary for heating is dependent on the pH of the product. For instance, sauces are heated in large kettles. Other examples of thermal processing include hot-fill operations for low-pH products and baking, which is carried out through continuous or batch operations. Cooking in ovens is a thermal process applied to meat products, while heat exchangers are used extensively in milk and juice processing.

CANNING

Canning is a well-known method for preserving foods through heating. The amount of heat applied to a canned product depends on particle size, container size, viscosity, pH, and water activity (Gould 1996). Low-acid foods (pH > 4.6) can be susceptible to the growth of *Clostridium botulinum*, a pathogen that produces toxins that can lead to serious illness and death. The US Food and Drug Administration (FDA) mandates that low-acid canned foods be processed using heat and pressure (retorted). In addition, manufacturers must file a description of their canning process with the agency. Thermal processing such as canning may cause changes in the texture and flavors of foods, but creates very safe products with long shelf lives.

In canning, producers must find three values (D, z, and F values) through processing experiments or published data, in order to arrive at the proper heating requirements. The D value is the time it takes at a specific temperature to kill 90 percent of the microbial population in a sample. The z value is the number of degrees required for the thermal death time curve of the microbial population to pass 1 log cycle. The z value is a measurement of microbial thermal resistance (Anonymous

2009). The F value is the number of minutes at a specific temperature required to destroy a specific number of organisms at a specific z value. The F value is the capacity of the heat treatment to produce a sterile product.

HIGH-PRESSURE PROCESSING

High-pressure processing has become more popular in recent years. This technology uses higher pressures in processing, which allows a reduction in processing temperature with the same kill effect on microorganisms. High-pressure processing has been explored in many areas of food production. The advantage of high pressure is that foods given a high-pressure treatment undergo fewer structural and appearance changes than occur with regular thermal processing.

ASEPTIC PROCESSING

Aseptic filling combines thermal processing and packaging in specialized materials, designed to ensure longer shelf lives. In aseptic filling, the process is totally enclosed and highly automated. Aseptic containers can be made from paperboard, foil, or extruded polyethylene (Gould 1996).

FILLING

Filling is the process of packing food into packaging materials. Filling is an important unit operation when it comes to customer satisfaction (Gould 1996). Underfilling and overfilling packaging containers can cause government compliance issues or company losses, respectively. The technology of filling can vary from hand packing to sophisticated rotary piston fillers. The type of filling equipment depends on the type of product and its packaging complexity. Products are filled based on net or gross weight (Fellows 2000).

CONTAINER CLOSURE

Container closing is important in all operations, especially canning. Hermetically sealed containers, those packed with airtight closures, are the key to safe canned products, since closures protect against leakage and microorganism contamination. Excluding oxygen from the package prevents molds and yeast growth. Metal cans are first sterilized through the use of hot water and steam, filled, passed through a steam tunnel, and finally the air is removed to create a vacuum. Filling glass jars is a similar process, but instead uses a steam capper to create a vacuum.

LABELING AND CODING

Labeling requirements should be carefully monitored and researched prior to production. Labeling includes all information located on the exterior of a package. Coding enables tracking of products throughout distribution. Date coding allows retailers to determine when a product should be taken off the shelves, and can assist in identifying and finding products affected by a recall. With sufficient tracking systems, manufacturers have the capacity to locate potentially unsafe or dangerous products. Spraying an individualized lot code onto packaging during packaging, with an inkjet, generally completes coding. Regulations governing labeling will be presented in Chapter 16.

IRRADIATION

Irradiation is a processing technique that uses radioactive waves to rid products of microorganisms. Although food irradiation has attracted consumer backlash, there are many advantages to this process. Irradiation uses little to no heating; therefore, the texture and flavor properties of food are not affected (Fellows 2000). Disadvantages of the process include worker safety, the possibility of resistance by microorganisms, and the public's fears of radiation and how it might affect their health (Fellows 2000). Irradiation has been used in the United States for eliminating insects on products such as wheat, potatoes, fruits, vegetables, tea, and spices, as well as use for destroying pathogens in pork, chicken, turkey, and red meats (Fuller 2011).

METAL DETECTION AND X-RAY DIFFRACTION

Metal detection and X-ray technologies are used to determine if any physical contamination has entered a food product. Because food processing equipment is mostly metal machinery, contamination by metal can occur. Metal detectors and X-ray diffraction technology can be important final steps in processing to ensure safety. Metal detectors must be calibrated routinely when they are used on a production line. Besides electronic detectors, gravity wells and mesh screening may also be implemented to remove foreign matter at the terminus of a production line.

SUMMARY

The unit operations discussed above are among the most widely used in food processing. The food industry relies on additional unit operations, and descriptions of these can be found in a variety of resources, including the material referenced in this chapter.

KEY WORDS

FIFO—FIFO is an abbreviation for "first in, first out"; it is an inventorying method that dictates using the first received items before using items received afterward.

Protective line equipment—equipment installed on a processing line in order to eliminate the likelihood of contamination from foreign substances.

Quality separation—a sorting, often carried out at receiving, of food raw materials and ingredients that applies item-specific parameters and quality traits as criteria.

Unit operation—a physical processing step that cannot be divided into smaller units and contributes to transforming raw materials into food products.

COMPREHENSION QUESTIONS

9.1. Define blanching. Name one test to test for adequate blanching.

9.2. Consider that your product concept will be produced at the commercial level. List the first 5 unit operations in its manufacturing process.

9.3. Name 2 physical and 2 chemical indicators of harvest maturity in fruits and vegetables.

9.4. Define the D, z, and F values used in canning.

9.5. Fill in the following blanks:

a. ________________ and ________________ are completed by

using heat and controlled relative humidity and airflow conditions.

b. ______________ ______________ has become more popular, making way for new packaging materials and longer shelf lives.

c. Coatings enhance food products by giving __________, altering __________, better the appearance, provide ___________, or increase the offerings of a food commodity.

REFERENCES

Fellows, P. J. *Food Processing Technology—Principles and Practice* 2nd ed. (Woodhead Publishing, 2000).

Gould, W. *Unit Operations for the Food Industries*. (Timonium, MD: CTI Publications, Inc., 1996).

Hui, Y. H. "Food Plant Sanitation and Quality Assurance." In *Food processing principle and applications*, J. S. Smith and Y. H. Hui, eds. (Ames, IA: Blackwell Publishing, 2004), 151–162.

CHAPTER 10

Regulatory Considerations

Learning Objectives

- Learn how city, state, and federal government regulate food.
- Understand the changes that the Food Safety Modernization Act brought forth in FDA regulated foods.
- Comprehend where to look up essential regulations.

AFTER the decision to develop a new product, it is necessary to research the regulatory requirements for each ingredient in it and to know every category under which it can be classified. Food producers have to comply with federal, state, and city policies, depending on the location of their operation.

Various aspects of food regulations are controlled by corresponding U.S. government agencies (detailed in Table 10.1), including the U.S. Food and Drug Administration (FDA); divisions of the U.S. Department of Agriculture (USDA); a division of the U.S. Department of Commerce; the Bureau of Alcohol, Tobacco, Firearms, and Explosives (ATF); the U.S. Environmental Protection Agency (EPA), and the Federal Trade Commission. These agencies have the right to enforce laws enacted by Congress, as well as their own regulations and policies, to protect the safety of consumers' health, safety, and economic well-being.

CITIES AND COUNTIES

City and county governments are authorized to establish and enforce standards of sanitation or local codes permitting or preventing the sale or production of certain items. Local governments may tax foods with higher sugar or sodium, in order to promote healthier options. Some local laws are not applicable to pre-packaged foods but are fully enforceable for food service establishments. City or county officials may play an integral part in uncovering sanitation issues in food processing or tracing the source of foodborne illness outbreaks. But, for the most part, municipalities are more involved in monitoring employee hygiene and the cleanliness in retail food service establishments (Bauman 1991).

TABLE 10.1. Regulatory Agencies and Their Responsibilities.

Agency	Responsibilities
Cities and Counties	Usually just involved in food hygiene and sanitation at the retail level. Involved mostly in local retail stores, restaurants, catering businesses, and other institutions within their territory.
State Agencies	Each state has its own food policy and enforcement agency which may be housed in the state department of agriculture, health, or consumer affairs; States may have their own regulations on some sanitary measures.
FDA	Requirements for manufacturing at large. Regulates all food, food products, non-alcoholic beverages and wine beverages containing <7% alcohol except: • egg products • meat including products with 3% or more red meat or red meat products • poultry including products with 2% or more poultry or poultry products • alcoholic beverages • public drinking water
	U.S. Department of Agriculture
Food Safety and Inspection Service (FSIS)	Regulates egg products, meat including products with 3% or more red meat or red meat products, and poultry including products with 2% or more poultry or poultry products.
Animal and Plant Health Inspection Service (APHIS)	Regulates fruit, vegetables, and other plants.
Federal Grain Inspection Service, (part of Grain Inspection Packers and Stockyard Association (GIPSA))	Conducts mandatory grading for grains including barley, oats, wheat, corn, rye, flaxseed, sorghum, soybeans, and triticale.
Agricultural Marketing Service (AMS)	Grades food products including meat and poultry, fruits and vegetables, cotton, tobacco, eggs, and dairy.
Agricultural Research Service (ARS)	Conduct scientific research on foods and plants to help provide safe healthy food as well as assessing the nutritional needs of the public.

(continued)

TABLE 10.1 (continued). Regulatory Agencies and Their Responsibilities.

Agency	Responsibilities
	U.S. Department of Commerce
National Oceanic and Atmospheric Association (NOAA)	Regulates fisheries, offers sanitation inspections, and grades fish and fish products.
National Marine Fisheries Service (NMFS)	Assesses the status of fish stock, ensures fishery regulations are met, and promotes sustainable fishing practices.
	U.S. Department of Treasury
Bureau of Alcohol, Tobacco, Firearms, and Explosives (ATF)	Regulates all alcoholic beverages except wine beverages with < 7% alcohol.
Environmental Protection Agency	Determines safety of pesticides and tolerance levels for pesticide residues.
Federal Trade Commission	Ensures the truthfulness of content claims along with FDA/USDA.

STATES

State regulatory agencies may be housed in the department of agriculture, department of health, or department of consumer affairs. State agencies generally have duties similar to those of federal agencies (e.g., inspecting facilities, ensuring sanitation and health standards are being met, and enforcing regulations). State agencies are more concerned with foods that will not enter interstate commerce, as they may be the only agency that oversees a company that does not sell beyond state borders. States work with federal agencies to control and trace interstate food safety problems and outbreaks of foodborne disease.

Case Study: New York City Bans Trans Fat

New York City's trans fat ban took effect in July 2007. Under this rule, "no food containing partially hydrogenated vegetable oils, shortenings, or margarines with 0.5 grams or more trans fat per serving may be stored, used, or served" within the New York City jurisdiction. The regulation does not apply to pre-packaged foods such as potato chips. What implications may this have on restaurants? How can suppliers better serve their NYC customers with this issue? How might this regulation change the way NYC inspectors do their job?

THE FOOD AND DRUG ADMINISTRATION (FDA)

The FDA is the primary agency with responsibility for food transported between states. The FDA is not responsible for meat or meat products with >3% meat or meat products or >2% poultry or poultry products; these are the responsibility of the USDA. The FDA oversees the periodic inspections of facilities, analysis of samples, and other regulatory procedures to guard the nation's public health.

FDA inspections occur less frequently than USDA inspections. Factory inspections usually consist of reviewing files, records, and presenting the facility and worker credentials. The actual inspection of the facility does include a walk- through of the grounds. The inspector may request to take samples, photographs, and even interview personnel. The inspector will then meet with a manger to review results. Companies should prepare for inspections by creating a plan detailing who is authorized to receive the notice of inspection and who will accompany the inspector. The plan can also spell out rules that are pertinent for a given facility.

A warning letter from FDA details information gathered by inspectors regarding a violation. This warning gives producers the opportunity to correct violations without facing enforcement actions by the agency, such as seizure or civil penalties.

Injunctions, a civil judicial process to stop or prevent violations of a law, can be issued when a health hazard is identified at a facility, significant repeat violations are found by an inspector, voluntary recalls are refused, and seizure is uneconomical. Injunctions are most common when there has been a history of hazardous activities that have not been resolved through voluntary measures.

Products may be seized when repeated violations have occurred, insanitary conditions are found, or the health of the public is judged to be in danger. Products that are found to be adulterated or misbranded may also be subject to seizure. When products are seized, they are held by the FDA until further notice. The FDA has made it clear in recent years that it has the intention to seize products if warning letter issues are not cleared up.

THE UNITED STATES DEPARTMENT OF AGRICULTURE (USDA)

The USDA is involved in many aspects of food inspection, quality grading, promotion, and research. The USDA regulates certain food products containing meat (>3% meat or meat products or >2% poultry or poultry products). The USDA Food Safety and Inspection Service (FSIS) has extensive oversight of meat, poultry, and egg facilities, with in some cases an inspector present when food is being processed.

The USDA Animal and Plant Health Inspection Service (APHIS) has a mission to protect and promote U.S. agricultural health through regulating genetically engineered organisms and administering the Animal Welfare Act, among other activities. To protect agricultural health, APHIS works to defend America's animal and plant resources from agricultural pests and diseases. The task of APHIS is important. For example, it monitors the Mediterranean fruit fly, a major agricultural pest. If this insect was left unchecked, its damage could result in several billions of dollars in production and marketing losses annually. Foot-and-mouth disease or highly pathogenic avian influenza are also issues that APHIS tries to control in domestic animals. If these diseases threaten the animal food supply, foreign trading partners may invoke trade restrictions, creating losses for U.S. producers. When a pest or disease of concern is detected, APHIS has developed emergency protocols and partners in state and regional areas, in order to quickly manage or eradicate the outbreak.

The Federal Grain Inspection Service (FGIS), a program under the Grain Inspections, Packers, and Stockyard Administration (GIPSA), facilitates the marketing of U.S. grain and related agricultural products through the establishment of quality standards. These standards help to assess grains, regulate handling, and manage a network of laboratories that provide official inspection and weighing services. Federal laboratories inspect grains that are meant for export, while state and private laboratories check grains that will be utilized domestically (U.S. Department of Agriculture, 2009).

The USDA Agricultural Marketing Service (AMS) is responsible for the grading of all products (excluding fish). The voluntary grading of products can be done if a company wishes to prove that its products meet quality standards set by the USDA. Many products have detailed grading sheets with specific testing criteria, which can be found on the website www.ams.usda.gov.

The USDA Agricultural Research Service (ARS) attempts to develop solutions to agricultural problems, assess the nutritional needs of the public, and help sustain agricultural practices. The ARS forms partnerships with other agencies, universities, and private corporations for the betterment of food and agriculture. The ARS administers and supports national research programs in the areas of nutrition, food safety, food quality, animal production and protection, natural resources, sustainable agriculture, and crop production and protection.

Bureau of Alcohol, Tobacco, Firearms, and Explosives (ATF)

ATF regulates the production, distribution, and sale of alcoholic beverages under the Alcohol and Tobacco Trade and Tax Bureau (TTB) https://www.ttb.gov/index.shtml. The Federal Alcohol Administration (FAA) Act of 1935 required those who engage in the business as a producer, importer, or wholesaler of alcoholic beverages to have a permit. The FAA Act also aimed to ensure that labeling and advertising of alcoholic beverages provide adequate information to the consumer concerning the identity and quality of the product. The agency thus focuses on the prevention of misleading labeling or advertising that may deceive consumers regarding a product. The mandatory warning statement on alcoholic beverages started with the passing of the Alcohol Beverage Labeling Act of 1988. The FDA has primary jurisdiction over the labeling of alcoholic beverages that contain less than 7 percent alcohol by volume. However, TTB has jurisdiction over some labeling requirements, most importantly the Government Warning Statement for any alcoholic beverage over 0.5 percent alcohol by volume. These requirements are specified in 27 CFR part 16.

Environmental Protection Agency (EPA)

The EPA sets tolerances for pesticides for use on crops, in manufacturing plants, and in homes. These regulations are also in effect for foods imported into the US. The agency regulates sanitizers and antimicrobial materials permitted for use in food processing facilities and homes (Bauman 1991).

A major remit of the EPA is to set and monitor public drinking water standards. To be deemed safe, public water systems must meet minimum standards, including treating water to below the maximum contaminant levels for chemicals, turbidity, and microorganisms (Nielsen 1998).

Federal Trade Commission

The Federal Trade Commission (FTC) shares jurisdiction with FDA and USDA to ensure the truthfulness of nutrient contents and health claims in food advertising. The FTC is involved with the prevention of trade restraints such as price fixing, boycotts, illegal collusion between competitors, and other unfair methods of competition.

If a new food product overstates the vitamin content on the package, both the FTC and FDA/USDA would have a case against the offending organization.

RULEMAKING PROCESS

Most federal rules move through a series of stages from initial promulgation to enforceable status. A proposed rule is first published in the Federal Register to explain the reasons behind new regulatory actions. The proposed rule acts as a draft of the eventual regulation. After the draft has been published, a period of 30 days is allowed for comments to be made by industry professionals, experts, and the public. Comments are carefully taken into consideration, and the rule may be modified at this time. Suggestions and questions provided during the comment period are generally addressed by the enforcing agency during the issuance of the final rule. The final rule is published in the Federal Register with an effective date for implementation. In order to make accommodations for smaller companies, enforcing agencies may grant exemptions or provide alternative effective dates, which allow extended compliance time, recognizing that the costs of meeting the regulation may be burdensome, especially if it requires a major capital outlay.

All rules enacted are categorized annually into the Code of Federal Regulations (CFR). The CFR is available in print and online through the U.S. Government Printing Office (www.gpo.gov). Title 21 of the CFR relates to products under FDA supervision, while 9 CFR lists regulations for food products under USDA. All rules for standard of identities, allowed ingredients, and rules regarding specific products can be found in the CFR.

REGULATIONS GOVERNING FOOD

In addition to the agencies mentioned above, many national laws directly governing food production have been passed by the U.S. Congress. Originally, at the outset of the twentieth century, such laws were fairly vague statutes intended to maintain food purity and forestall adulteration. Through the years, these laws, which are outlined in Table

TABLE 10.2. Food Regulations throughout Time in the United States.

Federal Pure Food and Drugs Act	1906	First law related to food supply. Only substances that are not likely to be injurious were allowed to be used in foods.
Federal Meat Inspection Act	1906	Requires mandatory pre- and post-slaughter inspections for meat processors. Established sanitation standards. Established recordkeeping procedures.
Grade "A" Pasteurized Milk Ordinance	1924	Gave standards for milk processing. Raw milk must: (1) be cooled to 7°C or less within 2 hr. of milking, (2) not exceed 100,000 per ml prior to comingling with other milk, not to exceed 300,000 per ml as commingled prior to pasteurization, (3) test negative for drugs, (4) have a somatic cell count less than 750,000 per ml.
Federal Alcohol Administration Act	1935	Began the Federal Alcohol Administration (now housed under the ATF). Requires permit to produce, distribute, or wholesale alcoholic beverages. Mandates labeling.
Food, Drug, and Cosmetic Act	1938	Prohibits adulteration and misbranding of foods. Authorizes the government to regulate food safety and quality. Requires food package to contain name of product, net weight, and the name and address of the manufacturer or distributor. Requires list of ingredients. Prohibits misleading labeling statements. Replaced the Federal Pure Food and Drugs Act of 1906.
Poultry Products Inspection Act	1957	Requires inspection of poultry products intended for human consumption. Ratites (such as ostrich) were added to this list in 2001.
Food Additives Amendent (contains Delaney Clause)	1958	Authorizes the oversight of health claims. Requires food additives to be approved by the government prior to use. Companies must prove that food additives are safe prior to use.
Fair Packaging and Labeling Act	1966	Joint effort between FTC and FDA. Requires companies to distribute accurate information on consumer goods. Authorizes regulations to prevent consumer deception (or to facilitate value comparisons) with respect to descriptions of ingredients, slack fill of packages, use of "cents-off" or lower price labeling, or characterization of package sizes.

(continued)

TABLE 10.2 (continued). Food Regulations throughout Time in the United States.

Egg Products Inspection Act	1970	Inspection requirements set for shell eggs and egg products (USDA). Required continuous inspection programs for plants that break, dry and process shell eggs into liquid, frozen, or dried egg products.
Rule on Mandatory Nutrition Labels with Claims	1973	Requires a nutrition label to be present on foods that have a health claim or added nutrients.
Safe Drinking Water Act	1974	Created drinking water standards enforceable by the EPA. EPA creates the standards, while states enforce them.
Nutrition Labeling and Education Act		Mandatory food labeling is required for most foods. Standardized serving sizes are established. Uniform health claims are created.
Public Health Security and Bioterrorism Preparedness and Response Act of 2002	2002	Requires the establishment and maintenance of records by persons who manufacture, process, pack, transport, distribute, receive, hold, or import food in the United States.
Food Safety Modernization Act	2011	Mandatory re-registration of companies in even years. Frequency of FDA inspections defined. Fees are defined for re-inspections.

Source: Based on information from Nielsen1998 and Bauman 1991.

10.2, have multiplied and now reach into all areas of food and beverage production and distribution.

Food, Drug, and Cosmetic Act of 1938

Food products that are imported, exported, or cross state lines are regulated by the Food, Drug, and Cosmetic Act (FD&C Act) of 1938. The FD&C Act details the prohibition of adulterated and misbranded food in all of the food supply. This regulation also gives the FDA oversight of foods with the understanding that all food is to be produced under reasonably sanitary conditions. The FD&C Act contains general requirements for all foods, drugs, and cosmetics, and also includes more specific regulations for selected foods.

With the understanding that crops cannot be grown without defects, the FDA maintains "defect action levels" which were described in Chapter Four. These are published in the Defect Levels Handbook available on the FDA website (www.fda.gov). An example of defect action levels includes the allowance of 30 or fewer insect fragments and 1 rodent hair per 100 grams of peanut butter. It is unlawful for processors to mix higher-defect products with those that meet the standard. The methods of analysis are also included in the handbook. The defect action levels can help determine if a product is adulterated.

Food Safety Modernization Act

The Food Safety Modernization Act (FSMA) was signed into law on January 4, 2011. The regulation's aim is to promote the safety of the food supply. In addition, the FDA's enforcement rights were outlined and better defined timing of inspections was outlined. The FSMA made changes to the FDA's enforcement abilities, as well, making it possible for the agency to mandate recalls. Companies experienced changes in recordkeeping procedures, fees, and company registration requirements.

Targeted Inspections

According to the FSMA, facilities will be identified according to risk factors associated with the types of food the facility handles, history of recalls and incidence of illness, and the effectiveness of the hazard analysis and preventative controls that the facility implements. Domestic high-risk facilities must be inspected at least one time in the 5 years after enactment, and not less than once every 3 years thereafter. High-risk facilities are those that have had previous recalls or outbreaks. All facilities not indicated as high-risk are to be inspected once in the 7 years after enactment and not less than once every 5 years after the initial inspection.

Hazard Analysis and Risk-Based Preventative Controls

Facilities must conduct a written hazard analysis in order to effectively analyze any known or foreseeable threats to food safety. Preventative controls are to be put in place to reduce or eliminate the probability of the identified hazards. Measures to diminish these risks could include clarifying critical control points. The developed plan has also to include corrective action measures, verification procedures, and recordkeeping activities. A designated team member in charge of the facility is required to re-evaluate the written analysis if any significant changes are made to processing or if new risks are introduced, or, at a minimum, every 3 years. This requirement took effect in July, 2010. An exemption for very small businesses was made.

Detainment and Suspensions

The FDA, through the enactment of FSMA, now has the right to take products into custody if there is reason to believe that the products may cause harm to humans or animals. In addition, the suspension of registration for companies is now allowed, if there is reasonable probability that the food produced by a cited company could cause illness or harm to humans or animals. If there are grounds to continue suspension after a hearing (which must be held within 2 days of issuance), the FDA would be required to supply a corrective action plan demonstrating how to amend the problem that led to the issuance of the suspension.

Recalls

In addition, the FDA now has the authority to mandate a recall. In the event of a recall, a $224 hourly fee will be imposed on the offending company for activities associated with the order. These activities could include: conducting recall audit checks, reviewing periodic status reports, analyzing the status reports and the results of the audit checks, conducting inspections, traveling to and from locations, and monitoring product disposition.

Fees

Beginning in 2012, an hourly fee of $224 was assessed for re-inspection. The re-visitation fee is imposed, if a follow-up visit is due to a deficiency cited in the regulations outlined in the Food, Drug, and Cosmetic Act. The fee is intended to cover costs incurred for ensuring that corrective actions have been implemented, and that the firm is in compliance on deficiencies found during a previous inspection. Time spent directly on re-inspection activities is also subject to fees, including compliance re-inspection at the facility, time spent making preparations and arrangements for the re-inspection, travel to and from the facility, analysis of records, analysis of samples, preparation of reports or examining labels, and performance of other activities found necessary to determine compliance of violation found during the initial inspection. FDA recognizes this may be a burden on some small businesses and has proposed guidelines for requesting reduced fees in certain cases.

Registration

All food companies must register with the FDA biannually, between October 1 and December 31 of each even-numbered year. The renewal process has been streamlined, with an expedited form for companies without changes since the previous registration.

United States Government Publishing Office. 2015. Electronic Code of Federal Regulations. Title 21 Part 117. Available from: http://www.ecfr.gov/cgi-bin/text-idx?SID=e9ca025764f8adff02bc93a2655d8450&mc=true&node=pt21.2.117&rgn=div5. Accessed August 2016.

HEALTH SAFEGUARDS

The U.S. government has created safeguards to reduce the possibility that adulterated food will be consumed. A food is considered adulterated if it "contains any poisonous or deleterious substance which may render it injurious to health" (US Code Title 21, Ch 9, section 342 (a)).

Food additives, which were described in Chapter 6, must be approved by the FDA prior to being introduced into a product. By definition, food additives are "any substance the intended use of which results or may reasonably be expected to result—directly or indirectly—in its becoming a component or otherwise affecting the characteristics of any food." Additives can be classified as generally recognized as safe (GRAS) or approved. Generally recognized as safe substances have been certified as safe either through scientific findings or through use before 1958. Other approved food additives can be used directly or indirectly with specific limitations. Food scientists and product developers have to read and understand regulations prior to finalizing formulas for new products, including the addition of vitamins and minerals.

Synthetic colorants must be made from approved batches tested and certified by the FDA (U.S. Food and Drug Administration 2007). These synthetic colorants are easy to pick out on an ingredient statement as there are only a few: FD&C Blue Nos. 1 and 2, FD&C Green No. 3,

FD&C Red Nos. 3 and 40, FD&C Yellow Nos. 5 and 6, Orange B, and Citrus Red No. 2. Naturally derived color additives do not require certification and can be added as detailed in 21 CFR 73 Listing of Color Additives Exempt from Certification. Examples of naturally derived colors are caramel color, grape skin extract, annatto extract, and dehydrated beets.

Foods can also be deemed as adulterated if they contain pesticide residues that are above the permitted levels or not authorized by EPA. The EPA sets the maximum levels or "tolerances," but these levels are enforced by a food agency. The USDA enforces meat, poultry, and eggs, whereas the FDA implements the limits on other foods. Tolerances set by the EPA are published in the Federal Register and later added to Title 40 of the CFR. Food packaging also is required to be made of approved materials. Packaging materials, for example, cannot include elements that will migrate or leach harmful chemicals into products.

Mandatory Food Safety Plans

The Food Safety Modernization Act mandates companies to determine hazardous functions in their business and spell out preventative measures. The hazard analysis should identify points in processing where products are likely to be contaminated. For each point of potential contamination, companies are required to implement preventative measures to help ensure their product is wholesome and unadulterated. This system is a modified version of the hazard analysis critical control points (HACCP) system, which is mandatory for meat, poultry, seafood, and juice producers. HACCP plans are configured for each product a plant produces, taking into consideration the chemical, biological, and physical hazards that could threaten the safety of the item. Hazards likely to occur in an operation are identified and controlled through processing standards and recorded. More about HACCP and Food Safety Plans will be covered in Chapter 19.

ECONOMIC SAFEGUARDS

Damaged foods may not be disguised as wholesome through coloring or flavoring. Food labels and labeling must not mislead the consumer. Misleading consumers can range from listing erroneous health benefits on the packaging, not providing the amount of product that is listed on the package, or using undeclared ingredients in the product. Food should be labeled using a common name that consumers can understand. The regulations set by the US government are in place to protect the economic interests of consumers and set a level playing field for producers.

Nutrition Labeling

To achieve national uniformity in labeling of food products, the U.S. Congress and FDA took action in 1990, which resulted in the Nutrition Labeling Education Act (NLEA). The act is designed to provide consumers with sufficient information to make informed decisions about their diet and to give food processors the incentive to improve the nutritional quality of their products (21 CFR 101.9). The NLEA preempts any existing state regulations and also authorizes states to take action in the federal courts to enforce the labeling law.

In May 2016, the most sweeping changes to the nutrition labeling regulations in over two decades were announced as finalized. The FDA initially announced their proposals to initiate modifications to the nutrition facts panels in 2014, and issued a supplementary rule in 2015. The FDA's new labels feature what they deem an updated design to highlight calories and servings, two important elements in making informed food choices. Mandated compliance with the new nutrition facts panels is required by July 26, 2018 for most food manufacturers, while those with less than $10 million in annual food sales will have an additional year to comply.

The law requires that labeling information be prominently displayed on the package in common terms that most consumers can understand. Required labeling information includes the size of font, type of font, location, and other information, which is detailed in 21 CFR 101.

Packaged food must have the name, street address, city, state and zip code of the manufacturer, packer, or distributor. The net amount of food in the package must be declared on the front panel of the food packaging in the English system and US gallons, but the metric system may also be used in addition to the English units. The common name of the food should be listed on the front of the package. For example, if a new dairy drink product developed by your company is named "Moo Moo Guzzler," then you would have to list that it is a chocolate flavored dairy drink. The ingredients of the food must also be listed by their common names in order of weight on the packaging. Further information about food labeling can be found in Chapter 16.

Exemptions to Mandatory Nutrition Labeling

Foods that have added vitamins or minerals or make claims about nutritional quality must have a nutrition facts panel displayed on the package. However, many food products are exempt from providing nutrition information, including foods manufactured by small processors with fewer than 200 employees and fewer than 200,000 units sold. Businesses must file an exemption notice with the FDA and claim a small business exemption based on the number of employees and units of products. No exemption is allowed for a company that has more than the required number of full-time employees, regardless of the number of units sold. Exemptions for certain food types are also made; these are covered in Chapter 16.

Sanitation

According to the FD&C Act, foods should not be exposed to unsanitary conditions that have the potential to contaminate the product. Food must be free of filth—rat, mouse and other animal hairs or excretions, whole insects, insect parts, or other materials of animal origin (Nelson-Stafford 1991). Foods also have the potential to be contaminated during transit, making collaboration with transportation carriers essential. As mentioned earlier in this chapter, the FDA sets tolerance levels on filth for foods, which can be found in the Defect Levels Handbook.

To outline the requirements needed to maintain a sanitary operation, the FDA published the Current Good Manufacturing Practice (cGMP) Regulations. These cGMP regulations detail expectations for personnel (21 CFR 110.10), plants and grounds (21 CFR 110.20), sanitary operations (21 CFR 110.35), sanitary facilities and controls (21 CFR 110.37), equipment and utensils (21 CFR 110.40), processes and controls (21 CFR 110.80), and warehousing and distribution (21 CFR 110.93).

Food Standards

Food standards have been created in the interest of both consumers and the food industry. "Standards of identity" define the types of food that can use a specific name, the ingredients that are allowed, and in some cases, the physical attributes that must be displayed. The goal in establishing standards of identity is to create a uniform guideline for certain foods, so that foods with the same name are similar in form.

Applesauce, for example, has a standard of identity stipulating that it should be a product "prepared from comminuted or chopped apples, which may or may not be peeled and cored, and which may have...one or more of the optional ingredients" (21 CFR 145.110). Optional ingredients that may be added are limited to water, apple juice, salt, organic

TABLE 10.3. Grading Standards for Dairy as given by USDA AMS.

Grade	Standards	Examples of Grading Symbols
AA, A, B, C	Official USDA grades for dairy products, such as U.S. Grade AA for butter and cheddar cheese, are based on nationally uniform standards of quality developed by the Standardization Branch. Grading standards vary with the product being graded, e.g., butter only has grades AA, A, and B, while cheddar cheese has all of the respective grades, plus C; Swiss and Ementaller cheese just use grades A, B, and C.	USDA U.S. GRADE AA WHEN GRADED PACKED UNDER INSPECTION OF THE U.S. DEPT. OF AGRICULTURE OFFICIALLY GRADED
Extra Grade or Standard Grade	These standards promote uniformity in Federal grading services and are sometimes used by dairy plants in their quality control programs. The official USDA grade shield indicates the product's quality level by use of letters such as AA, and A, or in this case the words "extra" and "standard." Examples of products graded with this system are cottage cheese, instant nonfat dry milk, and dry whole milk. As with the AA grading system, each product has a different grading system based on uniform standards.	USDA U.S. EXTRA GRADE PROCCESSED AND PACKED UNDER INSPECTION OF THE U.S. DEPT. OF AGRICULTURE
Quality Approved	Product specifications measure quality by establishing minimum acceptable requirements for dairy products not covered by an official grade standard. Specifications are a guide to quality for consumers, are routinely referenced in government procurement documents, and form a basis for trade across the United States. The official USDA quality approved shield can be applied to packages of dairy products meeting the requirements of a specification.	USDA QUALITY APPROVED U.S. DEPT. OF AGRICULTURE GRADING AND QUALITY CONTROL SERVICE OFFICIALLY INSPECTED

Source: Based on information from the USDA AMS Grading, Certification, and Verification website, which is located at: www.ams.usda.gov.

acids for acidification, nutritive carbohydrate sweeteners, spices, natural or artificial flavors, color additives to characterize (but not conceal damage) to food and erythorbic acid or ascorbic acid as an antioxidant preservative in an amount not to exceed 150 parts per million or ascorbic acid (vitamin C) in a quantity such that the total vitamin C in each 113 g (4 ounces) by weight of the finished food amounts to 60 mg. No other ingredients may be added to applesauce or it will be disqualified from using the name "applesauce." Products that do not meet this standard may be called by any other identifying name that implies the product is similar to applesauce—like "cooked apple slices." Meat product standards of identity are found in 9 CFR.

Fill of container standards give direction to companies on how far a container should be filled and how to measure this. Methods for determining the fill requirements for solid and liquid foods are given in 21 CFR. For example, shelled nuts sold in rigid containers should have a fill of 85 percent according to 21 CFR 164.120. Methods for determining what an 85 percent fill are detailed in the previously mentioned section of the CFR.

"Standards of quality," defined by the FD&C Act, stipulate minimum standards for the quality of certain products, in order for them to be sold. "Standards for grades" are different from standards of quality, because they offer quality determinations based on a scale. Voluntary grading is done by the USDA AMS. Quality standards were developed using measurable attributes that aim to describe the value of a product. Beef quality standards, for example, are based on marbling, color, firmness, and texture of a beef cut, as well as the age of the source animal. Standards for each product are outlined by the USDA AMS using their quality standards for grading (available at www.ams.usda.gov). There are eight grades for beef and three grades each for chickens, eggs, and turkeys. Standards for fruits, vegetables, nuts, and other specialty products add up to more than 312 standards. Eggs, for example, are graded AA, A, and B for their respective quality as well as size. Dairy grading symbols and classifications can be seen in Table 10.3.

Canned Goods

As mentioned previously, low-acid canned foods and acidified foods have special regulations due to their risk of harboring potentially harmful bacteria or toxins, especially *Clostridium botulinum*. The specifications for low acid and acidified foods are shown in Table 10.4.

TABLE 10.4. Classifications of Foods as Defined in 21 CFR 114.

Classifications of Hermetically Sealed Canned Goods	Specifications	
	pH	a_w
Low-Acid Foods	above 4.6	above 0.85
Acidified Foods	less than 4.6*	above 0.85
Acid Foods	less than 4.6	above 0.85
Water Activity Controlled Foods	Not considered	below 0.85

*pH is only less than 4.6 after an acidifying agent or acid food is added.

Low-acid foods are heat processed foods with pH > 4.6 and a_w > 0.85. Tomatoes or tomato products with a pH of less than 4.7 are not considered low-acid foods. Acidified foods are low-acid foods to which acidifying agents or acid foods have been added, in order to bring the pH < 4.6 (and a_w > 0.85.) Producers of low-acid and acidified foods must file a scheduled process for each product being manufactured. A "scheduled process" is a detailed form describing the processing method chosen for a given food that is designed to achieve and maintain an end-product that will not promote the growth of microorganisms. Information for filing a scheduled process is located on the FDA website: www.fda.gov.

DIETARY SUPPLEMENTS

A Dietary Supplement is an item meant for consumption that contains a "dietary ingredient" intended to supply added nutritional value to enhance the diet. A dietary ingredient is one or a combination of minerals, vitamins, herbs or other botanical substance, amino acids, concentrates, extracts enzymes, or probiota. Dietary supplements are consumed to aid in reducing risk of illness or long-term disease by increasing absorption of the essential nutrients found in dietary ingredients. Powders, liquids, capsules, tablets, or softgels are often the forms in which dietary supplements are produced for intake. Trendy classes of dietary supplements include products for weight control/loss, fat burners, appetite suppressants, muscle building, anabolic products, pre-workout and post-workout formulas, thermogenics, health maintenance and general well-being, multivitamins, immunity boosters, joint care, and nervous system/mood boosters.

An easy way to differentiate dietary supplements from conventional foods is that dietary supplement packaging must display a "Supplement

Case Study: Genetically Modified Ingredient Labeling in the EU

U.S. food companies that wish to export to the European Union (EU) must test their raw materials to ensure that no genetic modification has taken place. Proper raw material testing for certification against GM commodities is required because products in the EU must be labeled if they contain GM products (Fagan 1999). The United States and the EU agencies have drastically different opinions on how GM products should be handled. Some grocery chains in the United States are also pushing for GM labeling on products although the US government. What effect might this have if you are hoping to sell your product in this large chain? How would you label your product to tell customers that the product does not use GM ingredients?

How might the label "GMO free" be misleading?

What are the disadvantages to GM products? What are the advantages?

How do you feel about the use of biotechnology and GM ingredients?

Facts" panel, just as conventional food packaging must display a "Nutrition Facts" panel. Dietary supplements are NOT to be used as, or in place of, conventional food items or meals. It is essential that dietary supplements are labeled as such and only used in a way that complements the (conventional) diet.

REGULATIONS FOR DIETARY SUPPLEMENTS

Dietary ingredients and complete dietary supplement products are regulated by the FDA just as conventional foods are. However, dietary supplements are not conventional foods or "drug products," which means that they are regulated under the Dietary Supplement Health and Education Act of 1994 (DSHEA). Companies are responsible for proper labeling and for preventing misbranded or unsafe products from reaching the market, as well as certifying that those supplements or supplement ingredients are compliant with FDA and DSHEA regulations. FDA will then take action in the event a supplement or supplement ingredient is not compliant after it reaches the market.

As with other food products, five separate statements are mandated to appear on the label of dietary supplements and dietary supplement ingredient packaging. The statement of identity and the net quantity of contents statement must be printed on the principal display panel. The information panel should show the nutrition label, ingredient list, and name and place of business, of manufacturer, packer, or distributor. If space on the label is inadequate, there are special provisions on the "Supplement Facts" panel in 21 CFR 101.36(i)(2)(iii) and (i)(5).

21 CFR 101.3(a), 21 CFR 101.105(a), 21 CFR 101.36, 21 CFR 101.4(a)(1), and 21 CFR 101.5 and 21 CFR 101.2(b) and (d), 101.36(i)(2)(iii) and (i)(5), 101.5, 101.9(j)(13)(i)(A) and (j)(17)

The following are guidelines for creating a "Supplement Facts" panel from cited CFR sections:

- Dietary ingredients without DRVs and RDIs must be listed in the "Supplement Facts" panel on dietary supplement products.
- A producer can choose to share the source of a dietary ingredient on the "Supplement Facts" on a supplement panel.
- A producer is not mandated to disclose the source of a dietary ingredient in the ingredient statement for a dietary supplement in the event that it has already been listed on the "Supplement Facts" panel.
- A producer is mandated to disclose, on the panel of dietary supplements, the specific portion of a plant from which a dietary ingredient is taken from, in the "Supplement Facts".
- A producer may not list "zero" as an amount of nutrients in the "Supplement Facts" panel of dietary supplements.

21 CFR 101.36(b)(3) and (b)(2)(i), 21 CFR 101.4(h), 21 CFR 101.36(d) and (d)(1), and 21 CFR 101.9

- A producer must disclose names and quantities of the dietary ingredients comprising the dietary supplement in the "Supplement Facts" panel.

A producer must disclose the "Serving Size" and "Servings Per Container." In the event that "Servings Per Container" is the same net quantity as the contents, it is not required. 21 CFR 101.36(b)

- When present in measurable amounts, the following must be listed: total calories, calories from fat, total fat, saturated fat, transfat, cholesterol, sodium, total carbohydrate, dietary fiber, sugars, protein, vitamin A, vitamin C, calcium, and iron. If a claim is made about calories from saturated fat, the amount of polyunsaturated fat, monounsaturated fat, soluble fiber, insoluble fiber, sugar alcohol, or other carbohydrates must be declared.

21 CFR 101.36(b)(2)(i) (see 68 FR 41434 at 41505, July 11, 3003)

Ingredients

Dietary supplements and ingredients for dietary supplements do not require approval or pre-approval from the FDA before manufacture; they are reviewed by FDA only for safety, not effectiveness. It is the sole responsibility of a given company to produce a safe, quality product according to current labeling regulations and Good Manufacturing Practices. Should a dietary supplement be formulated using a new ingredient, the company is required to inform the FDA of the change and provide evidence that the ingredient is expected to be safe. The FDA will then review and either approve/not approve the ingredient. If the ingredient is GRAS, it does not need this approval.

Supplement Claims

There are three types of claims ordinarily stated on the labels of dietary supplements. They are structure/function claims, claims in relation to disease caused by nutrient deficiency, and general well-being claims. None of these claims are preapproved by the FDA. Therefore, should a dietary supplement label have this sort of claim, there must also be a "disclaimer" stating that the FDA has not evaluated the aforementioned claim. The "disclaimer" must further state that the stated dietary supplement or substance should not be expected to "diagnose, treat, cure or prevent any disease." Legally, only a medical drug may make such a claim. Marketing dietary supplements showing such claims is not permitted without providing the FDA with information regarding the honesty of the claim within 30 days of marketing the item. Claims regarding disease in relation to nutrient deficiency are allowed only if they also state the prevalence of the disease in the population of the United States.

GLOBAL

When products are created with the intent to sell beyond U.S. national borders, product developers need to be aware of international standards and regulations, as well as differences in taste preferences and consumer trends.

Importing Foods into the US

Companies importing food into the U.S. must follow all regulations of the U.S. government and meet all standards that domestic companies do. All imported food is considered interstate commerce, and is therefore subject to labeling and sanitary requirements. The FDA has no jurisdiction over the importing companies, but may reject a food if it does not comply with U.S. regulations. With the Food Safety Modernization Act signed in 2011, new requirements on importers called Foreign Supplier Verification Programs (FSVP) are required. Importers can import foods into the United States as long as the facilities that produce, store, or otherwise handle the products are registered with FDA, present prior notice of incoming shipments, and meet FSVP requirements. FSVP's tasks are to determine foreseeable hazards, evaluate risk through a hazard analysis, perform evaluations in order to approve suppliers, and conduct supplier verification activities including corrective actions. Importers are required to develop, maintain, and follow an FSVP for each food brought into the United States and the foreign supplier of that food. Imported food products are subject to FDA inspection when presented at U.S. ports of entry.

As a part of the Public Health Security and Bioterrorism Preparedness and Response Act of 2002 (the Bioterrorism Act), importing companies must register with the FDA and give prior notice of shipments. Having notice allows the FDA and border control agents to most effectively conduct inspections and protect the country against potential threats to the U.S. food supply.

Exporting Food From the US

Exporting food to other countries requires a knowledge of international importation policies, specifically the regulations that govern the product being exported to a specific country. The FDA will provide export certificates for food governed by them to indicate a specific product is marketed and sold in the U.S., meets all standards, and is eligible for export. The USDA operates the Foreign Agriculture Service (FAS), which works to expand and maintain access to foreign markets for U.S. agricultural products by removing trade barriers and enforcing U.S.

rights under existing trade agreements (U.S. Department of Agriculture Foreign Agriculture Service, 2012). Some countries require export certificates from the originating country. The Codex Alimentarius ("food code" in Latin) are open-ended rules that aim to "harmonize standards" for international trading (Walston 1992). The regulations are adjusted based upon recommendations of committees for various commodities. Product developers for foods that are or could be shipped internationally must at least meet Codex Alimentarius standards. It may also be important to recognize the religious and cultural background of purchasers of a product outside the U.S. For example, if your product is being exported to a predominantly Muslim region, the product may need to be certified by a specific agency to be considered halal. Foreign sourcing of raw materials requires research. Identifying non-U.S. buyers for food product ingredients can be a challenge, but trade shows, trade groups, and organizations are helpful in connecting buyers with sellers.

SUMMARY

From the outset of a project, developers must research and understand regulations that do and could govern a potential food product. These can cover almost any aspect of a food, from ingredient origins to special additives. Such knowledge increases the probability the final product will meet or exceed all legal guidelines, while overlooking such rules will add extra costs and postponements.

KEY WORDS

Fill of Container—standards that give direction to companies on how far a container should be filled and how to measure this. Methods for determining the fill requirements for solid and liquid foods are given in 21 CFR.

Food, Drug, and Cosmetic Act of 1938—regulates food products that are imported, exported, or cross state lines. The Food, Drug, and Cosmetic Act (FD&C Act) of 1938 prohibits the sale of adulterated and misbranded food in the entire food supply chain.

Food Safety Modernization Act—was signed into law on January 4, 2011. The FSMA aims to promote safety in the food supply, outlines the FDA's enforcement rights, and defines timing of inspections, and changed recordkeeping procedures, fees and company registration requirements.

Product recall—a recall is issued by a company in order to take a product off the market due to safety risks to the consumer.

Seizure—when repeated violations have occurred, insanitary conditions are found, and the health of the public may be in danger, products are taken and held, (i.e., seized, until further notice or proof of safety).

Scheduled process—a detailed form describing the processing method chosen for a food in order to achieve and maintain a food that will not promote the growth of microorganisms. The scheduled process also dictates controls for pH and other factors that discourage bacterial growth.

Standards for Grade—provide quality determinations based on a scale; these are different from standards of quality because they calibrate quality in terms of a scale.

Standards of Quality—minimum standards of quality a given product must meet in order for it to be sold commercially.

COMPREHENSION QUESTIONS

10.1. What agency under the USDA is responsible for inspecting meat and poultry products? Spell out the full name.

10.2. What is the maximum allowable fat content for ground beef? (*Hint*: Found in 9 CFR.)

10.3. Answer True or False to the following questions.

a. The FDA is responsible for inspecting egg processing facilities.
b. Regulations regarding food additives are the same for all countries.
c. Trans fat labeling is required.

10.4. The Pasteurized Milk Ordinance calls for raw milk to have which of the following standards regarding:

a. Temperature.
b. Bacterial limits.
c. Drugs.
d. Somatic cell count.

10.5. Name the official USDA grades for fruits and vegetables.

10.6. What changes did the Food Safety Modernization Act introduce into food regulations?

REFERENCES

Bauman, H. E. "Safety and Regulatory Aspects." In *Food Product Development From Concept to Marketplace*, E. Graf and I. S. Saguy, eds. (New York: Van Nostrand Reinhold, 1991), 133–144.

Fagan, J. "GM Food Labeling." *Nature Biotechnology 17*, no. 9 (1999):836.

How Safe are Color Additives? (Silver Spring, MD: U.S. Food and Drug Administration, 2007).

Nelson-Stafford, B. *From Kitchen to Consumer: The Entrepreneur's Guide to Commercial Food Production*. (San Diego, CA: Academic Press, 1991).

Nielsen, S. S., ed. "U.S. Government Regulations and International Standards." In *Food Analysis*, 2nd ed. Gaithersburg, Maryland: Aspen Publishers, Inc., 1998), 17–38.

"The Regulation to Phase Out Artificial Trans Fat in New York City Food Establishments," No. HPD1X25551. (New York: The New York City Department of Health and Mental Hygiene, 2006).

U.S. Department of Agriculture Foreign Agriculture Service (2012).

Walston, J. "C.O.D.E.X. Spells Controversy." *Journal Name 24*, (1992): 28–32.

CHAPTER 11

Packaging

> **Learning Objectives**
>
> - The purpose and functions of packaging.
> - Packaging materials commonly used in foods.
> - Active packaging applications.

PACKAGING acts as a barrier to protect food and is an important factor in the shelf-life, quality preservation, and marketing of many products. Packaging and labeling communicate the nutritional quality, name of the manufacturer, and health benefits and can act as a dispersing and dispensing unit. As such, packaging must be conceived and designed at the same time as the product it will accompany.

The functions of packaging are to contain, protect, preserve, distribute, identify, and provide convenience for consumers (Mauer and Ozen 2004). Packaging is a relatively low-cost way of protecting products from damages that can be incurred during shipping. Packaging also sends a message about what sort of product is within its walls. If a product created by a company is meant to be sold at a premium, but the packaging doesn't appear premium, consumers that have never purchased the product may pass it by for a more visually appealing product. During the development phases, potential packaging designs should be evaluated by consumers to test concept and compatibility with the product.

LEVELS OF PACKAGING

When you buy cookies at a grocery store, the cookie (food) is usually packaged inside a plastic tray or bag within a box or outer wrapper. The plastic tray or bag is referred to as the primary packaging, whereas the outer box or wrapper is referred to as the secondary packaging. Primary and secondary packaging are usually visible to retail consumers. When products are delivered to a store, they are packed in bigger boxes, which form distribution or tertiary packaging. Examples include corrugated boxes packed full, both to protect the product and to ease handling during transit and at the store. At plants, tertiary/distribution cartons may be stacked on a pallet. The pallet is referred to as the unit load or quaternary package. Figure 11.1 demonstrates how this might work with a

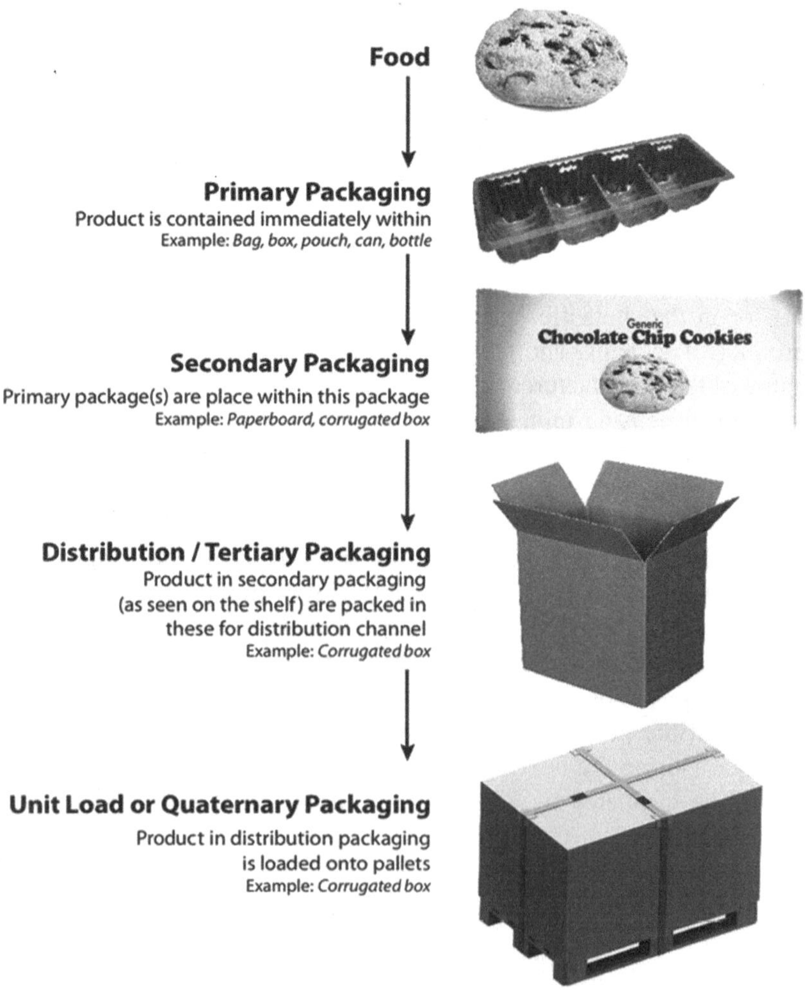
Food
Primary Packaging
Product is contained immediately within
Example: Bag, box, pouch, can, bottle
Generic
Chocolate Chip Cookies
Secondary Packaging
Primary package(s) are place within this package
Example: Paperboard, corrugated box
Distribution / Tertiary Packaging
Product in secondary packaging
(as seen on the shelf) are packed in
these for distribution channel
Example: Corrugated box
Unit Load or Quaternary Packaging
Product in distribution packaging
is loaded onto pallets
Example: Corrugated box

FIGURE 11.1. Demonstration of the levels of packaging for a cookie product.

cookie product that is packed in a plastic tray, which in turn has an outer wrapper packed in a bigger box.

STEPS TO DETERMINING PACKAGING

Step 1. Define Food Properties

In order to determine what packaging should be used, first consider the type of product you are planning to produce. The properties of the product, as well as regulations affecting it, will dictate packaging materials and design. This leads to questions. Is the product a solid, liquid, or gas? Is the liquid thin with good flow properties or thick? Is the product a powder? How large is it? The type of packaging will differ for products with variable flow properties or physical form. If the product is meant to be distributed frozen, what packaging is required? Is the product's shelf-life short? Does the product mold easily? Is the product highly acidic? Taking all of the product's properties into account, including ones that might change, is necessary to select the packaging material that is most fit.

The Food and Drug Administration (FDA) has specific "Definitions of Food Types and Conditions of Use for Food Contact Substances." These are divided into 2 groups; the first deals with food type (Table 11.1), and the second deals with the use conditions (Table 11.2).

Step 2. Define Package Technical and Functional Requirements

The developer must outline and list the properties and functions of the package, both in itself and in relation to the product. It is necessary to spell out what the packaging should be and how it is supposed to function. At this stage, an important consideration is the radius of distribution. A product susceptible to breakage by vibration or drops will incur significantly less damage when distributed in a 100-mile radius than it will with nationwide distribution. The way that individual packages are boxed and palletized can help eliminate some damage.

Step 3. Define Package Marketing and Design Requirements

Packaging communicates to consumers, and the package itself is a marketing tool. More sophisticated designs may require special packaging materials; therefore, packaging engineers should be involved in

TABLE 11.1. Types of Raw and Processed Foods.

Categories of Foods for Packaging
Non-acid, aqueous products; may contain salt, sugar, or both (pH above 5.0)
Acid, aqueous products; may contain salt, sugar, or both, and include oil-in-water emulsions of low- or high-fat content
Dairy products and modifications: Water-in-oil emulsions, high- or low-fat Oil-in-water emulsions, high- or low-fat
Nonacid, aqueous products; may contain salt, sugar, or both (pH above 5.0)
Aqueous, acid or non-acid products containing free oil or fat; may contain salt and include water-in-oil emulsions of low- or high-fat content
Low-moisture fats and oil
Beverages: Containing up to 8% alcohol Non-alcoholic Containing more than 8 % alcohol
Bakery products: Moist bakery products with surface containing free fat or oil Moist bakery products with surface containing no free fat or oil
Dry solids with the surface containing no free fat or oil (no end test required)
Dry solids with the surface containing free fat or oil

Source: http://www.fda.gov/Food/FoodIngredientsPackaging/FoodContactSubstancesFCS/ucm109358.htm

discussing the design, shape, and any special functions that are desired for the product's presentation. Another important consideration is the shelf display requirements for grocers. Will the package be displayed by a hanger, as some candies are? Will the product's package contain special features, such as easy-open or resealable closures? It may also be important to consider whether packaging materials can be recycled.

Step 4. Identify Legal and Regulatory Requirements

Legal restrictions can include regulations for the use of certain packaging materials or infringement of patented technologies. Like food additives, all packaging materials must secure approval by the FDA. Other considerations include religious restrictions, such as kosher packaging stipulations for Jewish customers.

Food additives that come into contact with food as part of packaging are considered "indirect food additives." They are regulated, as mentioned, in Title 21 of the U.S. Code of Federal Regulations (21 CFR) and include adhesives and components of coatings (Part 175), paper and paperboard components (Part 176), polymers (Part 177), and adju-

Case Study: Right-sizing a Package

When companies are thinking about what package sizes they should distribute, they must consider who potential customers will be. How often do you see family-size bags of prunes? Probably not very often, because prunes are generally thought to be sold to people from an older demographic. In addition, the numbers within an average family in the United States have been shrinking, which companies must also consider. Today's families may not need a mega jumbo sized jar of jam. Because of this trend, plus one that favors convenience, package sizes are moving toward smaller or individual packaging schemes or limited-calorie packages.

vants and production aids (Part 178). Additional indirect food additives are authorized through the food contact notification program and some may be authorized through 21 CFR 170.39. The FDA also maintains an "Inventory of Effective Food Contact Substance (FCS) Notifications." "The database lists effective premarket notifications for food contact substances that have been demonstrated to be safe for their intended use. The list includes the food contact substance (FCS), the notifier, the manufacturer of the FCS, the intended use, the limitations on the conditions of use for the FCS and its specifications, the effective date, and its environmental decision." http://www.fda.gov/Food/FoodIngredientsPackaging/ucm112642.htm

TABLE 11.2. Parameters that Affect the Packaging Materials Used.

Condition of Use for Packaging
Boiling water sterilized
Hot filled or pasteurized above 150°F
Hot filled or pasteurized below 150°F
Room temperature filled and stored (no thermal treatment in the container)
Refrigerated storage (no thermal treatment in the container)
Frozen storage (no thermal treatment in the container)
Frozen or refrigerated storage: Ready-prepared foods intended to be reheated in container at time of use: Aqueous or oil-in-water emulsion of high- or low-fat Aqueous, high- or low-free oil or fat
Irradiation
Cooking at temperatures exceeding 250°F

Source: http://www.fda.gov/Food/FoodIngredientsPackaging/FoodContactSubstancesFCS/ucm109358.html

Step 5. Select Potential Package Design and Materials

Designs for packages must meet all marketing, design, safety, and functional requirements. Materials will be chosen per the specifications of the design and the dictates of regulation. Packaging costs will be estimated at this step. Mock-ups can be made at this point and consumer preferences surveyed and measured.

Step 6. Establish Feasibility of Packaging with Equipment and Material

The packaging engineer should obtain sample packaging materials to determine whether a selected packaging material will function on the equipment in place. In such tests, the food should be in contact with the packaging material, to determine whether the packaging will change the product's properties and if it is able to provide for the minimum shelf-life requirements.

Step 7. Estimate Time and Cost Constraints

Will the cost of packaging be recouped by product purchases at various price points? Can any packaging cost be cut? Important factors in this phase are to schedule when the packaging materials will be needed and when they can be supplied.

Step 8. Shelf-life Testing and Market Testing

In products with extended shelf-life, it is critical to determine potential weaknesses in the packaging and to ensure it will hold up for the product's entire life. Consumers' input is valuable to establish their preference prior to moving forward with a certain design. The shelf-life and safety of the product need to be established prior to consumer testing. When the product design is well accepted by consumers and meets company specifications, the packaging and product can go into full production.

PACKAGING MATERIALS

Paper and Paperboard

Paper and paperboard are widely used for packaging. Paper and paperboard products include corrugated boxes and shipping boxes. Flour and sugar are sometimes packaged only in a paper wrapping. Benefits of paper are its low cost and light weight (Mauer and Ozen 2004). Ready-to-eat cereals, many snack products, cake mixes, and other foods are packaged in paperboard boxes. Because paper does not have many protective qualities, foods are often packed in a sealed plastic bag inside a paper box.

Paper can also be used for pouches of product that is not excessively moist.

Disadvantages of paper packaging are that it is less resistant to pests and is poor at blocking moisture and gas (Mauer and Ozen 2004). Paper expands and contracts with its environment and is easily distended. Uncoated paperboard will absorb grease and moisture and, therefore, should not be used for fatty and water-based products.

Metal

Metal is commonly used for canned foods and drinks and in metalized films for lining plastic. The four metals used in the food industry are steel, aluminum, tin, and chromium.

When using tin and steel, a layer of oil is usually added to reduce the risks of corrosion (Mauer and Ozen 2004). Steel is generally cheaper than tin.

FIGURE 11.2. Example of a 3 piece can.

FIGURE 11.3. Example of a 3 piece can.

The most common types of metal food packaging include three-piece cans, two-piece cans, and foil pouches. Three-piece cans are formed from a tinplate or steel cylinder (with a side seam) and two end pieces. The end pieces are curled and welded together to create a uniform container. Usually the body of the can has ridges to help increase strength and reduce the risk of collapse from impact or crushing (Mauer and Ozen 2004).

Two-piece cans are made from aluminum or steel with a single end piece. These cans are most familiar as the container for carbonated beverages. One advantage of aluminum is that it can be rolled very thin. Generally, the inside surfaces of metal cans are coated to prevent corrosion. This is sometimes done with bisphenol-A (BPA).

Aseptic boxes (for beverages) and pouches use metallic foils on the inside to protect the product. Metal foils provide a moisture, gas, and light barrier. Metalized films are also used in the packaging of snack products, such as granola bars, chips, and coffee. These can be vacuum sealed, as commonly seen in coffee packaging.

Metal is stable under thermal heating conditions and exhibits superior barrier properties. Metal is also recyclable and has high consumer acceptance.

Products commonly found in metal packaging are soups, nuts, canned fruits and vegetables, canned meats, and thermally processed, shelf-stable foods (Mauer and Ozen 2004) .

Glass

Glass is a good packaging material for many foods because it is non-reactive, meaning it does not leech chemicals into the product. Glass also enables the customer to see the product. Colored glass can be used for products that are light sensitive. Soda-lime glass is the most common glass for food packaging (Mauer and Ozen 2004). Disadvantages of glass include the risk of breakage and heavy weight, which contribute to higher distribution costs.

Plastics

Plastics are attractive as packaging material, because their components, polymers, can be custom formulated for a given product and also combined to take advantage of the chemical and mechanical properties of individual polymers. Plastics do not weigh very much, making them better suited for distribution. Plastics also do not break easily like glass. Plastic packages can be made with convenient attributes for consumers, such as resealability and flexibility, as in squeeze bottles. Plastics can be made opaque, which can help reduce deterioration caused by light. The food industry has come to depend on plastics to package and display many products. Product developers seeking to package a food in plastic should be familiar with the properties and nomenclature of plastics and polymers. In terms of potential uses, the important properties of plastic resins that should be learned and/or made available by a packaging supplier are as follows:

- Oxygen permeability (cc/100 $in^2 \times day \times atm$)
- Water vapor permeability (g/100 $in^2 \times day$)
- Resistance to acids, alkalis, and solvents
- Yield/thickness (m^2/kg: 1 mil)
- Tensile strength (kpsi)
- Elongation at break (%)
- Tear strength (gm/mil)
- Light transmission (%)
- Heat seal temperature and service temperature

Polyethylene

Polyethylene (PET) is the most widely used plastic for packaging.

Densities range from 0.89 g/cc to 0.96 g/cc. PET is preferred because of its light weight, inexpensiveness, impact resistance, and ease of fabrication. It also exhibits excellent water vapor and liquid containment properties, although it is not a good gas barrier, nor is it transparent.

Polypropylene

Polypropylene (PP) is a better barrier against water vapor than PET and is more transparent and stiffer. More difficult to fabricate than PET, PP is most commonly used for pouches and candy wrappers. It is heat resistant up to 133°C and, thus, can be used in microwaveable packaging.

OTHER PACKAGING TYPES

Aseptic Processing

As mentioned above, aseptic packaging has become a popular way to package soups, juices, and other liquid products. Aseptic processing produces a sterile product that is then filled into a sterile container in an enclosed and controlled environment. The processing temperatures for aseptic processing are usually very high, including an ultra-high temperature (UHT) process or a high temperature short time (HTST) method. Packaging materials and the product are sterilized separately. Aseptic processing reduces the effect of heat on the sensory properties of a product because of the short time it is exposed to elevated temperatures. Packaging is sterilized through heat, chemicals, or irradiation. Aseptic containers can be found in molded PET plastic or as boxes made from paper/paperboard, PET, and metalized foil.

Modified and Controlled Atmosphere Packaging

Modified atmosphere packaging (MAP) and controlled atmosphere packaging (CAP) change the atmosphere to which the food is exposed during its shelf-life. In MAP, the atmosphere is modified only at the time of packaging. In products with MAP, the gases inside the package are flushed out and replaced with a mixture of carbon dioxide, oxygen, and nitrogen. Vacuum technology is used to reduce the amount of air inside a package, thus prolonging sensory properties and the shelflife of products such as coffee. Controlled atmosphere packaging is used mostly for fresh produce. The storage atmosphere is controlled throughout transport via controlled release of compounds that keep the atmosphere at concentrations designed to be compatible with the product.

Active Packaging

Active packaging relies on inserts to control the environmental composition inside the packaging. Inserts include oxygen scavengers, ethylene scavengers, moisture regulators, and antimicrobial agents (Mauer and Ozen 2004). Oxygen scavengers absorb oxygen to prevent product deterioration due to the oxidation of lipids. Ethylene, a chemical that accelerates the ripening of fruit, can also be absorbed through scavengers. Ethylene scavengers are usually made from potassium permanganate, which creates acetate and ethanol through the oxidation of ethylene (Mauer and Ozen 2004). Moisture regulators are designed to reduce water activity and thus spoilage. Antimicrobial agents are released from packaging materials over time. Antimicrobials used in packaging include sorbates, benzoates, ethanol, and bacteriocins (Mauer and Ozen 2004) .

Issues and Concerns

When launching a new food product, food scientists should be aware of consumer trends and concerns with respect to packaging. These may include size, portability, ease of opening, color, environmental issues, migration of chemicals, and recyclability.

Case Study: Biodegradable Packaging Makes Noise

In an effort to cut down on waste in landfills, Frito Lay—the maker of SunChips—spent 3 years developing packaging that was biodegradable (Fournier and Avery 2011). The chip bags, though environmentally friendly, were very loud. The movement of the bag produced undesirable racket for the consumer; therefore the complaints rolled into the company. Because of these complaints, the company is back at the drawing board for biodegradable packaging and the product is back in less audible SunChip bags.

RECYCLED MATERIALS

Packaging materials from recycled glass and aluminum have already been established, whereas plastics continue to make progress in that area. Developers must be cautious in specifying recycled plastics. If recycled plastics are to be used to package a new food product, food scientists should check the "list of submissions for which FDA issued a favorable opinion on the suitability of a specific process for producing post-consumer recycled (PCR) plastic to be used in the manufacturing of food-contact articles." The list includes the date of a no objection letter (NOL) from the FDA, the company that made the request, the plastic material approved, and limitations on the conditions of use.

SUMMARY

Developers should treat product packaging with the same attention as the product itself, because similar design and regulatory requirements will guide the form, function, and materials selection of packaging. Additionally, the package must be seen as a vehicle to attract and instruct potential buyers. In practice, this will entail enlisting package engineers and marketers as part of the development team.

COMPREHENSION QUESTIONS

11.1. What are three roles of packaging?

11.2. Match the following foods to the packaging system used.

a. Pringles	_____ Aseptic
b. Juice box	_____ Vacuum
c. Hot dogs	_____ MAP

11.3. Describe the packaging for your product in terms of primary, secondary, and tertiary packaging.

11.4. Why would a product developer never describe a package only as plastic?

11.5. Define Controlled Atmosphere (CA) storage. What are common oxygen and carbon concentrations for both fruits and vegetables?

REFERENCES

Fournier, S., and J. Avery. "The Uninvited Brand." *Business Horizons 54*, no. 3 (2011):193–207.

Griffin, R. C., S. Sacharow, S., and A. L. Brody. *Principles of Package Development*. (Malabar, FL: Krieger Pub, 1993).

Jenkins, W.A., and J. P. Harrington. *Packaging Foods with Plastics*. (Lancaster, PA: Technomic Pub, 1991).

Mauer, L. J., and B. F. Ozen, B. F. "Food Packaging." In *Food Processing Principle and Applications*, J. S. Smith and Y. H. Hui, eds. (Ames, IA: Blackwell Publishing, 2004), 151162.

CHAPTER 12

Economic Feasibility Analysis

Learning Objectives

- How to determine if your new product idea is feasible.
- Understanding cost analysis.
- Understanding cash flows.

FIRMS engage in new product development to earn profits, which are realized when the expenses of production remain below revenue from sales. The expenses of production require cost analysis, which is essential in evaluating the potential profitability of a new product or venture. Product ideas must be examined for feasibility—from safety concerns to pricing analysis. The ability to translate an idea into a product that has an acceptable price range for the consumer is an absolute condition of success. Companies need to account for all costs as soon as they are realized. When actual figures are not available, estimated costs must be employed. Estimated average costs per unit are more reliable when as many empirically based actual costs are factored in.

To evaluate whether a profit is attainable, an economic understanding of total production cost is needed. Because profits from a new product are realized only when production costs are equal to or less than the price consumers are willing to pay, product developers must have a grasp of all production costs. Without this information, profitability cannot be assessed. Products entering the market will be competing with thousands of other food products. Ultimately, consumers decide which products survive via their purchasing decisions. Investment in a new product thus requires careful analysis of consumer purchasing patterns, with a stress on products competing in the same niche the developed product is designed to enter.

From concept to consumer, supplying a new food product involves many analytical steps. The first step is determining if consumers will buy sufficient quantities over an extended time period to justify investing in a processing plant. The second step is to develop an economic cost analysis to determine whether or not there will be a profit or loss in selling the product. This should be ascertained prior to beginning production. If there is a projected profit based on the best available information, then a business plan can be developed to continue with the product.

As mentioned, it is necessary to know that consumers will purchase the new product at a price equal to or greater than the cost to deliver it. It will also be beneficial to gather information defining the price range consumers will pay for the product and how this compares to the average cost to produce the product. Consumers choose which products they buy based on their needs, customs, income, and knowledge of alternative products. Price, as well as quality, plays a major role in the consumer's purchasing decision. Consumers have thousands of choices, but can actually buy and consume only a limited number of items per day, which means that many food products may not be purchased or may not be purchased in large quantities. Because consumers are the decision makers, managers must convince consumers to change their present preferences and to choose a new food product, by means of sophisticated marketing schemes and well-planned promotions. Consumers want to know that a new product is better than what they are currently buying and that they will be more satisfied with their purchase.

A cash flow analysis is necessary to estimate the total capital needs of the operation and how long operating capital will be needed until the product produces enough revenue to cover costs. Capital investments for buildings and equipment are normally needed to start a new business. However, it often takes as much operating capital as investment capital to build a processing facility and begin making products for sale. Internal capital investment continues up to, and even after, the product is sold. Cash from outside the business begins to flow only after consumers commence buying the new product.

NEW BUSINESS ANALYSIS

The goal of any business is to make a profit or a competitive return on investment. In order to estimate a profit per unit, managers need to understand how to analyze total annual costs and total income. To calculate these, all input costs and the amount of income from all products sold must be extracted from data or projected. Total input costs and projected revenues are needed for a detailed cost analysis.

Using cost analysis data, break-even costs and break-even volumes can be estimated. A break-even cost is the lowest price you can charge while covering production costs.

UNDERSTANDING COST ANALYSIS

All costs must be explicitly accounted for when completing a cost analysis. If they are not included, it is assumed that some other entity paid for them. Total costs (TC) are made up of two basic types, fixed and variable. Variable costs (VC) change during production periods, usually because of fluctuations in orders or changes in costs of inputs. Conversely, fixed costs (FC) do not change. For tax purposes, accountants and processing facilities generally use a period of one year for dividing fixed and variable costs. Financial records prepared by accountants should be consulted, if available, as they contain much of the information needed to do a cost analysis.

The estimation of production costs for cost analyses should be done before and after production has begun. In order to price products and manage costs, the most recent and empirically based costs should be used. When costs are estimated before actual production, it is imperative to input as realistic projections as possible. Actual cost figures can be introduced as they become available.

Profits can be defined as the amount of total revenue left after paying the total costs of production and marketing. Economic estimates should be done for a normal or average year and not just for the beginning of production. The fundamental formulas for a specific time period, usually one year, are as follows:

Total Returns	$TR = (Q \times Pm)$
Total Costs	$TC = FC + VC$
Profit	$P = TR - TC$
Breakeven	$TR = TC$ or $TR - TC = 0$
Cost per unit	$Pc = (TC/Q)$
Average market price	$Pm = (TR/Q)$
Break-even production	$Q = (TR/Pc)$

Where:

- (TR) = Total Revenues equals the sum of all sales received for one year priced at the door of the processing plant.
- (TC) = Total Costs equals the sum of all costs of production, management, and including an opportunity cost for one year.
- (P) = Profit equals the gross income left after all costs are paid. If this is zero, then the firm is at a break-even position but still should operate as all costs are being paid in addition to a return on investment that is acceptable to the investors.
- (Pc) = Average cost per unit.
- (Pm) = Average selling (market) price received per unit.
- (Q) = Total number units produced in one year.

These figures also coincide with an accounting year for tax purposes, and some of the same data can be used for both purposes. Some examples can be found in Table 12.1.

A spreadsheet can be set up for any type of cost analysis. Spreadsheets help analyze an investment by enabling one to visualize different profit outcomes that result from assuming and inputting many cost variables. To estimate profit, a manager needs to do a cost analysis for each new product before production is started and then make changes continuously after production has started. All cost analyses should use the latest and best information. This could be done daily, weekly, monthly, or annually, depending on the type of management decision being made. Consistent, accurate cost information is a necessary condition for calculating prices and, ultimately, profits.

TABLE 12.1. Costs of a Business.

Fixed Costs	Variable Costs	Production	Revenue
Depreciable: Equipment—Itemized Buildings	Labor wages: List per worker Labor Non-Wages: Social security, Worker's compensation	Units per day Units per year	Price per unit Units sold per year
Non-depreciable: Land, Building repairs, Property taxes, Insurance, Manager wages, Storage costs	Ingredients Packaging materials Equipment repairs Utilities Interest on loans	Inventory units stored	Shipping costs

TOTAL REVENUE

Total revenue (TR) is the income flow for one year to the food processor. Total revenue will depend on the price of goods and the number of new food items each consumer will buy. A goal of the business is to create repeat consumers who purchase the product more than once over a set period. Without repeat purchases, a new consumer must be found for each additional unit that's sold, which can result in lower profits, higher product prices, and increased outlays for promotion.

Demand for a specific food item tends to fluctuate with price. When there are multiple prices for a product, generally the higher prices will correlate with fewer units being sold. This assumes purchasers are aware of being able to buy a product at lower price. It also assumes that there are no changes in the price of similar product substitutes and that buyer income and tastes remain stable. Consumers have thousands of choices in retail markets and restaurants and are very much aware of lower "sale prices." Though not always rational, consumers expect to buy the most they can for the least cost to them.

Consumers can and will pay higher prices for unique products. Although uncommon in the food industry, distinctive food items appealing to a specific clientele can command a premium price. Examples are kosher or gluten-free food items. Consumers will buy unique or specialized products at a higher price if there is a positive and perceivable difference in quality. If the profit margin on such items is high, other entrepreneurs will likely mimic the product and enter the market with their own versions.

In the event processors need to increase TR, options include lowering a product's price in the hope of increasing the volume sold. A lower price should still remain above the cost of production. Provided the percent change in the price is less than the percent change in quantity sold, a lower price will result in a greater total return.

Evaluating how price changes affect profit is a driver for cost analysis. In a competitive market, the individual processor is a price taker,

$$TR = (Q * Pm)$$

Where:

- TR = Total revenue
- Q = Number of units produced throughout the year
- Pm = Market price for each unit throughout the year

meaning that they cannot set their prices above competitors' and expect their product to be purchased. Prices may be lowered to encourage the movement of inventory surplus, but this is usually for a short time. Having a drastically lower price for a product than competitors set is not in the interest of a business, if the product is routinely purchased at a higher price.

Total revenue projections prior to production should be based on the processing plant capacity for potential production volume. The average price of competing products can be used as the price for an item, as long as the product is representative in terms of cost. It is better to err on the conservative side with these figures than to be overly optimistic about future prices for products that have not been produced and sold to consumers. Thus, TR becomes a first estimate of the size of operation.

Actual TR is the total income received from the sale of a new food product in one year. Total revenue is calculated by multiplying the total number of items (Q) sold by the selling (market) price (Pm) for each item. The price received for each of the products will depend on the number of consumers that buy the product at the projected volume of production.

Projecting the quantity (Q) of a new food product that could be produced during one year is based on which variable factor is the most limiting. The limiting factor could be the capacity of the equipment, availability of raw materials, or anything constraining production. Management projections of production, transportation, and storage costs, along with the expected retail price, will be used to calculate the quantity expected to be sold.

The average Pm can be compared to the average cost figure for managers to determine if profits are being made on each item. To estimate the average Pm per unit for a year, the formula is as follows:

$$Pm = TR/Q$$

Units used for analysis should be as accurate as possible and coincide with the units of measure used for other business activities, such as cases, hundredweights, gallons, pounds, etc. The Pm per item may vary throughout the year, e.g., as a result of discounting, and these fluctuations must be reflected in the total income received. When more than one new product is sold, the income from each product should be kept separate, in order to compare average costs to average prices received for each item.

COST OF PRODUCTION

The other piece of a feasibility study is to estimate the cost to produce the new food item. Total income must cover total costs. One year is used as a basis for estimating costs of production, with the calendar dates based on the accounting time period. However, if costs for one week or some other time period are needed, the same procedures can be used as with the annual basis, except that all costs will have to be divided into the appropriate time periods.

As mentioned above, total costs (TC) are classified into two types, fixed (FC) and variable costs (VC). The difference between the two is based on whether or not each cost item or expenditure changes throughout the year because of variations in input. For example, building costs will remain the same whether there are 100 or 10,000 units produced. The same is true for machines that have a productive use of more than one year. Variable costs will change when volume of production changes, such as raw material inputs, labor, electricity, and packaging. Cost analysis is most effective when the data used to estimate cost are accurate and timely. The general equations are as follows:

$$TC = FC + VC$$

Where:

- TC = Sum of all costs incurred during the processing of a food item during a one-year period.
- FC = Fixed costs are not affected by changes in volume produced within the year.
- VC = Variable costs are directly affected by changes in volume produced.

To estimate an average break-even cost (Pc) per unit for a specific time period, the equation is as follows:

$$Pc = (TC/Q)$$

Break-even cost per unit (Pc) is the estimated average cost per unit over the course of one year, or some other designated time period required to cover the costs of production. Any Pm above this cost would result in a profit. When the average price received (Pm) is less than the average cost of production (Pc)—i.e., the product is not producible with a profit—managers have three options:

1. Do not begin production.
2. Begin production at a loss until problems are solved.
3. Raise the price of the product until all costs are covered, which entails the risk that it is priced higher than competing products and consumers will not purchase it.

To estimate an average break-even volume of production for an average Pm for the year, the equation is as follows:

$$Q = \left(\frac{TC}{Pm}\right)$$

Examples for each part of the profit equation will be explained in detail and how to estimate each of the variables. This can be done manually or it can be set up on any one of several computer spreadsheet programs that will do all of the calculations. This also helps when specific costs or prices of particular items are changed or when alternative equipment, volume, receipts, or any change is being considered. Data should be organized in a spreadsheet, which allows each part to become a separate analysis, and then combined into a final break-even price or volume analysis. The more detail in the spreadsheet, the easier it is to make a change. It is easier to add different cost items than it is to divide total estimates. There is no universal format, because each set of business circumstances is unique. Each spreadsheet should be compatible with the type of data available and be set up to provide information required for management decisions.

Fixed costs include items that are used longer than one year, such as equipment and buildings. These are "fixed" because for any given year, each item is used by the company, regardless of the production volume for that year. Depreciation should reflect use and expected lifetime of each piece of equipment. Building costs per year will remain the same. Land should be included in the FCs, if sales of the product are to help pay for the use of land. Annual salaries are also an FC, because typically they will be the same regardless of a company's output in a given year.

To estimate an annual FC, divide the total purchase price of the item by the number of years it will be used. This figure is calculated for each machine, building, and any other item that is used more than one year. These figures are the same from year to year unless new equipment is purchased. Other FCs include a manager's salary and opportunity cost.

The latter is the income assumed to be forfeited had an investment other than that in the new product been made, for example, had the invested money been placed in the stock market or simply allowed to earn interest in a bank.

Depreciation is a method of dividing the investment costs for long-term assets over the years those assets are used (see Table 12.1). To calculate total FCs, a complete list of all equipment and buildings must be developed. The date of purchase and total price paid for each item installed and the time the item first went into use should be listed to ensure accurate depreciation schedules. These data are also necessary for tax purposes.

To start the process of estimating total FCs, set up a table with at least four columns (Table 12.2). In the first column, list building assets and each piece of equipment that will be used longer than one year, regardless of the size and amount, and the date purchased. In a second column, list the price paid for each item, including shipping and installation. The third column contains the number of years each item will be used until replaced or discarded. In the fourth column, an annual cost of using each piece of equipment (depreciation) is calculated by dividing the total purchase price by the expected number of years of use. This is the most common for this type of analysis. There are many different ways to estimate depreciation, primarily for tax purposes. Use the one that makes the most sense for each situation.

These estimated depreciation figures are annual costs of machinery, equipment, and buildings. Machines will be used for different time periods based on their function and durability. Buildings are often depreciated over a 20- to 30-year period. This allocates the cost of each piece of equipment or building to a one-year period.

TABLE 12.2. An Example For Estimated Annual Fixed Costs.

Investment	Total Purchase Price	Life of Investment	Annual Costs*
Building	$200,000	20	$10,000
Equipment	$150,000	10	$15,000
Vehicles	$56,000	7	$8,000
Manager's salary			$40,000
Total investment	$406,000		
Opportunity costs	6%		$24,360
Total Fixed Cost (FC)			**$97,360**

*Depreciation is often calculated differently for tax purposes. The goal of tax depreciation is to minimize tax obligations. Straight line depreciation allocates cost over a fixed time period.

Greater production levels can lower average FCs if, for example, a greater volume is produced during the year with no change in building or equipment. Response time to production changes will depend on factors such as equipment capacity, availability of raw materials, labor, number of shifts, and management ability. A brief example of a firm that produces 200,000 units is as follows:

Total annual FCs amount to $97,360, which are the annual costs regardless of whether 1,000 units or 200,000 units are produced, with the total investment of $406,000 and an opportunity cost for the investment of, for example, 6%. This assumes that the investment has to return 6% or $24,360 in addition to all other costs to break-even or make a profit. The average fixed cost (AFC) per unit is $0.49 and is calculated as follows:

$$\begin{aligned} AFC &= \frac{FC}{Q} \\ &= \$97{,}360/\$200{,}000 \\ &= \$0.49/\text{unit} \end{aligned}$$

However, if only 1,000 units are produced, the AFC per unit increases to $97.36 per unit. This is one reason for the importance of estimating FCs. The average cost per unit decreases as the volume increases. This shows the importance of operating at or close to the equipment capacity, as long as the product continues to be sold.

VARIABLE COSTS

Variable costs include all inputs required to buy, process, package, and transport the product to where consumers will buy it. These costs will vary with the volume of production and include such items as labor and benefits, ingredients, packaging materials, cleaning supplies, equipment repairs, utilities, storage, transportation, and office personnel, as well as distribution and promotional outlays. All money spent during the production of the food item during the year should be included in the cost figures.

For this example, the equipment capacity is 200,000 units per year. Assume all the ingredients for each unit cost $2.00. The maximum cost would be $400,000 for ingredients. Specific ingredients can be set up with quantities and prices of each. Changes in any ingredient costs would automatically be reflected in a new cost for the receipt and product. Labor would be $90,000 for five people working eight hours a day for 50 weeks, plus $13,500 for fringe benefits. Many more VCs have to be included in an actual example, such as insurance, taxes, utilities, and more, depending on the product being produced. For the example in Table 12.3, the sum of all VCs is $605,300.

All cost items should be itemized as much as possible, so the economic impact can be estimated for hypothetical situations, such as "what if a new piece of equipment were installed." If there is a change in type of package or hourly wages, the costs can be easily evaluated using spreadsheets.

Each of these cost items can be used for all types of management decisions. The average variable cost (AVC) is the sum of these input costs divided by total production (Q).

Comparing average unit FCs and VCs, FCs are only $0.49 per unit, whereas VCs are $3.02 per unit. These individual cost figures are not as important as the two combined into a break-even cost of $3.51 per unit. Adding total annual FCs to total VCs equals $702,660. This is the total annual cost, i.e., amount that would have to be spent in one year, to produce 200,000 units. The $3.51 per unit average cost (Pc) is the figure that management compares to the Pm of the product. To return a profit in this scenario, the Pm of a product would have to be greater than $3.51 (Table 12.4).

If the Pm is, for example, $5.00 per unit, the volume needed to cover all costs would only have to be about 82,252 units per year. Gross income would be $1 million if every one of the units sold for $5.00 per unit at a production capacity of 200,000 units. The profit would be $297,340. If the Pm were set at $3.00, the volume sold to break even would have to be 234,220 units, which exceeds capacity. The loss

TABLE 12.3. An Example for Estimating Variable Cost.

Variable Costs	Number of Units	Cost/Unit	Annual Costs
Ingredients/Unit	200,000	$2.00	$400,000
Labor/Hour	5	$9.00	$90,000
Fringe benefits		15%	$13,500
Electricity/Month	12	$100	$1,200
Packaging material/Unit		$0.50	$100,000
Cleaning supplies/Month	12	$50.00	$600
Total variable costs (TVC)			$605,300

TABLE 12.4. An Example Estimating Total Cost, Break Even Cost, and Break Even Volume.

Variable Costs	Number of Units	Cost/Unit	Annual Costs
Ingredients/Unit	200,000	$2.00	$400,000
Labor/Hour	5	$9.00	$90,000
Fringe benefits		15%	$13,500
Electricity/Month	12	$100	$1,200
Packaging material/Unit		$0.50	$100,000
Cleaning supplies/Month	12	$50.00	$600
Total variable costs (TVC)			$605,300

would be $102,660. With a production capacity of 200,000, the management in this example needs to seriously consider other alternatives if the market prices of the new product were projected to remain below $3.51 (Pc) for a long time.

Using these formulas, an estimate can be calculated for an average annual cost that can be compared to the average annual price received for the product. These costs are based on actual or estimated volume or capacity of production.

In the real world, there are two Pmss. One is the projected or anticipated Pm, which managers have to use to make their production decisions before an item is distributed and sold. Second, the actual average Pm represents the price received based on the actual invoices from products sold. The projected price should be compared to actual prices to determine if pricing adjustments are needed for future production.

There are also two costs of production. One is the estimated cost based on the best information available. The second derives from actual

TABLE 12.5. Calculating Costs.

Total Costs	TC = $97,360 + $605,300 = $702,660
Average cost per unit	Pc = (TC /Q) Pc = ($702,660/200,000) Pc = $3.51/unit
Total revenue	TR = (Q * Pm) TR = (200,000 * $5.00) = $1,000,000
Profit	P = (TR - TC) P = ($1,000,000 - $702,660) = $297,340
Return on investment	ROI = P/Investment ROI = ($297,304/$406,000) = 73.2%
Average price received for products sold	Pm = (TR/Q) Pm = ($1,000,000/$200,000) = $5.00/unit

production figures after the product is sold. The projected costs should be compared with actual costs. Future expansion or product changes can be estimated more accurately when actual data from previous years are available. Once a new product has a production and sales "history," only a few variables have to be estimated, for example, the cost for new machinery.

CASH FLOW PROCEDURE

Once a market price for the product and average cost per unit are calculated, the data can be used to develop a cash flow analysis, which, in turn can be used to determine the amount of money a company may have to borrow for a year or other specific time period. In some cases, operating capital is needed only for a few months or weeks until a new product is sold. A cash flow analysis should be done before meeting with lenders. A *cash flow statement* is a projection or an actual record of the dollars coming in and the dollars going out of a business. It shows where the money comes from (the inflow of cash) and where the money goes (the outflow of cash). A cash flow procedure can estimate or project a cash flow analysis on a monthly, quarterly, or annual basis. For this analysis, a quarterly example will be used, although the same principles apply, regardless of the time period. A projected cash flow can be based on information from a cost analysis. Each expenditure and receipt is entered into the month or year in which it is expected to be made. This will provide budget information to determine the financial or cash position in any time period. Estimated costs and prices become actual cost information as the year progresses. The actual cash flow of a business provides information for making cash flow projections into the future. Projected cash flow reveals the ability of a firm to generate cash, clarifies cash requirements, and indicates how the two do or do not coincide. This type of analysis is often needed for a period of eight to ten years to predict long-term profitability and one to three years, usually on a monthly basis, to ascertain shortterm profitability and cash requirements.

Using data from the example above, a short-term cash flow for one year indicates the capital requirements for this new food product (see Table 12.4). Starting the operation requires buying a building and equipment and then commencing production. Assume that it takes six months to get the operation going but only at a level initially of 11 percent of capacity. This production is sold in the third quarter. Production can be increased to 25 percent of capacity and again sold in the fourth quarter. It takes time to get started, train all of the people that will be working, and get supplies, as well as find outlets for the product. A monthly cash-flow analysis can also be used if more detail is required. Let's assume the new food product can be sold for $5.00 per unit.

A cash flow analysis usually starts with inflows, which are the number of units expected to be sold each quarter multiplied by the projected price. In this case, the business takes six months to build and start production. An example is demonstrated in Table 12.6 for quarterly cash flows. The cash inflow is estimated by multiplying the number sold times the price/item. Cash inflow is only $111,500 for the third quarter and $250,000 for the fourth quarter for a total income for the first year of $361,500. The sum of the quarterly cash inflow and outflow for the first year can be used for the first year cash flow projections for a longer time period such as eight to ten years.

Cash outflows in the first quarter involve buying the equipment, buildings, and other items that are needed to construct a processing plant. In this time period, a manager's salary, an FC, is included. However, the VCs of processing, such as labor, are not, because processing has not commenced. This example would indicate that processing begins in the second quarter, but no product would sell until the third quarter. The net cash flow the first quarter is $416,000 and an additional $77,740 the second quarter, which represents expenses (outflows) for ingredients, labor, packaging, etc. There is a time lag between buying the ingredients and selling the products. The cash flow analysis will record the outflow and the inflow in the time period in which they were made, and the projected operating capital will indicate the required cash to continue to operate.

In this example, the net cash flow for the first three quarters is negative, meaning there is more cash being expended for the operation than there is income. However, in the fourth quarter there is a positive cash inflow of $88,675. This analysis shows the importance of knowing the amount of short-term loans that may be needed to buy ingredients (inputs), hire workers, and establish a market strategy. Negative cash flow is often overlooked in estimating how much operating capital will be required and for what time period.

It was demonstrated that this product had an average cost per unit of $3.51 and an average price of $5.00, which would in principle render it profitable. However, there would not be a positive cash flow after the first year if the selling price of the product remained at $5.00 per unit.

Profitability becomes apparent only when cash flow is projected into future time periods. In the current example, profitability is clearly demonstrated by having a projected operating balance of almost one million dollars at the end of the fifth year (Table 12.7).

SUMMARY

Economic feasibility analysis is important before major investments are made, especially in a competitive market. This analysis will provide an average cost per unit to be able to be compared with a Pm. The accuracy of both of these estimates becomes obvious if there is a small margin between them.

Cost analysis is time consuming and requires focused managerial effort. Such analysis can help identify problems at early stages of a project, before significant capital outlays are made.

Next, a cash flow analysis estimates the amount of operating capital required for operation and the length of time needed for the operating

TABLE 12.6. Quarterly Cash Flows.

Cash Inflow Items	Quarter 1	Quarter 2	Quarter 3	Quarter 4	Annual Cash Flow
Number sold			22,300	50,000	72,300
Price/item			$5	$5	
Total cash inflow			$111,500	$250,000	$361,500
Cash Outflow Items					
Buildings	$200,000				$200,000
Equipment	$150,000				$150,000
Vehicles	$56,000				$56,000
Manager's salary	$10,000	$10,000	$10,000	$10,000	$40,000
Variable Costs					
Ingredients		$44,600	$100,000	$100,000	$244,600
Labor		$10,035	$22,500	$22,500	$55,035
Fringe benefits		$1,505	$3,375	$3,375	$8,255
Electricity		$300	$300	$300	$900
Packaging		$11,150	$25,000	$25,000	$61,150
Cleaning supplies		$150	$150	$150	$450
Total Cash Outflow	$416,000	$77,740	$161,325	$161,325	$816,390
Net Cash Flow	($416,000)	($77,740)	($49,825)	$88,675	($454,890)
Interest 2% per Quarter		($8,320)	($10,041)	($11,239)	($29,600)
Projected Operating Balance	($416,000)	($502,926)	($561,926)	($484,490)	($484,490)

TABLE 12.7. Annual Cash Flow Example For A Firm Producing 200,000 Units.

Cash Inflow Items	Year 1	Year 2	Year 3	Year 4	Year 5
Number sold	72,300	200,000	200,000	200,000	200,000
Price/item	$5	$5	$5	$5	$5
Total cash inflow	$361,500	$1,000,000	$1,000,000	$1,000,000	$1,000,000
Cash Outflow Items					
Buildings	$200,000				
Equipment	$150,000				
Vehicles	$56,000				
Manager's salary	$40,000	$40,000	$40,000	$40,000	$40,000
Variable Costs					
Ingredients	$244,600	$400,000	$400,000	$400,000	$400,000
Labor	$55,035	$90,000	$90,000	$90,000	$90,000
Fringe benefits	$8,255	$13,500	$13,500	$13,500	$13,500
Electricity	$900	$1,200	$1,200	$1,200	$1,200
Packaging	$61,150	$100,000	$100,000	$100,000	$100,000
Cleaning supplies	$450	$600	$600	$600	$600
Total Cash Outflow	$816,390	$645,300	$645,300	$645,300	$645,300
Net Cash Flow	($454,890)	$354,700	$354,700	$354,700	$354,700
Interest 2% per Quarter	($29,600)	($38,759)	($13,484)	$13,813	$43,292
Projected Operating Balance	($484,490)	($168,549)	$172,667	$541,180	$939,175

balance to become positive. A complete financial analysis will cover outflows for initial capital expenditures needed to begin producing a new item plus the operating costs attendant on running a production line and distributing and selling the item. Often investors obtain capital for buildings and equipment and then are forced to go back to lenders for additional operating capital once production has started. To circumvent this step and secure sufficient funding, capital and operating costs should be presented at the same time, with a projected schedule for repayment.

KEY WORDS

Cash flow statement—a projection or an actual recording of the dollars coming in and the dollars going out of a business.

Profits—the amount of total revenue that is left after paying the total cost of production and marketing.

Total costs (*TC*)—sum of all costs incurred during the processing of a food item during a one-year period.

Total revenue (*TR*)—the income flow from all sources for one year.

COMPREHENSION QUESTIONS

12.1. Give an example of a fixed cost and a variable cost.

12.2. Why is it important to perform economic feasibility analyses?

REFERENCES

Beckman, M. D., Boone, L. E., & Kurtz, D. L. (1992). *Foundations of marketing* (5th ed.). Toronto: Holt, Rinehart and Winston of Canada. Alberta Agriculture. (2002) *Marketing Food In Alberta: An Access Directory*. p. 43.

Kijewski, V., Donath, B., & Wilson, D. T. (1993). Pricing-Think Value Not Cost. *The Best readings from Business marketing magazine: views from the trenches* (p. 225). Boston: PWS-Kent Pub. Co.

Guiltinan, J. P., Paul, G. W., & Madden, T. J. (1997). *Marketing management: Strategies and Programs* (6th ed.). New York: McGraw-Hill Companies.

Erikson, D. (1996). *Economic analysis of a new business-doing it right.* No. MF-2184). Manhattan, KS: K-State Research and Extension.

CHAPTER 13

Confidentiality and Intellectual Property Rights

Learning Objectives

- Understand confidentiality issues in teams.
- Know the meaning of a patent, trademark, and copyright.
- Understand the risks of trade secrets and how to protect them.

IN some industries, market competitors are desperate for data regarding rivals' future business directions, formulas, and proprietary processing techniques. Companies, therefore, must rely on the confidentiality of organizational knowledge to sustain product advantage and competitive edge. Because intellectual knowledge and know-how are a form of property, the owners of it have rights regarding its division and dissemination, just as they would with other possessions. There are four categories in which intangible possessions such as intellectual property can be protected: patents, trade secrets, copyrights, and trademarks. Intellectual property rights can be relevant to tangible inventions and creations associated with new products and packaging.

PATENTS

In order to promote the progress of technology, the government offers patent protection—an agreement between the public and inventors that only those granted permission can use their works. Patents can be issued only for new, useful, and non-obvious inventions. They are used occasionally in the food business to protect unique production processes; novel compounds; additives, such as flavor modifiers; or new methods to alter the properties of foods.

Patents protect the intellectual property of the inventor, and the patent holder has the right to exclude others from making, using or selling his/her invention, once a patent is granted. Patent protection can be exercised for a maximum of 20 years. Food additives and medical devices are sometimes allowed five extra years of protection, due to delays incurred from Food and Drug Administration (FDA) approvals. International patents are also available.

Patents in the food industry are primarily used for protecting creations in processing. Processing equipment and techniques must be unique throughout the industry, to receive protection.

Three types of patents exist in the United States—utility, design, and plant. Utility patents protect inventions or discoveries about processes, machinery, or new ingredients. Design patents protect novel designs for items to be manufactured. Plant patents can be used to protect newly discovered vegetation or newly generated plants in novel varieties. Plant and utility patents can be filed as provisional but after that must, within one year, fulfill all requirements to become non-provisional. See Table 13.1 for the distinction between provisional and non-provisional protection.

Provisional applications for patents grant the inventor a twelve-month period to finish the non-provisional patent applications. If a non-provisional patent is not filed within a period of a year, the application is automatically abandoned. A provisional application that fulfills the non-provisional application requirements receives the full benefits of patent protection.

The United States Patent and Trademark Office (USPTO) approves all non-provisional patents, once all requirements are met. Requirements for patent applications include the title of the invention, a description of the invention, a declaration of the uses, and sketches, if applicable. Inventors must also take an oath that they believe themselves to be the first creator of their invention. Considerations before filing a patent should include the following:

- Will the invention become obsolete before the 20 years is complete?
- Will the invention still have value by the time the patent is issued (approximately two years)?
- Will competitors be able to take advantage of the patent's information to further their work?
- Does the potential increase in revenue outweigh the cost?

Inventors are advised to seek legal assistance in preparing patent applications, because the process can be complex. Before filing a patent, inventors and companies should weigh whether the gains expected from

TABLE 13.1. Types of Patent Applications.

Type of Patent	Description
Provisional application	Offers protection of an inventor's creations for up to a 12-month period prior to submitting the complete non-provisional patent application
Non-provisional application	Offers full patent protection

an invention's protection are more valuable than the time and money spent to acquire it. The average cost of filing a patent is about $7,000. If the patent is not granted the first time, an applicant can file an appeal and request reconsideration. Even without a patent, the process or invention may be valuable intellectual property, which can be protected by intra-company measures, as is the case with trade secrets, which are discussed below.

Patent benefits must be enforced by the owner. If a competitor is infringing on a patent, the owner should ask the other company to cease their offending practices. Competitors who continue to exploit patent protections are liable for their actions and are at risk legally.

Searching for a Previously Filed Patent

Inventors are encouraged to search for previously filed similar patents prior to seeking their own patent protection. Patents that have been previously filed with the USPTO can be searched via an online database found at patft.uspto.gov. Other options for completing a patent search include Google Patent Search (www.google.com/patents) or contacting a librarian to assist. The USPTO also offers information about a patent's current ownership.

COPYRIGHTS

Copyright applies legal protection to original intellectual works that are tangible, such as plays, movies, music, choreography, pictures or graphics, literature, and audiovisual displays. Copyright is intended to prevent others from direct and largely unaltered copying of creative work. However, it does not prohibit others from describing a process by means other than full reproduction. Once placed into tangible form by their creator original works enjoy the assumed rights of copyright protection, even if they do not display a copyright notice.

Copyright laws do not protect ideas, scientific procedures, or technical information per se. Rather the laws protect the tangible forms in which these are presented and reproduced. In the food industry, a written description of a food processing procedure could be protected by copyright, but this would not legally preempt others from using the manufacturing process or describing the process in a different manner.

TRADEMARKS

A trademark is a word, symbol, picture, or any combination of those used to distinguish the goods and services of one individual or organization from those of another. Trademarks shield a name from use by competitors, especially product names and slogans. Trademarks can be used to identify the unique goods or services of a company and assure customers that the goods or services they are purchasing adhere to a standard. The USPTO is responsible for registering trademarks, although such registration is not required.

Trademarks are identifiable by the public through words, visual symbols, or colors that represent a product or company. Trademarks encourage market competition and assist consumers in making decisions by way of product and brand recognition.

TRADE SECRETS

Trade secrets, by definition, are information used to create a unique commercial product and that is deliberately kept from being known outside a company. Trade secrets can be found in business or ingredient transactions, finances, or technology. Because the law does not protect trade secrets, exposed trade secrets are an advantage to competitors. There is no legal restriction that keeps competitors from not using a leaked trade secret. Trade secrets do not contain patentable technology or processes and may not even be original to the organization, which is why it is essential to protect them from public disclosure. Even if trade secret information is not unique, it constitutes an element of a company's value.

In order to protect trade secrets, a company should require non-disclosure agreements to be signed by all employees. Companies should also provide a blanket closing e-mail message and written document footnotes stating that the information contained in transmitted documents may be confidential. Such e-mail notices and footnotes should be used on all company correspondence.

Employees must be made aware that trade secrets are vital company information and ought to be handled and communicated in ways that guard against even accidental or unintentional disclosure. Clean desk policies can help reduce trade secret leaks through contract or custodial staff. Physical facility barriers should be in place at research and development facilities. Keyed access needs to be set up for pilot plants and laboratories where innovation is encouraged. Cyber security should also be maintained on company intranet sites and internal networks. Employees should be reminded that talking in public about classified information can expose secrets to competitors.

When an employee leaves, it is necessary for a company to retrieve all privileged and proprietary information and papers from the individual before he or she leaves the premises. To ensure all rightful data are given back at the conclusion of a worker's employment, the company can request a signed statement from the employee stating that she or he has returned all information.

Trade secrets that are revealed through a breach of legal contracts are punishable by law. An employee may not receive information from competitors through bribery, theft, or a breach of secrecy, but reverse engineering of a product is allowed, as long as the process is based on publicly accessible data and product analysis.

Economic Espionage Act of 1996

The Economic Espionage Act (EEA) of 1996 made obtaining trade secrets through illegal means punishable by federal law. In a court, the presiding judge would consider if a non-disclosure agreement was breached, if protections were in place to reduce theft from outside parties, and the extent of the information disclosed.

Conspiring to obtain and use a trade secret to gain economic benefit or to damage another company's success is illegal. Companies disclosing information to the government about a violation of the EEA are not forced to disclose direct secrets in open court.

CONFIDENTIALITY

When researching a new concept, some sharing of the idea with knowledgeable individuals outside the company may be necessary. Outside scientists can provide specific advice and pointers, only if they understand the project and area of interest. Sharing an idea with external specialists before a product is in the market can create vulnerability. Other businesses with more assets can use your idea before your product and plan are fully developed. To minimize this risk, carefully check that advisors will keep your idea confidential. It is generally advisable to have a simple signed agreement of confidentiality. If you are considering entering discussions with potential competitors, seeking professional and legal advice is recommended, to draft a legally binding agreement of confidentiality.

WORKING WITH OUTSIDE SUPPLIERS

Product development often involves working with suppliers and other companies. One organization may enlist the help of another to develop a flavor system, seasoning packet, new ingredient, or additive. Companies should institute policies to protect themselves from trade secret loss or battles over whose intellectual property an original process or ingredient actually is. Companies in such a situation should set goals and intellectual property expectations prior to beginning a project. If at any time during a project, the agreement requires changes or an addendum, stop all work until a supplemental agreement is made. For legal purposes, jointly operating companies should each have the other sign non-disclosure forms.

SUMMARY

Protecting organizational intellectual property must be a company priority. Careless disclosure of secrets can lead to company losses and competitor advantage. If the organization can legally protect an asset such as processes or formulas, it is important to do so if it makes economic sense. Patents, trademarks, and copyrights protect differing works, but are all protected by the United States government. Trade secrets are not protected by the government directly and must be carefully secured.

Employees and contract workers must be instructed that the loss of intellectual property is serious, and in-house procedures must be implemented to prevent leaks.

KEY WORDS

Copyright—copyright law protects tangible works from being reproduced without authorization; it prevents others from copying a work by an author, but does not impede others from describing a process using other means.

Non-provisional application—submission of a patent to obtain full patent protection.

Patent—an agreement between the public and inventors that only those granted permission can use their works.

Provisional application—offers protection of an inventor's creations for up to a twelvemonth period prior to submitting a complete non-provisional patent application.

Trademark—a word, symbol, picture, or any combination of those used to distinguish goods and services of one individual or organization from those of another.

Trade secrets—information used to create a unique product or process that is closely guarded and not known by other members of industry outside a company.

COMPREHENSION QUESTIONS

13.1. Fill in the blank.

a. A ____________________ protects an invention.

b. A ____________________ protects an original artistic or literary work.

c. A ____________________ is a word or symbol or combination to identify the product or service as coming from a single source.

13.2. Name some strategies that companies use to protect their trade secrets.

13.3. What is the significance of the Economic Espionage Act of 1996?

REFERENCES

Buntrock, R. E. (2008). Patent searching made easy: How to do patent searches on the internet and in the library. *Choice, 45*(7), 1179.

Carr, C., Furniss, J., & Morton, J. (2000). Complying with the economic espionage act. *Risk Management, 47*(3), 21–24.

Kovach, K. A., Pruett, M., Samuels, L. B., & Duvall, C. F. (2004). Protecting trade secrets during employee migration: What you don't know can hurt you. *Labor Law Journal, 55*(2), 69–84.

Rourk, C. J. (1998). A short course in intellectual property protection. *Electrical World, 212*(9), 33.

CHAPTER 14

Shelf-Life Testing and Date Coding

Learning Objectives

- What is shelf-life and how is it determined.
- Importance of determining shelf-life.
- Methods of dating foods.

SHELF-LIFE encompasses several facets of food quality, including safety, nutritional value, and sensory properties. Food quality, in turn, influences the consumer's buying decisions. Thus, product shelf-life is critical in purchase decisions, including the possibility of repeated purchase. For many food companies, the ability of a food to retain its overall quality from the processing line, through distribution and marketing, and finally to the consumer, is the result of intensive studies to predict the "life" of a food. Shelf-life is the time frame during which a food product can reliably and demonstrably retain its quality characteristics. Shelf-life must be technically researched and determined for any new product.

INTRINSIC FACTORS

Certain factors intrinsic to a food's system and that affect how long it will retain its qualities cannot be controlled unless the food undergoes processing. In a few instances, such intrinsic factors may themselves "protect" a food from deterioration and thus function as built-in shelf-life extenders. Key intrinsic factors in foods are pH, moisture content, water activity (a_w), nutrient content, antimicrobial agents, biological structures, and oxidation/reduction potential.

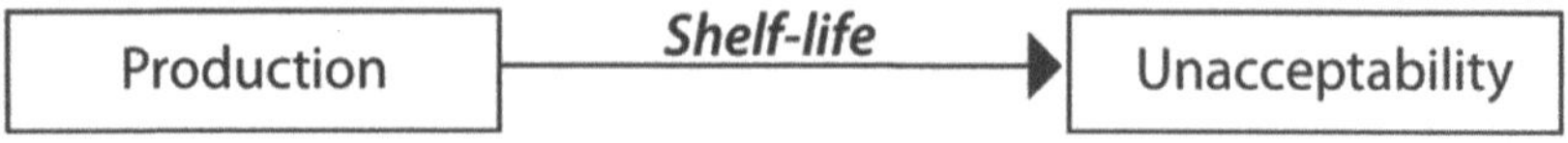

FIGURE 14.1. Demonstration of shelf-life time frame.

pH

pH is the index of acidity or alkalinity of a food ranging from 0 to 14. A pH value of 7 is considered neutral, whereas values of 0 and 14 are extremely acidic and basic, respectively. The lower the pH, the more acidic the food. Some acidifying agents, such as glucono-delta lactone, can be relied on to lower the pH of a food system without increasing the sour taste as much as other acids. A product developer needs to balance lowering the pH of a food for longer shelf-life with the effects of the added acid on the sensory properties of the food product.

The acidity or alkalinity of a food influences the type of microbial spoilage that will occur. Most bacteria do not thrive in acidic conditions; they prefer foods with a pH range between 6.6 and 7.5, e.g., red meat, chicken, fish, eggs, and vegetables. Spoilage of citrus fruits, tomatoes, and other food products with a lower pH often occurs as a result of mold and/or yeast.

Water Activity (a_w)

Moisture content and a_w are also a part of food composition. As indicated above, the two should not be confused. Water activity is the amount of unbound or "free" water in a system available to support biological and chemical reactions. Water activity ranges from 0 to 1, with pure water ranking 1. Most fresh foods have a_w values close to 1, whereas dry foods have values ranging from 0.2 to 0.6. Therefore, the objective of food dehydration is to reduce the water available to support biological growth. A food may have a high moisture content, but low a_w, due to other food constituents (sugars, salt, etc.) that bind the water ("moisture"), therefore rendering it unavailable. In such cases, sugar and salt serve as humectants, i.e., chemical compounds that bind water. In general, bacteria require higher aw for growth than yeast or mold. Most spoilage bacteria do not grow below a_w 0.91; however, halophilic (salt-loving) bacteria such as *Staphylococcus aureus* (*S. aureus*) have been known to grow at values as low as 0.75. Spoilage molds grow at much lower levels. Xerophilic (dry-loving) molds and osmophilic (preferring high osmotic pressure) yeasts have been reported to grow at a_w values of 0.65 and 0.60, respectively. For the most part, lowering the a_w of a food below 0.65 eliminates the majority of the spoilage microorganisms.

A food scientist must know how to manipulate the a_w of a new product for extended shelf-life. Managing the water in a food system is essential not only to control microbial growth, but also to improve the texture profile and sensory properties. Moisture migration will result in softening or hardening of a food, which can lead to retrodegradation or mold growth. A product developer can alter a_w in a food by means of various processing techniques, such as manipulation of time and temperature, humidity control, or additives such as solutes-coating agents, humectants, and hydrocolloids (See Chapter 6).

Nutrient Content

Nutrient content is another factor that influences spoilage. More nutritious foods tend to undergo more spoilage. This occurs because microorganisms require certain nutrients, such as vitamins and other growth factors. Food high in protein tends to undergo bacterial spoilage, because these microorganisms require a source of nitrogen. Examples include eggs, red meat, chicken, and seafood. Lipids or fats in food may also cause problems. Foods high in lipid content, especially unsaturated fats, may undergo oxidation. The loss of certain vitamins and pigments often results in fading color and other undesirable events.

Antimicrobial Agents

Foods such as eggs, cloves, and cranberries have built-in defense mechanisms, i.e., antimicrobial agents that are present naturally. Lysozyme, an enzyme in egg white, prevents the growth of gram-positive bacteria, which include *Listeria monocytogenes*, *S. aureus*, and *Streptococcus* species. The compounds benzoic acid and eugenol, present in cranberries and cloves, respectively, hinder the growth of mold and some bacteria.

Biological Structures

The natural covering, part of the biological structure of a food, affects shelf-life. Undamaged animal skins, as well as peels and shells in vegetables and eggs, provide protection against microbial invasion and deterioration.

Oxidation/Reduction Potential

Oxidation/reduction potential is the ease by which a substrate (food) loses or gains electrons; it is a function of oxygen tension, the partial pressure of oxygen molecules dissolved in a liquid, and certain other characteristics of a food. Oxidation/reduction potential is also influenced by the degree of oxygen penetration into a product. For example, steak has low oxygen penetration compared with ground beef which, because of its increased surface area, has a higher oxygen penetration level and, therefore, a higher initial microbial load. Based on the assumption that the inner portion of a steak is intact, and no oxygen has penetrated to the core, the inner portion of a steak may be "sterile."

EXTRINSIC PARAMETERS

In contrast to the previous elements that affected food quality from within the food itself, extrinsic factors impact a food from outside and include many environmental variables, such as temperature, time, relative humidity, presence of gases, physical stress, and other parameters, which need to be controlled or changed to extend shelf-life.

Temperature

Temperature is perhaps the most important extrinsic factor that must be controlled to minimize spoilage. By keeping certain foods hot and others cold, spoilage can be prevented or minimized. Certain microorganisms (mesophiles) prefer room temperature, whereas others (psychrophiles) prefer cold and are capable of existing in or on refrigerated items. Placing meat in the refrigerator may reduce the growth of mesophiles and at the same time promote psychrophiles, such as Pseudomonas. Temperature also affects numerous food-related chemical reactions. In particular, an increase in temperature often accelerates the rate of a chemical reaction.

Time

Generally, the duration of storage has an inverse relationship to food quality; in other words, spoilage occurs as time progresses. However, for some processes, time can contribute to a product's desired quality factors. Examples include fermented foods and beverages, such as wine, cheese, and soy sauce. Thermal destruction of microorganisms is based on time and temperature; the time/temperature relationship is the basis for microbial destruction in products such as canned goods. For this reason, time and temperature are often linked as a single extrinsic factor.

Relative Humidity

Relative humidity affects the a_w within food. Humidity is especially important if altering the a_w is the primary means of controlling spoilage within a food system. All foods are different with respect to supporting microbial growth and becoming dried out. High humidity may encourage the growth of molds on refrigerated foods. On the other hand, wet heat is more effective than dry heat in destroying microorganisms and inactivating enzymes.

Presence of Gases

Gas flushing with inert gases can also be an effective means of extending the shelf-life of foods such as potato chips, meat, and fruits. For example, controlled atmospheric storage of apples is accomplished by increasing the relative humidity and the level of inert gases (carbon dioxide and/or nitrogen) to about 85 percent and 5 percent, respectively. Temperature and oxygen levels are reduced to slow down respiration and retard physiological changes that accompany aging. Citrus fruits and bananas use ethylene gas to speed ripening and color development through the use of a controlled or modified atmospheric storage. Products utilizing vacuum package technology include meats, cheeses, and snacks.

Physical Stress

Proper handling of the food product is essential to avoid unnecessary spoilage from bruising and other physical damage that may occur during transportation and storage. Delicate food items must be packaged and transported in ways that reduce this type of abuse.

TYPES OF DETERIORATION

Physical Deterioration

Physical deterioration associated with aging is evident by signs such as color fading, moisture changes, and alterations in sensory properties, including aroma and texture. Although human senses are capable of distinguishing between desirable and undesirable characteristics in reference to color, texture, and aroma of foods, the senses alone are insufficiently reliable to determine a product's safety, nutritional value, or shelflife. A product that looks appealing may be a health risk. Loss of quality is the ultimate outcome when a product's intrinsic and extrinsic factors are out of balance.

As discussed in previous chapters, physical deterioration can be minimized through several techniques. Fruits and vegetables may be blanched before freezing in order to destroy enzymes that cause browning. Opaque packaging can reduce physical deterioration by reducing the effects of light. Additives may be used in some products to protect the loss of desired color.

Microbial Deterioration

Microbial deterioration occurs when spoilage microorganisms survive processing treatments and cause deterioration via multiplication and propagation. Microorganisms also can produce off-flavors and slime. To counter microbial growth, products undergo stringent ingredient quality controls with proper microbial testing prior to use, storage and processing times/temperature, and food additives.

Preservation of foods can be accomplished by using low temperatures (refrigeration), which slows down the proliferation of microorganisms. In reducing the temperature to freezing or subfreezing levels, most microbial activities may in fact cease. The reason for the occurrence of this phenomenon lies in the facts that all metabolic reactions of microorganisms are enzymatic, and the rate of enzyme-catalyzed reactions is dependent on temperature. Although some spoilage microorganisms are benign, pathogenic microorganisms may also spoil a food and decrease shelf stability. However, processing methods and techniques should destroy these harmful microorganisms. This leaves only thermoduric (heat-processing resistant) or thermophilic (heat-loving) bacteria that could survive cause food decomposition.

Chemical Deterioration

Chemical deterioration of food products often involves hydrolytic and oxidative reactions, which in some foods lead to rancidity. It is important to distinguish between hydrolytic and oxidative rancidity. Hydrolytic rancidity involves enzymatic reactions. An example of hydrolytic rancidity is evident when milk becomes sour. Pasteurization of milk eliminates pathogenic microorganisms but may not destroy all the microflora. Thus, even after pasteurization, thermoduric microflora can survive and over time multiply. These microorganisms may possess lipases or enzymes, which break down fat in the milk. As a result, free fatty acids are liberated, creating an acidic or sour flavor in the milk. Oxidative rancidity usually occurs when a fat (especially a highly unsaturated one) in the product contains many (poly) double bonds. Oxygen attacks the site of the double bonds, which in turn generates unstable free radicals that catalyze the production of more free radicals. Thus, a chain reaction is set up, which can quickly spread to all susceptible fatty acids. An increase in temperature and the presence of transition metals such as iron and copper can accelerate a chemical reaction like this.

Chemical deterioration of food can be controlled using a few strategies. The first is to complete raw ingredient quality checks at receiving. Second, reducing exposure time to amplifying factors can assist in minimizing this type of deterioration. Additives can also suppress harmful chemical reactions, such as added antioxidants that prevent the formation of free radicals. Lastly, opaque packaging materials decrease the risk of photolytic reactions, and modified atmosphere packaging reduces oxygen availability, and thus the chance of oxidative damage.

Extrinsic Biological Deterioration

Extrinsic biological deterioration involves contamination of food products via birds, rodents, or insects. These biological vectors can either eat foods directly or leave residues that transmit. That is, biological deterioration from outside a food will often lead to microbial contamination. A cockroach, for instance, can carry millions of microorganisms on the hairs of its legs.

Preventive measures, such as frequent cleaning, routine product monitoring, and high-quality packaging, can lower the likelihood of biological deterioration. In addition, extrinsic biological deterioration can be countered through the use of quality raw ingredients and pest control programs. Raw ingredient checks should be completed at the time of receiving. Pest control should be carefully maintained in a program that is customized for a food manufacturing facility.

Each mode of deterioration influences a food product's shelf-life. Loss of food quality can be attributed to any or all of the modes of deterioration previously described. Occasionally, the various modes of deterioration may occur simultaneously.

Although the previously described modes of food deterioration are the basis of food decomposition, numerous deteriorative factors exist. Temperature, light, oxygen, moisture, dryness, natural enzymes, microorganisms, industrial contaminants, time, and food-to-food interactions can adversely affect certain products. These factors are not isolated in nature. For example, microorganisms, rodents, and oxygen may all work together to compromise a food. Negative synergy of this type can spoil food in a warehouse, supermarket, or household.

SHELF-LIFE DATING

Because consumers feel they have the right to know about shelf-life, various dating systems have been implemented to provide information deemed necessary to purchase food items. The purpose of dating is to inform the consumer about the shelf-life of the product.

Different types of dating may appear on a product label. Thus, shelf-life information can be presented in several ways, including the following:

- *Pack date*: The date on which the food was manufactured.
- *Display dating*: The date the food was placed on the store shelf.
- *Sell by/pull date*: The date by which the food must be sold or removed from the shelf.
- *Best if used by dating*: The date prior to which the quality of the product is at its maximum.
- *Expiration date/use by date*: The date by which the food must be consumed or discarded.

There is no universally accepted dating system for food in the United States. Most perishable and semi-perishable commodities, such as dairy products and meat, carry one type of dating system on the label. It is important to be clear on the numerous relationships between dates and shelf-life. Equally critical is the necessity to distinguish what food properties are implied by shelf-life, including quality and deterioration factors, especially those pertaining to possible microbial growth.

For example, suppose one were to ask: Is a package of cupcakes dated two months ago fit for human consumption? The type of date (pack, sell, use by) is crucial in answering such questions. Because the pack date simply refers to the date of manufacture, the product would only be two months old and could probably be consumed as long as the package was intact. However, if the date were a use-by date, then indeed the contents might be unfit for human consumption.

SHELF-LIFE EFFECTS ON FOOD DISTRIBUTION AND MARKETING

One often posed question is whether longer shelf-life always has a positive impact. Benefits of extended shelf-life include ease of distribution and stocking, less frequent product rotation, and reduced waste. Although the advantages far outweigh the disadvantages, drawbacks such as quality deterioration and difficulty in tracking the product still exist.

CONSUMER EXPECTATIONS AND DEMANDS

Consumers' demands can also affect shelf-life planning. Processors have a responsibility for modifying conventional products in response to consumer demands for more healthful products. A conventional cookie formulation may contain 35 percent fat; however, the consumer may request an adapted recipe tailored to a fat content of only 5 percent. In addition, the new formulation must be palatable, cost efficient, and stable. In such a case, the product developer faces the problem of maintaining or extending the shelf-life of a lower-fat item.

Consumers fear the unfamiliar, e.g., additives. The absence of additives may result in inferior food quality, limited shelf-life and availability of certain foods, and more danger of microbiological contamination. The growing demand for natural and untreated foods with a long shelf-life has led to increased use of packaging, including specialized barrier and smart packaging. In some cases, such packaging can offset the removal of additives that extend shelf-life. Thermoformed packaging, gas flushing (carbon dioxide [CO_2]), vacuum packaging, and other materials for prolonging shelf-life have been used with successful results on a variety of bakery products, including cakes, breads, and croissants. Packaging technology can extend shelf-life and freshness without incorporating artificial preservatives into the product's formulation.

SHELF-LIFE TESTING

Testing shelf-life can be time-consuming and costly. Normally, a product might take weeks or even months to deteriorate, making a real-time shelf-life test a lengthy process. Accelerated test methods minimize time, expense, and possible risk of foodborne illness. Models, equations, and formulas are used, in conjunction with special chambers, to obtain accurate and quick shelf-life results.

For any given food product, it is important to find literature regarding the estimated shelflife. If a company produces a similar product, consulting documents regarding its shelf-life and modes of failure will be beneficial. Another important factor is the average time a product spends in distribution. Testing for the endpoint of a product in a real-time shelf-life test can be completed through random testing over the product's life. Accelerated shelf-life testing involves laboratory studies in which environmental conditions are accelerated by known variables, so that the product deteriorates at a faster rate. Based on the deterioration rate, formulas are used to estimate the actual shelf-life.

Temperature is a vital factor in the rates of reactions, because an increase in temperature accelerates the aging and quality deterioration of most foods. Many accelerated shelf-life testing methods use increased temperature to determine shelf-life. Other environmental factors, such as the gaseous atmosphere in which the product is tested or the gas composition in packaging, will affect the rate of deterioration.

Because shelf-life is the time in which a product has acceptable attributes for consumers, it is important to measure quality traits throughout testing. Physical, chemical, microbiological, and sensory changes must be monitored and measured throughout the entire shelf study. In shelf-life studies, sensory testing must be carried out with a question such as "Is this product acceptable?" Tests should be administered more frequently as the projected shelf-life nears its end, so that a more accurate and empirically verified shelf-life can be established.

In order to conduct a realistic shelf-life study, it is important to take into account the real-world logistics of storing and transporting food. During distribution, products can undergo significant abuse, whether temperature fluctuations or physical mistreatment. This is a challenge for companies to incorporate into shelf-life determination, but it can be done through the utilization of multiple test methods.

Methods for determining shelf-life include static tests, accelerated tests, and use/abuse tests (Fuller 2011). Static tests involve holding the product at set environmental conditions in which it will be distributed and testing samples over a set time interval. Shelf-life studies should be carefully planned and include a detailed sampling schedule. At pre-determined intervals, the product will be tested using sensory, physical, and chemical analyses. Accelerated shelf-life studies hold products under a range of conditions and subject each product condition to sensory (if applicable), physical, and chemical analyses at pre-determined intervals. Labuza (1982) recommends storage conditions for accelerated shelf-life testing. Use/abuse tests can help determine the amount of damage that a product may incur during shipping. The variety of use/abuse tests is innumerable, but a common variation is to distribute a pallet of food by normal carriers to a certain location, then have it sent back to determine packaging effectiveness and if the product could withstand abuse.

ACCELERATED SHELF-LIFE TESTING

Accelerated shelf life testing (ASLT) is a more rapid method than real-time tests for determining how long a product will be acceptable. Accelerated shelf life testing is based on principles of chemical kinetics, which are applied to quantify the effects that extrinsic factors have on the rate of deteriorative reactions. Tested products are subjected to controlled environmental conditions in which one or more of the factors is maintained at a higher level than normal. In the end, the "true" shelflife can be calculated. For this approach to work, a product developer should determine first what is the primary mode of failure for the product. It could be a physical property such as hardness due to staling in breads, a chemical property such as rancidity in potato chips, a microbiological property such as mold growth on a dried fruit, or a sensory property such as loss of flavor in a Fruit Roll-Up™.

Quality loss for most foods results from either a zero-order or first-order reaction. Products that undergo zero-order reactions have deterioration that is linear, whereas first-order reactions demonstrate logarithmic deterioration. For a given extent of deterioration and reaction order, the rate constant is inversely proportional to the time to reach a certain degree of quality loss.

The Q_{10} approach uses increments of ten degrees of temperature to determine shelf-life. The Q_{10} value is the factor at which a product deteriorates with a difference of 10°C. Typical Q_{10} values for foods are 1.1

TABLE 14.1. The Effect of Temperature on the Shelf-Life of Products at a Q_{10} Value.

Temperature		Shelf-Life (weeks)			
°C	°F	$Q_{10} = 2$	$Q_{10} = 2.5$	$Q_{10} = 3$	$Q_{10} = 5$
50	122	2	2	2	2
40	104	4	5	6	10
30	86	8	12.5	18	50

to 4 for canned foods, 1.5 to 10 for dehydrated foods, and 3 to 40 for frozen foods. As seen in Table 14.1, the Q_{10} value represents acceleration as related to temperature.

By determining the ratio of the shelf-life between any two temperatures separated by 10°C (18°F), the Q_{10} of the reaction can be found:

$$Q_{10} = \theta_{st}/\theta_{st} + 10$$

θ_{st} = Shelf-life at temperature T°C
$\theta_{st} + 10$ = shelf-life at temperature (T + 10)°C

Using the equation above, the differences give the Q_{10} value, which can be charted on a graph to determine the shelf-life at room tempera-

Example of Q_{10} value:

A company has been conducting accelerated shelf-life testing on a ready to eat cereal product. It is determined that the product fails quality acceptance at 6 weeks for a product tested at 40°C at 6 weeks, and at 18 weeks for a product tested at 30°C. What is the Q_{10} value? What is the shelf-life?

$Q_{10} = \theta_{st}/\theta_{st} + 10$
$\theta_{st} = 30°C$, $\theta_{st} + 10 = 40°C$
$Q_{10} = 18/6 = 3.0$

The Q_{10} is 3, but how do we calculate the shelf-life?

Since the product will be held at ambient temperatures (22°C), figure the percentage difference between the ambient temperature and the lowest test temperature: 22°C/30°C = 0.733

Take this number times your factor: 3 x 0.733 = 2.20

Take this factor times the shelf stability time found in the study for the same temperature: 18 x 2.20 = 39.6 weeks.

Will this product meet the company's goals of a one-year shelf-life expectation?

ture (22°C) over time. After you have calculated the Q_{10} at a certain temperature, you can determine what the shelf-life would be for ambient temperatures.

MICROBIAL CHALLENGE STUDIES

Microbial challenge studies simulate what happens to a product during processing, distribution, and subsequent preparation and handling, should the product become contaminated. Tests are performed through inoculating selected microorganisms into a food. The organism used to inoculate the food is dependent on the pathogens most likely to survive. For canned foods, a strain of *Clostridium sporogenes* is typically used, because of its similar characteristics to *Clostridium botulinum*. Challenge studies are generally performed on foods stored at refrigeration or room temperatures (shelf stable), as well as on foods vulnerable to spoilage organisms and/or pathogenic growth (pH > 4.6 or $a_w > 0.85$).

SUMMARY

Shelf-life determination allows companies to gather scientific data about when the quality of a food deteriorates and becomes unacceptable in terms of company and consumer standards. Effective shelf-life studies account for product distribution times. The type of date included on packaging is dependent on typical consumer usage practices.

KEY WORDS

Accelerated shelf-life testing (ALST)—a faster method than one in real time for determining how long a product will be acceptable.

Best if used by dating—the final date of the maximum quality of the product.

Display dating—the date the food was placed on the store shelf.

Expiration date/use by date—the date before which a food must be consumed or discarded.

Pack date—the date on which a food was manufactured.

Q_{10} *value*—the factor at which a product deteriorates with a difference of 10°C.

Sell by/pull date—the date by which a food must be sold or removed from the shelf.

COMPREHENSION QUESTIONS

14.1. What is the difference between intrinsic and extrinsic parameters? Give an example of each.

14.2. State the definition of the Q_{10} value and tell how it is used to define a product's shelf life.

14.3. Cite an example of each of the kinds of deterioration (physical, chemical, and microbial) that your product might be subject to.

14.4. Answer True or False to the following statements.

a. There is no universally accepted dating system for food products in the United States.
b. Accelerated shelf-life testing uses the Q_{15} value to calculate the shelflife of food.
c. Consumers' perception of the quality of a product over time should help determine the product's shelflife.

REFERENCES

Fuller, 2011.

Labuza, T. P. *Shelf-Life Dating of Foods.* (Westport, CT: Food and Nutrition Press, 1982).

Steele, R. (Ed.). (2004). *Understanding and measuring the shelf-life of food.* Boca Raton, FL: CRC Press LLC.

CHAPTER 15

The Essentials of Marketing Food Products

Learning Objectives

- Understand the basic marketing concepts.
- Know the differences among product outlets, retail and wholesale.
- Appreciate the 4 Ps of marketing.
- See how to create a marketing plan for a company.

MARKETING is the commercial activities that attend the transferring of food products from producers to consumers. Marketing a food product seems logical and reasonable, but finding consumers to buy a product requires executing a specific agenda of collecting accurate information, analyzing alternative market outlets, developing different product forms, pricing products to compete in the marketplace, and deciding the scope of the proposed market area.

The average income of people in the United States has risen over the past 20 years, but increased income has not translated into an increase in the quantities of food consumed. Per capita food consumption has changed very little in the last 50 years. Although the percentage of income spent for food has continued to decrease, the number of food services and prepared food products has increased. Wide variations in the level of incomes can be seen in a particular geographical location. Ranges of income levels are greater in urban areas where two-income families are more common. A higher income enables a family unit to buy more food preparation services. Thus, one goal of a new entrepreneur is to provide a food product that is readily usable by the modern family and to capture as much of the value-added market as possible. To attain a foothold in a market assumes the product is sold. However, a product can sell only when potential customers receive information about it. Communicating such information persuasively is one function of marketing.

ORGANIZING MARKETING FUNCTIONS

Buying and selling require rational and economically acceptable pricing. Sellers can offer a product for a very high price, but without willing buyers at that price, there will be no exchange of merchandise. Likewise, buyers can offer to buy a product for a very low price, but if the seller is unwilling to agree, there will be no transaction. For all transactions, there must be a willing buyer and willing seller who have to agree on the price, quantity, quality, and location of delivery.

Exchange Functions

The exchange function is the basic price-setting stage of the marketing process. The supply available at a particular time will determine the price buyers are willing to pay. The price then determines what the supply will be in the future. If the supply is low and consumers want more product, the price will be driven up. Based on this information, the processor will increase supply to take advantage of the higher prices. If the supply is more than the consumers are willing to buy at that price, prices will be driven down. A lower price might not cover all the production and marketing costs, which should lead to financial losses and a decrease, if not a halt, in production. When the supplies are at a level such that all units are purchased at the given price, the market is said to be in equilibrium.

As described above, when someone sells a product, they are transferring ownership to a buyer at a price that is acceptable to both seller and buyer. Prices received for products should be the same or greater than expected total costs associated with making the product. Total cost estimates also include a profit or a favorable return on investment for each entrepreneur. When buyers continue to buy products at these prices, the signal is to continue production.

Buying and selling are the basic exchange functions of marketing. The purchasing of products requires both parties to agree to an exchange of a specific product quantity and quality for an agreed price. If one party, such as a seller, has more knowledge than the buyer, the informational discrepancy between seller and buyer could result in a higher price being charged, e.g., a producer has specialized knowledge about ingredient costs, which a consumer could not easily discover.

As a rule, rational buyers and sellers will seek to understand forces that affect pricing and the market for a product. These will include availability, competing products, and claims made for similar products.

Middlemen, who transfer or sell but do not manufacture a product, will also consider their costs and income from exchange as part of their business. If they calculate that their total returns are equal to or greater than their total costs, they will handle a product. Middlemen will also try to sell more volume in their geographic area to lower their average fixed costs (FC) and, thus, increase their net return. This is assuming there is no change in FCs with additional sales volume.

Marketing efficiency will be optimized when all buyers and sellers have the same knowledge concerning alternative sources, uses, and prices. Consumer satisfaction will be maximized when they can choose between different products, qualities, and prices to maintain or improve their quality of living.

Physical Function

Food is a biological product; as soon as it is harvested or produced, it starts to deteriorate. Some products spoil faster than others. A major objective of the food industry is to deliver products to consumers in an acceptable state of freshness. Products must be physically processed, stored, and transported to the consumer in an acceptable form. Economic evaluation of a physical function, such as processing or transporting, will provide information to determine whether the developer will perform that function or hire someone else to do it.

Processing

All food products involve assembling, cooking, cutting, sorting, mixing, and/or packaging various ingredients into a product form that consumers will buy. Each of these steps adds value and, at the same time, cost. Even fresh fruits and vegetables have to be picked, cleaned, sorted, cooled, shipped, and displayed. A complete cost analysis for each physical function should be done to ensure that costs for additional processing will return a profit. Examples of value-added foods include applesauce, frozen vegetables, TV dinners, and many other items. Many forms of food must be modified to satisfy consumers' desires based on specialized tastes, religion, or ethnicity. Successful developers need to find the market niche of individuals willing to purchase their production and marketing services for a price that covers all costs.

Storage

All products have to be stored somewhere from the time they are produced until the time they are sold to the consumer. Various products will have different costs resulting from specialized storage facilities, such as frozen, fresh, or dry products and the length of time needed for each product. Storage will be required until these products are ready to be placed on a retail shelf. Consumers, as a general rule, may not have very much food storage capacity in their homes and, thus, make frequent purchases throughout the year.

Transportation

All products must be transported in one form or another from the original production location to the consumer. Costs of transporting products from a processing plant to a retail facility will depend on the distance and kind of transportation needed. Transportation costs will vary by location, type of transport, and volume of products. Sometimes there are several locations where a product has to be shipped. Special transportation equipment may be needed to maintain quality for such items as bread, fresh fruit and vegetables, and canned or frozen foods. Consumers can choose and pay for the final product only after it has been delivered to a location where they shop and at a price they are willing to pay.

Facilitating Function

The marketing system facilitates establishing quality standards, financing, risk bearing, and information for those who use them. All of these functions are outside the normal arena of local managers, but they should use this information to their advantage.

Consistent grades that are recognizable are established to indicate a food meets safety and quality standards. Industry, state and/or federal regulations help maintain safe, wholesome and consistent food products for consumers, who have every reason to expect wholesome and dependable products at the time of purchase. Consistent standards or a specific quality grade mean the same to both buyers and sellers, which also improves communication between them.

Maintaining constant standards for each food item requires additional costs for a quality control program from the time of procurement until the product is sold to the consumer. Product losses resulting from spoilage during storage and transportation have to be considered as a cost to the owner of the product and must be factored into total product cost estimates. Selling lower grades or partially deteriorated products in low-price outlets might offset revenue losses. But this is, at best, a temporary expedient.

Financing

Each firm in a marketing channel that buys ingredients and products finances products until they are sold. Each buyer assumes financial risks while products are processed, stored, transported, and sold to the next buyer in the marketing system. Each producer uses, and risks, capital until products in which it invests can be sold. It is only after the consumer buys the product that the total financial obligation for the product is settled.

Risk Bearing

During each stage of food production and distribution, owners of titles to a food bear two basic risks: price changes and product decay. Price risk can be minimized with various types of contracts, forward pricing, or other pricing techniques. Spoilage can be reduced with proper handling, storage, transportation, and scheduling.

Market Intelligence

Marketing firms, government agencies, and private brokers know what is happening in a marketplace. There are many ways small entrepreneurs can obtain information, such as websites, newspapers, trade magazines, catalogs, brokers, and company brochures. It is the responsibility of entrepreneurs to seek price and quality information that is best for their operations. Additional information should include nontraditional market outlets and alternative products that can be produced to meet different consumer requirements. Finding the right marketing combinations for niche products will depend on the kind and type of information that is collected about the industry.

Accurate pricing, volume, raw materials supply, and quality information are key to decision making. The marketing system provides information for specific commodity prices, quantity, overall competition, production patterns, and general price levels. Depending on the type of product, there are published price lists, private and/or public, that can be used as price guides. Identifying and selecting price lists will depend, in part, on the volatility of prices and ease of market entry by other producers.

A new cookie, for example, has little value without additional marketing activities, such as advertising and transportation. In addition, information must be collected and studied concerning competing cookie products. Sellers also need to consider the number of times consumers buys cookies in a week, month, or year. The number of consumers in an area and frequency of purchases determines the size of the market. This requires research by the cookie manufacturer or marketing agent to determine consumers' openness to buying a new cookie, especially when many different types are already available.

Summary

Thousands of new food products are constantly being developed for special niches. In reality, all food products can be substituted for one another if the price differential or specialty attraction causes the consumer to make the choice. In a competitive market, sales will depend on the success of convincing consumers to buy products at prices that satisfy them.

CONSUMPTION

The ultimate goal of production and marketing is to sell products to consumers. The task of public consumers is to select various food products that will be consumed by members of their household. Their selection will depend on their incomes, tastes, ethnic background, and knowledge of competing products. Satisfaction with the food product, store personnel, service, availability, and conveniences are also part of the experience of shopping. Thus, the purchase of a food product must be seen within a whole bundle of experiences that are evaluated by each consumer.

Because consumer demand drives sales, it is important to know if there is a need or desire for a new product prior to development. Also, the price range that consumers will pay for the product needs to be determined. In consumer studies, the price that consumers state they are willing to pay should be compared to the costs of production and marketing of the product. Prices for the products, as well as quality, also play a major part in the consumer's decision to buy any product. Each food product has a role in everyday food consumption, and it is the job of the food producer/processor manager to find it.

POPULATION TARGETS

Most people in the United States live in urban areas. Concentrations of people provide an opportunity to identify specific ethnic, religious, national, or other target demographics that can be the focus of niche marketing. Specialized consumers will provide stability for a product over an extended period of time. Usually, specialty products that appeal to a niche market are more stable than items intended for a wider audience. Selling to a broader swathe of consumers normally requires substantial volume and is subject to greater competition from all other food products. The volume of a food sold is increased only by a population increase or through expanded export markets.

MARKETPLACE OF ALTERNATIVE PRODUCTS AND CONSUMER PREFERENCE

Consumers have thousands of choices when shopping in a supermarket. If an entrepreneur wants to develop a new bread product, then proper considerations would include what alternatives are available to consumers. There are typically more than 100 different kinds of breads and rolls from which the consumer can choose. The number of times a product is purchased per year is also important. Products used daily or weekly by a household, such as bread or milk, do not need as large a population base as a product that might be purchased only once a year, such as a holiday-specific item. Production and availability of ingredients may also restrict year-round selling opportunities. For example, turkeys were long associated with, and bought only for, Thanksgiving and Christmas. But now turkey producers and processors have used marketing to alter consumer preferences for eating turkey any time of the year, in direct competition with beef, pork, poultry, and fish.

Advertising is an important factor in getting people to know about and purchase a product. New food products can be identified by the specific characteristics that separate them from competing food products. Advertising is a means by which information is passed to the consumer telling them of specific product traits, product superiority compared with competing products, and the satisfaction each purchaser will receive upon consumption. When a product is not distinguishable from others, then advertising becomes very expensive and may not result in increased sales.

Product developers and marketing managers must use market research to discover consumer preferences and product price points. Identifying close substitutes and competitive products is a prelude to development. Consumer demand information can be used to determine what to produce, when to produce, and where to sell.

The basic principles of supply and demand for individual commodities in a competitive market need to be researched to understand appropriate price points. A simplified definition of supply is that producers will produce greater volumes with increasing price levels, as long as sales continue. For example, if the cost to produce a specific product increases, producers will increase their output, and ideally sale volume, to increase their income. The definition of demand on the other hand is that consumers will buy less with increasing price levels. The role of the marketplace is to transmit consumer price signals to producers, so that they know how many units to produce.

The marketplace provides information to determine the price level and production volume that is needed to fulfill consumer's expectations and purchasing desires. Producers use price information from the sales market to decide the volume to produce based on the costs of production. Production changes cannot be made instantaneously, which can cause excess or shortage of the product in the marketplace. To move merchandise, products that are on the shelf but not selling can be sold at lower "sale" prices. The new price is a major factor for deciding future production based on costs of production. When the consumer price level is equal to the cost of the product for a given volume, the marketplace is said to be in equilibrium.

Production decisions are based on current prices along with prices projected when a product reaches consumers. The uncertainties of future prices cause managers to make "best-price estimates" based on their knowledge of consumer demand for their product or similar products. Careful analysis of consumers' wants and desires, combined with their incomes, and knowledge of their prior choices will help project reasonably accurate prices for specific food items. To remove some price uncertainties, advanced contracts can be developed. However, for certain products that set price or production levels, or both, delivery at a specific time and place may be more appropriate. Forward contracts can be developed for inputs and products.

In a freely competitive market, regulations or other artificial barriers should not restrict entry of new products. Each product competes on its own merits based on the willingness of consumers to continue to buy it over an extended period of time. In addition, the new food product will be produced based on the availability of inputs. All these factors become part of the decision-making process for managers in determining what form, how much, and when to produce a product and where to deliver it.

MANAGING MARKETING ACTIVITIES

The marketing manager should concentrate on marketing plans that will best serve the company and reach all targeted consumers. Managers think first of increasing sales, but to be successful, they must also think about selling costs, including the costs of promotion and distribution, i.e., moving products from the plant to the consumer. Consumers must be broken down by distribution channel, whether they buy from a roadside stand, catalog, or retail store.

Various marketing functions require estimating alternative costs for each function. The form of the food product will determine the extent each marketing function is used. Each function has a cost that is unique to each product. For example, if a product is processed and frozen, it has to be stored in a frozen state until consumers buy it. Frozen storage is more expensive than dry storage, but the freshness quality is maintained over a longer period of time. Product seasonality can be extended with various types of processing, such as freezing, canning, and drying. Fresh products need to be transported rapidly to consumers. Managers can organize marketing activities into three basic functions: exchange, physical, and facilitating functions.

COSTS AND PERSONNEL OF MARKETING ACTIVITIES

One person should be solely responsible for making marketing decisions. Without such specialized effort, the chances of success are lowered. Organizing a separate marketing activity for each new product is often the difference between success and failure. Information about the different functions and alternative outlets, different forms, and prices needs to be collected and analyzed. This requires a person to research the volume and the size of the proposed market area.

Often a new entrepreneur will not have the time and interest to develop a complete marketing plan. One means of establishing a marketing program is to engage a broker or other middleman to sell your product in conjunction with other products. A competent broker can provide access to markets that would not otherwise be accessible. Brokers have information concerning market outlets for many products. As specialists, they are able, for a fee, to sell products in market locations that would be difficult for a small firm to find. Information concerning alternative buyers, locations, prices, and similar products is a major input provided by brokers.

The primary job of a marketing specialist is to develop a marketing plan. Initial questions include the following: "Do consumers want or need the food product?" "In what form?" "Where are they located?" "What are the number and type of competing products?" "What prices are consumers willing to pay?" The marketing plan should include information about every market function required for the product to reach the consumer. Also, procedures need to be developed on how price information is to be collected for products. Information from consumers should include acceptable qualities, volumes, and prices.

The most difficult part of developing a marketing plan is estimating total marketing costs. Each marketing firm or production unit uses labor, management, land, and capital resources in various degrees of concentration. Expenditures should be included in a cost analysis and reflected in the difference between purchase and selling prices. Various marketing functions will have different costs, depending on how much of each is needed to move products from the place of production to consumers. Each entrepreneur must to evaluate information using estimates of cost and the pricing system to decide to continue operation. When a firm is in operation for a longer period of time, cost estimates can be based on actual expenditures, which are more accurate.

ORGANIZING TO SELL NEW PRODUCTS

Marketing managers need to decide what kind of a market territory they want to serve. Their selection will depend on different population concentrations, income levels, number of competitive products, and number of market outlets. Data like these should be used to develop the type of market organization that best serves consumers and sells the product. If these data are too difficult to collect using in-house resources, they can be purchased from marketing consultants and firms.

Manufacturers of new food products are faced with problem areas that are unique to each. For some products, delivery to sales outlets can be complicated, but for others the process is fairly straightforward. In any case, managers should gather the information needed to fully understand and be able to choose the most profitable alternative. To start this process, managers must have enough information about their consumers and target markets.

Identifying Target Markets

Who will most likely buy the product, how often will they buy it, what price they are willing to pay, and where will they be buying it? Managers have to collect market information in order to make the day-to-day decisions and define the target market, which comprises a demographic of those who are most likely to purchase the product. Some of the questions that should be posed are listed below.

- What quantity of a product are consumers willing to purchase?
- Who are the other manufacturers of similar products, and competing for the same consumers?
- What prices are consumers willing to pay for various quantities offered for sale?
- What is the speed with which products and information travel through the channels of distribution?
- How long does it take for a price increase to reach the producer?
- Based on changing price information from consumers, should production be increased or decreased?

PARTICIPANTS IN THE MARKETING PROCESS

There are many firms involved in the marketing process. This section focuses on "who" is active in conveying, broadly speaking, a product from the manufacturer to the purchaser. A variety of middlemen and organizations specialize in performing various marketing functions, and there is no limitation to the way they are organized. These participants include wholesalers, brokers, and retailers.

Wholesalers

Wholesalers sell to retailers, other wholesalers, and industrial users but do not sell in significant amounts to ultimate consumers. There are two main kinds of wholesalers, agent and merchant.

Agent wholesalers arrange to have products moved from processors to merchant wholesalers and retailers. They can also provide access to market territories that would be available only if the producer expended additional time and cost. This activity requires a great deal of specialization, and agent wholesalers charge fees for such services. For this fee, however, they can help provide a number of marketing solutions, such as alternative buyers, locations, prices, products, and novel outlets. In addition, some may specialize in a certain kind of product, in different market locations, or in a large number of different products in a specific location. Meanwhile, merchant wholesalers profit based on their knowledge of the market situation. Merchant wholesalers can provide great connections to consumers, because they are able to flow products through channels they understand, including wholesalers, retailers, and industrial purchasers. Their goal is to use their knowledge of a distribution system to "buy low and sell high."

Brokers

Brokers act only as representatives for their clients. Brokers' incomes stem from fees and commissions, which are payments for their knowledge of market outlets and contacts. Brokers do not assume physical control of the products, follow directions of each principal, and have less discretionary power in price negotiation.

Retailers

Retailers buy from many processors and wholesalers to develop a product mix that will attract consumers to their stores. They rely on consistent quality and availability of products. Retailers mark up their price on each product a given percent over what they paid for it, unless they are forced to lower the price to a "sale" level.

ALTERNATIVE RETAIL OUTLETS

Marketing alternatives can also include selling directly to retail outlets. Such arrangements need to be set up before full production, not after. These retail outlets include large chain stores, neighborhood stores, specialty stores, mail-order (Internet) sales, government contracts, roadside stands and door-to-door sales. Alternative retail outlets can help producers to reach a specific consumer group with product-specific incomes, ethnic preferences, and lifestyles.

Large Chain Stores

Chain stores offer exposure to a potentially enormous number of consumers. Large chain stores typically require great quantities of a product delivered at specific times and specific places at predetermined prices. They also require the product over an extended period of time. Often, these outlets charge for shelf space, a "shelving fee," in addition to the percent markup. This fee is a marketing cost to the producer.

Neighborhood Stores

Neighborhood stores will work with local producers if the managers feel their clientele will accept a new product. Each store has developed a clientele unique to that store, and new products are part of that image. Usually there are not a lot of different products, and selling in such a venue is a good way to see if consumers will buy a product.

Specialty Stores

Specialty stores are often single-line stores or discount houses which, like neighborhood stores, have a unique clientele. The products must match the clientele and image of the specialty store. Consumers patronize these stores because they want and know the quality and prices of various products carried by the store. Better quality products in these outlets are normally offered at higher prices, which reflects, in part, their higher costs.

Mail-Order (Internet) Sales

With mailorder outlets, sales volume can be controlled by the number and type of catalogs sent. When using mailorder catalogs, it is important to know the number distributed and the characteristics of the readers. For example, if 400,000 people receive a catalog and 3 percent of them order one product, there could be 12,000 orders. Producers need to understand and be prepared for the potential volume of mail orders. Conversely, there could be very few sales, and many products left over. Internet sales should be considered for food products that can be produced with minimal delay and shipped safely.

Government Contracts

Contracts may be concluded with government agencies to provide food to outlets such as prisons, military bases, and government cafeterias, thus possibly forming a consistent and predictable outlet for products. Contracts with government purchasing agencies can also be negotiated for large-volume sales, especially by smaller or minority-owned businesses. Government specifications must be met to secure these contracts.

TEST MARKETING

Regardless of the outlet chosen, products should be subjected to test marketing in order to gauge potential sales. The purpose of test marketing is to see how specific products compete with other brands and to gauge consumer reaction. Producers should work with retail managers to decide advertising and promotion strategies to spark consumer interest. Retail managers must have confidence in the product and be convinced it will sell in their establishment. Producers and retailers can entice customers to try new products by offering samples in a store, selling at reduced prices, or giving the product away. Immediate feedback should be sought from consumers to capture their thoughts, reactions, and suggestions for improvement. Producers should compare competing products by purchasing them and carefully noting prices and quality standards.

Location of products within any store is important, because certain locations receive higher traffic. Placement determines how many consumers will see the product. Work with retail managers to secure the highest exposure areas for new products, such as at the ends of aisles or at the checkout counter. In addition, there is a preferred height on store shelves where people can see a product without looking up or down. Placement in a favored area may require a fee.

CONSUMER FEEDBACK

Consumer feedback may be obtained by asking friends and neighbors to provide assistance when testing a new product. This is only a first step and should not be the test used to represent consumers. It is vitally important to seek consumer reaction to a product before full production begins. This process begins in a marketing plan. Ask consumers in a store the following questions;

- Do they like the product?
- Will they buy it again?
- How soon?
- Will they continue to buy it?
- What changes would they like to see in the product?

After full production is underway, a continuing program to obtain consumer reaction should be developed. Information should also be routinely gathered in each product outlet about sales volume, changes in competitors' offerings, lifecycles of the product, new products, and service to vendors and competitors.

Remember: General information will provide general results, and detailed information will allow for more detailed analysis and more accurate results. Each manager must decide what type of information is needed and how much to collect to make prudent plant management decisions. The more producers know about customers, the better chance they have of satisfying the customers.

PRICING COMPETITIVELY

One question is if the product is priced similarly to other competing brands but above costs of production. After consumers have been identified, a retail outlet has been located, and test marketing has been completed, producers determine at what price a product will sell and still be profitable. Price is the only means for generating income and profit for the producer and all marketing functions. There is no one method of setting prices. Costs of production do not determine the price that consumers will pay for the product. The market dictates acceptable pricing, because consumers are typically interested in the lowest-priced products at a particular quality and volume.

Marketing managers must find the price that satisfies both consumers and producers. Consumers are always willing to pay lower prices for any product. Producers are always willing to offer products for sale at higher prices. A market price for long-term production is established when the average price consumers will pay for any product is equal to or above the average total cost of production.

ADVERTISING

Advertising is often seen as synonymous with marketing. By definition, advertising is controlled communication between producer and consumer about a product. Through symbols and language, it conveys what a product or service can do for the consumer. The main thrust of advertising campaigns is to convince consumers that a particular product is unlike competing products and that quality of life will be improved if a product is purchased. Campaigns can focus on differentiating a product from similar offerings based on consumer-accepted quality differences. The goal is to persuade consumers to buy the product. Consumer response to a new product can be gathered by giving samples to consumers in stores or retail businesses.

Regardless of the quality of a product's advertising, it is important to remember that a product has to compete on its own. Brand preference cannot be established if a product fails to meet consumer expectations. Money for advertising should be budgeted into the overall product cost.

FREQUENCY OF CONSUMER PURCHASE

Frequency of consumer purchases is a main data point. Repeat purchases can assist in identifying and choosing successful sales outlets. Marketing managers need to understand how often consumers will be purchasing their products when determining production rates, transportation, storage, etc. The most common purchasing patterns are as follows:

- *Daily or several times per week*—Some products, such as milk, fresh fruit and vegetables, bread, and donuts, are usually purchased frequently, meaning the producer will have to deliver the product frequently. These products are perishable.
- *Weekly*—Products purchased weekly must have a three- to six-week shelf life. For these products, careful control of the production inventory is necessary. A producer must have the ability and capacity to store products between deliveries.
- *Monthly*—A larger consumer territory must be projected if the consumer only buys a product one time per month compared with one per week. Delivery to retail stores will be less frequent, and storage will need to be increased, either on the shelf or in a warehouse.
- *Seasonally*—Seasonal products are generally associated with a spe-

cific growing season and are usually sold only during the season they are available.

- *Annually*—Specific food products can be associated with a particular holiday, special event, or time of year.

PACKAGING

Packaging is a recognized mode of product promotion. Producers will not overlook the design and quality of external packaging, because it is the consumer's first impression of the food inside. Consumers are more likely to buy a product if the package is appealing to them. In fact, studies have shown that consumers will buy a product in a package they like and will not buy it in one they do not like, even when the product is the same.

Consumers decide the size package most suited to each product by selecting certain sizes when purchasing them. The size and type of package depends on knowing what the consumer finds convenient for each type of product. Consumers are more likely to buy a smaller package that is used immediately. A larger package can be considered even if the food is used frequently, just as long as it can retain its quality over several days.

The types of processing determine the length of time a product can be safely stored from the time it is processed until it is used, which in turn affects packaging design. Obviously, different packaged products demand different types of storage and transportation facilities. Fresh products have to move quickly to consumers. Dried products can be put into packets and moved through different marketing channels at a slower pace without affecting the quality of the product. They can also be shipped farther to reach multiple consumer areas. It is crucial that the package or containers maintain the same quality of the product from the time the product leaves the processor until it reaches the consumer, regardless of the type of storage and transportation required.

Marketing is used in this case to encompass all the steps that lead to final sales. It comprises planning and executing pricing, promotion, and distribution. From this definition, it is easy to see that marketing is more than just the process of selling a product or service. Marketing is essential and, without it, even the best products and services fail.

Marketing teams must study the marketplace to reduce the risk of failure. Exact analysis of customer needs and desires in relation to a product is called for, because when the needs of customers are unmet, companies fail. Developers may mistakenly believe that, with the proper amount of advertising, customers will buy whatever they are offered. Marketing consists of making decisions about the four Ps:

- Product
- Place/Distribution
- Promotion
- Pricing

Before a business owner can make decisions on the four Ps, he/she must devise a marketing plan to guide the decisions. A marketing plan involves a six-stage process that is commonly referred to as strategic marketing; a strategic marketing plan is an important part of a business plan.

MARKETING PLAN

A marketing plan should be developed and continuously updated for each product. This plan will include what, where, when, and to whom products are sold. This information should also be used to decide production practices, changes in products, where products should be sold for the greatest return, and the volume that can be sold. More specifically, a marketing plan provides an assessment of the product climate and guidance as to how the business will integrate a new product into the company's overall strategy.

Business Environment

An assessment of the current business environment of a particular area may be beyond the control of local managers. At the same time, marketers of a new product should be aware of the consumption, distribution, and marketing practices in the venue where the product is to be offered. The patterns of buying and selling are not easily changed for well-established products but can be more easily swayed with a new and unknown food product. Initial sales of a new product may have to overcome long-established business associations. If wholesalers have worked successfully with a given group of suppliers, it could be difficult to convince them to include a new product in their existing line, especially if it is similar to items they've handled for years.

One way to interest wholesalers or retailers is to demonstrate an increase in profitability for them, which can be difficult if there is no track record for a product. A completely new product should be placed into smaller markets that permit direct control of marketing, until a sales history and attendant data can be developed. With this information, it will be easier to convince wholesalers to consider the new item. Also, it will demonstrate that the new product has the possibility of being accepted by consumers for an extended time period.

Consumer Requirements

Important factors to consider when addressing consumers are market territory, population concentration, income level, and the number of market outlets.

Market territory is the geographical area or areas where the product is going to be sold. It must be determined whether it is local, regional, national, or international. The population number and density must also be taken into consideration. The number of visits people make per week to a certain store is also important information to seek. Where a product demands it, demographic data should include a breakdown of the number and location of specific ethnic groups. This will determine where to sell and the volume each sales site needs to maintain consumer satisfaction and at the same time keep the plant operating at a profitable level. Consumer household and other income levels must also be analyzed.

The marketing team should consider where consumers currently purchase similar product or products. All the foregoing factors must be quantified and added to the marketing plan.

Once the background research is done, work can begin on the strategic marketing plan, which is carried out in stages, as described below.

Stage 1: Mission Statement

The first stage in strategic marketing is the development of a mission statement. A mission statement is a brief description of a company's goals, generally no more than a few lines, that describes where the company is and where it wants to go.

A good mission statement should contain the following:

- Company purpose
- Target customers/markets
- Principal products/services
- Geographic domain

- Core technologies used
- Commitment to survival, growth, and profitability
- Key parts of the company's philosophy
- Company's desired images

Do not expect a mission statement to be developed quickly. It generally takes various revisions before a complete mission statement is written. A mission statement should reflect the objective and image the company wishes to portray.

Stage 2: Overall Company Objectives

Once a mission statement has been created, the company can develop objectives. Objectives are specific goals to be achieved by the business. Company objectives are plans that will help a company move toward the mission statement. A business normally creates both one- and three-year objectives. Examples of company objectives are as follows:

> To earn at least 20% after-tax rate of return on our net investment during this year
>
> OR
>
> To make our cookies the best-selling cookies in terms of units sold in Kansas

Types of Objectives

Objectives can focus on profitability, volume, stability, and other non-financial aspects of a business. Profitability objectives include improving net profit as a percentage of sales, total investment, or common stock share prices. Volume goals may be to increase market share, grow sales revenues, improve sales rank in the market, or enhance production capacity. Companies may also strive for greater stability, meaning less variance in annual sales volume, seasonal sales volume, or profitability. Improving stability helps organizations to better forecast the amount of money that will be coming into the business and to ease financial planning. Non-financial goals can center on any number of issues, including technological advancement, sustainability practices, and improved corporate image. No matter what its category, an objective should be suitable for the business, measurable, feasible, flexible, and motivat-

TABLE 15.1. Questions for the Creation of Marketing Objectives.

Suitable	Do they fit with the corporate mission?
Measurable	What will happen and when?
Feasible	Are they possible to achieve?
Acceptable	Do they fit with the values of the company and the employees?
Flexible	Can they be adapted and changed should unforeseen events arise?
Motivating	Are they either too difficult or too easy to achieve?
Understanding	Are they stated simply?
Commitment	Are employees committed to doing what is necessary to achieve them?
Participation	Are employees responsible for achieving the objectives included in the objective setting process?

ing and should include commitment and participation from employees. Companies need to ensure they do not set too many objectives, to avoid the risk of having objectives contradict and interfere with each other.

Stage 3: Competitive Strategies

Organizational objectives focus on internal motivation, whereas competitive strategies are developed to create advantages over the competition. Examples of creating a competitive strategy include offering buyers a standard product at a lower price or making a product different from those of the competition, based on attributes considered important to the customer.

Overall cost leadership is a strategy to reduce costs. Reducing costs allows the producer to have a greater competitive advantage in pricing finished goods, making the product more competitive with others like it. Reducing costs can be achieved through producing on a larger scale, designing products that are easy to manufacture or that use existing equipment, accessing low-cost raw materials, or extending a line of products.

Differentiation involves changing the product, so it is perceived as unique. Change can be based on technical superiority, quality, customer support services, or the appeal of more value for the money. Companies that use this strategy position themselves or their products as being different from their competitors in the eyes of consumers.

Niche marketing occurs when a product is sold to a small number of total potential customers. The specialty market is often referred to as niche marketing, because products are marketed to a very small group of buyers. Niche marketing requires the business owner to identify customers with similar demands and meet these specific needs extremely well. Niche marketing implies a company will earn a lower overall market share, but possibly higher profits on a product.

Stage 4: Marketing Objectives

Marketing objectives can be developed only after stages one through three have been completed. These should be designed to help a company attain overall objectives. The five basic marketing objectives are as follows:

- to achieve a viable level of sales or market share
- to increase market share
- to maintain market share
- to maximize cash flow
- to sustain profitability

Market share is a common term used in developing marketing objectives. It refers to the percentage of the total industry sales a company attains. For example, if a company sells 1,000 units of product, but total consumption for the good is 100,000 units, the market share is 1% (1000/100,000). Because market share quantifies how one company measures against its competitors, it is an important factor to consider.

Stage 5: Marketing Strategies

Marketing strategies outline how the planned marketing objectives will be achieved. For example, if the marketing objective is to increase market share, the marketing strategy will explain how the increase is to occur. A marketing strategy is a way to give marketing orientation to a business. A marketing orientation brings the customer into the center of the picture. All marketing objectives, whether profit, cash flow, or market share can be achieved only by increasing the number of users, increasing the rate of purchase, retaining existing customers, or acquiring new customers. How to achieve these goals is outline in Table 15.2.

Stage 6: Marketing Programs

Marketing programs are the detailed approaches to the four Ps (prod-

TABLE 15.2. Marketing Strategies and How to Achieve Them.

Marketing Strategy Goals	How to Achieve Goals
Increase the number of users	• Building willingness to buy • Increasing ability to buy
Increase the rate of purchase	• Broadening usage occasions for the product • Increasing level of consumption • Increasing rate of replacement
Retain current customers	• Maintaining satisfaction • Meeting what competition offers • Developing or increasing relationship marketing
Acquire new customers	• Bundling (selling products together, usually at a lower price than if bought separately) • Head-to-head market dominance • Head-to-head price/cost leadership • Differentiating the product • Serving a narrowly defined target market • Flankers (new brands designed to serve new segments)

ucts, place/distribution, promotion, and pricing). Decisions regarding the four Ps should closely follow the mission statement, company objectives, competitive strategies, marketing objectives, and marketing strategies.

PLACE: WHERE WILL THE PRODUCT BE OFFERED?

Distribution of products once they have been produced is important. Arrangements need to be set up before full production, not after. These include such outlets as large chain stores, mail-order sales, neighborhood stores, roadside stands, and door-to-door sales. Alternative retail outlets can help producers to reach a specific consumer group with income level suitably to the product, ethnic preferences that match the products, and lifestyles that are served by the products. Different retail outlets are usually defined by the size of store and variety of products.

Large Chain Stores

These stores can provide a better opportunity for a larger number of consumers compared with a local store. They offer thousands of choices of different products from which consumers must decide to spend their money. Large chain stores usually require large quantities of a product delivered at specific times and specific places at predetermined prices. They also require the product over an extended period of time. For providing access to large numbers of customers, they often charge a shelf space fee (i.e., shelving fee) in addition to the percent markup. This fee is a marketing cost to the producer.

Neighborhood Stores

These stores will often work with local producers if the managers feel their clientele will accept the products. Each store has developed a clientele unique to that store, and new products are part of that image. Usually there are not a lot of different products, and this is a good way to see if consumers will buy the product.

Specialty Stores

Products for specialty outlets were discussed previously. However, in addition, note that smaller distribution outlets can expedite customer feedback and concomitant product and pricing adjustments.

Mail-Order (Internet) Sales

Online (Internet) advertising must be coordinated with packaging and shipping procedures and should be used only for products that can be shipped safely.

Government Contracts

Contracts with government agencies typically involve a trade-off between adhering to stringent specifications for the produce and larger or long-term orders. Government specifications may lead to formulation changes.

Promotion

Promotional objectives vary for different products and situations. For example, producers must promote differently to brokers than to wholesalers. When promoting to a broker, the producer must promote what he/she wishes the broker to present to the wholesaler. When promoting to a wholesaler, the producer simply wants the wholesaler to purchase the product.

The five types of objectives for promotional activities are as follows: to provide information, increase demand, differentiate the product, accentuate the value of the product, and stabilize sales. Promotion can be carried out through advertising, publicity, and sales promotion. Advertising is the transmission of information via media channels whether it is free or purchased. Publicity is promotion at no cost to the company, which can be through news stories or media appearances. Sales promotion is any form of communication not found in advertising and personal selling, including direct mail, coupons, volume discounts, sampling, rebates, demonstrations, exhibits, sweepstakes, trade allowances, samples, and point-of-purchase displays.

Promotion Objectives

When designing a promotional plan, clearly spell out which objectives to use. It is possible to have more than one objective, but it is recommended that a company target its audience or run the risk of losing focus. All promotions should be clear on what the message will be, who the audience will be, and how the promotion will be measured for success and reach.

Promotional Strategy

Once the producer has reviewed all the possible promotional tools, he/she must devise a promotional strategy, which comprises defined goals and concrete types of promotion. Marketing managers should make note of what promotions are successful and which are less successful. Costs of promotion should be correlated to the size of the target audience reached, to get the best results with the least investment.

Cost of Promotion

Sales promotion has become increasingly affordable, as inexpensive, appropriate, and effective methods of promotion have emerged online. Although direct mail, window banners, and product demonstrations are all valuable promotional tools, social media outlets have become a major platform for reaching large audiences. Many social media outlets are free and can reach a large number of potential customers in a short amount of time. As their name implies, social media have the potential to ignite group interest in a product via rapid Internet sharing. Few promotions are more cost effective than word of mouth.

Type of Advertising

As noted above, advertising is the transmission of information about a product via mass media. Advertising can take place through print ads, television or radio spots, billboards, direct mailers, Internet site advertisements, or corporate advertising. Each advertising medium has advantages and disadvantages for the business and can reach a different group of consumers.

Newspapers

In general, newspaper advertising provides flexibility and a high amount of coverage. Newspaper ads often run for a short time and usually in a restricted geographic area. Their advantage is to be able to inform consumers in a local area where a product is likely to be purchased. A disadvantage is that newspaper readership is declining, with many readers in an older demographic.

Radio

Radio advertisements have low costs and are great for immediate promotional events. The audiences for radio stations can be tailored, thereby reaching a targeted audience. But, just as with newspaper advertisements, the effect of broadcast ads can be short-lived.

Magazines

A great advantage for magazine advertising is the audience selections it offers, because many magazines are specialized and have readerships that match certain categories. In addition, magazines are generally kept longer than newspapers. Although magazines have many positive factors, they are often inflexible in matters of space and timing. They are also facing stiff competition from online publications and new forms of consumer-specific Internet advertising, such as banner ads.

Outdoor Advertising

For quick communication of simple ideas, a company might consider outdoor advertising such as billboards. Outdoor advertising offers advantages when products are especially relevant or exclusively available in a limited geographical area. Newer outdoor advertising uses digital images and is comparable to TV ads minus sound.

Television

Television advertisements generally have mass coverage, especially during heavily watched events such as major sporting events. In addition, most advertisements are played repetitively, which helps induce product excitement. Television advertising can be geared to a local or regional market. However, it is expensive.

Direct Mail

Direct mailers sent via the United States Postal Service (USPS) provide flexibility of format, can give complete information, and offer personalization. In addition, they offer a great range of selectivity. For example, if you wanted to send out an advertisement regarding a new sales promotion in a single store, you could choose the geographical area or could just send it only to customers who have purchased from you at that store. The downfalls of this type of advertising are cost, dependency on a quality mailing list, and consumer resistance to "junk mail."

Cooperative Advertising

Cooperative advertising should be looked at as a way to enhance consumer awareness of a product (or brand) in a local market under both the brand and the retailer's name. Think of cooperative advertising as retailers helping to sell a product by paying part of the expense to promote the product in their stores. Examples of this can be seen in supermarket sales advertisements that offer special prices on specific products.

Internet Advertisements

Internet advertisements are a good way to reach a tailored audience.

Some websites have highly selective audiences, which may include bloggers. For example, a blog about eating gluten free has a highly selective audience made up of those who likely eat gluten free or live in a household with someone who does. A glutenfree blog may be the perfect place for a company that specializes in glutenfree products to invest in advertising. Internet advertisement may fluctuate in price because of differences in the number of visitors to a site or the number that might click on a banner ad. The advertisements must be catchy and use a focused message, as space is usually limited.

Media Rates

Promotional and media costs are the most difficult to allocate, because their effectiveness is hard to measure. Before looking at the dollar costs of different promotional media, a company should decide which media are most likely to reach the target audience, which media suit the product image, and whether any product-specific features make one medium more appropriate than another (e.g., when a visual demonstration is necessary). A promotional budget should be set before considering media rates. Common errors to avoid are trying to capture a broad market rather than a target audience, allowing the quality of a promotional piece to lapse to make it affordable, not including a measurement of effectiveness, and relying on just one type of media. With a company's free access to social media, a marketing manager should amplify the company's promotional material by providing more information online.

Trade Shows

Budgeting for and attending a trade show, and including this venue in the overall marketing plan, is a highly focused way to establish a presence in the marketplace, gain an overview of the current industry, and develop a list of serious buyers more quickly than would be possible with a traditional sales approach. Although trade shows are relatively expensive, they are widely used in the food industry. They offer the potential for a high return in sales and contacts if planned properly and presented well. Several months to a year may be required to obtain an exhibitor booth and a good location for it and to prepare the appropriate materials and displays.

Preparation for a Trade Show

After choosing a trade show that fits the business's current needs with the largest access to distribution, set goals for the organization to attain at the show. This will help in development of the presentation strategy and display. Set a budget allowing for enough personnel, accommodations, product, and travel. If the trade show is out of the country, allow for insurance costs and plan to spend a day in the host country before and after the trade show. It is advisable to choose professional design and marketing consultants to help prepare the materials for the booth. Effective material can also be prepared by the company. Keep in mind the target audience and the image the business wishes to project. A company should prepare a high-impact display to attract show attendees and clients, professionally prepared handouts, and samples of the product.

Trade show exhibitors should have a prepared and practiced sales presentation. Exhibit selling must be polished, brief, and informative. If the presentation lacks impact, the audience will quickly move on. Construct a system for recording leads. Several options include lead sheets for sales staff, a business card exchange system, or a sign-up sheet for more information. Most trade shows offer easy badge scanning systems that record contact information of visitors who are interested in receiving more information. Companies should also prepare business cards, if they are not already available, for each of the employees attending. Last, but not least, companies should ensure everyone at the booth is well informed about the company and its product, prices, and terms of sale.

At the Trade Show

Staff should plan to present products and work with customers the entire time in the booth. Ensure that adequate breaks are given so the quality of presentations remains consistent. Customers must relate a product to the individual situation. Sales staff should encourage customers to handle and taste the product and talk about the situation, so the most relevant points about the product can be presented. Encourage customers to take information and samples. Be sure to prepare a plan for follow-up, with deadlines for re-contacting interested parties. Follow-up should be immediate, and it is best to let customers know in advance when and how they can expect to be re-contacted.

Publicity

Publicity may provide free advertising for the producer through news stories found in newsletters, newspapers, magazines, and television. Sending a media release to radio, television, newspaper, and magazine offices can attain publicity. A media release is a onepage letter identifying a newsworthy event and outlining the who, what, when, where, and why of the story. The announcement of a new business, introduction of a new product, or any other success story related to a company is an occasion for a news release. The media will publish or announce the story as a news item, at no expense to the organization. Publicity is one of the most effective and least costly means of advertising.

Demonstrations

In-store demonstrations, sometimes referred to as product samplings, are an effective and inexpensive means to promote a new or existing product. There are three types of in-store demonstrations: (1) live demonstrations, (2) mobile demonstrations, and (3) static displays.

Live demonstrations include a staffed area with culinary activity, such as simple preparation. They are best with a new product that requires information or answers to questions or for a product that requires special preparation. One advantage of a live demonstration is you can encourage the customer to purchase the product.

Mobile demonstration is a form of live demonstration that occurs when a demonstrator walks through a store offering samples. The demonstrator usually has a base operation near the product sales display. Not all stores allow this type of demonstration.

Static displays include an area displaying the product and offering unattended samples. One advantage of a static display is cost. One disadvantage is that there is no control on how much sample is taken or on the purchasing decision. This type of demonstration requires consumer familiarity with the product.

Coupons

Coupons can be an effective way to increase sales and profits, but there are certain costs to consider, including physical distribution, mailing, placing advertisements, and paying the retailer a handling charge for redeeming the coupons. Managers must estimate various rates to determine the effectiveness of a coupon promotion. The estimates could be based on past performance or on experiments that run coupons in one city or in one part of a city. The rates that should be noted include the following:

- *Redemption rates*: The percentage of buyers responding to the incentive.
- *Displacement sales*: Sales made during a promotion that would otherwise have been made to regular buyers at the regular rate.
- *Acquisition rates*: Non-regular buyers who purchase the product during the promotion.
- *Stock-up rates*: Sales made during a promotion that are borrowed from future periods because the customer stocks up on the product at the discounted price.
- *Conversion rates*: The conversion of non-regular buyers into regular buyers.

PRICING

Pricing is much easier with one product than with many. When a single good only is produced by a firm, all FCs associated with the business are applicable to that one product. When several products are manufactured, company FCs must be assigned proportionately to each item produced.

Many companies want to have both extensive marketing programs and the lowest price. In most cases, this is not feasible, because the money for the marketing programs ultimately comes from consumer purchases which, with low prices, may not generate enough income to cover the expenses of accelerated marketing.

Traditionally, companies have used costs as the basis for setting prices, with little regard as to the value a customer places on a product or how competitors price analogous items. A market-driven company will also set prices based on value, while also being aware of costs. Target pricing involves studying the competition and the customer to identify a point at which the product must be priced to be competitive. Once the target price is identified, the company identifies a desired profit and works backward to calculate the cost at which the product must be produced to make a profit at the target price, and assuming different numbers or volumes of the item sold. These calculations must take into account the target profit margin, price reductions for retailers, costs of promotion, and future distribution costs. To properly calculate the costs, include current and future planned activities for distribution, promotion, and product development.

Setting Prices

To decide what price your new product should sell at, it is important to look at the breakeven analysis and the cost-volume-profit relationship. Breakeven analysis can be used as a tool for initially setting a product's price or for calculating the effects of a price change. It helps the owner/manager understand that, for certain prices, different levels of production are required to break even (i.e., to cover all variable and fixed costs).

The breakeven point is the point at which total revenue equals total cost. Below break-even, losses are incurred. Above breakeven, profits are realized. In the cost-volume-profit relationship, economies of scale measure the impact of changes in volume on FCs. In many cases, a company's ability to increase the volume of output allows the company to decrease the per unit cost. The experience curve effect is where variable costs (VCs) decline as volume increases. This can cause better results from increasing the volume of products. Experience curves may be due to more efficient production processes, higher discounts from greater volumes of purchases, and workers becoming more efficient at the process. "Sunk" costs, such as research and development, should be ignored when setting prices.

Pricing Strategies

Pricing strategies permit companies to study the role of varying prices in implementing marketing strategy. These strategies help investigate what the company wants to achieve by setting a particular price. Pricing strategies are not necessarily mutually exclusive, should be determined for each marketing strategy, and should be consistent with distribution and promotional strategies.

Penetration pricing is used when lower prices can result in an increase in growth in market share or an increased demand for the company's product. Penetration pricing is setting product prices low to stimulate sales. Other motivations for using penetration pricing are that it may drive up sales of complementary products purchased along with a lower-priced product. If a company knows its competitor's price structure is high and inflexible, penetration pricing can be a benefit.

Parity pricing is setting the price near or at competitive levels and using other marketing variables to drive sales. Parity pricing is best used when total market volume is not likely to grow with lower prices. If competitors can easily match any price decrease, parity pricing is more valuable than penetration pricing.

When a company can differentiate a product in terms of higher quality or special features, premium pricing should be utilized. Premium pricing entails setting a price above competitive levels. Premium pricing is best used when it is difficult for competitors to enter the industry. This pricing structure can also be used when consumers acknowledge one brand as having quality not attained by others.

Monitoring Costs

A multi-product company cannot get the information it requires from the conventional profit-and-loss statement. Instead, it needs to track costs for the company and for each product. Without product-specific information, it cannot tell which products are doing well and which need additional marketing support.

To gather all the relevant information, a company needs to track two types of costs, variable and fixed:

- *Variable costs* (*direct costs of manufacturing*): Costs specific to the manufacturing of the particular good or service under scrutiny (i.e., labor, raw materials, and supplies).
- *Fixed costs*: Ongoing costs that occur whether a business slows down for a period of time or is in full production (e.g., depreciation, insurance, taxes, selling and administration costs, utilities, and other costs).

Calculating Mark-Ups

When setting prices, companies must take into account their own costs as well as the various mark-ups required as a product moves toward the consumer. In the food business, mark-ups are usually calculated from the retail price working back, rather than from the cost working up. As a rule of thumb, retailers' margins average around 30%, with distributors' margins being as high as 30%, depending on what services are being provided.

The approach is similar when dealing with food service distributors such as Associated Food Distributors, but with allowances made for volume rebates. Volume rebate schedules are correlated with higher volumes, which means a higher percentage volume rebate is payable by the manufacturer or processor. Because rebates may entail a possible reduction in sales revenue, the processor must build in the rebate as an anticipated cost. However, the amount of the rebate will be invoiced and applied at year-end to the processor's total sales to the food service distributors.

The processor should not jump into a volume rebate schedule without first calculating the impact of the increased volumes in the form of lower per-unit costs. Many processors make the mistake of offering a volume rebate schedule that reduces profitability, because the volume rebate, i.e., sales revenue sacrificed, is greater than the cost savings of the increased output.

Pitfalls to Avoid When Devising a Marketing Plan

A marketing plan should try to account for the fickleness of the buying public. Producers need to understand the pitfalls of moving too many units into any one location based on a given price level, which can result in a surplus at that location. Conversely, if there are not enough units in a specific location and consumers want the product, they will pay higher prices to get it. Data that are available on sales of products at specific stores should be consulted.

Surplus

Products in a certain location and priced higher than consumers are willing to pay are called a surplus. Consumers may consider buying the surplus at a lower "sale" price. When this occurs, retailers will reduce the price offered for additional units they order and buy. The accumulation of surplus product is a signal to producers to send fewer units to that location. If surpluses continue, either new markets need to be found or production costs lowered.

Shortage

A shortage exists when consumers want to purchase more products than are available at specific locations at a given price level. When this happens, consumers who want the products are usually willing to pay a higher price which, in turn, can result in local retail managers offering higher prices to wholesalers to obtain additional volume. Rising prices are a signal to move more units to a "shortage" location. Pricing information from all locations should be combined to decide whether to expand production or to relocate units from one area to another.

SUMMARY

In the product development of food, it is important to remember that simply having a great product will not make it a success. Marketing is an essential piece of the product development process. Prior to production, marketing managers should have a good idea of what image a food will portray and how it will be viewed in the marketplace.

A detailed and well-researched marketing plan must be in place before starting to market a new food product. It will provide managers information about where to sell a product, when to ship it, why consumers buy it, and what price is acceptable to consumers and processors. Also, a plan will make it much easier to borrow capital. A well-developed marketing plan should demonstrate knowledge of the product, how much capital will be required, cost of production, specific market location, and an understanding of the consumers' purchasing activities. The plan must be accurate and reflective of a company's management skills.

The most difficult part of developing a marketing plan is estimating total marketing costs. Each marketing organization uses labor, management, land, and capital resources in various degrees of concentration. Each expenditure item should be included in a cost analysis. If this is done, the plan will provide an accurate picture of the total costs of producing and distributing the product—and persuading consumers to purchase. Obviously, the plan will attempt to account for all variables. Profit will accrue only when revenue from sales of the product exceeds the sum of all costs. Each sale is traceable to a consumer choice.

Often the reason for failure of some new products is not that they are bad products but that consumers were not convinced to give up their traditional food-buying pattern. Convincing consumers to consider a new food product and then to actually buy it is the objective of any marketing program.

KEY WORDS

Acquisition rates—percentage of non-regular buyers who purchase a product during a promotion.

Advertising—controlled communication between producer and consumer about a product.

Break-even point—point at which total revenue equals total cost.

Conversion rates—percentage of conversion of non-regular buyers converted into regular buyers.

Displacement sales—sales made during a promotion that would otherwise have been made to regular buyers at the regular rate.

Fixed costs—ongoing costs that are incurred whether a business slows down for a period of time or is in full production (e.g., depreciation, insurance, taxes, selling and administration costs, utilities, and other costs).

Market territory—the physical locations where a product is to be sold.

Redemption rates—the percentage of buyers responding to a promotional or price incentive.

Shortage—a situation in which fewer products are available at specific locations at a given price than there are customers willing to buy them.

Stock-up rates—sales made during a promotion that are borrowed from future periods because the customer stocks up on the product at the discounted price.

Surplus—a situation in which more products are located in a certain location and at a given price than there are consumers willing to pay to move that volume.

Target market—a group of similar people who are judged most likely to purchase a product and towards whom marketing will be aimed.

Variable costs (direct costs of manufacturing)—costs that change with the manufacturing of a particular good or service (e.g., labor, raw materials, and supplies).

COMPREHENSION QUESTIONS

15.1. Explain supply and demand.

15.2. Name the physical functions of marketing.

15.3. Who is the target market of the product you are developing? What outlets can be matched with those consumers? Where would you advertise in order to gain customers in your target market?

REFERENCES

Alberta Agriculture. (2002) *Marketing Food in Alberta*: An Access Directory. p. 43.

Beckman, M. D., Boone, L. E., & Kurtz, D. L. (1992). *Foundations of marketing* (5th ed.). Toronto: Holt, Rinehart and Winston of Canada.

Erikson, D. (1996). *Economic analysis of a new business-doing it right.* No. MF-2184). Manhattan, KS: K-State Research and Extension.

Guiltinan, J. P., Paul, G. W., & Madden, T. J. (1997). *Marketing management: strategies and programs* (6th ed.). New York: McGraw-Hill Companies.

Kijewski, V., Donath, B., & Wilson, D. T. (1993). Pricing-Think Value Not Cost. *The Best readings from Business marketing magazine: views from the trenches* (p. 225). Boston: PWS-Kent Pub. Co.

CHAPTER 16

Labeling

Learning Objectives

- Know the basic parts of a food product label.
- Realize what agencies oversee food labeling.
- Understand regulations governing labeling.
- Know the exemptions from nutrition labeling.

FOOD labeling laws cover "all labels and other written, printed, or graphic matter (1) upon any article or any of its containers or wrappers, or (2) accompanying such article," as defined in the Federal Food, Drug and Cosmetic Act. Packages and their labels should enable consumers to obtain accurate information as to the quantity of the contents and to assist value comparisons. As shown in many United States Food and Drug Administration (FDA) and Federal Trade Commission (FTC) proceedings, companies that include a website address on a label must consider their website as "labeling." During development, labeling needs to be considered in conjunction with package design.

The FDA enforces food labeling laws for most food products. For meat and poultry items sold in interstate commerce, labeling regulations are enforced by the Food Safety Inspection Service (FSIS) of the United States Department of Agriculture (USDA). If meat and poultry products are sold only within the state in which they are manufactured, labeling regulations are enforced by the state meat inspection service. A label is defined as "a display of written, printed or graphic matter upon the immediate container" of any article. To comply with label requirements, the label must be clearly visible on the outside of the package.

PARTS OF A FOOD LABEL

A food label can be separated into several sections, each with specific information and requirements. These sections include the Principal Display Panel, the Information Panel, and the Optional Panel.

Principal Display Panel

The Principal Display Panel (PDP) is defined as "the part of a label that is most likely to be displayed, presented, shown or examined under customary conditions of display for retail sale." Labels should be designed as large enough to accommodate all mandatory information on the PDP without crowding or obscuring. To determine the minimum type size of the net contents statement, the size of the PDP is based on dimensions of the package, which vary according to the package shape, as spelled out in Table 16.1.

The purpose of the PDP is to give consumers information about the product. This information must include the identity of the contents and the net quantity of the contents.

The identity of the contents is the Statement of Identity and must appear in bold type and be the name of the food as established by law or the accepted common or usual name of the product. This statement must be in a size reasonably related to the most prominent printed matter on the PDP and must be in lines generally parallel to the base of the package. If foods meet a Standard of Identity, the standard establishes the common or usual name of the food that is used on the package. If neither a Standard of Identity nor a common or usual name

TABLE 16.1. Principle Display Panel Size Requirements for Packages.

Type of Package	PDP Size Requirement
Rectangular	Height times the width of largest side
Cylindrical	40% of the height times the circumference
Special cylindrical containers (tall or short)	40% of the height times the circumference or the area of the lid (whichever is greater)
Other shaped packages	40% of the total surface
Tapered tube	40% of the height times the average of the top and bottom circumference
Bottles and jars	Exclude heels, necks, or shoulders in determining the height

exists for a food, an appropriately descriptive term or name commonly used by the public for the food may be used, such as "saltine" or "English muffin."

The Net Quantity of Contents Statement should accurately reveal the quantity of food in the package, exclusive of wrappers and other packaging materials. The weight of each food ingredient, including any water or syrup, is included in the net quantity declared on a label. In cases in which the packing medium is normally discarded, the drained weight is given, e.g., olives and mushrooms. If the food is liquid, the net quantity statement must be in terms of fluid measure (gallon, quart, pint, and fluidounce subdivisions and milliliters or liters). If the food is solid, semisolid, or viscous, or a mixture of solid and liquid, terms of weight are used (pounds or ounces and grams or kilograms). Also allowed is a numerical count of the contents, or a combination of count and weight or measure.

Common or decimal fractions may be used. Fractions are to be in halves, quarters, eighths, sixteenths, or thirty-seconds and are also to be reduced to the lowest terms; decimals are not to be carried more than three places. No qualifying terms such as "jumbo" or "full" may be used on the net quantity statement.

If the actual quantity falls below the printed declaration, the product is one of "short-fill" and is considered "misbranded." As such, it may be subject to confiscation by the FDA. Products with short fill are not allowed for retail sale but may be re-labeled for sale to federal, state, or local government operated institutions. For additional regulations concerning short fill, see 21 CFR 101.105.

The net quantity statement must be placed in the bottom 30 percent of the PDP, as shown in Figure 16.1. It must appear as a distinct item separated from other printed label information above and below by at least a space equal to the height of the lettering used in the declaration. The use of the term "net content" is optional. There are minimum sizes for type on the PDP description, which are established for the net quantity statement. This minimum size is based on the package space available for the PDP. In addition, letters may be no more than three times as high as they are wide, and letter heights are measured by uppercase or capital letters. If uppercase and lowercase or all lowercase letters are used, the lowercase letter "o" or its equivalent must meet the minimum standard. When fractions are used, each numeral is to be one-half the minimum height requirement. More information about all labeling regulations can be found on www.FDA.gov.

FIGURE 16.1. Example of a Principle Display Panel.

Information Panel

The Information Panel (IP) is defined as the "part of the label immediately contiguous and to the right of the Principal Display Panel as observed by an individual facing the Principal Display Panel." If this part of the label is too small to accommodate the necessary information or is otherwise unusable label space, e.g., folded flaps or can ends, the panel immediately contiguous and to the right of this part of the label may be used. Information panels commonly show a list of ingredients and manufacturer or distributor information.

Ingredient Declaration

Ingredient legends provide a list of the common or usual names of ingredients in descending order of predominance by weight. Ingredients must be listed by specific, not collective, names, except for spices, flavorings, and colorings. The ingredient legend must appear on either the IP or PDP.

For IP labeling, a print or type size that is prominent, conspicuous, and easy to read must be used. Letters should be at least one-sixteenth

(1/16) of an inch in height based on the lowercase letter "o," unless an exemption is permitted (21 CFR 101.2(c)(1)). The letters must not be more than three times as high as they are wide, and the lettering must contrast sufficiently with the background to be easy to read. Required information cannot be crowded with artwork or non-required statements. Statements that are not required are called "intervening material."

A common mistake in creating an ingredient legend is omitting "water" from the listing. Water added in making a food is considered an ingredient. The added water must be identified in the list of ingredients and listed in its descending order of predominance by weight. If all water added is subsequently removed by baking or some other means during processing, water does not need to be declared as an ingredient. When fruit is canned in juice from concentrate, the water used to reconstitute the juice must be declared. Water used to adjust the brix level in some foods does not need to be declared, as in adjusting the solids in a tomato paste from 28° to 24° brix.

Declaration of Trace Ingredients

If a substance is an incidental additive and has no function or technical effect in the finished product, then it need not be declared on the label as a trace ingredient. An incidental additive is usually present be-

FIGURE 16.2. *Demonstration of Principle Display Panel and Information Panel.*

cause it is an ingredient of another product produced on the same line. Sulfites are considered to be incidental only if present at less than 10 parts per million (ppm).

One type of incidental additive is a "processing aid," defined in 21 CFR 101.100(a)(3)(ii). Processing aids are either (1) "substances . . . added to a food during the processing of such food but are removed in some manner from the food before it is packaged in its finished form," (2) "substances that are added to a food during processing, are converted into constituents normally present in the food, and do not significantly increase the amount of the constituents naturally found in the food," or (3) "substances . . . added to a food for their technical or functional effect in the processing but are present in the finished food at insignificant levels and do not have any technical or functional effect in that food." Care must be taken in determining exactly when an ingredient is a processing aid or an ingredient that must appear on the label.

Spices, Flavorings, and Colorants

For labeling, a spice is defined as "any aromatic vegetable substance in the whole, broken or ground form, except for those substances which have been traditionally regarded as foods, such as onions, garlic and celery; whose significant function in food is seasoning rather than nutritional; that is true to name; and from which no portion of any volatile oil or other flavoring principle has been removed" (21 CFR 101.22 (a)(2)). As stated, spices, flavorings and colorings may be listed by the collective terms "spices," "flavorings" and "colorings," respectively. Exceptions to this include celery, garlic, and onion, which are considered foods and must be declared by their specific common or usual name. Paprika, turmeric, saffron, and other spices that are also colors should be declared as "spice and coloring" or by their common or usual name. The complete list of spices can be found in 21 CFR 101.22 and in Table 16.2.

Flavors generally comprise a carrier and the volatile components of specific ingredients or chemical substances derived to impart the flavor of a specific ingredient but not containing that substance. These are known as natural and artificial flavors, respectively. The need to formulate with a specific type of flavor depends on a product's desired consumer perception, claims of being natural, and organic status.

The term "natural flavor" or "natural flavoring" means the essential

TABLE 16.2. Spices as Defined in 21 CFR 101.22.

Allspice	Dill seed	Pepper, black
Anise	Fennel seed	Pepper, white
Basil	Fenugreek	Pepper, red
Bay leaves	Ginger	Rosemary
Caraway seed	Horseradish	Saffron
Cardamom	Mace	Sage
Celery seed	Marjoram	Savory
Chervil	Mustard flour	Star aniseed
Cinnamon	Nutmeg	Tarragon
Cloves	Oregano	Thyme
Coriander	Paprika	Turmeric
Cumin seed	Parsley	

oil, oleoresin, essence or extractive, protein hydrolysate, distillate, or any product of roasting, heating or enzymolysis, which contains the flavoring constituents derived from the ingredients of the name of the flavoring products (21 CFR 101.22(a)(3)). The significant function is to impart a distinct flavor rather than contribute nutritionally to the product. Products that are naturally flavored, but contain flavors other than that which the product is aiming to impart, must be labeled with a disclaimer stating that they contain "other natural flavors" or "natural and artificial flavors," depending on the case.

Additionally, if a food would generally be expected to contain an ingredient for the characterizing flavor, such as bananas in banana bread, and the product contains natural flavors and an insignificant amount of the characterizing ingredient, then the product's flavor on the PDP should display the word "flavored" in letters not less than one-half the height of the letters in the name of the characterizing flavor.

Artificial flavors must be labeled not only in the ingredient deck, but also on the PDP of products. Artificial smoke flavors must be declared as "artificial flavor" or "artificial smoke" flavor. No claim may be made that foods containing artificial smoke have been smoked or have a true smoked flavor.

Component Ingredients

Foods used in their entirety as an ingredient in a product of multiple food components may be listed two ways: (1) as parenthetical listings or (2) in order of predominance. In parenthetical listings, the ingredient

FIGURE 16.3. Example of a UPC code.

may be declared by its common or usual name followed in parentheses by a list of its own ingredients used in the formulation, i.e., catsup (tomatoes, vinegar, corn syrup). Using the order of subcomponents present in several ingredients may be combined and listed in their proper order of predominance. This requires the percentage of each component in a multicomponent ingredient be known, so proper order of predominance can be determined. Component ingredients should be part of multicomponent foods that have been previously combined.

Preservatives

The addition of a preservative must be listed by both the common or usual name and the description of its function, i.e., sodium benzoate (a preservative). Food additives are generally approved and characterized by their approved functions and can therefore easily be distinguished by manufacturers.

Manufacturer, Packer, or Distributor Statement

The name and place of business of the manufacturer, packer, or distributor of the food must be on the label and can appear on either the PDP or the IP. According to labeling regulations, the ingredient statement and the name and address of the manufacturer, packer, or distributor must be adjacent, with no intervening material (CFR 101.2 (e)).

The address shall include the street address, city, state, and zip code. Post office box addresses are not allowed. The street address may be omitted from the label if the business street address is shown in a current city or local telephone directory. This is required so that an interested party can locate the manufacturer, packer, or distributor. The requirement for including the zip code on the label applies only to packages intended for consumers. A minimum type size of one-sixteenth inch is required. If space is not available for the IP, required declarations may be included on the PDP.

Certified Organic by Statement

Products that are organic certified must also include a required statement directly below the distributor's information. Because product labels are approved by organic certification agencies, certification approval hinges on the correct placement. This required statement is "Certified organic by" with the name of the agency through which the manufacturer is approved. Generally, no information other than distributor information and contact information is allowed between the ingredient deck, distributor information, and the certified organic by statement.

Allergen Labeling

The Food Allergen Labeling and Consumer Act of 2004 (FALCPA) requires the declaration of 8 major food allergens—wheat, eggs, milk, fish, shellfish, tree nuts, peanuts, and soybeans. At the time of enactment, these allergens accounted for 90 percent of food allergies. Under this regulation, these allergens must be declared if present in the food either by listing explicitly in the ingredient deck or having a "contains" statement at the end of the ingredient deck.

Optional Panel

The optional panel is to the left of the PDP and provides space for items such as a company story or history statement, the Universal Product Code (UPC) bar code, and nutrition information.

Universal Product Code

The UPC is a series of bars of varying thicknesses used by electronic scanners to identify a product and the price set by the seller. This bar code is a 12-digit all-numeric code that uniquely identifies one item.

The code contains four parts. The first digit represents the manufacturer's retail category or function. The next five digits are the manufacturer's identification number and are unique to each individual manufacturer. The next five digits are the item number, unique to the product and its pack size. The twelfth digit is a check character used to verify the accuracy of the entire UPC. Universal Product Code bar codes had been obtainable through membership in the Uniform Code Council and can now be purchased on the internet for minimal cost. The European Article Number (EAN) is the standard adopted worldwide, except for the United States and Canada. The EAN codes look similar to UPC codes, except that EAN codes are 13 digits long. In June 2005, the Uniform Commercial Code (UCC) became the official GS1 member organization for the United States under the new name of GS1 US. For further information, one can visit https://www.gs1us.org/upcs-barcodes-prefixes.

NUTRITION LABELING

The Nutrition Labeling Education Act (NLEA) of 1990 revolutionized and standardized the presentation of nutrition information in the United States, but in the intervening years, the dietary habits and scientifically validated nutritional needs of Americans changed. Thus, in 2014, the FDA proposed changes to the nutrition facts panel. Rules for serving sizes and nutrition facts panel modifications were finalized on May 20, 2016, and published in the Federal Register on May 27, 2016. The majority of labels on the market will have the new nutrition facts by the compliance date of July 26, 2018; most manufacturers have two years to comply; those with less than 10 million dollars in food sales have three years to comply. The updates to the nutrition facts panels include modification of the design, nutrition declarations, and new serving size and labeling requirements for certain packages.

Nutrition Facts Panels

The Nutrition Facts Panel modifications highlight the number of calories in products and place new emphasis on the number of servings per container by increasing the font sizes required. The footnote is now changed to read as follows: "The % Daily Value tells you how much a nutrient in a serving of food contributes to a daily diet. 2,000 calories a day is used for general nutrition advice."

Size of Packages and Format

The requirements for providing nutrition information are based on the package size and label space. If a package is 12 square inches or less, the package is exempt from mandatory labeling and need not have any nutrition claims or other nutritional information. With this small size package, however, it is required that the manufacturer, packer, or distributor provide a telephone number in which the information can be obtained. With packages that are between 12 and 40 square inches, the nutrition facts may be displayed in a tabular format if the package shape or size cannot accommodate a standard nutrition facts panel. This size of package can utilize specific approved abbreviations. Packages with over 40 square inches of available labeling space must use the standard format, although some modifications can be made for unique shapes and limited space.

The Nutrition Facts Panel may be presented on any label panel when the total surface available for labeling is 40 or fewer square inches. Packages with more than 40 square inches of available space must place the nutrition information on either the PDP or IP, as defined in 21 CFR 101.2, unless there is insufficient space, in which case the nutrition facts may be placed on any panel that may be seen readily by consumers.

A few approved panel formats are permitted to display nutrition facts. Formatting differences allow flexibility for companies with small pack-

Nutrition Facts	
8 servings per container	
Serving size	**2/3 cup (55g)**
Amount per serving	
Calories	**230**
	% Daily Value*
Total Fat 8g	**10%**
Saturated Fat 1g	**5%**
Trans Fat 0g	
Cholesterol 0mg	**0%**
Sodium 160mg	**7%**
Total Carbohydrate 37g	**13%**
Dietary Fiber 4g	**14%**
Total Sugars 12g	
Includes 10g Added Sugars	**20%**
Protein 3g	
Vitamin D 2mcg	10%
Calcium 260mg	20%
Iron 8mg	45%
Potassium 235mg	6%

* The % Daily Value (DV) tells you how much a nutrient in a serving of food contributes to a daily diet. 2,000 calories a day is used for general nutrition advice.

FIGURE 16.4. *Nutrition facts panel format.*

ages. The standard format is the most commonly used format. The tabular label is a horizontal rendition of the standard format and can be used for packages that are wider than they are tall. Simplified versions of the tabular and standard formats are available for use if at least eight of the following nutrients are present in insignificant amounts: *calories, total fat, saturated fat, trans fat, cholesterol, sodium, total carbohydrate, dietary fiber, sugars, protein, vitamin A, vitamin C, calcium, and iron.*

For packages that are smaller, it may be necessary to use a linear format Nutrition Facts Panel. Examples of these formats can be seen in Figure 16.4. The declaration of certain nutrients (Table 16.3) is mandatory. When a product does not contain even minute amounts of a mandated nutrient, it can be omitted from the statement with a qualifying statement.

Dietary Fiber Definition

With the modification of the Nutrition Facts Panel format also came changes to the definition of specific nutrients. Dietary fiber changed to include only the following: (a) non-digestible soluble and insoluble carbohydrates (with three or more monomeric units) and lignin that are intrinsic and intact in plants and (b) isolated or synthetic non-digestible carbohydrates (with three or more monomeric units) determined by the FDA to have physiological effects that are beneficial to human health. The FDA explains that "intrinsic and intact" includes "non-digestible

TABLE 16.3. *Nutrients for Mandatory Declaration from 21 CFR 101.9 and 9 CFR 317/381.*

Specific Nutrient Declarations for Nutrition Facts Panels		
Mandated Declarations	**Nutrients**	**Voluntary**
Calories	Vitamin A	Poly-unsaturated Fat
Calories from fat	Vitamin C	Mono-unsaturated Fat
Fat content	Calcium	Fatty Acids
Daily values of total fat	Iron	Other Carbohydrates
Saturated fat		Sugar Alcohol
Trans fat		Soluble Fiber
Cholesterol		Insoluble Fiber
Sodium		Potassium
Total Carbohydrate		Other Vitamins
Dietary Fiber		Other Minerals
Sugars		
Protein		

carbohydrates that are created during normal food processing (e.g., cooking, rolling, or milling)." However, resistant starch that has been extracted and isolated is not intrinsic (part of the food matrix), and intact would be considered "isolated," non-digestible carbohydrates. The FDA further defined which fiber sources meet the definition; these include β-glucan soluble fiber, psyllium husk, cellulose, guar gum, pectin, locust bean gum, and hydroxypropyl methylcellulose. In order to have another fiber added to the list of approved isolated fibers, a company would need to prove "beneficial physiological effects" and submit a citizen petition to the FDA.

Added Sugar Definition

The FDA also requires the listing of "added sugars" in the new nutrition facts panel format. The daily values for added sugar for adults is 50 grams. Added sugars are defined as "sugars (that) are either added during the processing of foods, or are packaged as such." Added sugars come from sugars (such as cane sugar), sugars from honey or syrups, or sugars from concentrated fruit and vegetable juices. Added sugars from concentrated juices are those only in excess of what would be expected in same amount of single-strength juice of the same type.

Serving Size

A system has been established by the FDA based on the amounts of food/products per eating occasion called the reference amounts customarily consumed (RACC). The reference amounts are expressed in household units, such as 1 slice, and in discrete units, such as grams and ounces. Serving sizes must be declared in common household measures. This is defined in 21 CFR 101.9(b)(5) as a cup, tablespoon, teaspoon, piece, slice, fraction, ounce, fluid ounce, or other common household equipment used to package food products, such as a jar, tray, etc. Other stipulations include the following:

- *Cups*: Must be expressed in one-quarter or one-third cup increments.
- *Tablespoons*: Must be expressed in the whole number of tablespoons for quantities less than one-quarter cup but greater than or equal to two tablespoons; fractions such as one-third, one-half, and two-thirds may be used between one and two tablespoons.
- *Teaspoons*: Must be expressed in the whole number of teaspoons

for quantities less than one tablespoon but greater or equal to one teaspoon; one-quarter teaspoon increments are used for amounts less than one teaspoon.

- *Ounces*: Must be listed in 0.5-ounce increments.

The FDA updates to the serving-size regulations have some significant modifications. The new rules require that products that have less than 200% of the reference amount must be labeled as one serving. The thought is that consumers are likely to consume an entire package when the serving size is less than 200% of the determined RACC amount. The serving size on discrete packages, such as muffins or individually packaged products, which exceed 150% of the RACC but contain less than 200%, must add a second column of nutrition information to the left of the column that states the amount per package. Additionally, packages containing less than 300% of the RACC are mandated to have dual-column labeling as well. These labels indicate the nutrition per serving size and per package.

As an example, a company that produces cookies would like to determine the average weight of each cookie. The RACC for cookies is 30 grams. Therefore, if the company's cookies weigh 13 grams, it could claim that the serving size was two cookies (26 grams). The company would need to determine what size pack would be most suitable, noting that a dual-column label would be required for packages under 90 grams (300% of the 30gram RACC).

When serving sizes are stated on a package, rounding rules are stipulated by the FDA. For products containing two to five servings, the number of servings must be rounded to the nearest 0.5 serving. Above five servings, the servings per container should be rounded to the nearest whole number.

The reference amounts have been updated to reflect data from the actual consumption of products. The serving size of carbonated and noncarbonated beverages has been updated from 240 mL (8 fluid ounces) to 360 mL (12 fluid ounces), for example. The RACC amounts are published in 21 CFR 101.12. Product developers should always take into account the RACC value in order to understand prior to formulation how their products must be labeled.

Daily Values

The daily value percentages on nutrition facts panels are based on the daily reference values (DRV) and recommended daily intake (RDI). These values assist consumers in interpreting information about the amount of a nutrient that is present in a food and in comparing nutritional values of food products. Daily reference values are established for adults and children four or more years of age, as are RDIs, with the exception of protein. Daily reference values are provided for total fat, saturated fat, cholesterol, total carbohydrate, dietary fiber, sodium, potassium, and protein. RDIs are provided for vitamins and minerals, for protein for children less than four years of age, and for pregnant and lactating women. To limit consumer confusion, however, the label includes a single daily value term to designate both the DRVs and RDIs. Specifically, the nutrition labeling laws mandate the inclusion on packaging of the percent (%) daily values for various nutrients based on the target market daily value (DV). The only exception is that the % DV for protein is not required unless a protein claim is made for the product or if the product is to be used by infants or children under four years of age. The DV amounts for nutrients, including DVs and recommended DVs for food components, vitamins, and minerals, are listed in Table 16.4 for adults and children over 4 years of age.

CLAIMS

Companies must be cautious in wording claims on packaging regarding special nutritional and health functions of their products. Claims must be carefully composed to eliminate the chance of FDA seizure because of misbranding or misleading customers about the benefits of a product. The two types of claims covered in this chapter are nutrient content claims and health claims.

Nutrient Content Claims

Nutrient content claims are claims that state a food is made with or contains a nutrient in a specific amount. The FDA has trigger words that signal specific nutrient content claims. For example, a product is a "good source" of a nutrient means that it contains at least 10% of the DV of that specific nutrient. When the label makes a nutrient content claim, a statement referring the consumer to the nutrition label must be added. The nutrient content claim may have a type size no larger than two times the name of the product. There are claims for specific nutritional components, as seen in Table 16.5. A general outline of descriptors, such as

TABLE 16.4. Food Components Daily Values and Recommended Daily Values in 2016 Nutrition Facts Panel Updates.

2016 DV Updates	Infants 7–12 months	Young Children 1–3 years	Adult and Children < RDIs	Pregnant & Lactating Women
Calories	--	1000	2000	2,000
Total Fat	30 g	39 g	78 g	78 g
Saturated Fat	--	10 g	20 g	20 g
Cholesterol	--	300 mg	300 mg	300 mg
Sodium	--	1500 mg	2300 mg	2300 mg
Total Carbohydrates	95 g	150 g	275 g	275 g
Added Sugar	Adding to label	25 g	50 g	50 g
Fiber*	--	14 g	28 g	28 g
Protein	11 g	13 g	50 g	71 g
Biotin	6 mcg	8 mcg	30 mcg	35 mcg
Choline	150 mg	200 mg	550 mg	550 mg
Folate	80 mcg DFE[1]	150 mcg DFE[1]	400 mcg DFE[1]	600 mcg DFE[1]
Niacin	4 mg NE[2]	6 mg NE[2]	16 mg NE[2]	18 mg NE[2]
Pantothenic Acid	1.8 mg	2 mg	5 mg	7 mg
Riboflavin	0.4 mg	0.5 mg	1.3 mg	1.6 mg
Thiamin	0.3 mg	0.5 mg	1.2 mg	1.4 mg
Vitamin A	500 mcg RAE[3]	300 mcg RAE[3]	900 mcg RAE[3]	1300 mcg RAE[3]
Vitamin B_6	0.3mg	0.5 mg	1.7 mg	2 mg
Vitamin B_{12}	0.5 mcg	0.9 mcg	2.4 mcg	2.8 mg
Vitamin C	50 mg	15 mg	90 mg	
Vitamin D	10 mcg	15 mcg	20 mcg*	120 mg
Vitamin E	5 mg	6 mg	15 mg	15 mcg*
Vitamin K	2.5 mcg	30 mcg	120 mcg	19 mg
Calcium	260 mg*	700 mg*	1,300 mg*	90 mcg
Chloride	570 mg	1500 mg	2,300 mg	1300 mg*
Chromium	5.5 mcg	11 mcg	35 mcg	2300 mg
Copper	0.2 mg	0.3 mg	0.9 mg	45 mcg
Iodine	130 mcg	90 mcg	150 mcg	1.3 mg
Iron	11 mg*	7 mg*	18 mg*	290 mg
Magnesium	75 mg	80 mg	420 mg	27 mg*
Manganese	0.6 mg	1.2 mg	2.3 mg	400 mg
Molybdenum	3 mcg	17 mcg	45 mcg	2.6 mg
Phosphorus	275 mg	460 mg	1,250 mg	50 mcg
Potassium	700 mg*	3,000 mg*	4,700 mg*	1250 mg
Selenium	20 mcg	20 mcg	55 mcg	5100 mg*
Zinc	3 mg	3 mg	11 mg	13 mg

*Required to be labeled – does not have a DV/RDI value.

[1]Dietary folate equivalents: 1 DFE = 1 mcg food folate = 0.6 mcg of folic acid from fortified food or as a supplement consumed with food.

[2]Niacin equivalents: 1 mg niacin = 60 mg of tryptophan.

[3]Retinol activity equivalents: 1 RAE = 1 mcg retinol, 12 mcg β-carotene, or 24 mcg α-carotene, or 24 mcg β-cryptoxanthin.

TABLE 16.5. Nutrient Content Claims for Specific Nutrients.

Ingredient	Free	Low	Reduced
Total Fat	Less than 0.5 g of fat per serving and per reference amount	3 g or less per reference amount	At least 25% less fat per reference amount
Saturated Fat	Less than 0.5 g of fat per serving and per reference amount and less than 0.5 g trans fat	1 g or less per reference amount	At least 25% less saturated fat per reference amount
Cholesterol	Less than 2 mg of cholesterol per serving and reference amount, the food contains 2 g or less of saturated fatty acids per serving	20 mg or less per reference amount	At least 25% less cholesterol per reference amount
Sodium	Contains less than 5 mg of sodium per serving/reference amount and no added salt, can also be referred to as "unsalted" or "no salt added"	140 mg or less per reference amount	At least 25% less sodium per reference amount
Sugar	Food containing less than 0.5 g of sugars per serving and reference amount, contains no added sugars, must be labeled as a "low calorie" or "reduced calorie" food, or the term "sugar free" is accompanied in immediate proximity by a statement "not a reduced calorie food"	Not defined	At least 25% less sugar per reference amount
Calories	Less than 5 calories per serving, may also use "free of calories," "no calories," or "zero calories"	40 calories or less per reference amount	At least 25% less calories per reference amount

Source: A Guidance for Industry: A Guide for Food Labeling, a publication by FDA (2009).

"free," "lean," "light," and "reduced," have been redefined, so that consumers will be clear about their meaning (as seen in Table 16.6).

Health Claims

A health claim denotes any claim made on a label or in the labeling of a food that characterizes the relationship of any substance in the food product to a disease or healthrelated condition. Implied health claims include statements, symbols, vignettes, or other forms of communication that suggest, within the context in which they are presented, that a relationship exists between the presence or level of a substance in the food and a disease or health-related condition (*A Guidance for Industry: A Guide to Food Labeling 2009*). To help prevent the display of false claims, the NLEA established claims about foods that are linked to health benefits. These health claims are "qualified health claims" that

TABLE 16.6. Nutrient Content Claim Descriptors.

Claim Descriptor	Definition
Free	A product contains no amount or only a trivial amount of fat, saturated fat, cholesterol, sodium, sugars, or calories. Synonyms include "without," "no," and "zero"
Low	Used on foods that could be eaten frequently without exceeding the dietary guidelines for fat, saturated fat, cholesterol, sodium, or calories
Lean	"Lean" is used to describe the fat content of meat, poultry, seafood, and game meats. Defined as less than 10 g of fat, less than 4 g of saturated fat, and less than 95 mg of cholesterol per serving and per 100 g.
Extra Lean	Used to describe the fat content of meat, poultry, seafood, and game meats. Less than 5 g of fat, less than 2 g of saturated fat, and less than 95 mg of cholesterol per serving per 100 g.
Healthy	Foods must meet the criteria for "low fat" and "low saturated fat" and provide at least 10% of the daily value of vitamin A, vitamin C, iron, calcium, protein, or fiber
High, Excellent Source, or Rich In	Can be used if the food contains 20% or more of the daily value for a particular nutrient in a serving
Good Source	One serving of a food that contains 10–19% of the daily value for a particular nutrient
More, Fortified, Enriched, Added, Plus	Contains at least 10% more than the DV of the comparative item. Can be used for the level of protein, vitamins, minerals, dietary fiber, or potassium, but should not be used for certain meal items
Reduced	A nutritionally altered product contains 25% less of a nutrient or of calories than the regular or reference product. However, a reduced claim cannot be made on a product if its reference food already meets the requirement for a "low" claim
Less	A food that contains 25% less of a nutrient or calories than the reference food; "fewer" may also be used

Source: A Guidance for Industry: A Guide for Food Labeling, a publication by FDA (2009).

have been scientifically linked to a positive effect or decrease in the risk of disease.

Further, health claims are limited to claims about disease risk reduction and cannot be claims about the diagnosis, cure, mitigation, or treatment of disease. Health claims are required to be reviewed and evaluated by the FDA prior to use. An example of an authorized health claim is "Three grams of soluble fiber from oatmeal daily in a diet low in saturated fat and cholesterol may reduce the risk of heart disease. This cereal has 2 grams per serving" (*A guidance for industry: A guide to food labeling* 2009).

Qualified health claims must be approved by the FDA, which is accomplished through a petition. Organizations can submit their desired health claim and evidence to the FDA for approval. Approved health claims include the link between sufficient intake of calcium and vitamin D and a reduced risk of osteoporosis.

Accuracy of Claims

Added nutrients in fortified or fabricated foods (Class I) must present 100 percent or more of the label declaration. Naturally occurring (indigenous) nutrients (Class II) must be at least 80 percent or more. Other nutritional components of the label are considered third group nutrients, such as calories, sugars, total fat, etc., and must be no more than 120 percent of the label declaration.

TABLE 16.7. Qualified Health Claims.

Ingredients	Health Benefit	Qualifications to Use Claims
Calcium, Vitamin D	Reduction in risk of osteoporosis	• Must be "high" in calcium and Vitamin D
Tomatoes and/or Tomato sauce	Prostate, ovarian, gastric, and pancreatic cancers	• Cooked, raw, dried, or canned tomatoes can be used • Tomato sauces that contain at least 8.37% salt-free tomato solids
Green Tea	Cancer	• Green tea-containing foods when the food does not contain excess fat, saturated fat, cholesterol, and sodium • Must contain a minimum 10% green tea
Nuts	Heart disease	• Whole or chopped nuts that are raw, blanched, roasted, salted, and/or lightly coated and/or flavored • Nut-containing products other than whole or chopped nuts that contain at least 11 g of one or more of the nuts listed below per RACC; eligible nuts for this claim are restricted to almonds, hazelnuts, peanuts, pecans, some pine nuts, pistachio nuts, and walnuts • Should not exceed 4 g saturated fat per 50 g of nuts
Monounsaturated Fatty Acids from Olive Oil	Coronary heart disease	• Products including salad dressing, vegetable oil, and shortening must contain more than 6 g per RACC of olive oil

Source: www.FDA.gov.

Calculating Overages to Ensure Accuracy of Nutrient Claims

The accuracy of stated nutrients should be guaranteed (with a margin of error) throughout the complete shelf-life of the product. Product developers may have to calculate the percent overages of nutrients that deteriorate over time, such as vitamins. The degradation of vitamins is specific to nutrients, processing conditions, and the attributes of the food product and, therefore, must be carefully considered. Investigating research on vitamin degradation in specific products is recommended.

Misbranded Products

Failure to comply with labeling regulations may provide cause for the enforcing agency to bring action against a product and the manufacturer. Reasons for failure of a label to be prominent and conspicuous include, but are not limited to, the following:

- Failure of required information on PDP or IP
- Failure to use available space for prominence
- Use of available space for information that is not required or to give greater prominence to some required information
- Minimum type size requirements are not met
- Insufficient background contrast
- Obscuring design
- Crowding with other written, printed, or graphic material

NUTRITION DATABASES

Software is available to help companies calculate the number and proportion of nutrients of foods in development. Nutrition databases can help companies formulate products, especially when they have specific nutritional goals or make health benefit claims. Software programs are also available to generate nutrition facts panels and ingredient legends. The USDA keeps a nutritional database with vast amounts of information about products on the market and standard food items. It is called the USDA National Nutrient Database for Standard Reference and can be found at http://ndb.nal.usda.gov. When using databases, it is a good idea to perform periodic checks by sending a product to an analytical laboratory and comparing results with the database. We use databases extensively in our laboratory for new food product development and nutrition labeling. At the same time, we also rely heavily on analytical moisture and salt analyses, and % brix measurements, and we often have to override values due to cooking losses, especially if unaccounted for by yield measurements. Setting the correct moisture content is by far the most important factor to ensure accuracy of nutrition information.

EXEMPTIONS FROM LABELING

Packaged products must meet all labeling requirements. Products that are unwrapped until selected by the consumer are exempt from labeling requirements. Foods sold through vending machines must meet all the requirements for labeling, except they are exempt from mandatory nutrition labeling.

Mail-order products are considered packaged consumer foods sold directly to retail customers. They are subject to the same requirements as products sold through supermarkets or other retail outlets. Mandatory information must not be misleading or false and must be visible to the customer prior to opening the package, even though the package itself may not be available prior to purchase from a catalog. Required information may appear on the shipping container or on a separately packaged inner container. Retail and in-store bakeries fall into two different types of categories:

1. Self-service sales
2. Displayed for sale unwrapped and packaged as ordered by the customer

Many food products are exempt from providing nutrition information. These include foods manufactured by small processors with fewer than 100 employees and fewer than 100,000 units sold. The number of employees is based on the average number of full-time employees a company has over a twelve-month period. In all cases, the exemption is forfeited if an explicit or implied nutrition claim or any other nutrition information is provided on packaging or in advertising. Businesses must file an exemption notice with the FDA and claim a small business exemption based on the number of employees and units of products. No exemption is allowed for a company that has more than the required number of full-time employees, regardless of the number of units sold. Other exempt products include the following:

- Foods served in restaurants or other facilities where food is served for immediate consumption
- Foods that contain insignificant amounts of all of the nutrients and food components required on the nutrient declaration
- Raw fruits and vegetables
- Foods in small packages with a total available label area less than twelve square inches

Under current FDA laws and regulations, no label approval is needed prior to the food product's distribution. It is the responsibility of the food producer to comply with current food labeling regulations. Both the FDA and USDA offer informal reviews of a food product's label.

DIETARY SUPPLEMENTS

The law defines dietary supplements in part as products taken by mouth that contain a "dietary ingredient." Dietary ingredients include vitamins, minerals, amino acids, and herbs or botanicals, as well as other substances that can be used to supplement the diet.

Dietary supplements come in many forms, including tablets, capsules, powders, energy bars, and liquids. These products are available in stores throughout the United States, as well as on the Internet. They are labeled as dietary supplements and include, among others, the following:

- Vitamin and mineral products
- Botanical or herbal products—These come in many forms and may include plant materials, algae, macroscopic fungi, or a combination of these materials
- Amino acid products—Amino acids are known as the building blocks of proteins and play a role in metabolism
- Enzyme supplements—Enzymes are complex proteins that speed up biochemical reactions

Five statements are required on the labels of dietary supplements: (1) the statement of identity (name of the dietary supplement), (2) the net quantity of contents statement (amount of the dietary supplement), (3) the nutrition labeling, (4) the ingredient list, and (5) the name and place of business of the manufacturer, packer, or distributor. All required label statements must be located on the front label panel (the PDP) or on the IP (usually the label panel immediately to the right of the PDP, as seen by the consumer when facing the product), unless otherwise specified by regulation (i.e., exemptions).

Claims made on dietary supplements can be substantiated or unsubstantiated by the FDA. A health claim is an explicit or implied characterization of a relationship between a substance and a disease or a health-related condition. This type of claim requires significant scientific agreement and must be authorized by the FDA. The claim can be a written statement, a "third party" reference, a symbol, or a vignette. A "qualified" health claim is supported by less scientific evidence than an "authorized" health claim. The FDA requires that qualified claims be accompanied by a disclaimer that explains the level of the scientific evidence supporting the relationship. The FDA will permit the use of a qualified health claim provided that (1) The FDA has issued a letter stating the conditions under which it will consider exercising enforcement discretion for the specific health claim; (2) the qualified claim is accompanied by an agencyapproved disclaimer; and (3) the claim meets all the general requirements for health claims in 21 CFR 101.14, except for the requirement that the evidence for the claim meet the validity standard for authorizing a claim and the requirement that the claim be made in accordance with an authorizing regulation.

A "structure/function" claim describes the role of a substance intended to maintain the structure or function of the body. Structure/function claims do not require preapproval by FDA. You may make the following types of structure/function claims under section 403(r)(6) of the Act:

- A statement that claims a benefit related to a classical nutrient deficiency disease and that discloses the prevalence of such disease in the U.S.
- A statement that describes the role of a nutrient or dietary ingredient intended to affect the structure or function in humans, or characterizes the documented mechanism by which a nutrient or dietary ingredient acts to maintain such structure or function
- A statement that describes the general well-being from consumption of a nutrient or dietary ingredient

When making a structure/function claim, a manufacturer must (1) have substantiation that such statement is truthful and not misleading, (2) include the disclaimer, and (3) notify the FDA no later than 30 days after the first marketing of the product that the statement is in accordance with 21 CFR 101.93. One of the following disclaimers (exactly as shown) must be placed below the claim on the label:

- *Singular*: "This statement has not been evaluated by the Food and Drug Administration. This product is not intended to diagnose, treat, cure, or prevent any disease;"
- *Plural*: "These statements have not been evaluated by the Food and Drug Administration. This product is not intended to diagnose, treat, cure, or prevent any disease."

Additionally, companies should consider if their dietary supplement requires them to submit a New Dietary Ingredient notification to the FDA prior to launch. These dossiers are meant to serve as proof that the ingredient is reasonably expected to be safe under the conditions of use recommended or suggested in the labeling. A New Dietary Ingredient notification is required when a new ingredient is being used that was not on the market prior to October 15, 1994. Manufacturers are responsible for determining whether the ingredient was on the market, because there is no list stating what was used prior to that date. If a New Dietary Ingredient notification is required, the information must be given to the FDA at least 75 days in advance of the product being introduced into interstate commerce.

SUMMARY

Law, regulations, and policies regarding labeling are complex and vary depending on the facility producing the food, the intended consumer, packaging, and method of sales. Ensuring that your label meets all standards is important to eliminate the risk of noncompliance. Claims are carefully regulated; therefore, companies should verify that their product meets all guidelines before printing a misleading claim. Labeling requirements vary based on the number of employees, of units sold, the arena for sales, the customer, and many other factors. Thorough research of label requirements can save companies from going through substantial work later or having to recall a product for mislabeling.

KEY WORDS

Added sugars—sugars (that) are either added during the processing of foods, or are packaged as such, which include sugars, sugars from honey or syrups, or sugars from concentrated fruit or vegetable juices.

Dietary fiber—Non-digestible soluble and insoluble carbohydrates (with three or more monomeric units) and lignin that are intrinsic and intact in plants; isolated and synthetic nondigestible carbohydrates (with three or more monomeric units) demonstrating that such carbohydrates have a physiological effect(s) that is beneficial to human health; or (3) isolated and synthetic non-digestible carbohydrates (with 3 or more monomeric units) that are the subject of an authorized health claim.

Dietary ingredients—include vitamins, minerals, amino acids, and herbs or botanicals, as well as other substances that can be used to supplement the diet.

Information Panel (IP)—legally defined as that "part of the label immediately contiguous and to the right of the Principal Display Panel as observed by an individual facing the Principal Display Panel."

Nutrient content claims—claim on a label that states a food is made with or contains a nutrient in a specific amount.

Principal Display Panel—legally defined as "the part of a label that is most likely to be displayed, presented, shown or examined under customary conditions of display for retail sale."

COMPREHENSION QUESTIONS

16.1. What is the Principal Display Panel?

16.2. Name two of the three spices that also add color.

16.3. Match the following claim with its definition.

a. High	___	25% reduction
b. Good	___	At least 33% less calories, 50% less fat, or both
c. Reduced	___	20% or more of the DRV or RDI of nutrient
d. Light	___	10% to 19% of the DRV or RDI of nutrient

16.4. A company is producing a flavored juice drink with 100% DRI of Vitamin C. It has previously been found that the pasteurization process for the drink destroys 25% of the total ascorbic acid.

a. How much Vitamin C should be added to an 8,000 fluid ounce batch?

b. The drink is given a shelf-life of twenty weeks at refrigeration.

The company studies show that 20% of the vitamin C content is lost at the end of that period. Re-calculate the amount of vitamin C that should be added to the 8,000 fluid ounce batch so that the apple juice's vitamin contents can remain at 100% throughout the entire shelf period.

16.5. When does water not have to be declared as an ingredient in food products? Give two specific examples.

REFERENCES

A Guidance for Industry: A Guide to Food Labeling. (Silver Spring, MD: U.S. Food and Drug Administration, 2009). Accessed October 17, 2012, http://www.fda.gov/Food/GuidanceComplianceRegulatoryInformation/GuidanceDocuments/FoodLabelingNutrition/FoodLabelingGuide/default.htm.

CHAPTER 17

Controlling the Quality of New Food Products

Learning Objectives

- Understand the basic concepts of quality control.
- Know how to create a quality-control system.
- Appreciate what is gold standard quality control.

QUALITY control consists of actions taken by food processors to adequately monitor a food product, providing a product that is safe, compatible with the market, and accepted by consumers. Quality assurance is the control, evaluation, and auditing of the overall food processing system. Quality control is critical when launching a new food product, because it establishes product reputation, increases efficiency, ensures product safety, and provides evidence of food regulation compliance. Quality control needs to be implemented in three stages during processing:

1. Control of raw materials
2. Control of the processing line
3. Inspection of the finished product

IMPORTANCE OF QUALITY CONTROL

The failure to meet quality standards in food products will result in no purchases by consumers or bad publicity and is therefore important in the food industry. Consumers expect consistency in the products that they buy. Product and company reputations are upheld by exceptional quality control. Quality control systems help manufacturers maintain consistent product quality and sensory properties, reduce production costs, eliminate defects, and increase productivity. Even when products meet company specifications, slight differences between batches are possible as variability of ingredients and processing is inevitable. Successful quality systems ensure product safety by eliminating any potential of food poisoning and related risks. Firms can reduce the chances of recalls through strict maintenance of quality control measures.

Quality control also increases process efficiency with the use of information provided through analysis of quality control labs. Efficiency can be increased in regard to material and output. Analysis of quality control documents may unveil patterns in manufacturing quality throughout processing and suggest changes in processing speed, duration before sanitation, hygiene, or sanitation issues. Worker safety and hygiene are also a part of maintaining quality standards.

Quality standards should be articulated and followed in the development of each product. Research and development technologists must concentrate not only on physical and sensory properties of the new food, but also shelf-life and regulatory requirements. Processing equipment and process rates also influence quality attributes. A quality representative should assist in product development, if applicable. Quality issues that ought to be addressed in the development stages are tolerance, hazard and mode of failure analysis, shipping test and evaluation, and the creation of specifications for ingredients, process, product, and packaging.

QUALITY CONTROL DURING THE DEVELOPMENT STAGE

The first step in quality control is finding out what attributes are acceptable to a consumer, and what is unacceptable. Consumers sometimes base their likes and dislikes on popular culture, making them hard at times to track. A list of product requirements is made from these attributes, and interested parties examine how they can measure these attributes during the production process. Some attributes consumers like are more complicated than others. For examples, if consumers prefer their store-bought cookie to be free of palm oil, the ingredient listing will give them the knowledge that the product being offered meets this expectation. Consumers might also prefer a moist, chewy cookie, but how will this be measured? Quality control personnel, product developers, and process engineers have to work together to find out how a moist, chewy cookie correlates with steps in the production process. Quality control activities can use sensory analysis, instrumental analysis, or more simple visual analysis to determine acceptability. Consumer preferences should be determined through consumer product liking tests, in-home use tests, or focus groups.

The quality control specifications that should be addressed during food product development include (1) physical and sensory properties, (2) product function and nutritive values, (3) process equipment and process rates, (4) packaging and packaging equipment, (5) composition, (6) microbiological limitations, (7) shelf-life, (8) labeling and coding, and (9) regulatory requirements (Stauffer 1988). The quality control program established by a processing facility or company should cover all aspects of the production process including material handling, packaging, storage, and all processing procedures. Companies can reduce costs and eliminate unforeseen production problems with a solid quality control program.

Pilot plants can be used to determine the performance of the food and ensure that standards are attainable prior to full production. Pilot plant manufacturing can lead to setting superior standards, due to tighter control, smaller batches, and ideal production environments. Pilot plants usually do not experience processing problems that lead to stoppages of the line and product holding times. Standards that cannot be met in a pilot plant are unlikely to be met in a production facility.

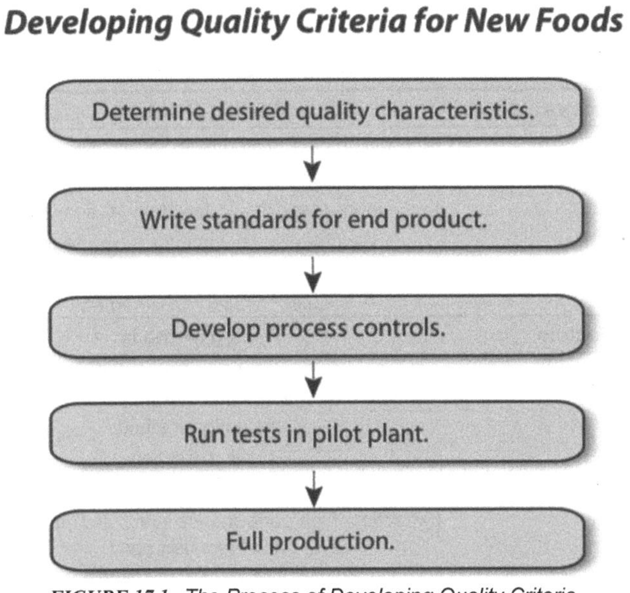
Developing Quality Criteria for New Foods
Determine desired quality characteristics.
Write standards for end product.
Develop process controls.
Run tests in pilot plant.
Full production.

FIGURE 17.1. The Process of Developing Quality Criteria.

QUALITY CONTROL TOOLS

Methods for establishing quality control measures include physical, chemical, sensory, and microbiological testing. Chemical and physical tests for delineating quality attributes are laid out in Table 17.1.

Developing Product Specifications

New food products should have product specifications that detail the attributes of the food as well as its defects. To create product specifications, the quality of raw materials and their specifications must first be determined. Attributes needed to create processing stability and the desired product quality should be decided upon through coordination of the research and development and quality control departments. After the important attributes have been indicated, a uniform testing method must be found. Finding accurate testing methods can be difficult, as many of the tests may need to be rapid, in-line assessments. All labeling and packaging guidelines should also be included in the product specifications. The regulatory status of all ingredients should be noted.

Product specification records may also contain defect information. Examples of defective foods can come from the processing operation or through consumer complaints. It is important to characterize defect

TABLE 17.1. Physical and Chemical Quality Factors and Testing Methods.

Physical Factors	Testing Methods
Color	Spectrophotometer, colorimeter, or Munsell color system
Viscosity	Viscometer, Bostwick consistiometer
Texture	Finger feel, mouth feel, texture analyzer
Container	Weight, volume, vacuum, seal integrity
Symmetry	Weight, volume, length, width, diameter
Defects	Count or size measurement
Chemical Factors	**Testing Methods**
Moisture	Karl Fischer titration method, oven drying, vacuum drying, desiccation, dielectric method, infrared analysis, microwave absorption method
Fat-Oil	Ether extraction
Protein	Kjeldahl Method
Carbohydrates	Extraction, high performance liquid chromatography, gas chromatography
Ash	Dry ashing, wet ashing, microwave ashing

TABLE 17.2. Raw Materials and Quality Attribute Tests.

Raw Material	Quality to Test	Test Procedure
Grains		
Flour	Baking performance	Bake testing
	Protein	Kjeldahl method
Meat		
	Color	Colorimeter, Munsell Color system
	Shear/Tenderness	Warner Braxler
Fruits and Vegetables		
	Maturity	Brix, Brix/Acid ratio
	Color	Colorimeter
	Texture	Texture analysis instrument
General		
	Smell	Sensory
	Infestation	Visually
	Taste	Sensory testing
	Visual appeal	Sensory

traits, so that plant quality control departments have the criteria to uniformly discriminate between good and defective ingredients.

MATERIAL CONTROL

Raw materials form the foundation a product is built on. Therefore, reliable and consistent ingredients are the first quality control essential. The purchaser of raw materials should assess the quality of the materials from each supplier and set tight quality expectations. Buying high-quality raw materials can reduce downtime, enable a processor to reduce the amount of inventory on hand), and eventually lead to cost savings (Stauffer 1988).

Departments should work together to ensure that the raw materials being purchased are of sufficient quality. Purchasing, quality control, production, and research and development all have a role in finding suppliers that can provide a consistent product that meets company standards at the volume needed for continuous production. Material control begins at the product development stage by defining material selection criteria and selecting vendors (Stauffer 1988). Through well-tailored and realistic material selection criteria, the purchasing company can exclude products and providers that may not meet expectations.

Selecting a supplier can also include performing a quality audit on the vendor's production facilities and reviewing their quality control programs. Quality audits may also occur on a periodic basis, even after a product is in production.

When materials are received at the production facility, a quality evaluation procedure should be in place to assess the products prior to their being accepted into the plant. Immediate inspection of raw materials can help alleviate any question of faults. Elements of control in receiving can include visual inspection, sampling, verification of identification marks, checking the carriers, and logging deliveries (Hui 2004). Below are samples of documents attesting to the quality of received materials.

Example of a Certificate of Analysis (CoA) for a Newly Developed Organic Sorghum Syrup

- *Color*: Light to medium brown
- *Flavor*: Sweet with slightly grainy
- *Solids*: 70–72%
- *Maximum Moisture*: 28%
- *Density*: 11.15 lb/gal at 90°F
- *Viscosity*: 500 CPS at 90°F
- *pH*: 3.5–4.2
- *Sulfur dioxide*: maximum 3%
- *Microbiological*:
- *Aerobic Plate coun*t: < 200 CFU/yeast: < 10 CFU/g
- *Molds*: < 10 CFU/g
- *Coliforms*: < 10 CFU/g
- *E. coli*: negative in 30 g sample
- *Salmonella*: negative in 100g sample
- *Aflatoxins*: < 10 ppb
- *Pesticides*: None detected
- *Heavy Metals*:
- *Arsenic*: < 20 ppb
- *Lead*: < 10 ppb
- *Shelf-life*: 1 year in cool dry environment

Example of a Letter of Guarantee (LOG) for a Newly Developed Organic Sorghum Syrup

"Our business is committed to providing you with Organic Sorghum Syrup that is of the highest quality and that complies with the requirements of the FDA and with the USDA's Organic certification program.

"We guarantee that our raw material was produced without the use of any pesticides and that it is free of any hazardous biological or chemical contaminants. It is delivered to you in approved packaging material, intact, undamaged, clean, and clearly labelled.

"We value your business and ask that you contact us immediately should you see anything wrong with our product."

CONTROLLING QUALITY DURING PRODUCTION

The main share of quality control procedures takes place in the production facility to ensure that, as they are being made, products meet consumer standards. Sampling plans need to be established. Processes for testing quality control should be written so that are easily understood by operators and testers. Unwritten plans lead to confusion and misunderstandings. Control of processes will entail numerous procedures: inspection of raw materials, verification of processes, identification of materials (generally done using a labeling or tag system), calibration of test equipment and processing instruments, and documentation.

QUALITY CONTROL SYSTEMS

Quality control systems ultimately define how consumers perceive your product. Is a company satisfied with being a purveyor of inexpensive packaged goods? Or does it offer a premium product? Companies selling lower priced goods may have more flexibility in quality standards for items such as packaging, and may allow more variability in products. Higher-end products demand greater quality control. A written policy should be constructed to address the quality of the products that the company produces and specify who is responsible for controlling quality control systems. In large organizations, quality personnel are located at the corporate offices and in the manufacturing plant.

Corporate quality assurance representatives may assist in determining quality control settings for new product launches, monitor the quality of products being made at plants, and attempt to harmonize product attributes of items produced in different manufacturing facilities.

In a manufacturing plant, quality representatives will be responsible for keeping the product within the outlined specifications. Quality personnel can help detect issues with the product or the food while it is being processed. Product that does not meet quality specifications is reworked, diverted, or sent to other uses.

For cases where products are found to be outside of the established specifications, the manufacturing facility should have written corrective action procedures. Identifying the reason(s) why a food is not of a specified quality starts by assessing the quality reports.

SAMPLING PLANS FOR NEW PRODUCTS

Sampling must be done regularly to evaluate the quality of raw materials and product lots. Because every piece of food cannot be tested when high volumes are being produced, sampling is done to get an idea of the quality. Quality control will be only as good as the sampling plan. Samples should, to the greatest extent possible, give an accurate glimpse into the characteristics of the foods being produced.

For each quality attribute to be measured, a sampling procedure should be considered. The optimum sampling point during processing should be determined. Procedures for collecting samples are important for certain attributes, like moisture, which can be skewed. If a sample for moisture is transported through a plant without being sealed in an airtight bag or container, the sample may dry out. The frequency and sizes of sample gathering should also be clarified.

In a few instances, a 100 percent sampling is applicable. Many operations use automatic weight checkers to inspect 100 percent of the weights of products (Hubbard 1990). Many operations apply sophisticated tools, such as optical scanners, to detect missing labels or other defects.

Spot checking is an important part of a good sampling plan. Spot checking consists of infrequent, unplanned checks, which provide a more thorough examination of the operation. Because sampling plans operate on scheduled sample times, operators come to recognize and perhaps unconsciously adjust to the pattern of sampling. Because periodic sampling checks are often made by line technicians, it is important to obtain and check independent results, in order to unveil discrepancies. Discrepancies between quality control personnel and line technicians can be signs of problems in processing. Such discrepancies may also indicate instrument failure or the need to calibrate instruments.

Examples of sampling plans for new products are discussed in the publications by Kohl's and Maynard, cited in the references.

CONTROL CHARTS

Control charts are used to test if an operation's processing is operating within the boundaries of a targeted quality. Control charts should contain upper and lower control points, plus a center line that can be used as a target.

X-BAR AND R CHARTS

X-Bar and *R* charts are statistical tools that can be used to depict quality control parameters, such as pH, moisture, percent solids, pounds, or any other units that may be applicable to a process. *X*-bar and *R* charts are beneficial when trying to understand and control the quality of raw materials and finished product quality (Hubbard 1990).

An *X*-bar represents the average value of measurements (represented by *X* with subscripts such as X_1, X_2, X_3, X_4, etc.). *X* bar charts graph a series of X bar data measurements, which are averages of sample sets.

In the following example, the weights of a finished ready-to-eat cereal product are weighed after the dryer to test for consistency and to ensure that the weights correspond with the product specifications for proper fill of the packaging materials. Attaining consistent weight of product is needed to design and fill packaging. It is vital to stay within regulatory confinements (eliminating low package fills) and not accidentally give away product (overfilling). For each sample set, five weights are taken as seen in Table 17.3. The *X*-bar calculations are a

TABLE 17.3. Calculations for X-bar and R charts for Ready to Eat Cereal Finished Weights.

	grams/cup of product						
Sample Set	1	2	3	4	5	Average (X-bar)	Range (r)
1	32	34	33	36	33	33.6	4
2	28	32	33	34	34	32.2	6
3	30	31	30	33	31	31	3
4	38	37	37	33	35	36	5
5	34	34	35	32	32	33.4	3
6	40	40	39	37	40	39.2	3
7	28	32	24	30	29	28.6	8
8	33	32	31	34	33	32.6	3
9	34	35	36	36	36	35.4	2
10	36	32	33	34	36	34.2	4

simple average of all of the weights, while the range (r) is calculated by subtracting the largest value in the sample set from the smallest value.

The X-bar chart in Figure 17.2 shows that at times, the product fill has gone above the upper limit. Products that are overweight may cause packages to have low fill volumes leading to the need to add additional product to the package. When the product has a low weight, it is important to ensure that automated packaging lines are able to properly seal the packaging material since improperly sealed packaging materials can cause product quality to deteriorate, which will affect shelf-life. The X-bar chart shows the changes in averages over time, while the R chart depicts how subgroups are changing.

The R chart in Figure 17.3 depicts the ranges of the readings taken. Some of the ranges are quite high, which could indicate inconsistencies in the process. Perhaps at sample 7 (big spike in ranges), there could have been a process change or halt in processing, which caused the ranges to spike.

X bar and R charts are preferred because they are easy to prepare, simple to understand, and helpful when diagnosing and locating problems (Hubbard 1990). These charts can be used to test the stability of the operation and make process improvements. Other charts are used to evaluate attributes such as defects, sensory qualities, and color throughout processing.

DEVELOPING A GOLD STANDARD

Quality and sensory programs go hand-in-hand in determining standards for food products. The primary goal of product sales entail pleasing a customer by means of sensory traits. Therefore, sensory testing becomes an essential part of quality control. Sensory judges should be well trained on the stipulations of the quality program, but the standards themselves should be derived from consumer testing. A "gold standard" represents the best available product from which all others are judged. The gold standard can be determined through a combination of management decisions and consumer testing data. Consumer research must poll enough people to produce statistically significant results and thereby provide adequate data to arrive at the best overall product with the most desired attributes. Desired attributes are compiled and used to establish product and processing specifications. Upper and lower quality limits for the attributes should be established. Analytical measurements and sensory tests must be carried out for each attribute. Instrumental

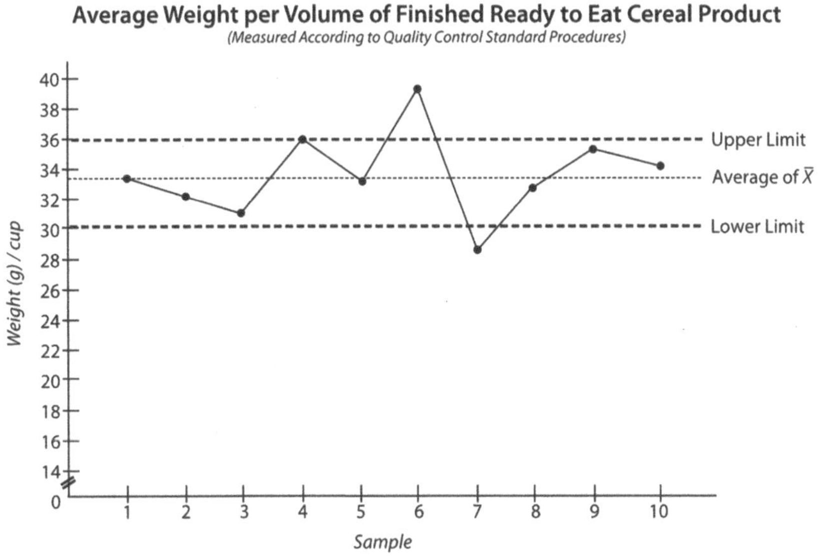

FIGURE 17.2. Example of X-bar chart for sample set.

measurements should be substituted if the sensory evaluations cause fatigue or are repetitive, unpleasant, or dangerous.

To maintain the gold standard, production samples have to be collected and used to monitor quality. Products can be compared against the gold standard by maintaining an accessible gold standard sample, if applicable, or keeping detailed notes of the gold standard. Photographs of gold standard food may also be helpful if visual appeal is required. Testing against the gold standard can consist of pass/fail tests, differ-

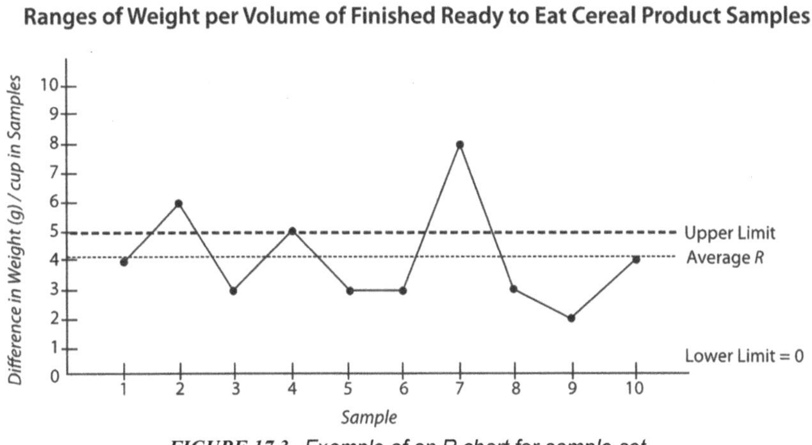

FIGURE 17.3. Example of an R chart for sample set.

ence testing, quality ratings/scoring, or descriptive analysis. Gold standards help to maintain and meet high expectations for quality.

ADDRESSING CONSUMER COMPLAINTS

When consumers contact a company with product complaints, issues should be handled quickly and carefully. Systems for handling consumer complaints vary between organizations, but consumer complaints should be relayed to the quality control department to ensure their knowledge of the issue. Product complaints frequently relate to flavor, odor, foreign material, appearance, net volume or weight, health effects, deterioration, ingredient questions, and allergen information (Hubbard 1990). Consumer affairs personnel should obtain the package code date or other identifying mark from the package of a questioned product, so that recurring instances from the same facility or lot can be documented. All consumer complaints need to be filed by category and assessed by the quality department to determine areas of weakness or repeating issues. Valid complaints may lead to the need to reevaluate a product's formulation and quality procedures.

SUMMARY

The quality of products assist in increasing the probability a product will be purchased more than once. Quality control parameters and sampling plans must be developed to define, monitor and sustain product quality, and enable product success. Evaluation of quality programs should be done on a regular basis, and customer complaints scrutinized as possible clues to quality deficiencies.

KEY WORDS

Gold standard—represents the best available product in terms of which all others are judged.

R charts—represents the range of values for each of the measurements. *R* bar charts graph a series of *R* measurements, which show the range of each sample taken. *R* charts are used to reveal variability in a process.

X bar charts—represents the average value of measurements (represented by *X* with subscripts such as X_1, X_2, X_3, X_4, etc.). X bar charts graph a series of X bar measurements, which are averages of sample sets.

COMPREHENSION QUESTIONS

17.1. What is a sampling plan and how is it used to determine acceptable quality levels?

17.2. A granola bar is within company specification if the chocolate drizzle covers an average of 25% of the bar with a standard deviation of 5%.

a. Explain what actions would be taken if a lot of product has an average 22% drizzle and why.
b. Explain what actions would be taken if a lot has an average of 34% drizzle and why.

17.3. Describe some quality attributes that can be controlled in your raw materials and product. Give examples of tests that you could use.

17.4. Answer whether the statements are True or False:

a. Control of raw materials is important from a food quality standpoint
b. Rapid methods for determination of food quality are not important.

REFERENCES

Gould WA & Gould RW. 1988. Total Quality Assurance for the Food Industries. *Timonium, MD: CTI Publications.*

Hubbard, M. R. *Statistical Quality Control for the Food Industry*. (New York: Van Nostrand Reinhold, 1990).

Kohls, Richard L., *Marketing of Agricultural Products*, The Macmillan Company, New York, NY, 1967.

Maynard, H.B., *Handbook of Business Administration*, (New York: McGraw-Hill Book Company, 1970), 8–87.

Stauffer, J. E. *Quality Assurance of Food Ingredients, Processing, and Distribution*. (Westport, CT: Food & Nutrition Press, Inc., 1988).

CHAPTER 18

Safety Concerns for New Food Products

Learning Objectives

- How companies ensure safety in their new products.
- The most prominent pathogenic microorganisms.
- How to prevent food safety breeches.

FOOD safety concerns make news: Someone found metal or a mouse in a food product, a nationwide outbreak of foodborne illness is causing death, or high levels of arsenic are present in apple juice or rice. Food safety issues affect every new food product and include microbial contamination, physical contamination or extraneous matter, product tampering, pesticide residues, and natural toxicants.

MICROBIAL CONTAMINATION

In recent years, a number of widely reported outbreaks of foodborne illnesses caused by microbial contamination have increased public awareness and concern about the safety of food. The CDC estimates that 1 in 6 Americans get sick as the result of foodborne microbes—which adds up to 48 million people in the United States alone (*Estimates of foodborne illness in the United States* 2012).

Almost any food can supply nutrients that support the growth of microorganisms; thus, in a sense, microorganisms compete with humans at all stages of the food chain. Under the right conditions, some microorganisms cause human illness; others cause foods to spoil, rendering them inedible.

The Problem of Foodborne Illnesses

Foodborne illnesses generally cause temporary disorders of the digestive tract; however, they can also lead to more serious consequences. Precise costs of foodborne illnesses are unknown, but recent estimates range from $4.4 billion to more than $33 billion annually from the 14 most common illnesses, which account for 95% of cases of sickness and 98% of deaths (Hoffman *et al.* 2012). Because of ineffective and under-resourced monitoring procedures and widely variable costs of illness, data on actual cases and outbreaks of foodborne illness are inaccurate and greatly under-represent actual incidence and costs.

The majority of cases of foodborne illnesses are not reported because the initial symptoms of most foodborne illnesses are not severe enough to require medical attention, a medical facility or state does not report cases that are diagnosed properly, or the illness is not recognized as caused by food. It is estimated, however, that in the United States, each year, about 9.4 million episodes of foodborne illness occur, about 55,961 people are hospitalized, and about 1,351 deaths occur that are traceable to 31 major foodborne pathogens (Scallan *et al.* 2011). Bacterial pathogens are the most commonly identified cause of foodborne illnesses. They are easily transmitted and can multiply rapidly in food, making them difficult to control.

The Centers for Disease Control and Prevention (CDC) in Atlanta, Ga., has targeted four pathogens (*Escherichia coli* [*E. coli*] 0157:H7, *Salmonella enteritidis* [*S. enteritidis*], *Listeria monocytogenes* [*L. monocytogenes*], and *Campylobacter jejuni* [*C. jejuni*]) as those of greatest concern. The CDC also are concerned about other bacterial pathogens, such as *Vibrio vulnificus* and *Yersinia enterocolitica*, that can cause serious illnesses, and *Clostridium perfringens* and *Staphylococcus aureus*, that cause less serious illnesses but are very common.

Viral pathogens are often transmitted by infected food handlers or through contact with sewage. The hepatitis A and Norwalk viruses have been shown to cause foodborne illnesses.

Public health officials believe that the risk of foodborne illnesses is increasing. Because of a national and international production and distribution system, products that may be contaminated can reach a greater number of people. In addition, new and more virulent strains of previously identified harmful bacteria have appeared in the past several decades. Some of these organisms are resistant to usual controls, such as refrigeration.

Employee turnover, lack of training and supervision, and other factors in the foodservice industry can increase the risk of foodborne illness. Mishandling or improper preparation at any step in the food system, including the home, can be the culprit causing serious illness.

In general, animal foods such as beef, pork, poultry, seafood, milk, and eggs are more frequently identified as the source of outbreaks in the United States than non-animal foods. Increasingly, however, produce such as apples, lettuce, potatoes, onions, garlic, sprouts, berries, melons, and tomatoes have been associated with foodborne illnesses.

Not Just the Flu

Many foodborne illnesses are brief and cause flu-like symptoms: nausea, vomiting, and minor aches and pains. In a small percentage of cases, more serious illness or death can result. Foodborne infections can spread through the bloodstream to other organs. Complications also result when diarrhetic infections act as trigger mechanisms in certain individuals, causing an illness such as reactive arthritis to flare up. In other cases, no immediate symptoms appear but serious consequences eventually develop. About 2 to 3 percent of all cases of foodborne illness lead to serious consequences.

Salmonella can lead to reactive arthritis, serious infections, or death. In recent years, *Salmonella* outbreaks have been caused by the consumption of many foods of animal origin, including beef, poultry, eggs, milk and dairy products, and pork, with cases also implicating peanut butter. The largest outbreak occurred in the Chicago area in 1985 and involved more than 16,000 laboratory-confirmed cases and an estimated 200,000 total cases. One institution that treated 565 patients from this outbreak confirmed that 13 patients developed reactive arthritis after consuming contaminated milk. In addition, 14 deaths may have been associated with this incident. More recent outbreaks include a peanut outbreak in

Case Study: Jack-in-the-Box Outbreak of 1994

An outbreak in 1990s at the Jack-in-the-Box fast food chain affected more than 700 people. Fifty-five patients, including four children who died, developed hemolytic uremic syndrome, which is characterized by kidney failure. The culprit in this incident was *Eschcerichia coli* (E. coli) 0157:H7, most commonly transmitted to humans through eating undercooked ground beef. *E. coli* 0157:H7 can cause kidney failure in young children and infants.

late 2008 that led to 529 illnesses, 116 hospitalizations, and possibly 8 deaths. The peanut butter was used by many national and multinational companies, resulting in numerous recalls. A huge *S. enteritidis* outbreak in late 2010 involving shell eggs resulted in approximately 1,939 illnesses from two producers of eggs in Iowa.

Listeria can cause meningitis and stillbirths and has a fatality rate of 20 to 40 percent. All foods may contain these organisms, particularly raw poultry and unpasteurized dairy products. The largest outbreak occurred in 1985 in Los Angeles, primarily in pregnant women and their fetuses. More than 140 cases of illness were reported, including 13 cases of meningitis. At least 48 deaths, including 20 stillbirths or miscarriages, were attributed to the outbreak. Soft cheese produced in a contaminated factory environment was confirmed as the source. A more recent outbreak occurred in the summer of 2012 involving cantaloupe grown in Colorado, which was responsible for 147 illnesses and 33 deaths.

Campylobacter has been implicated in Guillain-Barre syndrome, which is now one of the leading causes of paralysis from disease in the United States. *Campylobacter* infections occur in all age groups, with the greatest incidence in children under one year of age. Most cases occur individually, primarily from eating poultry, not during large outbreaks. About 4,250 cases of Guillain-Barre syndrome occur each year, and about 425 to 1,275 cases are preceded by *Campylobacter* infections.

Growth and Prevention of Microorganisms

Microorganisms grow rapidly. A single microorganism can grow into a large load by cellular division, in which 1 becomes 2, 2 becomes 4, 4 becomes 8, 8 becomes 16, and so on. This is called logarithmic growth. The time it takes a bacterial cell to reproduce is called the generation time.

If we start with the twentieth generation containing 524,288 bacteria, it takes only one further generation to reach 1,000,000 bacteria, which is a large enough population to cause spoilage to begin in food products. If the equipment, personnel, and product are clean, the initial numbers of bacteria will be lower, and we may begin with the fifteenth generation of 16,384. In this instance, the shelflife will be five times longer than in the prior case where a bacterium multiplied to the twentieth generation.

Four distinct phases mark the bacterial growth curve: lag, log or growth phase, stationary or resting phase, and death phase. Bacteria need about four hours to adapt to a new environment before they begin rapid growth. In handling food, this means we have less than four hours to make a decision to cool the food, heat it, or eat it. For example, when chicken arrives at the dock of a fast food outlet, at a restaurant, or at your home, you must decide whether to heat and eat it, refrigerate it at the proper temperature (chicken freezes at 28°F) for a short period of time, or wrap and freeze the chicken for longer storage. If you don't decide, bacteria will enter the log phase of growth, multiply rapidly, and cause spoilage and possible illness, if the chicken is eaten.

Spoilage bacteria produce the slime, toxins, off-colors, and odors associated with food spoilage in the log phase of growth. Pathogenic bacteria can grow and produce large numbers of toxic compounds, and these are usually not detectable as off odors, bad flavors, etc. Remember, the four hours bacteria remain in the log phase is approximate and cumulative.

As microorganisms grow, they tend to form colonies of millions of individual cells. Once a colony forms, the food available to each cell is limited, and excretions from these millions of cells become toxic to other microbes. This is the stationary phase. Some of the cells now begin to die.

To prevent bacterial colonies from forming, keeping initial bacteria levels low is important. A food product that starts with 100 microorganisms per gram may have a shelf-life of twelve days before it develops off odors, slime, and spoilage. When the initial number is 5,000 per gram, the shelf-life of that same foodstuff may be shortened to seven days. Because so much depends on the initial number of bacteria, temperatures, and handling practices, calculating a specific shelf-life for a category of food products is difficult.

Good personal hygiene, sanitizing equipment, controlling temperature, and using chlorinated water are all practices that help keep initial bacterial counts low.

Different microorganisms require different combinations of the factors listed in Table 18.1 under the acronym "FATTOM," which stands for food, acid, time, temperature, oxygen, and moisture.

Food

Like all living things, bacteria require food to live, but they need

TABLE 18.1. Requirements for the Support of Microorganisms.

Requirements for Microorganism Growth (FAT TOM)	
F	Food to meet growth requirements
A	Acid conditions to support growth
T	Time at conditions to allow growth
T	Temperatures that support growth
O	Oxygen (or no oxygen) depending on organism
M	Moisture

only very small quantities. A smudge of protein or fat left on the wall of a processing plant, grease on the blade of a knife, or food residues on the wheel of a can opener or on a cutting board are a feast for microorganisms, as well as for larger pests.

Acidic/Basic Conditions

Every microorganism has an optimal pH (acid) concentration for growth. Yeasts and molds favor more acidic conditions than do bacteria.

Time. Different types of microbes grow at different rates. Under ideal conditions, certain bacterial populations can double in as short as nine minutes; others require hours. Bacteria that reproduce most quickly will dominate.

Temperature

Temperature is probably the single most important factor in preventing microbial food spoilage. Generally speaking, the cooler a food is kept, the longer shelf-life it will have. A thermometer in the refrigerator is a necessity. Maintain the temperature at 35° to 40°F. However, foods such as tomatoes and lettuce will freeze or be damaged at 32° to 33°F.

Different bacterial species require different temperatures for maximum growth. Some bacteria will grow at refrigeration-level temperatures. Others will only grow at moderate temperatures. Warm-loving bacteria grow at temperatures above 140°F. At temperatures above or below their optimum, bacteria will grow and reproduce at a slower rate. Food spoilage bacteria grow best at environmental temperatures of 70° to 100°F. A good rule of thumb is to double the shelf-life of a food that needs refrigeration; each time the temperature can be lowered by 18°F.

That is, for every 18°F decrease in storage temperature, food will last twice as long.

Oxygen Use

Microorganisms are considered aerobic if they can use oxygen, anaerobic if they grow best without oxygen, and facultative if they can grow well with or without oxygen. Understanding the oxygen characteristics of a specific microbe targeted can help you understand the type of prevention techniques.

Moisture

All living things require moisture, and bacteria are no exception. Perishable foods requiring refrigeration usually have very high moisture contents. Moist food left for long periods of time still provides adequate moisture for bacterial growth. Bacteria need water because their only means of obtaining food is by absorption. This process cannot be accomplished without moisture, which explains why foods such as dried milk, dried soups, and cereals do not spoil microbiologically. Microorganisms exist in such foods, but they can't eat.

Companies should perform challenge studies when producing processing parameters and periodically throughout the life of a product. Challenge studies are a method by which a product is inoculated with bacteria prior to processing, then allowed to go through the processing procedure. The objective is to determine the success that the processing technique has in eliminating the bacteria. The bacteria chosen for the study should be similar to those that would be expected to thrive in the product.

Bacterial Causes of Foodborne Illness

Bacillus cereus

The disease: Two distinct syndromes may occur. In one, the toxin produced results in diarrhea, and in the other (the emetic), the toxin causes vomiting. Generally, the diarrheal toxin is associated with consumption of puddings, starchy sauces, or vegetables such as mashed potatoes. The emetic syndrome is most frequently associated with cooked rice.

The organism: *Bacillus cereus* forms heat-resistant spores, so it can survive the initial cooking of starch-based products. The spore can then germinate if cooked products are not kept hot (140°F or higher) before serving.

Control: Avoid holding freshly cooked hot grain foods and vegetables any longer than necessary before serving. Keep cooked foods hot to prevent spore germination or refrigerate and chill rapidly. Reheat previously cooked rice and vegetable dishes to 165°F prior to serving. Avoid slow cooling and reheating.

Campylobacter jejuni

The disease: *Campylobacter jejuni* has been recognized for years as a cause of abortion in sheep. *Campylobacteriosis* or *Campylobacter enteritis* in humans is now more common in the United States than *salmonellosis*. Common symptoms include profuse and sometimes bloody diarrhea, nausea, cramps, headache, and fever. Onset is within two to five days after eating contaminated food. The illness may last two or three days, but it can last weeks or months with complications such as meningitis, cholecystitis, urinary tract infection, and reactive arthritis. Death is rare. The organism, *C. jejuni*, is found in the intestinal tract of animals, with an almost 100 percent occurrence in poultry. Raw meats and poultry are important sources, along with raw milk and untreated water supplies. The majority of cases have occurred after a person consumes raw milk, undercooked poultry, or raw meat.

Control: The organism requires reduced oxygen levels and can survive several weeks of refrigerator temperatures. It is easily killed by heat and is inhibited by acid, salt, and drying. To control *C. jejuni*, drink only pasteurized milk; avoid cross-contamination of cooked or ready-to-eat foods by utensils, equipment, or cutting surfaces not properly cleaned and disinfected after contact with fresh, uncooked meats or poultry; and use good personal hygiene. Wash hands after handling raw meats to avoid transmitting organisms to other foods and utensils.

Clostridium perfringens

The disease: Ingestion of food containing large numbers of vegetative cells of *Clostridium perfringens* (*C. perfringens*) is necessary for illness to occur. In the intestines, the vegetative cells can form spores and release toxins. Diarrhea and severe abdominal pain are the usual symptoms. Nausea is less frequent. Fever and vomiting are unusual. Death is uncommon but has occurred in older, debilitated people.

The organism: Spores of *C. perfringens* are found in soil. The organism is also part of the normal intestinal content of animals and humans. *Clostridium perfringens* requires protein for growth and will grow with or without oxygen. Spores are common in raw foods, and they are heat-resistant. Cooking foods will destroy vegetative cells, but not necessarily the spore forms of the bacteria. In addition, cooking drives off oxygen, kills competing organisms, and heat shocks the spores. Then, the remaining spores may germinate, resulting in rapid growth of new vegetative cells, especially in foods that have been allowed to cool slowly with inadequate refrigeration. If food is inadequately reheated, ingested organisms could then cause illness.

Control: Illness can be prevented by proper handling of foods, particularly meats, poultry, stews, roasts, meats, pies, casseroles, and gravies. Cook items and then cool them rapidly in shallow pans in the refrigerator. Avoid cooling gravy, stews, or chili in deep cooking pots. If foods are to be held hot, keep the temperature above 140°F. Thoroughly reheat leftovers (to 165°F) before eating. Use good personal hygiene.

Clostridium botulinum

The disease: Foodborne botulism results from eating food in which *Clostridium botulinum* (*C. botulinum*) has grown and produced neurotoxin. The toxin is absorbed and binds to nerve endings. It causes vomiting and diarrhea, fatigue, dizziness, and headache. Later there is constipation, double vision, and difficulty speaking and swallowing. Involuntary muscles become paralyzed. Cardiac and respiratory failure, and ultimately, death occur. Today, because of rapid treatment, botulism is fatal in fewer than 10 percent of cases. Infantile botulism, affecting infants under fourteen months, is another type of botulism that was first identified in 1976. This disease can occur after infants ingest bacterial spores that colonize and produce toxin in the intestinal tract. Spores have been found in honey and syrups and have been implicated in some cases of infantile botulism. Other nonfood items may be sources of spores. Symptoms of infantile botulism include constipation followed by lethargy, poor feeding, weakness, drooling, weak cry, and loss of head control.

The organism: *Clostridium botulinum* spores are widely distributed in soils, shore, and bottom deposits of lakes and streams, gills and viscera of fish, and seafood. They can be found on fruits and vegetables, as these items often are in contact with the soil. Spores have also been found in honey and corn syrup. Meats and vegetables can provide nutrients for growth and toxin production.

Control: Conditions favoring growth and toxin production by *C. botulinum* include high moisture, low-salt, low-acid (pH greater than 4.6), low-oxygen foods such as canned or vacuum-packed products, and storage at room temperature. Foods commonly involved include canned vegetables, fish, meats, chili sauce, chili peppers, tomato relish, and salad dressing. The majority of outbreaks have been caused by home-processed foods. Other foods include foil-wrapped baked potatoes held at warm, not hot, temperatures (above 140°F); cooked onion also held at warm temperatures; and garlic in oil mixtures stored at room temperature. *Clostridium botulinum* spores are heat-resistant. Therefore, canned meat, poultry, fish, and low-acid vegetables (i.e., corn, beans, spinach, beets) require pressure canning to achieve a high enough temperature (240° to 250°F) for sufficient time to destroy spores.

Escherichia coli 0157:H7

The disease: Many types of *E. coli* can cause gastrointestinal disease in humans. One type causes infantile diarrhea; another can cause traveler's diarrhea, associated with travel in foreign countries. Another type causes a dysentery-like illness similar to shigellosis, and a fourth type, 0157:H7, produces hemorrhagic colitis, a severe illness characterized by bloody diarrhea and severe abdominal cramps. Hemolytic uremic syndrome (HUS) can be a complication in children and is a leading cause of acute kidney failure. *Escherichia coli* bacteria are classified by their O and H antigens (e.g., *E. coli* O157:H7, *E. coli* O26:H11). Another classification is Shiga toxin–producing *E. coli* (STEC) O157 or non-O157 STEC. In the US, there have been outbreaks of non-O157 *E. coli* including O111, O26, O45, O145, O104, O6, O51, O103, O27 and O84. The USDA added as adulterants Shiga–toxin producing *E. coli* (STEC) serogroups O26, O45, O103, O111, O121 and O145. Like *E. coli* O157:H7, if any of these serogroups are found in raw ground beef, the culprit product is subject to recall. Although rare, non-O157 STEC outbreaks tend to primarily be due to contaminated food and person-to-person transmission.

The organism: This organism is a normal component of the gastrointestinal tract. The major source of the bacteria in the environment is the feces of humans. Feces and contaminated water are the most likely sources for food contamination. For years, *E. coli* was considered harmless to health and was used as an indicator of fecal contamination in food and water.

Control: Foods that have been implicated in *E. coli* 0157:H7 outbreaks of foodborne illness include mold-ripened cheeses, inadequately cooked ground beef, lettuce, and unpasteurized apple beverages. Good sanitation practices in the manufacture of products such as cheese, good personal hygiene when working with food, cooking meat thoroughly (155°F is the 1995 Food Code recommendation for food service and 160°F is the FSIS recommendation for consumers at home), and avoiding recontamination after cooking or processing will control *E. coli* 0157:H7.

Listeria monocytogenes

The disease: *Listeria monocytogenes* causes listeriosis. Before the 1980s, it was associated with abortions and encephalitis in sheep and cattle. The disease in humans begins with nausea, headache, fever, and vomiting. In severe cases, meningitis, stillbirth, and perinatal septicemia can occur. The disease is rare in non-pregnant healthy adults; however, adults with the following conditions are more susceptible: neoplasm, acquired immunodeficiency syndrome (AIDS), alcoholism, Type 1 diabetes, cardiovascular disease, renal transplant, and corticosteroid therapy. The mortality rate is about 30 percent in the unborn, newborn, or immune compromised. Outbreaks have been associated with consumption of milk, certain soft cheeses, and coleslaw made from contaminated cabbage that had been fertilized with infected sheep manure. Post-pasteurization contamination can also cause outbreaks.

The organism: *Listeria monocytogenes* is widely distributed in soil, vegetation, water, and animals. The organism can survive for long periods in soil, silage, feces, and milk and other dairy foods. It grows well in sewage. Use of sewage sludge and effluent on edible crops is hazardous, as is the use of manure from infected livestock.

Listeria is capable of growing at refrigerator temperatures, and it is sensitive to heat. It also tolerates high concentrations of salt. Because of its wide distribution in nature, its ability to survive for long periods, and its ability to grow under refrigeration, *L. monocytogenes* could be an important cause of foodborne illness in the future, particularly as the popularity of ready-to-eat, refrigerated foods continues to increase.

Control: To control the organism, one must inhibit its occurrence in raw food materials and follow good sanitation practices in food processing plants. Use pasteurized milk and avoid post-pasteurization contamination of milk. Cook foods thoroughly.

Salmonella

The disease: *Salmonellosis* is the classic example of foodborne infection. There are actually three types of diseases caused by *Salmonella*: Enteric fever caused by *S. typhosa*, in which the organism, ingested with food, finds its way into the bloodstream and is excreted in the stools; septicemia caused by *S. cholerasuis*, in which the organism causes blood poisoning; and gastroenteritis caused by *S. typhimurium* and *S. enteritidis*, a true foodborne infection. In the latter case, large numbers of organisms are ingested with food and cause localized infection of the intestinal tract with no invasion of the bloodstream.

Symptoms of *salmonellosis* include nausea, vomiting, headache, chills, diarrhea, and fever. In most cases, the disease is short-lived, and the person recovers. It can be fatal, however. Those at greatest risk include the very young, the aged, and those whose health status is poor. Mortality rate from enteric fever is high. *Salmonella typhimurium* is the common cause of enteric fever, but any of the more than 2,000 different Salmonella organisms are capable of causing enteric fever. In addition to the acute effects of *Salmonella* infection, it is now known that serious chronic rheumatoid or cardiac problems may occur after recovery from the acute disease.

The organism: *Salmonella* are widely distributed in both wild and domestic, warm and cold-blooded animals. It is estimated that some 40 percent of all poultry are contaminated.

Meat and poultry are the most important sources of *Salmonella*. Because Salmonella are very heat-sensitive, they are destroyed by normal cooking and pasteurization processes. They can, however, survive long periods of time in dried or frozen foods. When frozen foods are thawed, these organisms can grow again.

Control: In homes and foodservice sites, *salmonellosis* can be prevented by proper handling of meats, poultry, and other animal foods. Keep raw foods away from cooked foods, avoiding cross-contamination. Cook animal foods thoroughly and hold at either cold (below 40°F) or hot (above 140°F) temperatures. Avoid drinking unpasteurized milk. Thaw turkeys, roasts, fish, and other meats in the refrigerator, not on the countertop. A number of recent outbreaks of salmonellosis have been due to processing errors, particularly in the handling of milk, cheeses, and deli meats. Problems of this nature are controlled by more attention to sanitation and quality control at the processing plant.

Shigella

The disease: *Shigellosis*, also known as bacillary dysentery, is caused by several bacteria of the genus *Shigella*. Symptoms include diarrhea, abdominal pain, vomiting, and fever. Generally, foodborne shigellosis involves a short incubation time (seven to thirtysix hours), but symptoms persist three to fourteen days. As few as ten to one hundred organisms have been shown to cause illness. Secondary infections occur frequently. Recently, *shigellosis* has become a problem in daycare centers.

The organism: *Shigella* organisms are generally considered fragile. They are readily killed by heat used in processing or cooking, and they do not survive well in acidic foods (pH below 4.6). They can survive for extended periods, however, in certain foods. Most outbreaks result from contamination of raw or previously cooked foods during preparation in the home or in foodservice settings. Often, the source of the contamination is traced to a carrier with poor personal hygiene. In fact, the "4 Fs" involved in the transmission of Shigella are food, finger, feces, and flies.

Control: Because infected food handlers are the most likely source of contamination of food by *Shigella*, good personal hygiene is necessary to control the organism. Other control measures include use of properly treated water, sanitary disposal of sewage, and control of flies and rodents.

Staphylococcus aureus

The disease: *Staphylococcus* organisms are capable of producing very heat-resistant enterotoxins. The toxins, rather than the actual bacteria, are responsible for causing foodborne illness. Common symptoms include nausea, vomiting, cramps, sweating, chills, weak pulse, shock, and lowered body temperature. Recovery usually occurs within two days.

The organism: *Staphylococcus aureus* is found in the nose and throat and on the hair and skin of more than half of the healthy population. Infected wounds, lesions, boils, and mucus spread by coughs and sneezes of people with respiratory infection are other sources of contamination. Any food that requires handling in its preparation can become contaminated. The skins and hides of animals can also harbor *Staphylococcus* organisms and may contaminate foods at slaughter. Foods that best support *S. aureus* include protein-rich foods such as meats, poultry, and fish; cream sauces; salads such as ham, turkey, and potato; puddings; custards; and cream-filled pastries. *Staphylococcus aureus* bacteria are not a problem in raw foods, because other harmless bacteria crowd them out. The harmless bacteria may be destroyed in heated foods, leaving a niche for *S. aureus*, should the food become contaminated. In addition, many cooked foods are handled and prepared in final form after cooking, which enables the food handler to contaminate foods whose harmless bacteria have already been destroyed. In mayonnaise-type salads (e.g., ham, egg, etc.), the acidity of the mayonnaise inhibits the growth of staphylcocci. But because other low-acid ingredients are mixed with the mayonnaise, the acid level may be diluted sufficiently to support growth of *S. aureus*. Salt and sugar added to certain food systems also inhibit growth of other organisms, but do not inhibit *S. aureus*. The microorganism grows well at body temperature but can grow at both colder and hotter temperatures. Heat processing and normal cooking will kill *S. aureus* organisms, but heating does not destroy the enterotoxins.

Control: Because *S. aureus* bacteria are common and widespread in humans, preventing contamination of food is virtually impossible. A food becomes contaminated when held at warm temperature for a sufficient time to permit enough bacteria to grow and produce a level of enterotoxin to cause sickness. Thus, time and temperature control are two of the most effective ways to control staphylococcal intoxication.

It is important to use good hygiene to help prevent Staphylococcus contamination. Cook foods thoroughly. Then, cool foods in shallow containers in refrigerators. Keep meat salads, potato salads, cream pies, puddings, and pastries chilled until served. Avoid leaving foods at room temperature for more than two hours.

Yersinia enterocolitica

The disease: *Yersinia enterocolitica* (*Y. enterocolitica*) causes yersiniosis. The most common form causes various symptoms of gastroenteritis, but more serious forms can lead to polyarthritis, septicemia, and meningitis. Death from gastroenteritis is rare, and recovery, if there are no further complications, occurs within one or two days.

The organism: *Yersinia enterocolitica* is commonly found in a wide variety of animals, food, and water sources. Pigs are the most important animal source. Food sources include raw milk, meat, poultry, shellfish, vegetables, and tofu.

Certain strains of the bacteria produce disease, but it appears that many of the strains are nonpathogenic. *Yersinia enterocolitica* can grow at refrigerator temperatures but grows best at room temperature. It is sensitive to heat and is destroyed by adequate cooking and by pasteurization of milk.

Control: Post-pasteurization contamination is the most frequent cause of food-borne outbreaks. Thus, preventive measures in processing plants need to include strict adherence to procedures for keeping perishable products, such as tofu and milk, clean, and cold.

Vibrio

Three *Vibrio* species are considered separately because each is responsible for a different disease syndrome, and their modes of causing foodborne illness also differ.

Vibrio cholerae

The disease: Cholera causes thousands of deaths each year, primarily in Asian countries. Since 1978, however, there have been numerous reports of cholera in the United States, most of which have been traced to consumption of raw oysters and clams. *Vibrio cholerae* (*V. cholera*) colonizes the small intestine and causes large volumes of fluid to be secreted. Diarrhea results in loss of body fluids and accompanying minerals.

In severe cases, cardiovascular collapse and death may occur in a day's time. Organisms are excreted in large numbers and can be transmitted through contaminated water supplies and by foods obtained from those waters, particularly seafood.

The organism: Humans are the only natural sources of this organism. The organism is most commonly spread through water. *Vibrio cholerae* does not multiply in water but can survive for up to two weeks. It is salt tolerant, heatsensitive, and destroyed by cooking.

Control: *Vibrio cholerae* is controlled by the use of clean water and by thoroughly cooking seafood.

Vibrio parahaemolyticus

The disease: *Vibrio parahaemolyticus* (*V. parahaemolyticus*) causes an illness characterized by severe abdominal pain, nausea, diarrhea, and vomiting. It is the most common foodborne illness in Japan.

The organism: *Vibrio parahaemolyticus* has been found in warm coastal waters of countries throughout the world. Most disease outbreaks occur during warm seasons. Growth of organisms occurs while seafood is being held for consumption. It does not grow under refrigeration. The organism is salt-tolerant, but it is very sensitive to heat and is destroyed by cooking.

Control: Refrigeration and proper cooking are important means of controlling *V. parahaemolyticus*. Consumption of raw fish and shellfish poses risks. After cooking, it is important to avoid cross-contamination between raw and cooked seafood. In the United States, this has been the most frequent cause of *V. parahaemolyticus* infection. In Japan, however, the illness frequently involves consumption of raw seafood.

Vibrio vulnificus

The disease: *Vibrio vulnificus* (*V. vulnificus*) causes two clinical forms of illness, one affecting the blood (septicemia) and the other causing seawater-associated wound infections (progressive cellulitis). The death rate is 61 percent for those with septicemia and 22 percent for those with wound infections.

The organism: *Vibrio vulnificus* is common in marine environments and has been found in water, sediment, plankton, oysters, and clams. It is heat-sensitive and grows best in warm temperatures. Cooking destroys the organism.

Control: Refrigeration and cooking of shellfish are important control measures. In addition, avoid contaminating existing cuts or causing new wounds to hands while cleaning and harvesting shellfish.

Viral Causes of Foodborne Illness

Viruses are submicroscopic agents that cause a wide range of disease in both plants and animals. Because they are not complete cells, they are not capable of growing and multiplying like bacteria. Viruses that infect the gastrointestinal tract are usually transmitted by food or water. Human infection results from the following:

- consumption of food contaminated by a food handler who was carrying the virus

- consumption of raw seafood taken from waters polluted by human wastes
- drinking polluted water

Norovirus

Norovirus is currently the number one cause of foodborne illness in the United States. It is a very contagious virus that anyone can get from an infected person, from contaminated food or water, or by touching contaminated surfaces. Symptoms include stomach pain, nausea, and diarrhea. Prevention is through prohibiting sick employees from handling food, hand washing hygiene, washing of fruits and vegetables, cooking seafood thoroughly, and cleaning and sanitizing contaminated surfaces.

Hepatitis A Virus

The disease: Hepatitis A is usually a mild illness with symptoms of sudden onset of fever, nausea, loss of appetite, and abdominal discomfort and is followed by jaundice. The incubation time may be 10 to 50 days. During the middle of the incubation period, it can be transmitted to others. Usually, recovery is complete in one to two weeks. Person-to-person transmission, as well as foodborne and waterborne transmission, occurs. Adults are more susceptible to this illness. Foods become contaminated by food handlers who do not follow good personal hygiene practices or by contaminated water.

Cold cuts, sandwiches, salads, fruits, shellfish, and iced drinks are commonly implicated in outbreaks. Contamination of foods by infected workers in food processing plants and restaurants is common.

The organism: The hepatitis A virus is made up of a single molecule of RNA surrounded by a small protein capsid.

Control: Wash hands thoroughly after using the restroom or diapering infants. Also, harvest shellfish only from unpolluted waters.

Norwalk Virus

The disease: Norwalk virus is a recently discovered foodborne virus. The illness it produces is mild and characterized by nausea, vomiting, diarrhea, and abdominal pain. Headache and low grade fever may result. Water is the most common source of outbreaks. Shellfish and salad ingredients are the foods most often implicated.

Control: Use good personal hygiene and avoid handling food when ill.

Summary of Microbial Contamination

This brief overview of microbial contamination does not even skim the surface of the microbiological concerns regarding food. As a product developer, it will be important for you to research the types of contamination that have previously been associated with the type of product being created. Action plans and the awareness of what steps are needed for safe production are vital in preventing recalls, foodborne illness outbreaks, and monetary losses for the organization.

PRODUCT TAMPERING

Tampering with products can be eliminated by incorporating tamper-evident seals into the packaging scheme. Tamper-evident packaging such as seals around bottle tops are now common in the food and drug industries. Tamper-evident packaging includes jars with a "safety seal," clear tape around the tops of bottles, and tearaway tops in resealable packaging.

PESTICIDES AND OTHER CHEMICAL CONTAMINANTS

Pesticide levels are set by the United States Environmental Protection Agency, which develops tolerance levels for pesticides on food crops. Pesticides are regulated by the FDA, but the tolerances are set by the EPA. All pesticides used on food must be approved.

Case Study: Tylenol's Safety Seal Now a Norm

In 1982, Tylenol capsules laced with potassium cyanide killed 7 people in the Chicago area as the result of product tampering on store shelves. As a result, Johnson & Johnson recalled all 31 million bottles of the product (a loss of more than $100 million dollars). Tylenol was praised for their commitment to product safety, but the company was still faced with how to eliminate product tampering. Johnson & Johnson created a tamper resistant capsule. The United States Food and Drug Administration (FDA) followed with some regulations (mostly in the drug industry) mandating the use of tamper-evident break away components (such as the tape around the tops of bottles).

Other residual components that end up in food include sanitation solutions, antibiotics, and indirect additives from packaging. Sanitation solutions should be carefully used and labeled in a food production facility. Standard operations for cleaning and sanitation should be well described in written documents. Employees in charge of sanitation should be trained. Antibiotics, sometimes used in animal feed, have been found on animal carcasses following harvest. Packaging materials, too, have been implicated in leaching harmful chemicals into packaged foods. A recent example is bisphenol A (BPA). Bisphenol A, used for canned food liners and plastic bottles, was found to leave trace components in food products, while BPA itself has been linked to increased risk of cancer in animal studies.

NATURAL TOXICANTS

Natural toxicants are chemical elements or compounds naturally present in foods that can be harmful to humans. Natural elements, such as arsenic, are found in foods. Trace compounds are dependent on the growing region, soil, irrigation water, previous pesticide use, growing practices, and type of crop. Much of the exposure to arsenic is through water, grain products, rice and rice products, fruit and fruit juices, and dairy products (Yost *et al.* 2004). Arsenic is a natural part of many foods and water sources, but exposure should be limited as elevated exposure to inorganic arsenic has been linked to heightened risk of bladder and lung cancers (*Arsenic in Drinking Water Linked to Bladder, Lung Cancer* 2001).

Other natural toxicants include food allergens. The eight major food allergens that must be labeled on United States products are wheat, soy, eggs, milk, peanut, tree nuts, fish, and shellfish. Some consumers can have life-threatening reactions to these ingredients; therefore, it is of great importance to note the ingredients on food packaging. Major recalls of foods occur due to the failure to list allergens. In an effort to protect consumers, some companies have started listing potential allergens as well (i.e., the statement, "this food has been made on equipment that also processes wheat, tree nuts, peanuts, etc."). If a company is producing two products on the same line and one has allergens and the other does not, the company must implement allergen cleanup procedures in order to produce food uncontaminated by an allergen or list the possibility of allergen contamination.

SUMMARY

Contaminants in food can lead to recalls, negative press, and financial losses. Companies should make efforts to receive high-quality safe food from producers as well as to have safety plans (covered in Chapter 19) to help ensure all product risks are controlled. As consumer awareness of unsafe foods and contaminants grows, it is important for food companies to move quickly to understand the safety risks and health threats associated with each product.

KEY WORDS

Natural toxicants—chemical elements or compounds naturally present in foods that can be harmful to humans.

COMPREHENSION QUESTIONS

18.1. Define water activity and briefly relate it to microbial growth and chemical reactions.

18.2. What microorganism is typically used for microbial testing of canned goods?

18.3. Discuss the relation of pH to microbial growth in foods.

18.4. Fill in the blanks in the following statements.

a. ______________ contamination can be detected using an in-line detector after packaging.

b. ______________ ______________ bacteria are common and widespread in humans; preventing contamination of food is virtually impossible.

c. ______________ ______________ can cause meningitis and stillbirths, has a fatality rate of 20 to 40 percent, and is especially at risk in ______________ ________ ______ ______________

d. Pesticides are regulated by the ____________, but tolerances are set by the _________.

18.5. Name the eight major allergens that must be labeled on food products in the United States.

REFERENCES

"Arsenic in Drinking Water Linked to Bladder, Lung Cancer." *The Nation's Health 31*, no. 10 (2001):5.

Hoffman, S., M. B. Batz, and J. G. Morris. "Annual Cost of Illness and Quality-Adjusted Life Year Losses in the United States Due to 14 Foodborne Pathogens." *Journal of Food Protection 75*, no. 7 (2012):1292–1302.

Jenkins, S., N. Raghuraman, I. Eltoum, M. Carpenter, J. Russo, and C.A. Lamartiniere., C. A. (2009). Oral exposure to bisphenol A increases dimethylbenzanthracene-induced mammary cancer in rats. *Environmental Health Perspectives, 117*(6), 910–5.

Scallan, E., R. M. Hoekstra, F. J. Angulo, R. V. Tauxe, M. Widdowson, S. L. Roy, *et al.* "Foodborne Illness Acquired in the United States—Major Pathogens." *Emerging Infectious Disease* XX, no. XX (2011): XX-XX.

Yost, L. J., S. Tao, S. K. Egan, L. M. Barraj, K. M., Smith, J. S. Tsuji, et al. "Estimation of Dietary Intake of Inorganic Arsenic in U.S. Children." *Human and Ecological Risk Assessment 10*, no. 3 (2004):473–483.

CHAPTER 19

Pre-Requisite Programs, Food Safety Plans, HACCP, and Audit Systems

Learning Objectives

- Learn the requirement of pre-requisite programs.
- Know what commodities have mandated HACCP.
- Recognize how audit systems work and their importance.

ALL new products must comply with safety standards. Processes should be built on food safety programs such as the Hazard Analysis and Critical Control Points (HACCP) system. The HACCP system is widely used in the food industry, but mandated in seafood operations, meat, poultry and juice. The HACCP system does not stand alone—it must be used in coordination with pre-requisite programs that define and spell out procedures for cleaning, sanitation, maintenance, and other operational duties.

PRE-REQUISITE PROGRAMS

Pre-requisite programs establish and apply basic standards for the environmental and operational conditions that must be in place to produce safe products. All pre-requisite programs should be revised and revisited periodically, especially with the introduction of a new product. Pre-requisite programs are not limited to food safety objectives and may include other compliance issues such as net content compliance. Pre-requisite programs help companies meet their primary goal: To produce a safe, wholesome, and quality product.

Good Manufacturing Practices

Good Manufacturing Practices (GMPs) are mandated general main-

TABLE 19.1. Differences between HACCP and Pre-requisite Programs.

Program	HACCP	Pre-Requisite Programs
Purpose	Food safety	General operations
Scope	Specific	Multiple area/lines
Cost of deviation	Deviations have serious consequences	Deviations may not be serious

tenance regulations that are essential to produce wholesome products. Good Manufacturing Practices account for employees, equipment, processing, and environmental conditions within an operation. Good Manufacturing Practices are also referred to as "current" Good Manufacturing Practices (cGMPs). Good Manufacturing Practices were established in 1969 and originally were very specific. In 1986, they were revised to be more "umbrella" regulations, making them relevant to a larger number of operations. The regulations were in 21 CFR 110 detailing cGMPs, but under the Food Safety Modernization Act (FSMA), cGMP can be found in 21 CFR part 117, Subpart B. The updated GMPs include the following:

- Protection against allergen cross-contact.

TABLE 19.2. 21 CFR Current Good Manufacturing Practices Categories.

Part	Subject
General Provisions	
117.10	Personnel
Buildings and Facilities	
117.20	Plant and grounds
117.35	Sanitary operations
117.37	Sanitary facilities and controls
Equipment	
117.40	Equipment and utensils
Production and Process Controls	
117.80	Processes and controls
117.93	Warehousing and distribution
Defect Action Levels	
117.110	Defect Action Levels

- Updated language (e.g., "must" instead of "shall"). Certain provisions containing recommendations were deleted.
- Required cleaning of non-food contact surfaces as frequently as necessary to protect against allergen cross-contact and contamination of food, food-contact surfaces and food packaging.
- GMPs for holding and distributing human food by-products for use as animal food.

21 CFR states that all personnel tasked with maintaining sanitation must be educated in food safety practices. All employees must be aware of cGMP. It is important for plant managers to teach the basics of this regulation in a form employees can understand. It may be beneficial for companies to have employees sign that they have read and understand the statements.

Personnel should be aware of disease control and maintain adequate cleanliness through all phases of food handling. Hair and beard restraints should be used where appropriate. Companies should produce strict and detailed return to work policies for all employees who miss work as a result of sickness.

Clean outer garments are important and are sometimes provided by companies. A proper place to store street clothes should be provided. The ability to store personal belongings assists employees in complying with company policies, such as a prohibition of jewelry or street shoes.

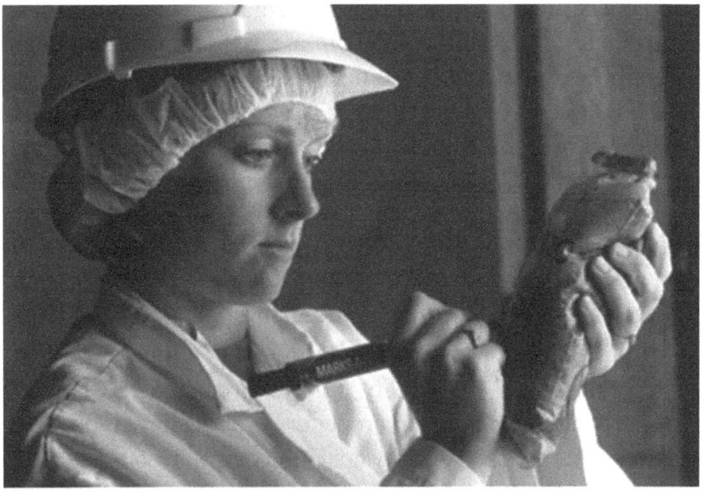

FIGURE 19.1. *Wearing hairnets and clean clothing is very important to eliminate unwanted contamination. Photo by Jack Dykinga, courtesy of USDA ARS.*

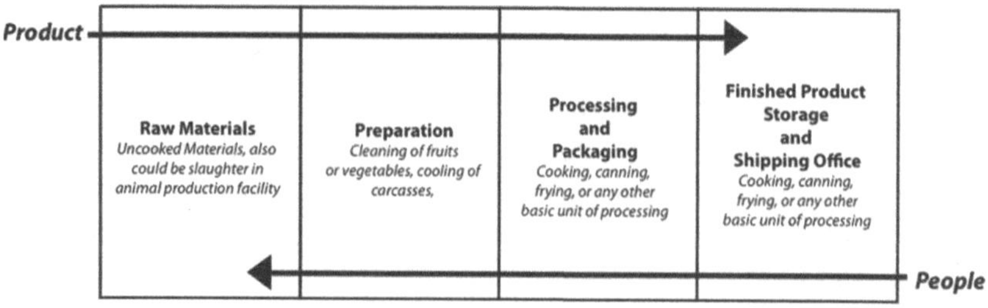

FIGURE 19.2. The flow of people and product should be opposite of one another to prevent contamination of finished products.

Many companies provide steel toe shoes, or other work shoes that are not to be worn outside of a plant facility.

To prevent cross-contamination, buildings and processing facilities should be designed so that people and their tasks flow back from the finished product to the raw materials, in as shown in Figure 19.2; i.e., product flow should be opposite of the flow of employees. If employees must move from raw to finished product, sanitation procedures need to be mandated so that raw materials do not come in contact with processed or finished states of the product.

Equipment and utensils should be easily cleaned and be chosen with a view to offsetting the risk of metal contamination. Instruments for measuring processing parameters must be regularly calibrated.

Raw material handling must be done with care. Proper handling requires inspecting damaged boxes, being on the lookout for foreign material, and checking the temperature of refrigerated and frozen products. Storage of materials should be done in a way that prevents contamination. A great example of this would be storing chicken below ground pork and whole cuts of beef in the refrigerator based on heating temperatures of 165°F, 160°F, and 145°F, respectively. The chicken will be heated to the highest temperature; therefore, it should be stored on the lowest part of the refrigerator. This reduces the risk of chicken contaminating the ground pork or cut of beef, which will not be heated to 165°F.

In all cases, refrigerated foods should be kept at 40°F or less. Frozen food should remain frozen. Hot foods should be kept above 140°F. All cooking times should be based on both time and temperature.

Sanitizers and other potentially hazardous chemicals should be labeled properly and have written procedures for use based on the manufacturer's recommendations. Physical objects that could accidentally fall into a product should be eliminated if at all possible. This means restricting the use of jewelry, hairpieces with metal, or other small items.

Policies can be put in place, such as not permitting any items to be worn on clothing or placed in pockets above the waist.

Good Manufacturing Practice systems should be written documents describing policies and procedures that employees are expected to follow. All employees should be taught these procedures. Employees must be able to read and understand the procedures, which may require employers to post reminders with descriptive pictures and in multiple languages.

STANDARD OPERATING PROCEDURES

Standard operating procedures (*SOPs*) are descriptions of specific tasks to be carried out in a particular operation. Standard operating procedures vary with each manufacturing facility and piece of equipment. For example, some equipment is designed for cleaning in place, whereas other machinery must be completely disassembled, to maintain sanitary conditions. Standard operating procedures are critical in the first phase of new product development. These detailed task descriptions work along with GMPs to support a new product and a company's HACCP plan. Standard operating procedures are also used in conjunction with GMPs to train employees about procedures in a processing facility.

Standard operating procedures should define 6 attributes as described in Table 19.3. Each piece of the SOP helps alleviate any questions about the process of doing a single task. Standard operating procedures are a set of explicit instructions on how to carry out a specific operation, whereas GMPs are procedures to be carried out by a plant to prevent adulteration. Proper SOPs offer enough detail that any employee can easily perform the task described.

The United States Department of Agriculture Food Safety and Inspection Service (USDA FSIS) mandates sanitation standard operation procedures (SSOPs) for meat and poultry operations. Sanitation standard operation procedures address pre-operational and operational sanitation procedures to prevent direct contamination or adulteration. Each company and facility must develop its own set of SSOPs addressing pre-operational and operational sanitation. The FSIS verifies whether each plan is working or if the facility needs to update their SSOP to reflect changes, such as the purchase of new equipment.

Pre-operational sanitation comprises procedures to clean a facility, equipment, and utensils. These SSOPs should include detailed descrip-

TABLE 19.3. The Information That a Standard Operating Procedure Should Answer for Each Specific Task.

Information	Clarification	Example SOP: Controlling Time & Temperature During Preparation
Who	Who is going to perform the job or task	Foodservice employees should be trained on this SOP as well as using and calibrating thermometers.
Why	The purpose for competing the task	To prevent foodborne illness by limiting the amount of time that potentially hazardous foods are held at dangerous temperatures during preparation/processing.
What	Identifies what the task is	Chill ingredients that should be kept cold, such as ready to eat meats and pre-cut fruits and vegetables; limit the time that potentially hazardous food is kept at room temperature.
How Frequent	When it will be performed and how often	At least 2 internal temperatures from each pan of heated foods.
Critical Time Limits	Specifies any time limit for the task	As foods are kept at heated or cooled temperatures, their temperatures should be taken at least every 2 hours or as otherwise defined.
Corrective Action	Identifies what to do if the task was not completed or performed incorrectly	If the temperatures are not taken, then the food will be discarded after 4 hours (or another appropriate defined time).

tions of how to disassemble and reassemble equipment. Cleaning and sanitation procedures must also be described step-by-step.

Operational sanitation denotes procedures that eliminate the chance of contamination during processing. Equipment cleaning that takes place during production is one SSOP that is required. Employee hygiene, such as the procedure for cleaning should an employee vomit in the processing area and when an employee can return to work following a fever, can be described in operational sanitation as well. An SSOP for product handling in both raw and cooked areas is also included.

The implementation and monitoring of SSOPs help maintain compliance with FSIS and company sanitation. Designated employees should be appointed to carry out preoperational and operational checks through organoleptic, chemical, or microbiological assessments. Safety managers should also hold scheduled and unscheduled checks of all SSOPs, to ensure accuracy and employee understanding.

When deviations occur from the SSOPs, a corrective action protocol for each specific task is needed. Corrective actions should have the goal of ensuring that direct product contamination has not occurred. All corrective actions should be pre-defined in the SSOP and, when implemented, should be recorded.

The Importance of Pre-Requisite Programs

Standard operating procedure and GMP plans guard against defects in new and existing products. Having sound pre-requisite plans helps to create safe and quality new products, which will assist in attracting repeat wholesale buyers and retail consumers. Good Manufacturing Practice programs can ensure that all grounds, facilities, and employees meet the basic needs of safety, whereas SOPs spell out the procedures for keeping products safe, an ideal that should never be compromised. Pre-requisite programs are managed as a system of their own.

HAZARD ANALYSIS AND CRITICAL CONTROL POINTS

Hazard Analysis and Critical Control Points is a common sense technique to control food safety hazards. It is a preventive system of hazard control rather than a reactive one. Food establishments can use it to ensure safer food products for consumers. It is not a zero-risk system, but is designed to minimize the risk of food safety hazards. The objective of the HACCP system is to make products as safe as possible by thoroughly assessing risks in an operation, identifying hazards, establishing controls, and monitoring these controls. It has almost become the norm

Handwashing GMP

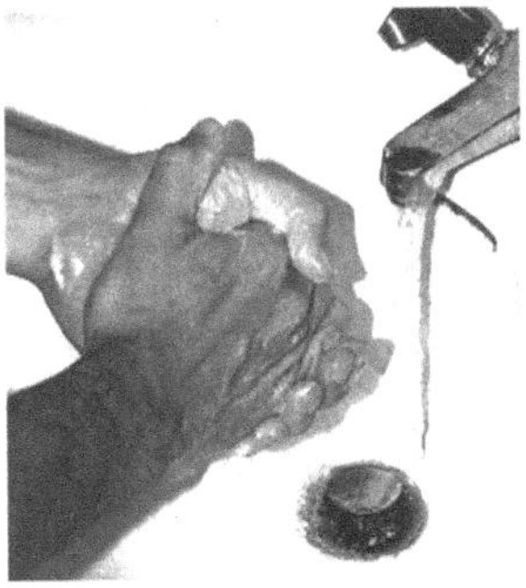

1. Use water as hot as the hands can comfortably stand.
2. Moisten hands, soap thoroughly, and lather to elbow.
3. Scrub thoroughly using brush for nails.
4. Rub hands together using friction for 20 seconds.
5. Rinse thoroughly under running water.
6. Dry hands using a single-use towel or a hot air dryer.

FIGURE 19.3. An example of a hand washing GMP that might be utilized at a manufacturing facility.

to develop an HACCP plan for every new food product developed by a manufacturer. Besides helping make a safe product, HACCP plans are routinely required by buyers of new products and are often audited by representatives of these organizations. Hazard Analysis and Critical Control Points is not a stand-alone program but is one part of a larger system of control procedures that must be in place in order for HACCP to function effectively. These control procedures are prerequisite programs.

The success of an HACCP program depends on both people and facilities. Management and employees must be properly motivated and trained if an HACCP program is to reduce the risk of foodborne illness. Education and training in the principles of food safety and management commitment to the implementation of an HACCP system are critical and must be continuously reinforced. Personnel issues, such as instilling food worker commitment and dealing with high employee turnover and communication barriers, have to be taken into account when designing an HACCP plan.

The National Aeronautics and Space Administration (NASA) and the United States Military Natick Laboratory first developed HACCP. Pillsbury was the first company to use HACCP as it prepared foods for the United States Space Program. Safe food for astronauts was essential to prevent illness, and the space program demanded that the company achieve close to a 100% probability that the food was not contaminated. As Pillsbury saw the success of the system, it decided to enact HACCP principles companywide (Corlett 1998).

The hazards, whose risks are addressed by HACCP, are categorized into three categories: biological, chemical, and physical. Examples of each are given in Table 19.4.

The HACCP system has been refined since Pillsbury first put the program into place, adding an emphasis on process control and recordkeeping. Process control involves the maintenance of raw materials, production, environment, personnel, storage, and distribution. Recordkeeping should paint a comprehensive history of the product, and report all practices to ensure safety. In 1985, the National Academy of Sciences (NAS) recommended that HACCP be adopted by all regulatory agencies and mandated for food processors. The National Advisory Committee on Microbiological Criteria for Foods (NACMCF) had been researching and drafting the principal points of the system through the investigation of the work at Pillsbury, courses offered on the system, and a publication of the NAS. In 1989, the HACCP principles were standardized by the NACMCF.

TABLE 19.4. HACCP Aims to Define the Possible Hazards in a Company's Food Processing Procedure.

Hazards Occurring in Food Processing	
Biological	• Bacterial, parasitic, or viral contamination
	• Bacterial growth
	• Bacterial, parasitic, or viral survival
	• Bacterial toxin production
	• Bacterial, parasitic, or viral cross-contamination
Chemical	• Nonfood-grade lubricants
	• Cleaning compounds
	• Food additives
	• Insecticides
Physical	• Stones
	• Glass
	• Metal fragments
	• Packaging materials

Even before a company can create an HACCP plan, there is work to do. It is important to establish support from the company and management prior to enforcing this preventative system. Hazard Analysis and Critical Control Points cannot be implemented without full cooperation of the entire facility and operation. After support for the program is established, a multidisciplinary HACCP team should be formed, including operations supervisors, line operators, engineers, sanitation personnel, quality- control staff, and representatives from purchasing, receiving, and distribution.

A team leader trained in HACCP is appointed as the coordinator. The team will together research and identify areas in which hazards should be controlled and will help to define measures to do so. The HACCP coordinator must have management skills and resources to implement the system. Resources may include knowledge, a contact list of regulatory and other experts, basic forms and, of course, a competent team. Outside experts can be called in to advise and assist in determining the best HACCP plan but should not write the plan. An in-house team's writing of the plan creates a sense of ownership for plant personnel.

Prior to creating an HACCP plan, the team must assemble to describe the food and its distribution, identify its intended use and who the consumers will be, develop a flow diagram, and verify the diagram. The description of the product should include the name, recipe, formula, and ingredients, as well as the shelf-life and distribution channels. The intended use for consumers is also important to define. For example, is the product ready-to-eat and meant for the general public or is it a cook-and-eat product geared toward infants?

The HACCP team should create a flow chart like the one in Figure 19.5 and indicate all product descriptions and specifications for each product. The flow diagram should be a simple, clear description of the steps in the process of turning raw products into the finished food product. Walking the processing floor and determining if any steps are missing should complete verification. Only steps that are within the control of the facility should be included.

After the team has a product description and flow diagram, it can begin addressing the seven principles of creating a plan. The entire plan should be recorded in forms similar to examples at the FDA, USDA, and other commodity group websites. These seven principles are as follows:

1. Conduct a hazard analysis
2. Identify critical control points (CCP)
3. Establish critical limits for CCP
4. Establish monitoring procedures
5. Establish corrective actions
6. Establish verification procedures
7. Establish recordkeeping procedures

Principle 1: Conduct a Hazard Analysis

Conducting a hazard analysis takes the work of the whole HACCP team. Using the processing steps, significant hazards that are likely to occur should be described along with current control measures. Hazards should be identified within each individual's area of responsibility. Are there hazards that are not being controlled? Hazards must be a risk significant enough that if not controlled, there is a probability it could jeopardize the product at any stage of processing. Areas of inquiry during a hazard analysis include the following (Corlett 1998):

- Ingredient risks
- Intrinsic elements of ingredients
- Procedures used for processing
- Microbial load of the materials
- Facility design

- Equipment design and usage
- Packaging
- Sanitation procedures
- Employee health, education, and barriers for contamination
- Conditions of storage to end-user
- Intended use of the product
- Intended consumer

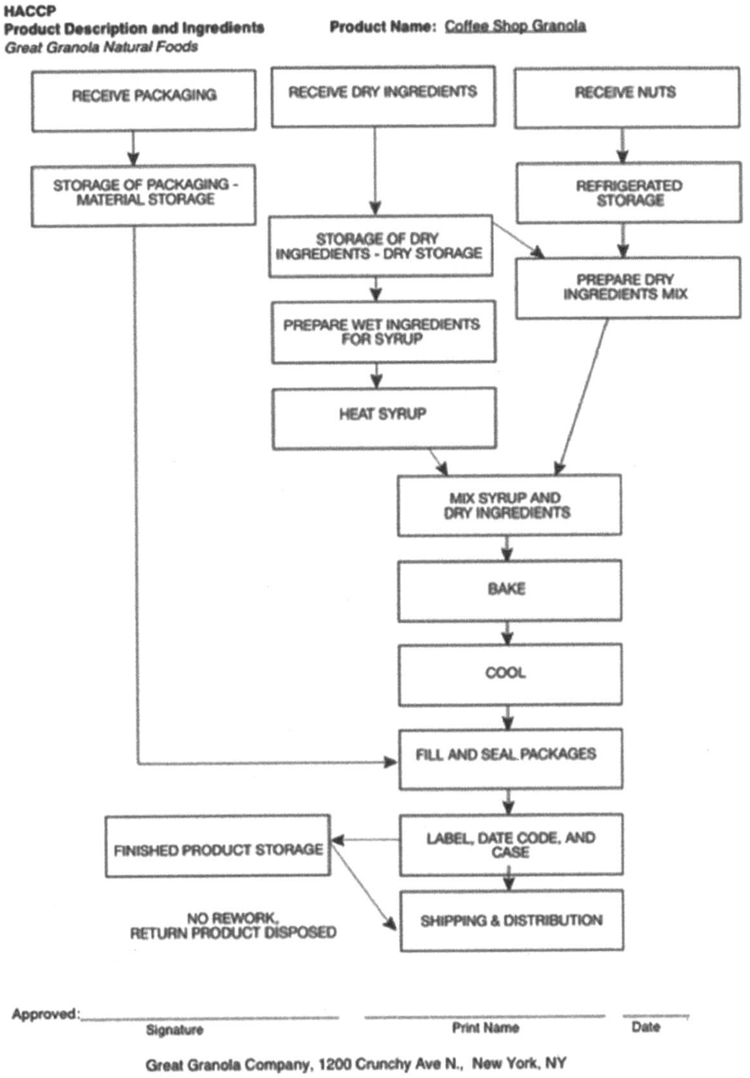

FIGURE 19.4. *Process flow sheets should be used to help create a HACCP plan.*

HACCP
Hazard Analysis
Company Name

Product Name: ____________

Process/Step	Potential Hazards Introduced, Controlled, Enhanced or Reduced at this Step		Is this Hazard Reasonably Likely to Occur?	Justification for Decision to Determine Significance	Control Measure
	Biological:				
	Chemical:				
	Physical:				
	Biological:				
	Chemical:				
	Physical:				

Approved: ____________ ____________ ______
Signature Print Name Date

FIGURE 19.5. *Example of a hazard analysis form. A modified version of forms by Boyle and Aramouni, 2003.*

Principle 2: Identifying Critical Control Points

Using the processing steps and hazards defined in Principle 1, the team should determine each point, step, or procedure at which a control can be applied and a food safety risk that can be prevented, eliminated, or reduced to an acceptable level. The points that are crucial in reducing risk are defined as critical control points (CCP).

A CCP can be located at any step in receiving, processing, storage, or distribution. Critical Control Points are meant to be the most important controls in the process because they provide an opportunity to manage the most critical hazards in the operation. For example, raw meat products will invariably include a CCP for cool storage, because this is an important control to keep microbial growth and spoilage organisms from ruining the product. A CCP to keep raw meat under refrigerated temperatures should be listed. At any one stage of processing, hazards that are controlled in a later step do not need to be labeled as CCPs.

Principle 3: Establish Critical Limits for CCP

For each CCP, critical limits need to be established. Critical limits are quantitative or concrete measures for controlling the operations for the CCP. Critical limits should be based on scientific literature and/or regulatory standards. In the CCP of keeping raw meat refrigerated, a critical limit that would be proper to set would be to store the meat at or below 40°F. Critical limits must be susceptible to quantifiable measurement by instruments, observation, or recordkeeping that shows thresholds are reached.

HACCP
Critical Control Point (CCP Form)
Company Name

Product Name: ____________________

Process/Step	Hazard	Q1a. Do preventive measures exist for the identified hazard(s)? If no--go to Q1b. If yes--go to Q2.	Q1b. Is control at this step necessary for safety? If no--not a CCP. If yes--modify step, process or product and return to Q1a.	Q2. Does this step eliminate or reduce the likely occurrence of a hazard(s) to an acceptable level? If no--go to Q3. If yes--CCP	Q3. Could contamination with identified hazard(s) occur in excess of acceptable levels or could these increase to unacceptable levels? If no--not a CCP. If yes--go to Q4.	Q4. Will a subsequent step eliminate hazard(s) or reduce the likely occurrence to an acceptable level? If no--CCP. If yes--not a CCP.	CCP No.

Approved:______________________ ______________________ ________
Signature Print Name Date

Company Address, 123 N. Street, Manhattan, KS 66502

FIGURE 19.6. Example of a critical control point form for Principle 2. This example is a modified version of forms from Boyle and Aramouni, 2003.

An example of a critical limit not measured through instrumental means is a company with a CCP at receiving for patulin. Patulin, a toxic substance produced by molds, can occur in apple juice when old or dropped apples are used. A critical limit to control this step would be a letter from a company guaranteeing that the apples purchased do not contain patulin levels above 50 parts per billion (the actionable limit set by FDA) and do not contain apples that have dropped from the tree. Letters like this stating a product does meet certain specifications are called "letters of guarantee" (LOG). Letters of guarantee, then, should be provided with every load of apples in order for that shipment to be verified as meeting the critical limit. When a shipment is outside of the critical limits, it is deemed to be out of control.

HACCP
Identifying Critical Limits and Monitoring Actions
Company Name

Product Name: ____________________

Process/Step CCP	Hazard	Critical Limit	Monitoring Procedures			
			What will be measured?	How will the CL be measured?	Who will monitor the CL?	How often will the CL be measured?

Approved:______________________ ______________________ ________
Signature Print Name Date

Company Address, 123 N. Street, Manhattan, KS 66502

FIGURE 19.7. An example of a critical limit form and monitoring actions, HACCP principles 3 and 4. This example is a modified version of forms by Boyle and Aramouni, 2003.

Principle 4: Establishing Monitoring Procedures

Critical limits should be monitored using written procedures (perhaps an SOP) applied at a pre-defined frequency by a designated person. The monitoring questions on the form presented in Figure 19.8 help to define exactly how monitoring procedures will be carried out. Developing forms for critical limit monitoring is important, in order to eliminate questions about whether or not a given procedure is in control or not. In-line technicians may be responsible for monitoring pH and water activity (a_w) or for performing a visual inspection at designated times during their shifts. Having designated personnel monitoring critical limits helps to create clear expectations on how monitoring procedures should be carried out.

Principle 5: Establishing Corrective Actions

What does a line technician or HACCP coordinator do if a product tests outside the critical limit? The person must take corrective actions, which need to be in place prior to any deviation from standards. Options for corrective actions include reprocessing, holding the product for further analysis (microbiological, chemical), or destroying the product. When a product does not meet heating standards, the product can in some cases be reprocessed to meet the correct temperature. If an apple cider company does not receive their letter of guarantee, they may tag the product with an identifier that states not to use the product or hold it until the supplier can provide documentation. If no reprocessing or holding can take place, the product may have to be destroyed or put to waste.

Corrective actions should include step-by-step procedures (SOPs) for how to perform the desired actions and what the appropriate action is for every scenario. There can be more than one corrective action for each CCP. In fact, the corrective actions should cover every possible deviation that can be brainstormed by the HACCP team.

Principle 6: Establishing Verification Procedures

Critical limits for CCP should be verified as satisfactory through validation measurements. If a facility has a biological CCP for pathogens, a challenge study using inoculated product could be carried out to verify that pathogens are being destroyed. Internal personnel and third-party auditors should complete periodic audits of the HACCP system. Verification procedures may include the monitoring of instruments and equipment used to measure critical limits. Calibration should occur at a specified frequency. For high-usage instruments, such as thermometers, calibration may be scheduled for each shift. Some instruments may need to be sent to the manufacturer once a year or so to ensure working quality. Specific personnel should be appointed to execute verification procedures. A verification sample form combined with principle 7 (recordkeeping) in Figure 19.10.

Principle 7: Establishing Recordkeeping Procedures

Records must be kept of all HACCP operations. In the event of a regulatory audit, the saved documents can provide evidence that a company's procedures are in place and operating per schedule. Recordkeeping and documentation should cover all information about product safety, including test results, calibration records, inspection reports, and monitoring record (Corlett 1998).

HACCP Summary

Whether or not HACCP is mandated for your product, it is essential to understand the basic procedures for determining hazards in your operations. Many facilities, even those where it is not mandated, have adopted the HACCP system as a preventative strategy to keep products safe. New products should, at a minimum, undergo a hazard analysis in which actionable methods for controlling the most critical attributes are

HACCP
Corrective Action
Company Name

Product Name: ____________

Process/Step CCP	Hazard	Critical Limit	Corrective Actions			
			What caused the deviation?	How will the process be corrected?	What measures will be implemented to prevent recurrence?	What is the product disposition?

Approved: ____________ Signature ____________ Print Name ____________ Date

Company Address, 123 N. Street, Manhattan, KS 66502

FIGURE 19.8. *An example of a critical limit form and monitoring actions, HACCP principles 3 and 4. This example is a modified version of forms by Boyle and Aramouni, 2003.*

HACCP
Identifying Verification and Recordkeeping Procedures **Product Name:** ____________
Company Name

Process/Step CCP	Records	Responsibility	CCP Verification		
			What equipment needs to be calibrated, and what is frequency of calibration, of equipment used to monitor the CCP?	What direct observations of monitoring activities and corrective actions will occur, and at what frequency?	What records will be reviewed and at what frequency?

Approved:____________ ____________ ____________
Signature Print Name Date

Company Address, 123 N. Street, Manhattan, KS 66502

FIGURE 19.9. An example of a form listing records and verification procedures. This example is a modified version of forms by Boyle and Aramouni, 2003.

established. HACCP cannot stand alone, and should always be combined with sound pre-requisite and quality programs.

FOOD SAFETY MODERNIZATION ACT

The Food Safety Modernization Act (FSMA) was signed into law on January 4, 2011, by President Barack Obama. The regulation is aimed to change the focus to preventing contamination rather than responding to it. Since its signing, FSMA has produced many final rules, including Preventive Controls for Human Food, Produce Safety, and Preventive Controls for Food for Animals, with each bringing reforms that relate food safety management practices in companies.

Preventive Controls for Human Food

On September 10, 2015, the FDA published its final regulation for human food. This final rule titled, *Current Good Manufacturing Practice, Hazard-Analysis and Risk-Based Preventive Controls for Human Food*, is found in the Code of Federal Regulations (CFR) under title 21. Previously, the cGMPs for human food were found in 21 CFR §110, but the new rule is now found in 21 CFR §117. This rule applies to a facility that "manufactures, processes, packs, or holds food for sale in the United States if the owner, operator, or agent in charge of such facility is required to comply with, and is not in compliance with, section 418 of the Federal Food, Drug, and Cosmetic Act. . . ." Facilities subject to this rule are required to comply with updated cGMPs found in Subpart B of 21 CFR §117 and have a food safety plan. Facilities are also required to do a reanalysis of their entire food safety plan at least once every three years or must reanalyze a portion of the food safety plan when a significant change in the activities conducted at the facility occur, when new information about a potential hazard is discovered, or when the facility finds the preventive controls or food safety plan as a whole is ineffective. All facilities under this requirement are expected to comply with the cGMPs, but some facilities may be exempt from subparts C and G, which state requirements for the food safety plan and the supply-chain program, respectively. Exemptions to this final rule can be found in 21 CFR §117.5.

The Food Safety Plan

The structure of the FDA mandated food safety plan is very similar to HACCP with some minor differences related to preventive controls, a supply-chain program, and a written recall plan. Requirements for the food safety plan can be found in 21 CFR §117 subpart C and include the following: A written hazard analysis identifying biological, chemical, and physical hazards; written preventive controls; a written supply-chain program; a written recall plan; written monitoring procedures for the identified preventive controls; written corrective actions; written verification procedures; and mandatory record-keeping.

Preventive Controls

Preventive controls are defined as risk-based procedures, practices, or processes that significantly minimize or prevent hazards. There are four types of preventive controls: process, sanitation, allergen, and supply-chain. Process preventive controls are controls in which hazards identified in the hazard analysis are controlled by a process step. For example, cooking and cooling processing steps can be used to either kill or control the growth of foodborne pathogens. Sanitation preventive controls are controls in which hazards are controlled only through sanitation. For example, sanitation is needed to control pathogens when ready-to-eat (RTE) products are exposed to the environment before they are packaged or to control food allergen cross-contact in a facility that produces products with different allergens. The latter could also be categorized as a food allergen preventive control. Unlike the other preventive controls, allergen preventive controls have two requirements: Preventing allergen cross-contact and ensuring allergen labeling of finished food. Allergen preventive controls can work with other types of preventive controls to achieve both requirements. Supply-chain preventive controls must be applied when an identified hazard at receiving will not be controlled at any other step in the process. These preventive controls can include a certificate of analysis (CoA) or a letter of guarantee (LoG). If supply-chain preventive controls are identified to control a hazard, a supply-chain program is required to be written and carried out. Requirements for a supply-chain program can be found in 21 CFR §117 subpart G.

Applying Regulations to a New Product

Product developers must keep in mind how safety regulations affect the facility where an item is manufactured, as well as other products made at that location. For example, if a company that makes granola products plans to develop a granola bar coated in yogurt, it must realize that to process such a product the company would be introducing a new allergen into their facility. The developers might consider changing the product to chocolate coated, if they already make a product with chocolate in it. If the company decides to move forward with the yogurt-coated product, it would be expected to reanalyze the food safety plan and write a separate plan for the new type of granola bar.

Steps to Developing a Food Safety Plan

Much like an HACCP plan, a food safety plan mandated by the FDA also has preliminary steps that are recommended before developing a full food safety plan. By choosing to take the following preliminary steps, a company will find developing a food safety plan becomes an easier task.

Preliminary Steps (Recommended)

1. Assemble a food safety team.
    - Assembling a team including individuals with different specialties and experiences provides knowledge of daily operations. This team approach reduces the risk of missing any food safety hazards as well as encourages ownership of the plan.

Another key to a food safety team is management commitment to ensuring that resources dedicated to developing the plan are appropriate.

2. Describe the product and its distribution.
   - The product description should include the following:
     —Product name(s)
     —Important food safety characteristics (i.e., pH, a_w, preservatives)
     —Ingredients
     —Packaging type
     —Shelf-life
     —Storage and distribution
3. Describe the intended use and consumers of the food.
   - This can be included in the product description. The following questions should be considered by the food safety team:
     —What is the intended use of the product (i.e., retail, food service, further processing)?
     —What is the potential for mishandling and unintended use?
     —What handling and preparation procedures are required of the end users? Is the product ready-to-eat, or does it need preparation such as reheating, cooking, etc.?
     —Who are the intended customers of the product?
     —Is the product intended specifically for use by immune-compromised individuals or other susceptible groups?
4. Develop a flow diagram and describe the process.
   - A process flow diagram provides a visual of all the process steps within the facility's control, including reworked product, by-product, and diverted product. A written description can be added to explain what happens at each processing step and provide more detail than a flow diagram.
5. Verify the flow diagram on-site.
   - Because the steps in the flow diagram are used to conduct the hazard analysis, it is critical that every step in the process is addressed and present in the flow diagram. The flow diagram should be checked and verified on site while the product is being processed.

Contents of a Food Safety Plan (Required)

1. Hazard Analysis
   - A hazard analysis is crucial to the success of a food safety plan. A properly written hazard analysis identifies hazards (biological, physical, chemical [including radiological]) that require a preventive control. A hazard analysis also identifies processes or operations requiring improvement.
2. Preventive Controls
   - Process
     —Controls applied at processing steps that require science-based minimum or maximum values, often called CCPs.
   - Food Allergen
     —Allergen preventive controls are primarily to eliminate allergen cross-contact and to ensure accurate allergen labeling of the finished product.
   - Sanitation
     —The hazard analysis might identify hazards that require stricter sanitation controls including environmental pathogens, pathogen transfer through cross-contamination, and food allergen cross-contact. These will require sanitation preventive controls.
   - Supply-Chain
     —Supply-chain controls are applied when a hazard is identified at receiving and is not controlled later in the process. Controls of this nature are often in the form of a certificate of analysis (CoA) or a letter of guarantee (LoG). If supply-chain preventive controls are identified, a written supply-chain program is required.
3. Critical Limits
   - Critical limits are parameters that must be met to control a hazard. For most process controls, the critical limit will be a measurable parameter, where other preventive controls will be based on a qualitative criterion.
   - Critical limits are required only if/when a preventive control is identified.
4. Monitoring Procedures
   - Monitoring procedures ensure and document that food safety

hazards are being controlled properly. Monitoring requires four elements:
—What is being monitored?
—How is it being monitored?
—How frequently is it being monitored?
—Who is monitoring it?
- Monitoring procedures are only required if/when a preventive control is identified.

5. Corrective Action Procedures
   - Corrective actions are to be taken when a critical limit of a food safety preventive control is not met. Corrective action procedures must address steps taken to do the following:
     —Identify and correct a problem.
     —Reduce likelihood of re-occurrence.
     —Evaluate affected product for safety.
     —Determine the disposition of the affected product.
   - Corrective actions are only required if/when a preventive control is identified.
6. Verification Procedures
   - Verification provides evidence that a safety plan is properly implemented and operating correctly.
   - Verification procedures are required only if/when a preventive control is identified.
7. Validation Procedures
   - Validation procedures demonstrate that the food safety plan and its identified controls are actually controlling the hazards. Validation procedures can include the following:
     —Scientific experiments on set dates
     —Expert analysis and opinion
     —In-plant observations or tests
   - Validation procedures are required only if/when a preventive control is identified.
8. Supply-Chain Program
   - A supply-chain program is required only when a hazardous suspected in what is supplied to a company. Generally, a supply-chain program requires the following:
     —Use of approved suppliers.

- Determination of supplier verification activities, third party audits
  —Conducting supplier verification activities.
  —Documentation of supplier verification activities.
  —Verification of a supply-chain-applied control by an outside entity (when applicable).

9. Recall Plan
   - Since the FDA has the power to mandate a recall, recall plans are now required only when a preventive control is identified. A recall plan is required to include steps to do the following:
     —Notify direct customers ad consignees
     —Notify the public, when appropriate
     —Conduct effectiveness checks
     —Execute disposition of unsafe food
10. Records
    - Incidents and monitoring data must be recorded in writing. During an audit, written proof that hazards are being controlled the way they are written in the plan is paramount. The following are required records:
      —Food safety plan
      —Implementation records
    - Preventive control monitoring data
    - Corrective actions taken
    - Verification activities
    - Validation documentation
    - Supply-chain program implementation
    - Training

AUDIT SYSTEMS

Audit systems provide checkpoints for companies and allow for outside firms to critique them on their attention to food safety risks. Facility audits should take place internally and by a third party. Typical audits consist of a review of records, in addition to a facility walk-through. Auditing agencies will usually look at the following (Corlett 1998):

1. GMPs
2. Basic food handling

3. Consumer complaint records
4. Incidence of product holds and safe disposition of held product
5. Establishment of a quality assurance system
6. Laboratory testing procedures and their effectiveness
7. Review of regulatory inspection results and actions
8. HACCP system and SSOP verifications

In May 2000, following a number of food safety scares, a group of international retailer CEOs identified the need to enhance food safety, ensure consumer protection, and strengthen consumer confidence. They launched the Global Food Safety Initiative (GFSI), a non-profit foundation, which sets requirements for food safety schemes through a benchmarking process to improve cost efficiency throughout the food supply chain. Global Food Safety Initiative benchmarks existing food standards against food safety criteria and also develops mechanisms to exchange information in the supply chain, raises consumer awareness, and reviews existing good retail practices. Once formal recognition has been given to a standard, the certificates gained from an audit to a GFSIrecognized standard are accepted by many international suppliers and regional/national retailers. The GFSI has recognized different food safety schemes, including those introduced by the British Retail Consortium (BRC), the International Organization for Standardization (ISO), and Safe Quality Food (SQF).

Audit systems are important for manufacturers, because retailers are requiring such certifications to accept foods into their operations. Recognizing the potential harm from a foodborne illness originating in a product they sell, large retailers have focused on the safety of their product suppliers, to reduce the risks to them.

British Retail Consortium

The BRC is a safety and quality-focused manufacturing scheme and auditing system. Companies that wish to be certified under the BRC are licensed through third-party "Certification Bodies." Before scheduling an audit, companies undertake a preliminary self-assessment. An optional pre-assessment is also available in preparation for the audit. Completed audits are given a grade of A, B, or C. If the audit is unannounced, it is distinguished on the certification with an asterisk (*).

Safe Quality Food

Safe Quality Food provides independent certification that a supplier's food safety and management meets international and domestic food safety requirements. Safe Quality Food enables suppliers to assure customers that their food is handled according to the highest possible standards. This system is tailored for manufacturers, wholesalers, and distributers, but it can be applied at all levels of the food supply chain. Safe Quality Food codes are divided according to producer types. For example, SQF 1000 is designed for primary producers/farmers, whereas SQF 2000 is geared toward manufacturers, distributors, exporters, brokers, and retailers. Each code is divided into three levels of certification, intended to show the level of development of the supplier's safety and quality systems.

International Organization for Standardization

The ISO develops international standards for most industry sectors, as well as for a variety of cross-sector, horizontal procedures (such as metrology and generic management systems). ISO 22000:2005 specifies requirements for a food safety management system, which is used when an organization in the food chain needs to demonstrate its ability to control food safety hazards.

AUDITING AGENCIES

In many cases, the agencies that create auditing systems do not actually do the auditing themselves. Third-party auditing agencies are generally responsible for completing the audits. All auditors need to be accredited. For example, AIB International, an auditing agency, is "authorized grade" on these systems: BRC Global Standard, ISO 22000, FSSC 22000, and SQF 2000. AIB also offers HACCP Accreditation. Other private entities provide SQF 1000 and SQF 2000 certification audits globally and are also approved by BRC Global Standard for Food Safety Issue 5. They can also be approved training sources for SQF, BRC, FSSC 22000, and other certification processes.

KEY WORDS

Critical control points—crucial points in processing that are essential for reducing risk.

Good Manufacturing Practices (*GMP*)—mandated general maintenance regulations that are essential to produce wholesome products, found in 21 CFR 110.

Operational sanitation—procedures that eliminate the chance of contamination during processing.

Pre-operational sanitation—procedures that are completed to clean a food facility, equipment, and utensils.

Pre-requisite Programs—the components of an operation that set up basic grounds for environmental and operational conditions to produce safe products.

Standard operating procedures (SOP)—descriptions of specific tasks to be carried out in a particular operation that vary with each manufacturing facility and piece of equipment due to specialized issues.

COMPREHENSION QUESTIONS

19.1. Name four areas that Good Manufacturing Practices (GMPs) address.

19.2. Assume your product (or a product) is ready for large-scale production. Write a Standard Operating Procedure for the first step in your production process.

19.3. Name the commodities that require HACCP Plans as required by FDA and USDA.

19.4. Why is the flow of product and people important in production facilities? Draw a flow of product diagram for a product you are currently developing.

REFERENCES

Aramouni, F., and L. Boyle. "Example HACCP Forms." (Manhattan, KS: KSU Department of Animal Science and Industry, August 12, 2003). Available at: http://www.oznet.ksu.edu/meatscience/HACCP/forms.htm.

Aramouni, F., and L. Boyle "PowerPoint Lectures." (Manhattan, KS: KSU Department of Animal Science and Industry, August 12, 2003). Available at: http://www.oznet.ksu.edu/meatscience/ASI690/ASI690Campus.htm.

Corlett, D. A., Jr. *HACCP User's Manual*. (Gaithersburg, MD: Aspen Publishers, 1998). *Preventive Controls for Human Food Participant Manual*, 1st ed.(Food Safety Preventive Controls Alliance, 2016).

"Electronic Code of Federal Regulations. Title 21 Part 117." (United States Government Publishing Office. 2015). Accessed August 2916, http://www.ecfr.gov/cgi-bin/text-idx?SID=e9ca025764f8adff02bc93a2655d8450&mc=true&node=pt21.2.117&rgn=div5. A.

CHAPTER 20

Pet Food Product Development

Learning Objectives

- Define and understand what a pet and pet food are.
- Know the regulatory side of pet food.
- Learn about pet food products on the market.
- Understand current pet food trends.
- Learn the steps involved in product development for pet food.

PETS have become a huge part of people's lives. Nielsen (2016) has suggested that 95% of pet owners consider their pet part of the family. In the USA, 66.9% of all householders share their home with a cat or dog (AVMA, 2012). According to the American Veterinary Medical Foundation, or AVMA (2012), 36.5% of households own dogs and 30.4% own cats. According to the American Pet Products Association (APPA), 23 billion dollars were spent on pet food in 2016 (APPA, 2016). In the United States, people believe their companion animal is a family member (Berryman *et al.* 1985; Nielson 2016). Because of this familial connection, owners want their companion animals to live long, healthy lives (Jellison 2004), a goal food can help achieve. Properly developed and produced pet foods can have a big impact on ownership cost, risk to relinquishment, and overall satisfaction. Thus, the developer has a significant responsibility to both pet and owner.

Further, as a business enterprise, new product development plays a key role for pet food companies. There are various definitions for pet food. Legally, the Food and Drug Administration (FDA) defines it as food or drink for animals. As is the case with human foods, the Federal Food, Drug, and Cosmetic Act requires animal food to be safe to eat, produced under sanitary conditions, and to not be adulterated in any way. The rules regarding pet food are more specifically defined by the Association of American Feed Control Officials (AAFCO), as a commercially developed feed that is prepared and distributed for consumption by dogs or cats (AAFCO 2016). Although AAFCO's remit excludes companion animals like rabbits, gerbils, and hamsters, for the purpose of this chapter, foods for these animals, the so-called specialty pets (AAFCO, 2016) will also be addressed. Overall, pet food can be summarized as a food produced through various means to feed a companion animal, which may include cats, dogs, birds, reptiles, horses, and other animals that are kept by people for companionship and not for food consumption (Aldrich 2015). Pet food may or may not resemble a food item found in the wild environment of progenitor species. Also, pet food may be a snack or treat, or it can be a complete and balanced diet suitable for sustaining the animal for a lifetime. This creates a multitude of possibilities and technical challenges.

Idea Generation

One of the first steps in product development is idea generation. To generate ideas, the company needs to understand who its market is, what the market needs, or where the gaps are in the current set of products. Most companies will have a marketing group that conducts consumer research, in order to validate new product assumptions. In some cases, it's as easy as following human food trends, since many new pet foods simply mirror human food trends (Nielson 2016). Once the marketing team or leadership of the organization decides on an idea for their particular market, they will conceptualize the product's characteristics, including ingredients, packaging, shape, size, color, flavors, and other properties of the product.

Project Evaluation

Before work begins, the product development team should discuss the product idea, developmental steps, resources, and budget to ascertain if the product is feasible. Developing new products is time consuming, resource intensive, and costly. At this point, the team will either decide to keep going with the process, make a course adjustment, or terminate the project if it is unrealistic. When deciding whether or not to go forward, the team must consider costs for purchasing new science or technology, formulation of the product, prototyping, and taking the product from the bench top to a pilot plant. They must also consider the costs for scaling the product from a pilot plant to a production facility, animal evaluations, packaging, artwork on the packaging, test marketing, and the initial distribution to stores. The team must also consider that the pilot plant may have limited capacity when running the product, compared to a full-scale production facility.

Concept Brief

The concept brief is a written contract, product summary, and/or blueprint for the project along with details about the timeline and deliverables. The concept brief will contain information about what the product is. For example, product name, product description, packaging size, shape, specific claims (grain-free, non GMO, natural), and will contain a product purpose statement (e.g., puppy, performance, adult). Research regarding competitor products and their positioning should be factored into the equation. Pet food developers need to make sure that they are not infringing on other companies' intellectual property, patents, or contracts. The concept brief should also outline an action plan, validation steps, and budget, with responsibilities for each member on the team, and contain a timeline for the product. The product brief should also outline product attributes like the guaranteed analysis, ingredients, feeding guidelines (e.g., age and weigh bracket, food intake), and any regulatory wording needs to comply with government regulations. The validation portion of the product brief should include chemical analysis, microbial work, pH, bulk density, or any other analysis on the food. Pet food companies may also perform animal validation on the product, which refers to palatability testing, digestibility studies, stool quality, urine pH, metabolizable energy, and verification of any claims the product may make. The concept brief is usually a working document that everyone signs into, and it should be understood that course changes may be necessary as the project moves forward.

PET FOOD REGULATIONS

As with human foods, very distinct rules and regulations exist, wherein one can market and make claims about pet foods. The concept brief and the product development team must make sure that they are in compliance. At the federal level, pet food is regulated by the United States Food and Drug Administration (FDA) in the code of federal regulations 21CFR500. Pet foods are required to have a principal display panel on their packaging. The principal display panel must include product name, product brand, species designation, quantity statement, guaranteed analysis, ingredient statement, nutritional adequacy statement, feeding guidelines, calorie statement, and name and address of the manufacturer. The pet food must also provide a nutritional adequacy statement indicating whether it is for a treat or intermittent feeding, or for a particular animal life stage. Finally, the ingredients must be listed in descending order of amount used. AAFCO has a list of common names for certain ingredients, which can be referenced when creating the ingredient statement.

There are certain rules a company must consider when developing the name for their product. If the name of the product says "100%," then the food must consist of only that ingredient, with the exception of preservatives, vitamins, minerals, and nonnutritive additives. If the term "with" is used in the name, then 3% or more of that ingredient must be in the product. If a named ingredient includes the words "dinner, platter, entrée, formula or recipe," at least 25% of the named ingredient must be in the product, excluding water for processing. If two ingredients are named, then the first ingredient is the predominant one. Any ingredient in combination with the first ingredient must be more than 3% of the overall ingredient amount. If the term "meat" is used in the name, the meat ingredient must make up 95% of the total formulation or 70%, if excluding water for processing.

When nutritionists are formulating the diet, they typically follow AAFCO's nutrient profile and guidelines. Nutritionists may also follow the Nutrient Requirement of Dogs and Cats (NRC) when formulating the amount of calories for cats and dogs. The formula for calculating calories for a cat is $60 \times$body weight (kg), and the formula for a dog is $132 \times$ body weight (kg)0.75 is referenced from the NRC. If there are feeding guidelines on the package, the food must have been dispensed during a formal study and have passed the feeding protocol. The feeding guidelines depend upon the life stage of the animal species to which the product is aimed. For example, if the package says "growth," it means the product is for puppies or kittens. "Maintenance" means the food is for adult animals.

Pet food is regulated at the state level as well. These state feed officials work with pet food companies to ensure that pet food products are not adulterated, pet food meets the label, and that the pet food is uniform. Each state has its own feed control laws and regulations. Pet food companies must follow these regulations whether they sell at a veterinarian office or at a state retailer. Many states require product registration before a company can sell a product in that state. The label may have to meet requirements of state laws to prevent mislabeling to inform the consumer correct information about the product. State employees can also inspect manufacturing facilities. For example, the Kansas Department of Agriculture requires manufacturers, importers, corporations, or people that sell or distribute commercial feed in Kansas to have a commercial license for each manufacturing facility. Commercial feed in Kansas includes livestock, pets, pet treats, and specialty pets.

Another group that pet food companies will rely on when formulating cat and dog food is AAFCO. AAFCO is made up of officials from all states, members from the government, veterinarians, and other individuals. AAFCO writes model bills for food and feed that state legislators use for reference when writing pet food regulations. However, AAFCO is not a federal or state regulator. AAFCO writes an annual book that has nutritional standards for complete and balanced diets derived from the Nutrient Requirements of Cats and Dogs. AAFCO has information on guaranteed analysis which includes a minimum for crude protein, minimum for crude fat, maximum for crude fiber and maximum for moisture. When these guaranteed analyses are put on pet food labels, the product must meet these guidelines. Other guaranteed analyses that a pet food company may place on their label, but are not required, include ash for dogs, amino acids, fatty acids, vitamins, and minerals.

PILOT PLANT OPERATIONS AND FACILITIES

Most pilot plants have separate unit operations rather than one uniform process. Typically, the equipment is smaller and the process may take longer than it would in a full-scale production facility. The equipment in a pilot plant may be more limited than large scale production equipment. For example, when comparing a pilot plant extrusion facility to an extrusion processing facility there may be differences in feed rate control, steam water control, drying and conveying process, and ingredient handling. A canning facility will have smaller retorts, limited ingredient handling, and less capacity for filling and sealing.

Analysis of Pet Food and Validation of the Product

Pet food product development will normally have the added step of animal validation. Costs that companies pay for animal validation cover a variety of tests for palatability, stool quality, digestibility (metabolizable energy), studies on life stages (maintenance, growth, and gestation-lactation), dental, hairball, urine pH, and glycemic index. Other tests include proximate analysis (moisture, crude fat, crude protein, crude fiber, and ash) and any other analysis on the label. All of these studies cost thousands of dollars in order to validate claims on packaging. Some companies may do in-home testing.

Companies conduct palatability testing to determine whether or not the animal likes a product. They want to validate that the food, whether it be kibble, treat, or a canned product, is acceptable to the animal. If the food is not acceptable and the animal will not eat it, the food will not meet nutrition requirements.

Some companies may do a preference test to compare their product to a competitor's. However, when running a preference test, the data must be studied closely to look to see if animals have bowl bias. This means the animal will eat food from only one particular bowl. Typically, bowl bias is obvious when the product is being eaten out of one of a limited number (e.g., either the bowl on the left or another on the right). Dogs who are used for palatability tests typically are trained and qualified for the testing. Dogs biased towards eating only on one side are removed from palatability testing.

A further reason animal testing is crucial to new products is for validation and safety. Such testing is used as a "disaster" check. If animals have runny stools or vomit after eating a new product, a company would not risk placing the product on the market. Animals such as dogs or cats may be used for digestibility testing for a new product. Developers may want to see the overall nutrient utilization of a product. This is done by having a group of cats or dogs ingest the product, after which scientists analyze the animals' fecal output.

Not only is it important for pets both to accept (eat) and digest the food but it is also important to please the consumers who purchase the product. Pet food companies have only one chance from consumers to buy their product. If a consumer (i.e., a person's pet animal) does not like the product, it will never again be purchased by that individual. Acceptability of the product by the pet is extremely important because consuming the product is how the animal will ingest its daily nutrient requirements.

Product Launch

Once the product has met regulatory guidelines, been validated, been brought up to production scale, with a well-designed package, the product will be brought into launch. This is the period when the roll-out of production is complete and product inventory is in the warehouse ready to be distributed to retailers. Customer service should be in place for areas such as product characteristics, technical support, statistics, record keeping, and communication.

COMMON TYPES OF PET FOOD OUT ON THE MARKET

There are numerous types of pet food on the market. One of the most common types is dry pet food. Dry pet food, with a moisture content less than 10%, typically has a shelf-life of 12 months when stored under ambient conditions. Dry kibble includes powders, granular meals, crumbles, pellets, baked biscuits, and nuggets that have a high concentration of grains. Most dry kibble goes through a preconditioner that mixes, heats, and reduces pathogens. Then, the ingredients are sent through an extruder where the starch is gelatinized, and the kibble is formed at the die. Once the kibble exits the extruder, it is dried and coated with liquids, such as fats, oils, or flavors. After the kibble has been coated in a liquid, it can also be coated with dry powder. Dry kibble is coated using tumble drums, curtain spray, augers, and spray systems. Once the kibble has been processed, it typically is measured to make sure it is uniform. Tests completed during processing include bulk density, color, shape, and texture analysis.

Another common type of pet food is wet pet food. Canned/wet pet food has a high moisture content and a pH around 6. Canned pet food must be commercially sterile and packed in a hermetically sealed container. This means the product must have achieved conditions with heat application that renders the food free of pathogenic and spoilage microorganisms capable of growing in the food at shelf-stable temperatures. Typically, wet pet food products achieve commercial sterilization with thermal processing through a retort. Types of packaging that can undergo the retort process include cans, pouches, trays, and tubs. Processing with steam allows temperatures above 100°C to be used. Commercial sterilization can be achieved at 121°C for 15 minutes, which leads to the complete destruction of microorganisms (Wehling, University of Nebraska-Lincoln). Commercially sterile cans on average have a shelf-life of two years. Other wet products include raw and refrigerated products. These products are high in meat content and flavor, while having low energy density due to dilution with water. Salmonella in raw pet food diets is a concern (Finely *et al.*).

Intermediate moisture pet food, sometimes referred to as semi-moist products, is another option. Humectants and preservatives are added to this type to prevent mold growth, since the water activity in intermediate moisture pet food is around 30%. Typically, semi-moist products are given to pets because of the soft texture and the product's resemblance to meat. Intermediate moisture foods often include dyes, and undergo cold-forming extrusion with high-barrier packaging.

Injection molding is used to process another type of pet food. Injection molded treats are made from plasticized proteins and starches or resins, which are melted in the injector and then formed into a specific shape. These products are rigid and require chewing to be broken down for digestion.

A wide variety of treats exist on the market that are nonessential to a pet's diet. Some categories of treats include extruded treats, rawhides, jerky treats, and baked treats. Extruded treats may resemble human foods such as bacon or other meats and are typically high in starch. Dental treats are typically extruded as well. Rawhides originated from the leather and tanning industry. The rawhide is wetted and cut then dried. The rawhide can be transported frozen, chilled, or fresh. Rawhides are trimmed, cured, or jerked and then dried in rooms, smokers, or baking ovens. Jerky treats are dehydrated meats high in protein and cured through the use of salts and preservatives to prevent mold growth. Baked treats include cookies, dog bones, hearts, and other shapes made from dough that is baked. Typically, baked treats are mass produced using a rotary molder. The dough is forced into cavities and molded into shapes. The formed pieces drop from the mold onto a moving chain belt and are baked in a tunnel oven.

REGULATIONS FOR ANIMAL WELFARE AND ANIMAL TESTING

When working with animals for experiments including feeding trials, the company must follow the Animal Welfare Act and minimize distress on the animals throughout the scientific process. The Animal Welfare Act is a federal law that covers animal research. The Animal Welfare Act regulates research, testing, teaching, and transport of animals. The law sets minimal standards for warm-blooded animals in areas such as housing, feeding, handling, and veterinary care.

The Institutional Animal Care and Use Committee (IACUC) plays an integral role with research groups as they act as an agent to oversee research facilities. The committee consists of at least three members, which must include a veterinarian from the facility and one member not affiliated with the facility to represent the general interest of the welfare of the animal.

A researcher will determine if there is a need to fill out an experimental IACUC protocol in the following situations: if the animal is covered under the Animal Welfare Act, if the researchers are part of the Association for the Assessment and Accreditation of Laboratory Animal Care, if the research is supported by the National Institute of Health, or if the experiment involves the use of invertebrates.

Once the researcher has determined that an IACUC protocol is necessary, the researcher will have to contact the committee and start the paperwork process. The IACUC committee looks at the Animal Welfare Act and applies the regulations to the documentation and paperwork. For example, the protocol consists of a section on methods and materials. The methods section contains materials addressing animal welfare issues that include non-alternative animal methods, animal species justification, and justification for the number of animals being used. The paperwork also requires the research to address living conditions and veterinary care for all the animals in a study. Lastly, the protocol also requires the names and qualifications of all the personnel who will be working with the animals. All of the names must be listed because all of the personnel working with the animals need to go through a training process and must have animal experience. Not only will the researcher fill out the research protocol, but they will also have to fill out the facility animal care and use a program that will have to be approved by IACUC.

The USDA enforces the Animal Welfare Act. Not only does a researcher have to comply with IACUC when testing with animals, but they must use the animals licensed and registered with the USDA. The animal facilities must also be inspected by the Animal and Plant Health Inspection service.

For example, if a researcher is using dogs for a digestibility experiment, the dogs in the study are required to be obtained from sources authorized by the USDA. Laboratory dogs are typically bred for research and are bred from USDA licensed breeders. Some of the qualifications for USDA licensed dogs include defined health, pedigree, and being up to date on vaccinations. When the USDA-licensed facility houses these dogs, it is required to submit an annual report on the use of the animals for research, testing, and teaching.

Besides such requirements of the Animal Welfare Act, if animal research is funded by the United States Public Health Service (PHS), the researcher must adhere to the Public Health Service Policy on Humane Care and Use of Laboratory Animals. The PHS policy applies to institutions with federal funding from a PHS agency such as Centers for Disease Control, FDA, or National Institutes of Health (NIH). If the researcher is developing a product being tested by animals that is sponsored by PHS, they must provide the Office of Laboratory Animal Welfare (OLAW) a written Welfare of Assurance of Compliance. The Office of Laboratory Animal Welfare is an agency that ensures animals are treated humanely and receives reports from IACUC if a researcher violates any animal welfare regulations. If a researcher does violate the animal welfare law, and IACUC reports the violation to OLAW, the research group's funding grant may be suspended or retracted.

FOOD SAFETY MODERNIZATION ACT

The Food Safety Modernization Act's (FSMA) regulations are now being enforced for pet food. Before FSMA, the government had no authority to mandate recalls, mandate product holding, ensure hazard monitoring, control safety of imported goods, or shut down bad facilities. Even though no pets have become sick due to foodborne illness, FSMA is enforced for pet food because the FDA does not want pet owners to contract a foodborne illness traceable to a food designed for their animals.

According to FSMA, the "owner, operator, or agent in charge of a facility, shall in accordance with this section evaluate the hazard that could affect food being manufactured, processed, packed or held by a facility." This is important because pet food companies are held accountable when producing pet food. Accountability of pet food processors falls under the general provisions for all registered facilities. Under the bioterrorism act, manufacturers, processors, packers, or holders of animal food are all groups that must be registered as a facility. Any human food facility that makes co-products has to follow 21 CFR 117, if the food safety plan has hazards for animals. The hazard analysis and risk based preventative controls are similar to Hazard Analysis and Critical Control Points (HACCP). Hazard Analysis and Risk-Based Preventive Controls (HARBPC) also takes into account pet food containing three types of hazards, (e.g., the physical, chemical, and biological). To comply with FDA regulations, companies must follow these FSMA regulations before any new pet food can be launched on the market. When developing a new food, the team must work with the production facility to make sure they are meeting all of the new FSMA regulations.

Other Companion Animals and their Diets

Besides dogs and cats, other companion animals require specialized foods. These animals include rabbits, ferrets, birds, and fish. Herbivores such as rabbits, guinea pigs, and chinchillas need high-fiber diets with pellets, treats, water, and hay. Timothy grass and orchard grass are the main types of hay that herbivores need. If herbivores are given pellets and hay, it is recommended to feed the hay on top of the pellets. Rabbits are hind gut fermenters that are coprophagic, meaning that they get additional nutrients from the fermentation in their hindgut, which results from consuming their own feces.

Birds need high-energy feeds that contain fatty acids such as linoleic, linolenic, and arachidonic acid. Commercial formulated seed diets consist of corn, oats, barley, wheat, and grass. A potential problem with commercial seed diets is that a domestic bird may pick out what looks best and not eat everything. Pelleted diets may be a better source for birds because they have known nutrient requirements that are compressed into a pellet.

Fish need a wide range of foods since some are carnivores, others are herbivores, and some are omnivores. Omnivores are best for captivity and can consume aquatic plants, smaller fish, algae, plankton, and insects (Karr 2013). Herbivores need 15% to 30% protein, carnivores need at least 45% protein, and young fish need 50% protein. Fish meal and other seafood products are good sources of long-chain fatty acids. For fat, carnivores need less than 8%, while herbivores need less than 3%. Carnivores need a low-fiber percent because they lack fermentation capabilities where herbivores need 5% to 10%. Fish need vitamins A, C, D, E, H, and vitamin B complex. They also need calcium and phosphorus. Fish diets may include flakes, meat/live foods, plants, and vegetable matter. Fish should be fed 0.5 to 1.0 percent weight per day. There are several types of fish food, including floating food and fast or slow-sinking. Floating is for fish like catfish and carp. Slow sinking is for fish like salmon and trout. Fast sinking is for shrimp. Factors to look at in fish food include piece density, nutritional quality, and water stability. Fish flakes are better for smaller fish. For larger fish, pelleted fish foods are better, and they are often extruded.

SUMMARY

In order to be successful in developing a new pet food, the team must take the time to research the product idea. It will need to conduct research on the target market, costs to develop the product, technology to make the product, and government regulations. After the product development group has completed preliminary research, they must develop a detailed concept brief to guide them when creating the new product. At the end of the day, the product must be palatable to, and digestible by, the animal, in compliance with government regulations, and have appeal to pet owners.

KEY WORDS

Animal welfare—the state of the animal and the treatment of animals under human care (AVMA).

Companion animal—animal that has been domesticated.

Concept brief—working document that outlines an action plan, discusses validation of a product, contains a project budget, outline responsibilities for each member on the team and contains a timeline for the product.

COMPREHENSION QUESTIONS

20.1. What is pet food?

20.2. Who regulates pet food?

20.3. What is a concept brief and what does it consist of?

20.4. Why is it important to test pet food before putting it on the market?

REFERENCES

AAFCO 2014. Official publication of the Association American Feed Control Officials.

Aldrich, C. Greg. Personal Communication Kansas State University Department of Grain Science (2015).

APPA. "American Pet Products Association. Pet Industry Market Size &

Ownership Statistics: 2015 Sales within the U.S. Market." (2015). Accessed November 20, 2015, http://www.americanpetproducts.org/press_industrytrends.asp.

AVMA. "American Veterinary Medical Foundation. U.S. Pet Ownership Statistics: 2012." (2012). Accessed 14 Dec 2016, https://www.avma.org/KB/Resources/Statistics/Pages/Market-research-statistics-US-pet-ownership.aspx.

Berryman J.C., K. Howells, and M. Lloyd-Evans. "Pet Owner Attitudes Towards Pets and People." *Vet. Rec. 117*, no. XX (1985): 659-661

Deng, P. and Swanson K., Future aspects and perceptions of companion animal nutrition and sustainability. *J of Ani Sci.* 2015.

Food and Drug Administration Department of Health and Human Services Subchapter Food for Human Consumption. 21 C.F.R. § 113.3. 2016.

Human Health Implications of Salmonella Contaminated Natural Pet Treats and Raw Pet Food by Rita Finley, Richard Reid-Smith, J. Scott Weese and Frederick J. Angulo November 2005.

Jellison, J. "New Study Shows People and Pets Can Succeed Together in Fighting the Obesity Epidemic; Researchers Announce Results of First-ever, Year-long People and Pet Weight Loss Study." (PR Newswire Association LLC, 2004). Accessed December 19, 2016, http://go.galegroup.com/ps/i.do?&id=GALE|A124651636&v=2.1&u=ksu&it=r&p=AONE&sw=w&authCount=1;

Kansas Department of Agriculture. Accessed December 16, 2016, http://agriculture.ks.gov/divisions-programs/acap/feed/feed-licenses. .

Lisa Karr, L. Personal Communication University of Nebraska Lincoln Department of Animal Science (2013).

National Research Council. 2006. *Nutrient requirements of dogs and cats.* Washington, D.C.: Washington, D.C.: National Academies Press.

Nielson, "The Humanization of Pet Food. How Far Are Pets Willing to Go?" 2016.

Randy Wehling, R. Personal Communication University of Nebraska Lincoln Department of Food Science and Technology.

Appendix A: Guide to the Code of Federal Regulations

AFTER food laws are signed, the enforcing agency issues a proposed rule, which is known as a Notice of Proposed Rulemaking (NPRM). The proposed rule is then published in the Federal Register, where the public is allowed to view it and make comments regarding the possible implications of the new regulation. After a comment period of at least 30 days, an official rule will be published in the Federal Register. In practice, comment periods for food regulations range from 6 months to 1 year. The final rule will have information regarding the dates it will become effective for companies. Small companies, in some cases, have a longer period to comply than larger organizations. The Food and Drug Administration (FDA) sometimes issues guidance documents to assist companies in understanding how the new rules will affect their business and its responsibilities. After the final rule has been issued, the regulation will be filed in the Federal Register and become permanent law. All permanent laws are codified in the Code of Federal Regulations (CFR), where they are filed with other laws on a particular subject. Rules and regulations regarding food and drugs are listed in Title 21 in the Code of Federal Regulations, while rules regarding animals and animal products are found in Title 9.

The Code of Federal Regulations (CFR) is available online, and can be accessed through www.fda.gov and the Government Printing Office's website (www.gpo.gov/fdsys). To find specific regulations regarding a product, use the search tool available on the site. Guidance regarding rules can be found on the websites of the United States Department of Agriculture (USDA) and FDA.

Appendix B: Creating a Focus Group Moderator's Guide

WRITING a moderator's guide begins by defining the purpose and outcomes of the focus group. A purpose statement should be written in order to make the goals clear to all who are assisting in the coordination of the test. After a purpose has been defined, questions must be carefully crafted. Elements to understand before writing a moderator's guide include:

- Clear purpose statement.
- Outline of issue areas.
- Questions of importance for each issue area.
- A logic path for the line of questions.

Steps to creating a focus group moderator's guide:

Step 1: Understanding the client's purpose for the qualitative research.
Step 2: Outlining the 4-6 key issue areas.
Step 3: Crafting critical questions for each issue area.
Step 4: Submitting draft guides for client approval.
Step 5: Fine-tuning guide with client input.

Before Writing the Guide

A moderator must have client's responses to select questions before a guide can be started. The questions the client has to answer include:

- What has led to the need for research?

- If you could ask only one question of respondents, what would that be?
- How does qualitative market research fit into the research continuum—what happened before this project—what will happen after this project?
- How does this qualitative market research project fit into business strategy planning?
- How will this research support decision-making?
- What will be different when the research is over?
- How will the research results be used and by whom?
- What happens if the answers fall into responses like these:
  —"I love this product/service."
  —"I hate this product/service"?
- Who/what kinds of people should be represented in the focus group?

How to Write Guide Questions

Guides should always be written with the respondent in mind. Writers and moderators must be careful not to interject their own opinions and bias into the discussion. If conscious efforts are not made to eliminate bias, the questioner may inadvertently influence the respondent's reply. The writer of a guide must take into account the viewpoint of the speaker and the intended audience. Below are three ways to phrase questions that consider different points of view:

1. The moderator's point of view
   "*People in other groups have been split on the issue of Nutrasweet in soft drinks. How do you feel about it?*"
2. The respondent's point of view
   "*Should Nutrasweet be banned from soft drinks?*"
3. The client's point of view
   "*What do you people think about Nutrasweet in soft drinks?*"

Flow of the Guide

There is a natural flow for discussion guides, and that flow adheres to guidelines, including the following:

- Move from general to specific questions *within each issue area.*

- Move from easy-to-answer to difficult-to-answer queries *within each issue area.*
- Vary the question stems *within each issue area.*
- Vary the question types *within each issue area.*
- Where appropriate, vary the activities required of respondents within each issue area.
  —*Examples*: Use interventions such as paper and pencil exercises or notate key lists on the easel or have respondents react to specific stimuli such as picture sorts, animations, or finished ads.

Writing Questions

Step 1: On 5 pieces of paper, write the name of the five issue areas that the group will discuss.

Step 2: *Start with Issue Area A*: usually background questions. Allow 6–10 minutes for this section in terms of the time it takes for the room to answer the questions.

- Write a *general* question about the topic that anyone in the room can answer.
- Writer another general question that has probes. Again, anyone can answer the question. It is easy and non-threatening.

Step 3: Move toward specific questions that relate only to that issue area.

- Include a brief intervention, e.g., writing on the easel, private writing, or raising hands to indicate a "vote."

Step 4: *Move on to Issue Area B*: Write one general question and then move to specific questions. Allot 10-15 minutes for this section in terms of how long it takes to answer the questions. Include a 2-4 minutes of interventions to keep the section "interesting."

Step 5: *Move on to Issue Areas C & D*: Write one general question for each and move on to specific questions. Allot 40-60 minutes for these two sections combined.

Step 6: *Write a traditional closing issue area*: Issue Area E and write in a plan for a false close so you can meet with the client.

Editing a Guide

1. Now that you have a first draft, go back and revisit questions that

might require more probes or more instructions [to the moderator or to the respondents]. Add those probes/instructions.

2. Check format to ensure it is easy to read and key data is in caps or bolded.
3. Submit a fully edited draft to the client for review. Prepare for further editing or possible sign-off.
4. Usually the initial draft is to discover how close you've come to interpreting the purpose of the study, which will be found in the "right" formulation of questions for respondents. Remember: The guide is in all likelihood the first time the product concept has been rendered as an actionable item.

General Subjects to Consider for Focus Group Questions:

1. General product/service usage [behavioral].
2. Likes/dislikes of products/services.
3. Reactions to concrete stimuli (e.g., pictures, ads, products, posters, concept statements, etc.).
4. Creating an idea together.
5. Brand images.
6. Perceived motivational aspects.
7. Advantages/disadvantages of products/services.
8. Perceived attributes [products or service].
9. Importance/relevance to consumers.
10. Believability/credibility.
11. Perceived target users.
12. Similarities/differences to existing products/services.
13. Image of self as user.
14. Unmet needs.
15. Perceived problems/barriers.
16. Others as determined by the special nature of a specific project purpose.

Focus Group Moderator's Guide Example

Month Day, Year | Snack Product Guide

PURPOSE: To explore consumer perceptions of various grain-based extruded snack products.

INTRODUCTION

A. Hello. My name is __________ and I am an employee of _________. The researchers have asked me to moderate today's *2-hour* group discussion, but I am not involved directly in the outcome of the research. Our purpose today is to talk about snack foods. We'll be doing several things today: participating in group discussion, tasting, and commenting on some snacks in development.

B. Feel free to make negative or positive comments about any of the items we will be discussing. This is a free-flowing discussion and there are no wrong answers. The results of today's discussion will be useful to the researchers who are developing new snack foods.

DISCLOSURES

A. *Facilities, observers, anonymity*. I want to tell you some things about this room. Like many other research facilities in the United States, this room has a one-way mirror. A few of the researchers involved in this project are on the other side of the glass. They want to hear your comments firsthand, so they can help with interpretation and won't have to wait for my report. Your comments also are being audio-taped so that I can pay attention to the discussion instead of note taking. I am concerned about what is being said, not who made which comments. Your name will not be used in any report about this project.

B. *Voice opinions*. Your presence here is very important to the success of this project. I want to thank you for your time, your opinions, and courage in voicing your point of view.

C. *Allowance to leave the room*. At any time you may leave the room to use the restroom, get a drink, etc. But in order to maintain the group, I ask that only one person be up or out at a time.

D. *Allergens*. I will be asking you to sample some grain -based snacks later on. Please let me know if you have any allergies at this time.

GUIDELINES FOR DISCUSSION

Now, in order to make this session work as a research session, here are some guidelines to follow:

A. Please talk one at a time and with a voice as loud as mine. I need to be able to pick up your voice on the tape.
B. Avoid side conversations. Usually side conversations involve some interesting comments so I ask that any comments you make, make them to the entire group.
C. I need to hear from everyone in the group, and let's allow everyone equal time so that nobody talks too much or too little.
D. There are no wrong answers, but there are different viewpoints. Say what you believe, whether or not anyone else agrees.
E. It's okay to disagree, but don't put anyone down for thinking or saying things differently than you.

INTRODUCTIONS

A. Before we start talking about snack foods, I'd like to meet each of you. Please introduce yourself to the group. Tell us three things: (1) your name; (2) your favorite food; and (3) who or what lives at your home with you. Let's begin at my left and go around the room.
B. Thank you for sharing that information with the group.

SNACKS IN GENERAL

A. Let's begin our discussion about snack foods by thinking about your favorite snack foods. What are they? (List on easel, markers various colors).
B. What is it about these foods that makes them "snack foods?" What characteristics? (color, flavor, aroma-smell, textures, nutritive?)
C. What time of day do you eat snack foods?
D. How many times a day do you eat them?
E. Where are you when you are most likely to eat them?
F. What temperature are snack foods most likely to be?
G. What else are you doing when you eat snack foods?
H. Are there things that signal that it's time to eat a snack food?
I. What are the emotional issues of eating snack food?
J. Are snacks good for you?

IDEAL SNACK

A. If you could design the perfect snack food, what characteristics would it have?
B. Let's talk about how it would taste.
C. Tell me what ingredient would be most important.
D. Describe the mouth feel, texture, etc.
E. What nutritional value would it have?

EXTRUDED GRAIN-BASED SNACKS

Now we are going to talk about snacks made from grain.

A. What snacks made of grain do you eat now?
B. Which do you like most?
   1. What do you like about them?
   2. Do you want them crunchier, less crunchy?
   3. Saltier, less salty? What flavor is best?
   4. Which color is most appealing? What does it remind you of?
   5. What memories do you associate with this snack?
   6. What nutritional benefits do grain snacks provide?
   7. Is there anything negative about snacks made from grain?

EXTRUDED GRAIN PRODUCTS TO SAMPLE

Participants are shown samples of a new product and at a pre-determined point are encouraged to taste them.

A. Appearance
   1. Which of the products have the best appearance?
   2. How would you describe the appearance of the best products? What does __________ tell you about the food item?
   3. Size, shape?

B. Flavor/Taste
   1. Which product has the best flavor?
   2. Describe the flavors of the best products? What do those flavors remind you of? Associate with other positive things?

   3. Which do you like the least? Tell me what you don't like about the flavor.
   4. What suggestions do you have for improving the flavor? Adding salt, sugar/cinnamon etc.?

C. Texture
   1. Which products do you like best based on the texture?
   2. Describe the texture of the best products.
   3. What is it about the texture that appeals to you most?
   4. Which textures are least desirable?

D. Nutrition
   1. Which products would provide the best nutrition?
   2. How would you describe the nutritive value of these products?
   3. What clues do you have about the nutritional value?
   4. What nutritional benefits would you want these products to provide?

E. Usage
   1. Would you eat this product as a snack? Why? Why not?
   2. What time of day would you eat it?
   3. How would you eat it? Where?

OVERALL PREFERENCE

A. Sort samples into 3 groups by preference: Most, average, least (use scorecard).
B. Of your "most preferred," please sort them, most preferred to least.

CLOSING (EXCUSE SELF TO GET FINAL QUESTIONS FROM OBSERVERS)

A. What final comments do you have about these snack products?
B. Thank you for participating.

Appendix C: Guide to Product Development Competitions

MULTINATIONAL companies, trade organizations, and special interest groups sponsor competitions to induce excitement for their products, to support interests of consumers, and to provide a competitive opportunity for students and professionals.

When you are brainstorming ideas for a competition, ensure that they fall into the category and follow all rules for the contest. When deciding on an idea, ask if the idea follows market trends or fills a gap in the market. To do this, conduct a small, informal focus group or a consumer study with 20 or 25 people. In a focus group, you can discuss the idea and perhaps make changes to your product before the competition deadline. Understanding consumer perception of a concept is an essential piece in marketing the product—even when the consumer is a judging panel.

After you have determined the product you will create, start experimenting to find a suitable formula for a prototype. Examining several flavor combinations or differing formulas is advisable if time allows. These formulas can be tested using consumer panels.

A clever product name and slogan will make your product more appealing. Providing a package mock-up with a nutrition facts panel and ingredient statement will convey your product vision to potential consumers and contest judges.

Determining your target market is an important piece. Go to local grocery stores if your product will be sold in a retail setting, or research competing products. How will the price of your product compare to competitors'? How will your new product be differentiated from products already on the shelf?

Guidelines for Competition Success

As simple as it sounds, probably the number one reason that teams are not successful is they do not follow directions! Carefully read the competition rules and deadlines so that your product is the highlight of the competition. In addition, follow all guidelines outlined in the Code of Federal Regulations regarding your product. If fortification with vitamins is in your product description, ensure you are not exceeding the allowable amount. All ingredients and additives should be checked against the regulations, just as a new product being developed commercially would be researched, to ensure accuracy and legitimacy. It is also advisable to conduct a search to ensure the product does not infringe filed patents.

Appendix D: Metric Conversion Charts

Weight

								Often Rounded To
1 t	=	1/3 T	=	1/6 fl oz	=	4.9 ml		5
3 t	=	1 T	=	1/2 fl oz	=	14.8 ml		15
2 T	=	1/8 cup	=	1 fl oz	=	29.6 ml		30
4 T	=	1/4 cup	=	2 fl oz	=	59.1 ml		60
5-1/3 T	=	1/3 cup	=	2-2/3 fl oz	=	78.9 ml		80
8 T	=	1/2 cup	=	4 fl oz	=	118.3 ml		120
10-2/3 T	=	2/3 cup	=	5-1/3 fl oz	=	157.7 ml		160
12 T	=	3/4 cup	=	6 fl oz	=	177.4 ml		180
14 T	=	7/8 cup	=	7 fl oz	=	207.0 ml		210
16 T	=	1 cup	=	8 fl oz	=	236.6 ml		240
1 pint	=	2 cups	=	0.473 l	=	473 ml		470
1 quart	=	2 pt	=	0.9464 l	=	946 ml		950
1 gallon	=	4 quarts	=	3.785 l	=	3785 ml		3800
1 liter	=	1.057 quarts	=	0.264 gallon	=	1000 ml		

Weight Measures

1 g	=	0.035 oz	=	0.001 kg	=	1000 mg
1 mg	=	0.001 g				
1 oz	=	28.35 g (often rounded to 28 g)				
1 lb	=	16 oz	=	453.59 g	=	0.454 kg
1 kg	=	2.21 lb	=	1000 g		

The volume weight of water is a commonly used reference point for other food measures.

1 T water	=	15 g	=	0.001 kg	=	15 cc
1 cup water	=	237 g				
1 fl oz water	=	29.54 g (often rounded to 30 g)				
1 liter water	=	1 kg	=	453.59 g	=	1000 g
1 quart water	=	946 g	=	1000 g		

Index

About the Authors

DR. FADI ARAMOUNI was born and raised in Beirut, Lebanon. He received his BS in Biochemistry in 1977 and his MS in Food Technology in 1980 from the American University of Beirut. Dr. Aramouni earned his PhD in Food Science in 1986 from Louisiana State University. He joined the Kansas State University Department of Foods and Nutrition in 1989, then the Department of Animal Science and Industry in 1995. Since July 1999, his responsibilities have been primarily in extension; however he also teaches course such as Research and Development of Food Products, Principles of HACCP, Advanced HACCP Principles, and Fundamentals of Food Processing. His honors from the College of Agriculture include the Outstanding Faculty Award, graduate teaching award, and faculty member of the semester.

KATHRYN GODDARD DESCHENES is from Ellsworth, Kansas. She received her BA in Food Science in 2011 and received her MS in Food Science in 2012 from Kansas State University. She has won several national awards in Food Product Development competitions, including first prize in the 2008 Almonds Board of California "Game Day Snacks for Men" and the grand prize at Disney's Healthy Snack for Children in 2009. Kathryn has managed activities at the Kansas Value Added Foods Lab from 2009 to 2013 as well as provided technical assistance to food companies in product development, ingredients and packaging, regulatory compliance, and packaging technologies. Kathryn also did an internship at Kellogg's in Battle Creek, Michigan, for 6 months. She is currently a regulatory compliance manager for a food company in Idaho where she resides with her husband, Joshua.